D0579779

MY PEOPLE

The Story of the Jews

MY PEOPLE

The Story of the Jews

by Abba Eban

BEHRMAN HOUSE INC.

RANDOM HOUSE

The author and publishers wish to acknowledge the devoted help
of the following in the preparation of this volume: Cilli
Brandstatter and Neal Kozodoy for research and editorial aid;
Pat Appel and Marcus Cohen for photographic research; Betty
Binns for the design and photo editing.

EIGHTH PRINTING

Published in the United States by Behrman House, Inc., New York,
New York and Random House, Inc., New York and simultaneously
in Canada by Random House of Canada Limited, Toronto

Library of Congress Catalog Card Number: 68-27328

Manufactured in the United States of America

Foreword

*T*HIS book is the fruit of sporadic labor extending over seven years. It is no secret to many of my readers that during that period I have had many things to do apart from writing this book. I owe it to myself and others to explain why I should have wandered into a well-plowed field to sow a seed and add a furrow of my own.

A special role was thrust upon me at an early public age and has clung to me ever since. My vocation has been to explain the Jewish people to a confused and often uncomprehending world. The central fact in modern Jewish experience has been the renewal of Israel's statehood. The utter singularity of Jewish history, its rebellion against all historic laws, its total recalcitrance to any comparative system of research, have all been brought home to me at every stage. I have also come up against the impossibility of understanding, and therefore of explaining, the current Jewish reality without a constant probing of ancient roots. There is no other modern nation whose motives of existence and action require such frequent reference to distant days. This is true of Israel in the Diaspora, as it is of Israel in the community of nations. And when all is said and written, the Jewish career remains an unpenetrated mystery. The mark of interrogation is written everywhere. The problems can be illuminated but never solved. I recall Kierkegaard's words: "Life must be lived forward, but can only be understood backward."

A writer owes his readers the effort of objectivity. But the title of this book is a frank confession that the story is written from within, by one who feels passionately committed to the strange destiny which he is trying to elucidate. This is not only or mainly a record of the uncommon events which compose my people's story. It is largely a personal reflection on those events and a particular response to their origins and echoes. That every word has been pondered and written in Jerusalem may also give this book a special dimension. Much of the awe and wonder of the story lies in the experience of renewal. The journey has come back to where it first began.

Abba Eban

Jerusalem
September 1968

CONTENTS

MY PEOPLE

The Story of the Jews

1 ❧ The Age of the Patriarchs

*I*SRAEL'S history opens in a twilight zone where fact and legend meet. The legend has entered so deeply into human experience that it has acquired its own reality. What men believe to have happened in the Middle East has been no less formative in world history than that which is known to have occurred.

Fact and legend come together to describe Israel's emergence into a Middle East dominated by the river empires of the Nile and the Euphrates. Around these opulent waters it was possible to build settled societies which were not dependent on the unequal fortune of the skies. Those who lived in the green valleys were immune from the nomadic destiny which, elsewhere in the Middle East, sent thirsty men in anxious quest of pasture from year to year.

At Israel's birth Egypt had many centuries of stable, national life behind her. The Pharaohs were not only the lords of a dynasty, they were also the patrons of a majestic culture. The pyramids bear witness to their instinct for grandeur. Hieroglyphic inscriptions on walls and tombs show their intense ambition to conserve and transmit experience. Massive statues and stylized mural paintings reflect a lofty artistic imagination which finds expression through the veil of a stereotyped technique. The political sway of Pharaonic Egypt ranged from the sources of the Nile in Nubia (Sudan), across the Sinai wilderness into Canaan and Syria. Sometimes a Pharaonic expedition would reach far westward into Libya. But to the north and east of the Nile Delta, Egyptian power was constantly blocked by the empires which rose, one after the other, in Mesopotamia—the land between the Tigris and Euphrates rivers.

Here the people of Sumer began the known history of a region which, under successive occupations, was to breed and accommodate many empires and cultures. In the third millennium B.C.E., Sumer was overrun by the martial Akkadian race which swept from the East beyond the two rivers to found the mightiest empire then known to man. The next wave of invasion came from the West. The vigorous Amorites undermined the power of the Akkadians and established successive dynasties culminating in the rise of Babylon.

When Hebrew history begins, Sumer, Akkad, and Babylon have already left their primitive epochs far behind. Agricultural villages have evolved into city-states alive with varied commerce and sophisticated crafts. A system of numbers gave precision to Babylonian life and thought. Cuneiform (wedge-shaped) writing far excelled the Egyptian hieroglyphic in flexibility of use. Sumer, Akkad, and Babylon built lofty, ornate temples in devotion to the gods of air and sun and sky. Their skill included the construction of irrigation canals which stretched the zone of cultivation beyond the immediate proximity of the river banks. Babylonian florescence is most vividly revealed in the life and work of Hammurabi who, in the twenty-first century B.C.E., gave himself the proud title "King of Babylon, Sumer, and Akkad and of the four quarters of the world." His achievements in military conquest and mercantile expansion were overshadowed in later history by his formulation of a detailed legal code, part of which has come down to us in a well-preserved statue discovered in 1901 and now exhibited at Paris in the Louvre. Hammurabi describes his reign with the pride common to most statesmen—but with much greater brevity. "Lasting water I provided for the land of Sumer and Akkad. Its separated peoples I united. With blessings and abundance I endowed them. In peaceful dwellings I made them live."

The Hebrew tribes, according to the Biblical story and all other extant records, came out of Mesopotamia. They were not primitive desert nomads, but the product of a region in which Sumer, Akkad, and Babylon had built a long tradition of civility and enterprise. By the time of their conquests in Canaan they had first been steeped in Mesopotamian cultures, and then exposed to Egyptian ideas. But the home in which they settled and which they were to endow with eternal fame lay between the empires which bestrode the ancient

This copper-mask effigy of an Akkadian king found at Nineveh exemplifies the face of those Semites whose civilizing genius dominated the great empires of Akkad, Babylon and Sumer in the Fertile Crescent.

East. After their birth in Babylon and their sojourn in Egypt, we find the Hebrews struggling for a fragile but memorable lease of nationhood in a corner of land between the Nile and the Euphrates, serving sometimes as a bridge, at other times as a wedge, between the two; living in the shadow of one or the other—but ultimately surviving and outshining both.

Historians called these lands the Fertile Crescent. The name exaggerated its qualities. For every inch of verdure, there are countless discouraging acres of sand and rock. The theme of the Fertile Crescent in ancient history is constant movement. Populations, armies, nomad tribes, traders, and caravans pass across it in unending spasms. The Fertile Crescent occupied the intermediate fringe between the two main centers of ancient history. Its destiny, then and always, was to be a crossroad where the traffic of goods and the commerce of ideas would interact and converge—only to branch out again into new and varied combinations.

The corner of the Crescent occupied by the Hebrews seldom knew the stability of Egypt and Mesopotamia. Those who were there at any given time were usually on the way to somewhere else or on the point of submergence. The Biblical literature and other records contain long, tedious lists of ethnic names which, in most cases, are all that stand between their owners and oblivion. Suddenly we find a group of tribes migrating from Mesopotamia, striking root in the southwest corner of the Fertile Crescent, developing a separate and distinct peoplehood and ultimately bequeathing to posterity a double gift: a moral law within a unique vision of history, and a body of splendid and passionate writing revered over the centuries by more people than have ever come under the spell of any other literature.

Fathers of
a People
The unity of the Hebrew people has been sustained throughout the ages by a vision of descent from a single ancestor. The narrative in Genesis of Abraham, Isaac, and Jacob is presented in the language of national myth. It evokes the memory of an age in which gods walked intimately with men and intervened in the daily commerce of their lives. But if the style is legendary, the language fabulous, the context and background accord with authentic history. We know that in the time of Hammurabi in Babylon and thereafter there were endless migrations of families and tribes along the fringes of the Fertile Crescent. Abraham and his family

are portrayed in the Biblical account as moving from Ur of the Chaldees in southwest Mesopotamia to Haran, a center of Amorite settlement in northwestern Mesopotamia. It was here that he received divine instruction to leave his land and kinsmen for a new country in which he would found an historic lineage of his own. "And I will make of thee a great nation, and I will bless thee and make thy name great and thou shalt be a blessing."

Obedient to the divine voice, Abraham moves into western Palestine, the land of the Canaanites. The territory "from Dan to Beersheba" is promised to him as an inheritance. We know that the dominant element in this territory was Semitic. The broken configuration of the land, its diversity of soil and climate, and the mingled ethnic stocks which formed its population—all made for a dispersed and uncohesive social pattern. It was a land of many small, unstable sovereignties. The "kings" with whom Abraham negotiated his sales of land and purchases of wells could hardly have been more than tribal patriarchs like himself. The territory of Canaan is in some green parts propitious to permanent settlement. Elsewhere it offers nothing but a sparse living to nomadic families content with a pastoral life. Abraham, Isaac, and Jacob move between the sedentary life of towns—Shechem, Hebron, Beersheba, and Gerar—and the watering places in the wilderness. Their life is neither completely settled nor totally nomadic; the Palestinian soil invites semi-permanent establishment and tillage. A strong tie of kinship inspires their family and tribal life, but their wanderings are in search of subsistence, not in quest of territorial nationhood. Later the Hebrew tribes enter the stream of international trade, represented in Joseph's time by caravans coming from Gilead with spices, balm, and myrrh. When hunger threatens in a dry season, Abraham moves southward to the Nile Delta, only to go back to Canaan as soon as the pasture grounds turn green.

In Hebron a family burial ground is acquired in the Cave of Machpelah. On Abraham's death his son Isaac shows a loyal concern for tribal solidarity, insisting that his own younger son, Jacob, marry kinswomen so as not to sever family ties. Isaac's twin sons Esau and Jacob are portrayed in terms of personal and economic conflict. Esau is a "cunning hunter, a man of the field" and Jacob (Israel) "a quiet man, dwelling in tents." From Jacob's wives, Leah and Rachel, and from their handmaidens, twelve sons are born: Reuben, Simeon, Levi, Judah, Issachar, Zebulun, Dan, Naphtali, Gad, Asher, Joseph, and Benjamin. Their descendants form the "tribes of Israel," and "Children of Israel," or the

"Israelites." Their social identity is now sharply defined. They eschew marital alliances outside their group, and they see Canaan as their land and inheritance. When famine drives them into Egypt they regard themselves as "strangers" or "sojourners" in temporary exile from their home. Their distinctiveness is constantly ascribed to their vision of a monistic God presiding over natural events and human fate—in contrast to the chaotic polytheism of Mesopotamian and Egyptian thought.

The Hebrew Ideal

Spiritual reasons are adduced both for Abraham's migration and for the intense cohesion and solidarity of his descendants. There is indeed no other convincing explanation. We must remember that the Mesopotamia in which Abraham was born was the center and pinnacle of contemporary civilization. It far outstripped Canaan in the sophistication and refinement of its arts. Law and commerce gave its social organization a stability not to be found elsewhere. We can only conclude, in accordance with the Genesis narrative, that Abraham's migration was inspired by protest and affirmation. protest against the incoherence of Mesopotamian life and thought —and affirmation of a new and satisfying answer to the riddle of man's destiny.

The story of the Patriarchs is told in Genesis immediately after the account of the Creation and the Flood. This narrative is rich in details familiar from Babylonian tradition. Similarly, the Joseph narrative is replete with names and legends of Egyptian origin. But that which separates the Patriarchs from their contemporary background is more decisive than that which relates them to the life and manners of their times. Israel's history emerges from the mists in a posture not of continuity, but of revolt. There is a new intuition about man and nature, and a fierce rejection of contemporary mythologies with their pluralistic pantheons of warring deities. The unity and transcendence of God are novel and disruptive ideas which transform every aspect of experience and create new categories of thought. The departure of Abraham from the land of his birth symbolizes a radical secession from pagan ideas. In their stead Israelite religion postulates the universal rule of a single purposeful intelligence, a God who acts with a moral purpose, whose fundamental attribute is goodness.

A nation writes its history in the image of its ideal. The story of the Patriarchs, from Abraham's migration into Canaan to the

A shepherd's haven, the landscape of the "Promised Land" scintillates beneath a brilliant sky full of the play of cloud and light, where sunblanched rock and lush greenery, hill and vale are the stark scenic contrasts.

sojourn of Jacob and his sons in Egypt, has worked with peculiar strength in the Jewish imagination. It is not a chronicle of remote, superhuman warriors. It does not resemble the vision of a resplendent heroic world such as the Greeks and other ancient peoples saw as their original state. The stories of Abraham, Isaac, Jacob, and Joseph are permeated by a sense of divine destiny. But they also contain much simple, earthy lore reflecting a recognizable way of human life in which combat and cunning are mitigated by the gentler and softer affections. In subsequent literature and memory the Hebrew nation looked back to its first ancestor as the prototype of two virtues: goodness and warmth in human relations and utter resignation, beyond mere humility, to the divine will. Both Christian and Muslim traditions accept the historic authenticity of Abraham and admit him as their spiritual ancestor. But to the Jews he is the first and unique Patriarch, the model of Hebrew excellence. Inspired by his covenant and welded together by the memories of three generations descended from his loins, the Children of Israel, precariously settled in Egypt, cross the frontier into established history in the middle of the second millennium B.C.E.

2 🐍 A Nation Is Born

THE BIBLICAL narrative springs into sharp movement and color in its portrayal of the Israelite family evolving as a nation on foreign soil. It tells how the tribal community founded by Abraham and his line is torn by feud. Joseph, because of the jealousy of his elder brothers, is removed to Egypt. A famine in Canaan sends his brothers southward in their turn. By that time Joseph, unknown to them, has risen in the service of the Egyptian monarch. He has stored the surplus produce of seven abundant years in precaution against the seven years of famine which are to follow. After a dramatic reunion with his brothers, Joseph sends them back to Canaan, bidding them return with their aged father Jacob. The brothers establish themselves in Goshen on the east of the Nile Delta. Centuries are to pass before their descendants once again see the land of their fathers and their own promised inheritance. At the beginning of their sojourn in Egypt they are free men, secure in the peace of an agricultural life in a watered zone far from the anxious droughts of Canaan. At its end they are oppressed slaves in flight from tyranny and persecution.

Other sources confirm the feasibility of this narrative in its main outline, if not in picturesque detail. We know that by the seventeenth century B.C.E. Semitic tribes, called the Hyksos, overran Egypt from the north and east. Since they themselves were foreign to Egyptian culture they may well have shown tolerance to the autonomous social life and religious creed of the Israelite settlers in Goshen. The rise of a foreigner like Joseph to viceregal power would be credible at a time when Egyptian nationalism was in eclipse.

The lack of secure harvest in Canaan must have brought other waves of Israelites to Egypt where they would naturally have joined the related Semitic groups. Contact between Egypt and Canaan was particularly intimate and constant during the Hyksos regime. Canaan was under virtual Egyptian suzerainty. There was much intermarriage, and the Israelites in Egypt adapted themselves easily to the prevailing political institutions. Yet the social and cultural life of the Israelites in Goshen seems to have been segregated and sheltered. The ritualistic rigidity of the Egyptians was not easily penetrated; and the separation between Egyptians and Israelites was ratified by a kind of reciprocal understanding. Even during Joseph's regime, according to the Bible, "the Egyptians might not eat bread with the Hebrews; for that were an abomination unto the Egyptians." These barriers encouraged the Israeli tribes to keep Canaan vivid in their memory and to cherish their ties with their Hebrew kinsmen to the north.

But it was primarily in their religious perceptions that the Israelites stood distinct and apart from Egyptian society. The narrative in the Book of Exodus portrays the collapse of their security under the tyrannical rule of a Pharaoh who may be safely identified as Ramesses II (ca. 1250 B.C.E.). The Hyksos monarchy fell early in the sixteenth century B.C.E. Egyptian nationalism reasserted itself. It was marked by intolerance and exclusiveness. The Israelites living in Goshen were deprived of their freedoms, reduced to slavery, and pressed into forced labor for the construction of new cities. They were neither welcome to stay nor free to go. In the depth of their humiliation and suffering there arose in their midst a leader who became the founder both of Israel's nationhood and of Israel's religion.

Moses was born and bred into Egyptian life and tradition. But he was of Hebrew ancestry; the persecution of his kinsmen moved him to ardent and creative anger. He gave the Hebrew God YAHWEH a distinctive and majestic character in his people's consciousness. He organized the straggling semi-nomad tribes for concerted revolt. He appealed to the dim but unbroken memory of pastoral freedom in the "Promised Land." In the ultimate assertion of his political and spiritual dominance he took the Israelites out of their Egyptian birthplace, led them, a turbulent multitude, queru-

The cold command of Ramesses II making sacrifice
of an Israelite, a Negro and an Asiatic to the
Egyptian god Amon in a brilliantly carved relief.

In ancient times, pagans worshiped gods in many forms, animal and human. Here the Egyptian fertility goddess, the great pregnant hippopotamus Toveris of the 26th dynasty.

lous and skeptical, across the Sea of Reeds, through the wilderness to the threshold of Canaan where they were to build a nation and bear undying witness to their faith.

The emergence of this faith has been accurately described as "a revolution in the world view of man." All previous and contemporary religions saw human destiny as subject to the laws of nature. Just as the natural cycles return to their point of origin without claim of progress, so was human life conceived as an endless ordained procession passing through birth and life—back to a starting point in darkness and chaos. The gods themselves were subject to human passions, instincts, and lusts. They were associated with natural emanations—sun, light, air, fertility, rain. Since natural forces are diverse and numerous, the pagan concept of divinity was pluralistic to the point of chaos.

Abraham had broken with the idolatrous element in paganism. He would not worship stocks and stones. But his God was not unique, omnipresent, or fully transcendent. He was the deity of Abraham's family, not of other families, still less of all mankind. When things went wrong He would assert His power to put things right. The Mosaic concept of divinity is less intimate and naive, more austere, but far more sublime. Moses is capable of an unprecedented exercise in abstraction. He can envision a God above nature, immune from human passion and natural vicissitudes. The pagan concept of history as tied inexorably to the wheel of repetition imparts a profound melancholy to most of ancient thought. Its somber theme recurs much later in history in the despairing cry of the Roman philosopher, Marcus Aurelius: "Up and down, to and fro, round and round, this is the monotonous and meaningless rhythm of the universe." Against the characteristic fatalism of pagan civilizations, Hebrew thought, from Moses onward, conceives God as the author of natural forces, exempt from their cyclical rhythm. The divine purpose fulfills itself not in nature, but in human history. Progress, not repetition, is the law of life. In the Mosaic tradition God applies to Himself a new epithet: "I AM THAT I AM," the one whom no definition can exhaust, the omnipresent helper of the people, "who is afflicted in all their afflictions and in His love and in His pity redeems them."

Once human destiny is separated from the cycle of nature, it breaks loose from the fatalistic chain of recurrence. Man has the capacity to "reject evil and choose good." He is thus endowed with a unique and active dignity, beyond the reach of any other element in nature.

We can only understand how revolutionary these concepts were by comparing them to the Egyptian and Mesopotamian environment in which they grew. The relics and monuments of pagan cultures include hybrid representations of "gods" with human heads and animal bodies; of bulls with wings, and birds with the bodies of quadrupeds. The equation of gods with brute beasts degrades divinity even below human level. The presence of such idolatries demonstrates that with all its external sophistication Egyptian culture was plunged in a deep confusion of spirit. Magical and orgiastic rituals flowed naturally from an unharmonious vision of nature.

Moses referred to the simpler, cleaner codes of his ancestors which were doubtless similar to those of the Midianite nomads among whom he had spent his early manhood. His religion, to be sure, falls short of prophetic Judaism in its full evolution some centuries later. The Mosaic deity is still the patron of Israel alone. The concept is anti-idolatrous, ethical, but by no means yet fully universal. "*You* shall not have any God but Me." The exhortation is in the singular. The object of its address seems to be wholly national, as was the case in all contemporary faiths. Similarly, Egyptian and Babylonian magic can still be detected in the stories of serpents being turned into rods, of a "bush that burns and is not consumed," and of plagues produced by incantation. The carrying of the "ark of the covenant" into battle reflects a primitive view of a portable deity confined in space, so that if the ark were lost divine protection could not be expected. But all these symbols and imageries, some of them primitive in origin, are brought by the Mosaic religion into the service of a transcendent vision of great nobility, and committed into the keeping of a people which had been chosen for a special burden of spiritual responsibility.

From Servitude to Freedom

The author of the new religion was also the leader of his people's national liberation. Moses was deeply touched by the affliction of his people in Egyptian bondage. He imparted to them the conviction that their freedom could be secured by revolt—against both Egypt's secular domination and against her spiritual corruption.

A Nation Is Born

Uniting the Israelites in the worship of a single God he manages, without physical authority or sanction at his command, to lead them in a forty-year journey across the Sinai desert into Canaan amidst a constant growth of their spiritual and national identity. The Exodus from Egypt is not only a liberation from servitude. It is the crucial event in Israel's self-conception. It is a people's constitutive moment. In later generations, whenever prophetic voices warned Israel against the loss of its identity or the erosion of its values, they appealed to the unifying and exhilarating memory of the departure from Egypt.

Beyond its particular stature in Israel's history the Exodus was to become a symbol of national and social liberation in many cultures and tongues. In the words of Henry George: "From between the paws of the rock-heavy Sphinx rises the genius of human liberty; and the trumpets of the Exodus throb with the defiant proclamation of the rights of man." When Benjamin Franklin and Thomas Jefferson were consulted on the emblem of the future American Union, they suggested that the seal of the United States should represent the Children of Israel fleeing across the parted waters of the sea on their way to freedom. This portrayal was to be surmounted by the slogan, "Resistance to Tyrants is Obedience to God." In the National Convention of Revolutionary France, popular leaders spoke of themselves as inheritors of the new "Canaan." Whether they sought liberation from a foreign yoke or from the degradation of poverty, men were to use the imagery of the Exodus to symbolize a possibility of swift transition from "servitude to freedom, from darkness to light." Thus the Exodus, in addition to its specific role in history, emerges as a dynamic social myth able to describe and inspire the revolutionary impulse in many times and in distant lands.

In the Wilderness There are three hundred years of Israel's history, between the sixteenth and thirteenth centuries, for which the Bible is our only source. Egyptian records never refer to Israel's sojourn. This may be because the period of Hyksos domination was considered too inglorious to be described. Today it is generally accepted that Hebrew migration to Egypt took place in the eighteenth century B.C.E. or after and that the Exodus occurred later than the fourteenth century, probably during the reign of Ramesses II (1290–1225). Both the descent into Egypt and the departure probably occurred in various

A Nation Is Born waves. The number of Hebrews who left Egypt is equally uncertain.

The Biblical version of six hundred thousand men, with their wives and families, seems vastly exaggerated. It is unlikely that such a number could have found a livelihood in the Sinai desert. It is more likely that the Israelites who marched across the sea to the wilderness of Sinai comprised a few thousand.

The Exodus began at the northeastern end of the Nile Delta. The Bible narrative leads the Israelites straight to Mount Sinai. To this day the location of Mount Sinai (or Mount Horeb) is a mystery which some modern scholars claim to have solved among the granite mountains in the southern Sinai peninsula. From there, the group moves to the Oasis of Kadesh (some fifty kilometers southwest of Beersheba). Thence they probably intended to move straight up to Canaan. The shorter route through the Philistine country was closed to them by Egyptian fortifications on the coast. The attempt to enter Canaan from the south was equally unsuccessful. Here the Canaanite defenses blocked the entrance to the Negev, and the Israelite effort to break through was repulsed by the King of Arad. After this defeat they were forced to return to the desert and to wander from oasis to oasis. Their main center remained at Kadesh Barnea where they lived the customary desert life, nomadic and uncertain.

The Biblical narrative is divided on the events leading to the conquest of Canaan. While the Book of Judges speaks of a long and gradual penetration, the Book of Joshua describes a swift and brilliant campaign by a military leader who subjugated many parts of the country. Most authorities agree that one version does not exclude the other. The military assault of Joshua was an important stage in a longer struggle in which each tribe played its particular local role. It is difficult to reconstruct the conquest of Canaan with any certitude. There are no contemporary inscriptions, and Biblical sources are inconsistent. Recent excavations have shed some light on the conquest of various Canaanite towns, such as Hazor. The capture of Jericho and Ai, on the eastern approaches to Jerusalem, appear to be legendary tales, since both cities had been destroyed long before the fourteenth century.

Return to Canaan

Joshua followed an unconventional strategy. He penetrated Canaan from its eastern flank, and the conquest resulted in settlement in Transjordan. Now, the Israelites in Egypt had had no tribal organization and it is hard to ascertain which tribes took part in the

Exodus or in the conquest. The capture of the lands west of Jordan is even more obscure. There was no immediate or total occupation of the country. Apart from the territories in Transjordan the areas occupied were mainly those of the mountains of Ephraim (Samaria), the Lower and the Upper Galilee. There the Israelites had to confront the most formidable of the Canaanites, the King of Hazor, "who was strong because he had war chariots made of iron, whereas the Israelites had only light weapons. . . ." Hazor, situated at the crossroads from Sidon to Bet Shan and from Megiddo to Damascus was the leading Canaanite city in the North. Its political influence was commensurate with its strategic importance. Joshua's victory over the King of Hazor at the waters of Merom was understandably hailed as the crown of his military career. But even thereafter many Canaanite cities in the plains remained intact behind their walls and the cities in the coastal strip were never conquered.

The Israelites after the conquest lived with their neighbors in an uneasy relationship. Their victories may have led to accessions by defeated clans and cities which came over to be incorporated into the Israelite structure. Once the military victory was stabilized Israel began her national life.

The Bible does not represent the Israelite entry into Canaan as a conquest by an alien people. The process is described as the return of tribes who, in the distant but unforgotten past, had dwelled in the land. The people who now returned had never seen the "Promised Land," but they had dreamed of it for generations. This home had been vivid in their memory and as the only place in which their divine mission could be fulfilled.

The Land The land between the Mediterranean and the Arabian desert, bordered by Syria in the north and the Sinai peninsula in the south, compresses a great diversity of climate and landscape within a small space. Between the River Jordan and the coast there is the fertile valley of Esdraelon (Jezreel) and the once richly forested hills of Galilee and lowlands (Shephelah) in which abundant crops have rewarded patient cultivation. The coastal plain was in ancient days a highway for armies and merchandise passing from the empires of the Tigris-Euphrates valleys to those of the Nile Delta.

The River Jordan, rising in the Lebanese foothills, sinks 680 feet below the level of the sea into Lake Galilee. Sixty-five miles farther south it descends into the Dead Sea, 1290 feet below maritime level.

*The olive tree, ancient and twisted but fruitful and evergreen,
rises out of the Negev wastes, its yellow-white flowers a
promise of beauty, its oil-rich fruit the promise of plenty, its
olive branches the promise and symbol of peace.*

This valley then rises to a point some 300 feet above sea level before it sinks again into the Gulf of Aqaba (Eilat) on the Red Sea shore. Along this southern line the climate is tropical, the scenery volcanic. In the Judean hills to the north and west there is a regular winter rainfall. It is a broken, varied land seemingly destined by nature for tribal fragmentation and hostile to centralized control. What is common to all its parts is the bright clear quality of its light, sharpening the edges of mountains against the sky, giving an ever-changing design to the folds and hollows, and illuminating the sea with dramatic shifts of color as the sun ascends and falls. With all its smallness the country offers sharp contrasts of wilderness and fertility, a sense of space and distance which comes from Palestine's high position between the great desert and the great sea.

The land was called by many names. For the Akkadians it was part of Amurru ("West" in Akkadian), or land of the Amorites. To the Egyptians it was Retenu, but they also called it Canaan during the eighteenth and nineteenth dynasties. This is the name given to the land by the Hebrews.

The Bible describes the Canaanites as one people among other inhabitants of the Land of Canaan. At other times, however, "Canaanites" is used as a collective name for all the sedentary dwellers in Palestine before the Hebrew conquest. It is evident that Canaan before the Israelite conquest was a country without a political identity, yet it was marked by a strong vitality of culture. Indeed, Canaanite culture at the time of the conquest embraced the entire coastland of Palestine and Syria, from the Egyptian frontier south of Gaza to the northern boundary of Ugarit (southwest of Antioch). Several languages were spoken in this small area and five systems of writing came into use. Akkadian cuneiform and Egyptian hieroglyphs were the international scripts of the period. But there were other scripts which were even more revolutionary in their influence —for they are the oldest alphabets ever to have been used. One, consisting of 32 letters, was current mainly in the Syrian harbor town of Ugarit. The other was probably invented in southern Palestine: a 22-letter alphabet which is the source of the alphabets of modern languages—Phoenician, Hebrew, Greek, and Roman.

3 ❧ Israel in the Land

*T*WO CENTURIES (1230–1023 B.C.E.) divide the conquest of Canaan from the establishment of the monarchy under Saul. These are described in the Bible as the "days when the judges ruled."

When Israel entered Canaan she was not yet a nation. Her formative period still lay ahead. The transition from a semi-nomadic to an agricultural society, the transformation of political organization, and the evolution from tribe to nation, were all to be influenced by contact with the populations of Canaan and by the diversity of the Israelite community itself. The land too was to impress its stamp on Israel's social evolution.

Palestine's geography worked in favor of a tribal organization. It was a small country. But within a compact space it found room for a kaleidoscopic range of landscapes, climates, and geographic features, some forty distinct climatic and geographic units having been identified within its limited borders. These range from the snow-capped Mount Hermon to the Dead Sea, the lowest place on earth. Hill dwellers and residents of the plains naturally reflected their diversity in separatist tribal units.

Canaanite enclaves continued to exist—especially in the valley of Esdraelon and in the Jerusalem hill country. The consolidation of the tribes was thus rendered difficult. There must have been periods of peaceful relations among Israelites and Canaanites, and we know that some merging of cultures took place. The Israelites had settled among a civilization higher than their own, whereas they themselves still constituted a heterogeneous society reflecting many differences.

The material condition of the Israelites slowly improved. They became a nation of small farmers. They learned to build water cisterns. In their dire need for more soil, they showed resourcefulness in reclaiming land from desert and forests. Their towns—few and badly fortified—were of rural character, unlike the strongholds of the Canaanite and Philistine towns. Israel's strength depended on the number of men under arms who could be mustered in case of need. More often than not tribal loyalties seemed to have prevailed against Israel's larger interests. "In those days," as the Bible reports, "there was no king in Israel; every man did that which was right in his own eyes."

The political organization of ancient Israel was expressed in a religious bond. A federation of the twelve tribes was formed around a central sanctuary. One religious center was established in Shiloh, though both Gilgal and Shechem are mentioned as places where the tribes assembled for war or worship. In Shiloh they had deposited the Holy Ark. Here they acknowledged one and the same God; and here they celebrated festivals with the symbol of God's presence in their midst.

The Days of the Judges   In times of crisis the people applied for help to a judge. He was a general custodian of the public interest—seer, military leader, and deliverer all in one. He was a man chosen by God for his mission, endowed with divine spirit. The Book of Judges is our only record for this period. It is very fragmentary and details of the rule of the Judges are few. Of some, like Othniel and Ehud, who were not involved in any military crisis, we know little but their names. On the other hand, Deborah and Jephthah, Samson and Gideon, Eli and Samuel, have made history. No judge ever ruled over the whole of Israel. The evolution which led to the establishment of national unity was caused not so much by internal as by external developments. The Philistine crisis was an emergency that the tribes could not meet.

The Philistines were an Aegean people. They had been driven out of their homes on Crete and on the shores of Asia Minor by invaders from the North. Failing in their attempt to penetrate into Egypt, they obtained a foothold on the Palestine coast where they

consolidated their strength around five cities: Gaza, Ashkelon,

*Ancient and powerful foes of Israel,
the Philistines practiced the warlike skills of the
Hittites and the peaceful crafts of Crete. Here a
Philistine bowl excavated at Tel Zipor.*

Ashdod, Ekron, and Gath. The Philistines occupied some of the most fertile country of the region, and their resources were abundant. They had superior arms. They had inherited the Hittites' secret knowledge of how to make iron and to weld it into weapons. Their physical appearance too was overpowering. Men of great stature were not uncommon among them.

Some of the Israelite tribes were under constant pressure from the Philistines and were forced to cede them territory. In the face of this common danger, the Israelite tribes were compelled to present a united front, but were beaten in battle at Aphek. This disaster took on the proportions of a national catastrophe when the Ark, brought into battle, fell into the hands of the enemy (ca. 1050). The lesson was plain: if they were to resist Philistine domination, the Israelites had to have a national leader.

The Monarchy   There are many contradictions in the narratives relating to Saul's elevation and the role Samuel played in it. The Israelites had demanded of Samuel: "Behold, you are old and your sons do not walk in your ways. Choose a king for us to judge us like all the nations." But Samuel warned them of the dangers of monarchy:

> This will be the manner of king who will reign over you; he will take your sons and appoint them to his chariots. And he will appoint captains over thousands and captains over fifties; and set them to till his ground, and to reap his harvest, and to make his instruments of war. And he will take your daughters to be his confectioners and cooks and bakers. And he will take your fields and your vineyards and your olive groves, indeed the best of them and give them to those who serve him. And he will take a tenth of your seed and of your vineyards, to give to his officers. And he will take your manservants and your maidservants, and your best young men and your asses, to do his work. And you shall be his slaves. . . . The people refused to listen to Samuel, and they answered: Nevertheless we will have a king over us that we may be like all the nations, and that our king may judge us and lead us into battles.

In the end, however, Samuel listened to the voice of the people. He set out, full of foreboding, to select a king.

The man whom Samuel chose to be Israel's first king was Saul, the son of Kish, a farmer in Benjamin, the smallest of the Israelite tribes. He was a "young man and handsome, and among the Children of Israel there was not a handsomer person than he. And from his shoulders and upward he was taller than any of the people."

Saul's reign was principally taken up with the struggle against the Philistines. He used the first years of his rule to build up a strong and efficient army; many of his soldiers were drawn from his own tribe, Benjamin.

A spectacular victory at Michmash led to the expulsion of the enemy from the Benjaminite and Ephraimite territories. Punitive or retaliatory raids were carried out against other neighbors. These included the Moabites, the Ammonites, and Arameans to the east and southeast, and later, the Amalekites in the south. These victories enhanced the pride of the Israelites. The peril of foreign invasion remained, however, one of the dominant factors in national affairs for a full generation to come.

Saul filled the gap between the primitive organization under the Judges and the establishment of a full monarchy under David. He is, perhaps, the most tragic figure in the Biblical story. Of complex character, he was unable to profit from his relationship with Samuel and David. He was suspicious to the point of paranoia. He suffered from fits of terror and from depressions of melancholy. His authority, however, had a marked religious character which no doubt contributed toward the union of the nation under his aegis and organization.

Little is known about the administration of the state under Saul's rule. It seems that the unification of various parts of his state remained imperfect. His absolute authority extended only over the center of the country, while the border districts came only gradually under his power. His residence was his native town, Gibeah, in the land of the Benjaminites.

Saul and David Recognized by the tribes of the center and the north, Saul had one internal enemy, the powerful tribe of Judah, which chafed at its eclipse by Benjamin. David, the son of Jesse, a Judean farmer, enjoyed great consideration in Saul's military household. He had risen to prominence while still a boy, after defeating the Philistine giant Goliath in single combat, "with a sling and a stone." Since then, "David went wherever Saul went." He played the harp for him, married the king's daughter, and was the loving friend of the king's son, Jonathan. His daring raids on the enemy became the
Israel in the Land themes of popular ballads.

Saul became alarmed at David's ascension to popular favor. "Saul has slain thousands," the people sang, "but David, his ten thousands." Saul began to suspect the young man of political rivalry. Toward the end of his reign, Saul became obsessed with the idea that if he could rid himself of David, all would go well. He saw traitors everywhere.

Finding his life in danger, David escaped to his native district in the hill country of Judah. For the next few years he lived as an outlaw. Saul made several attempts to hunt him down and showed little mercy to any of his sympathizers. The Biblical narrative brilliantly captures the spiritual and mental torment of this unlucky monarch:

> . . . When Saul returned from following the Philistines, he was told, "David is in the wilderness of Engedi."
>
> So Saul took three thousand chosen men, and went to seek David among the rocks of the wild goats. He came to the sheepcotes along the way where there was a cave, and Saul went in to cover his feet.
>
> Now David and his men were lodged inside the innermost parts of the cave. David rose, and noiselessly cut off the skirt of Saul's robe. But afterward David's heart smote him, and he said to his men, "The Lord forbid that I should do this to my master, to stretch out my hand against the Lord's anointed." David checked his men with these words, and would not let them rise against Saul.
>
> When Saul left the cave, David also went out, and called after him, "My Lord, the King."
>
> Saul looked behind him, and David bowed with his face to the earth and said, "Why do you listen to men who say, David seeks your hurt? See the skirt of your robe in my hand; I cut it off, yet did not kill you. I have not sinned against you, yet you hunt my soul to take it. The Lord judge between us and avenge me, but my hand shall not be upon you. As says the proverb of the ancients, Wickedness proceeds from the wicked. After whom does the king of Israel come? Whom do you pursue? After a dead dog? After a flea? The Lord judge between us."
>
> When David finished speaking, Saul said, "Is this your voice, my son David?" And Saul lifted up his voice and wept. And he said, "You are more righteous than I, for you have rewarded me with good, whereas I have rewarded you with evil."
>
> And Saul went home. But David and his men returned to the stronghold.

David was forced to take refuge among the Philistines, in the campaigns against whom he had made his name. He was living at Ziklag, under the protection of the King of Gath, when Saul with Jonathan and two other sons fell in battle on Mount Gilboa in a vain effort to stem further Philistine incursion. The King was wounded on the battlefield by Philistine archers. He begged his armor-bearer to make an end of his life. The man refused. Saul took his own sword and fell upon it. David mourned the tragic death of the King and his three sons in a noble elegy:

> How are the mighty fallen! Tell it not in Gath, nor in the streets of Ashkelon; lest the daughters of the Philistines rejoice, lest the daughters of the enemy exult.

> O mountains of Gilboa, let there be no dew, let there be no rain upon you, for there the shield of the mighty was cast away—the shield of Saul, as though he had not been anointed.

> From the blood of the slain, from the fat of the mighty, the bow of Jonathan turned not back, and the sword of Saul returned not empty.

> Saul and Jonathan, beloved and loving, in their life and in their death they were not divided! They were swifter than eagles; they were stronger than lions.

> O daughters of Israel, weep for Saul, who clothed you in scarlet, who adorned your garments with gold. How are the mighty fallen in the midst of battle!

> O Jonathan, I am distressed for you, my brother Jonathan. Your love to me was more wonderful than the love of women.

> How are the mighty fallen, and the weapons of war perished!

David Becomes King

Saul was succeeded by his son, Eshbaal, who removed the royal residence to Mahanaim, east of the Jordan. David was now in a position to lay his claim to kingship. He reentered the country with his veteran warriors and seized Hebron, very probably with the aid of the Philistines, who were not averse to seeing their enemies weakened by internal struggle. The Judean tribesmen looked to David as their chieftain and were ready to accept him as king.

But David's ambitions were greater. He wished to complete the task begun by Saul and to unite all the tribes of Israel, and not Judah alone, under his crown. Israel's position, after the Philistine victory at Mount Gilboa, was desperate. But the Israelites were determined to have a kingdom of their own. Thus the division of Israel into two kingdoms had in a sense already virtually taken place, symbolically summing up the schism between Israel and Judah and prefiguring the subsequent organizational severance.

In order to seize and consolidate his power, David had to resolve both domestic and foreign problems. On the one hand, he had to unite Judah under his sole authority, and on the other, in order to incorporate Israel, it was necessary to engage in constant warfare. In most of these battles, David's army was victorious. Eshbaal's position was undermined by the treason of his commander, Abner, who made open overtures to David. It seems that Abner had personal quarrels with Eshbaal. He had taken the concubine of the dead King Saul. According to the customs of those days, this was a royal prerogative. Abner realized that David, both as military and political leader, was far superior to the mediocre Eshbaal. Thus Eshbaal became more and more isolated; one by one his closest followers and friends deserted him.

Despite their resentment of the south, the northern tribes came to recognize that the interests of the nation would best be served if David became ruler of a united Israel. David was forced to act when Abner was treacherously murdered by David's military commander Joab, while Eshbaal found his death at the hands of two of his officers. His reign had lasted but two years.

After the death of Eshbaal, the tribes of Israel, represented by their notables, came to Hebron and offered the throne to David. David had achieved his aim. He became King over a united nation.

The Philistines saw the significance of David's elevation quite clearly. He was still too weak to start an effective offensive against them, and therefore they acted swiftly, invading Judah and threatening its capital, Hebron. David withdrew to Adullam, where he remained until he could consolidate his forces. From his stronghold he undertook a number of raids against the Philistines and finally defeated them decisively at Gath.

After expelling the Philistines, David's next objective was Jerusalem (then called Jebus) which had remained in the hands of the Canaanites. This situation interfered seriously with communication between the north and the south, thus hindering the unification of Judah and Israel, which was David's central aim. He also wanted to make Jerusalem his capital.

When David took up residence in Jerusalem, the citadel became known as the City of David. All that the city lacked was religious prestige. Canaanite Jerusalem had had its own holy places. David, wishing to link the national prestige of the new capital with the religious traditions of Moses, transferred to Jerusalem the Ark of the God of Israel and made plans for the building of a magnificent

temple to house it. This task he left, according to the advice of the prophet Nathan, to his successor.

Jerusalem, the City of Peace, the City of David, was to remain the sentimental and spiritual center for the Jewish people throughout history, and later to become its capital again. From its place in Jewish history all its other renown has flowed.

The Wars of David

After his decisive victory over the Philistines, David began a series of foreign expeditions. He took advantage of the temporary weakness of Egypt to the south and of Assyria to the north, to build a powerful border kingdom. He then secured his borders by a succession of wars against neighboring states.

David's rule lasted forty years, but each year was a year of war. However, he rewarded his people with victories over the Philistines and over Ammon, Moab, and Edom. He built alliances with Phoenicia and the King of Tyre; he placed a garrison in Syria; Moab and Amalek were subdued (the latter finally); and the land of Edom was annexed. Thus the entire Mediterranean coast, except for Phoenicia and small parts of Philistia, had been made tributary, and Transjordan, as far as the Arabian Desert to the east, also acknowledged David as king. David was not only a brilliant military leader but a very gifted statesman as well. Parallel to his military expeditions, he built up a network of alliances. His authority was recognized from the borders of Egypt and the Gulf of Aqaba to the banks of the Euphrates. In order to uphold his power, David had to maintain a standing army, the nucleus of which was the Kings' Guard of the "Gibborim" (Heroes). The command was controlled centrally in Jerusalem and was directly under the King's authority. Its commander-in-chief was Abner, the King's nephew.

South of the walls of Jerusalem, in the shadow of the Mount of Olives, recent archaeology has unearthed not only the original city of Ophel which David wrested from the Jebusites but also the burial ground of the family of Jesse.

While David was preoccupied by military cares, he also found time to set up a new administration. Manpower and money were obtained by taking booty and tributes from conquered peoples, and by taxation and forced labor at home. Yet the monarchy established by David was constitutional in spirit. The rights of the sovereign were limited by public opinion as voiced by the prophets.

The last years of David's reign were troubled and disturbed. The royal household was convulsed by cruelty, jealousy, and intrigues. David was worn out by a life of constant hardship; he aged prematurely. His sons by various wives quarreled among themselves. Ultimately his own son, Absalom, broke from him in open revolt, supported on this occasion by a part of the population. The rebels were outwitted and defeated by David's militia under its commander Joab. Absalom, the King's beloved son, was killed by Joab himself.

To future generations, David was an inspiring figure. His personality and achievement were the driving force behind Ezra and Nehemiah when they turned from exile to rebuild the Temple and the city of Jerusalem five hundred years after David's death. Nearly three hundred years after Nehemiah, the Maccabees in turn drew strength from the memory of David, the wise ruler and great Psalmist, who had achieved in fact the independence dreamed of in later generations.

The Biblical tradition attributes to David many qualities, but none more endearing than his gift for poetry and music. In all probability, he composed some parts of the Psalms ascribed to him. David's loves and hates, his virtues and human failings, have gripped the imagination of peoples across many centuries. He is an authentic figure both of history and of drama.

King Solomon

"Let Zadok the Priest and Nathan the Prophet anoint him King over Israel, and blow the trumpet and say, 'Long live King Solomon!'" Thus King David, on his deathbed, arranged for his succession, choosing his youngest son by his favorite wife, Bathsheba.

Court intrigues and murder marked the beginning of Solomon's rule. Fearing an eventual rival, he had his brother Adonijah executed. (The pretext, as was so often the case, was Adonijah's demand for a woman from the late King's harem.) This done, "the kingdom was firmly established in Solomon's hand." It fell to Solomon to complete the building of the kingdom which his father had begun. While the work of consolidation under him was a gigantic success, his rule also laid the seed for the disruption which was to follow in time.

Solomon's reign was unmarred by wars; he did not acquire new territories for Israel. But with great diplomatic skill he made his country an equal among the great powers of his time. He entered into friendly alliances with these powers, often achieved or cemented by marriages with foreign princesses. His marriage to Pharaoh's daughter even brought him a useful dowry in the form of the town of Gezer, which was important for opening the way to the Mediterranean.

Israel's rise to prominence must be seen against the background *Israel in the Land* of the ancient Near East at about 1000 B.C.E. Egypt's power was

A terracotta plaque from Tel Asmar in Babylonia showing harp which was a familiar musical instrument mentioned in the Psalms of David.

The relics of a house at Megiddo built during David's reign, 11th-10th century B.C.E.

at a low point. Mesopotamia was divided into several states, not one of which was strong enough to venture outside its own territory. David's plans for expansion filled a power vacuum in Western Asia. Not a single state in the region was powerful enough to obstruct Israel's expansion.

Solomon was a determined builder. He fortified towns of strategic and economic interest: Hazor and Megiddo on the route from Egypt to Damascus; Tamar, the gate of the caravan route leading to the Red Sea and Haran, shielding Jerusalem from the south. Though Israel was mainly an agricultural people, little prone to commerce on a large scale, Solomon saw great possibilities in the development of trade. He built a magnificent fleet and established Ezion Geber on the Gulf of Aqaba as the home port. From there, his ships undertook mysterious voyages to the lands of Ophir (probably southern Arabia or perhaps India) bringing "gold and ivory, sandalwood and precious stones, apes and peacocks." Solomon also permitted Hebrew sailors to join foreign expeditions; they sailed the Mediterranean as far as Tarshish (Spain). Thus he made his country one of the chief transit places for commerce from east to west and from north to south.

Nelson Glueck has suggested that the visit of the Queen of Sheba to Jerusalem must have been connected with a diplomatic mission concerning the expansion of Israel's trade routes at the expense of other nations. Solomon's shipping lines were damaging the lucrative business of the Queen's caravan trade. She therefore hastened to Jerusalem with precious gifts in the hope of putting her personal charms in the service of arriving at a trade agreement. The Bible assures us that "King Solomon gave to the Queen of Sheba all that it pleased her to ask, besides which he gave her according to his royal bounty."

One of Solomon's outstanding economic enterprises was the building of copper mines and refineries for the smelting of metals near the river Timna in the Negev. These mines were rediscovered by the modern Israel army three thousand years later and are again producing for the people of Israel.

Solomon surrounded his kingdom with all the external signs of a great power: he built numerous luxurious palaces for which he had to import skilled workers and raw materials. He crowned his building activities with a magnificent Temple, erected on Mount Moriah, which he adorned with sculptures and works of art. Zadok was appointed High Priest. This event inaugurated a hereditary Priesthood which was to last for a thousand years. Solomon dedicated the Temple with much splendor on the Feast of Tabernacles (about 953) declaring, "I have surely built Thee a house of habitation—a place for Thee to dwell forever."

The reign of Solomon saw great material progress. New cities and villages came into existence. The population doubled in size, to a figure of 800,000. However, the general prosperity did not affect all of Solomon's subjects. The people had to pay heavily for his extravagances, and Solomon was forced to take unpopular measures in order to meet his ever-increasing expenses. He must have been so short of funds at one time that he ceded twenty towns in the Galilee to his ally, the King of Tyre, for a sum of 120 talents. In order to improve the efficiency of his administration, he had the country reorganized into twelve districts, thereby disregarding the conventional division of the tribes. He appointed *netzivim* (overseers) to supervise such internal affairs as the enrollment of the citizenry for forced labor and the payment of taxes, a yoke which weighed heavily upon the population. Such policies naturally alienated large sections of the populace, which was accustomed to a less rigid form of life and, instead, found itself under the iron rule of an absolute monarch.

Increasing contact with foreign nations led to a mingling of populations. Together with foreign princesses came alien religious ideas. The worship of Baal and other Phoenician deities spread throughout Israel; their shrines and altars became a common sight. Solomon's cosmopolitan tolerance, in fact, opened the way to apostasy.

The magnificence of Solomon's rule was marred by dissatisfaction on the part of the populace. Solomon was criticized for his habit of according preferential treatment to his own tribes in the south, thereby embittering the north. The northern tribes rebelled when forced labor was imposed upon them, and their leader Jeroboam had to flee to safety in Egypt. With Solomon's death the disruption of national unity could not be halted.

Solomon, despite the shortcomings of his reign, stands out in history as the ruler who united in one person the sagacity of a judge and the gifts of a worker and thinker. The Biblical annalists have glorified his enterprise and lavished admiration upon him. They attributed to him all the qualities which have come down to us in a wealth of legends, in proverbs and in psalms, in love songs and in magic spells.

It is irrefutable that Solomon achieved the reinforcement of the monarchy; no bloody wars stain his success. But an excess of political and economic power brought a neglect of other spheres: the glory of the state transcended all human and national considerations. It is true that foreign marriages fostered valuable alliances, and that the ceding of cities enabled the mobilization of funds; but such policies weakened the national fiber. Toward the end of Solomon's reign, the prophet Ahijah denounced the King's excessive toleration of foreign cults and encouraged instead the separatist tendencies of the ten tribes. The eventual disruption of the kingdom was further advanced by the resurgence of Egypt and the emergence of a strong Assyria. A period of weakness among neighboring powers had favored Israel's meteoric rise to national strength. This moment was now over. The era of the united kingdom had lasted for the reigns of only three monarchs—Saul, David and Solomon.

4 ❧ The Fall of Israel and Judah

SOLOMON'S oppressive policy had antagonized northern Israel. During the last years of his reign, the early rumblings of revolt were already audible. With his death, an explosion was unavoidable. The country split into two political units which were henceforth to have their separate histories. They were akin in blood, but their relation was to alternate between rivalry and alliance, and, on occasion, to erupt in war. Israel, the larger and wealthier of the two kingdoms, determined the foreign affairs of both, reducing Judah to the status of a vassal. But the Northern Kingdom itself lacked cohesion. It was composed of many tribes, and was constantly torn by civil strife. Northern Israel was to survive for two hundred years before disappearing from history almost without a trace.

The destiny of Judah was to be quite different. Smaller and less wealthy, her population was more homogeneous and less exposed to foreign influences. She had the advantages of a stable dynastic tradition and of a religious unity symbolized in the Temple of Jerusalem. Her geography made her less vulnerable to foreign aggression.

Upon the death of Solomon, his son, Rehoboam, was proclaimed king in Jerusalem. Following a precedent created by his father, Rehoboam hastened to Shechem to receive the acclamation of the northern tribes. This was his doom. The elders to whom he presented himself laid down conditions before they would acknowl-

36

edge his rule: He must reduce taxes and abandon forced labor. Rehoboam reacted with stupidity and arrogance. He took counsel with his advisers who exhorted him wisely, "If you will be a servant to the people, and speak good words to them, then they will be your servants forever." But Rehoboam preferred the attitude of his younger counselors:

> Speak thus to the people: You say, "Your father made our yoke heavy, therefore lighten it for us." But you shall find my little finger thicker than my father's loins. And now, whereas my father burdened you with a heavy yoke, I will add to your yoke. My father chastised you with whips, but I will chastise you with scorpions.

The Biblical narrative tells the sequel in concise words:

> Jeroboam and all the people returned to Rehoboam on the third day, as the king had appointed. And the king answered the people roughly, and spoke to them after the counsel of the young men. When the people of Israel saw that the king would not listen to them, they said to him, "What portion have we in David? We have no inheritance in the son of Jesse. To your tents, O Israel! Now look to your own house, David!" And the people departed.

> Rehoboam reigned over those who dwelt in the cities of Judah; but when he sent Adoram, who was in charge of the tribute, the people of Israel stoned him to death. And King Rehoboam fled to Jerusalem.

> So Israel rebelled against the House of David. And they summoned Jeroboam to the congregation, and made him king over Israel. And the House of David was followed by the Tribe of Judah only.

The Northern Kingdom

The first of the nineteen kings to rule Israel during the ensuing two centuries was the leader of the rebellion, Jeroboam, who, on Solomon's death, had returned from exile. He had once before attempted to revolt, during Solomon's reign, but had been forced to flee and seek asylum at the court of Pharaoh Shishak I. Of his administration little is known. Tirzah, near Shechem, was his capital. But the Temple in Jerusalem held the people's loyalty and affection. To compete with Jerusalem's attraction, Jeroboam set up Israel's own shrines at the two extreme ends of his country: in Dan and in Beth El, where ancient religious traditions still lingered in popular memory. Jeroboam is denounced in the Book of Kings for having opened the way for the reintroduction of the Baal cult and other forms of idolatry in Israel. There may well be some factual basis for this assertion. Religious purity had never been complete in Israel, but was always diluted by the presence of foreign populations, and Jeroboam may have adjusted his policies to this reality.

Jeroboam's monarchy lasted for twenty-one years—a long reign in the history of the north, where tribal jealousies, usurpations, and civil strife led to frequent changes of monarchial power. After him, the country had only two periods of respite: the first, after the establishment of the house of Omri, and the second, with the succession of Jeroboam II (793–753) of the line of Jehu, which was to last for a hundred years. But the general history was one of dynastic crises accompanied by social unrest. Foreign invasions ravaged the land and heavy tributes to alien powers drained its resources.

Political recovery set in with the establishment of the Omride dynasty (876–842). It is certain that Omri and his successors, by resolute politics, prolonged the existence of the Northern Kingdom. Omri was the first ruler to establish friendly relations with Judah. This gave him a free hand to conduct his foreign relations. He succeeded in reconquering much of the lost territory. He also reestablished close ties with Phoenicia, and strengthened the alliance by marrying his son Ahab to Jezebel, a daughter of the King of Tyre. His aim was to resist Aram, the emerging power centered in Damascus.

With peace and relative prosperity came a trend toward urbanization. Samaria became the new capital and gave its name to the whole kingdom. It surpassed all the other cities in size and economic power. But in urban society deep social antagonisms were sharpened. Prosperity was restricted to an upper class. The common people, farmers and artisans, found the gap between themselves and their masters widening. Frequent droughts, together with other plagues, added to the plight of the poor.

In this situation, religious crisis cast a deepening shadow. From her native land, Jezebel had brought a pagan religion which she not only openly practised herself, but tried to foist on others with missionary zeal. A temple to her god, Baal Melqart, was erected in Samaria, and wholesale apostasies occurred, especially among the old native population. For this Jezebel incurred the intense hatred of the prophets.

Opposition to the new paganism was led by the prophet Elijah and his group of rebels. They accused Ahab of participating in the idolatrous cult of Jezebel, and thereby of doing "more to provoke the anger of the Lord God of Israel than all the kings of Israel who were before him."

But the prophets did not constitute the only opposition to the monarchy. Dissatisfaction had in the meantime spread to the army, especially during Ahab's war against Aram, a country which had been gaining prestige and power. Ben Hadad II, king of Aram, had invaded Samaria and demanded surrender in a degrading ultimatum. Ahab was prevented from surrendering by his elders, who forced him to resist, and Ben Hadad was driven back. A year later, however, he attempted another invasion, this time joining battle in the plain of Jezreel. He considered the God of Israel to be a mountain god and felt more at ease on lower ground. His great armies were opposed by the inferior troops of Israel, which looked to him like "two little flocks of goats." For six days the two armies stood poised for battle. When it broke out on the seventh day, the Israelites drove the enemy within the gates of Aphek, and brought the walls of the city crumbling down upon them, burying many of the Aramean soldiers in the ruins. Though Ben Hadad was taken prisoner, Ahab showed clemency and let him go free. Later, he made an alliance with Aram, in an effort to thwart the looming danger of Assyria.

But the struggle for the succession, led by dissidents in the Israelite army, went on, and was finally won by Jehu, Ahab's able general. On usurping the throne, Jehu murdered the hated Jezebel and all Ahab's descendants. He then founded his own dynasty which was to last for a century (842–745). No illustrious deeds mark the years of his reign, in which Israel was constantly threatened by Aram. Jehu could, at best, secure an intermittent peace by paying heavy tribute to Assyria, the new power arising as a rival to Aram. This event is represented on a famous obelisk discovered in the Assyrian palace of King Shalmaneser which shows delegations of men kneeling before the Assyrian monarch.

In Samaria's desperate struggle for survival, Assyria served for a time as a deterrent to Aram's aggression. Jehu murdered not only the whole house of Omri and its supporters, but all the priests and prophets dedicated to the Baal cult. His revolution thus had a religious character. It was inspired by the pious fervor which had seized the country under the influence of Elijah, the thundering prophet from Gilead, and was maintained by his follower, Elisha.

The Kingdom of Judah Two tribes had joined in forming the Southern Kingdom: Benjamin and Judah. The latter gave the kingdom its name.

Judah's good fortune lay in her comparative isolation and in her small size. She was less important than Israel either as foe or

as ally in the power struggles of the Near East. She was threatened mainly by the expansionism of her southern neighbor, Egypt, which, with the founding of the new dynasty by Shishak, was emerging to new heights of power.

In the fifth year of Rehoboam's reign, the armies of Shishak already stood at the gates of Jerusalem. They apparently had no plans for occupying the capital, but the invasion spread over the whole country, devastating it from one end to the other. Total defeat was averted only by the payment of heavy tribute.

The war with Egypt continued under Rehoboam's successor, Asa, who also had to deal with the aggression of the Northern Kingdom. Asa was successful in averting both dangers. He withstood the Egyptians and, by bribing the King of Aram to attack Israel, he relieved the pressure on Judah from the north.

Jehoshaphat, Asa's son, did much to restore Judah's fortunes, extending his influence as far as Aqaba and southern Edom. The relationship between Israel and Judah also improved. It was strengthened by a marriage bond: Jehoshaphat's son Jehoram married Athalia, the daughter of Ahab and Jezebel. But this bond was to antagonize large sections of the Judean population. With Athalia came foreign gods. The Baal cult made fewer inroads here than it had in the Northern Kingdom, but many in Judah could not forgive the disruption of the nation's religious unity. On her husband's death, Athalia tried to usurp the throne, but as a foreigner, she evoked little support and was finally assassinated. An infant son of Jehoram was anointed king, while the Priesthood gained influence and introduced reforms to consolidate the ancient pieties and restore the national unity.

The two kindred countries of the south and north were at daggers drawn again.

The End of the Northern Kingdom

Under Jehu's successors, the agony of the Northern Kingdom was to last for another hundred years. As a pathetic vassal of Aram, it could endure only at Assyria's pleasure.

Of the later kings, Jeroboam II stands out as a brilliant ruler who, during his forty-year reign, brought the kingdom to its former power and wealth. He even succeeded in reconquering lost territory at the expense of Damascus, which was vying with Phoenicia for supremacy over all Syria. But the increase of wealth and the sharpening of class distinction brought moral corruption.

The Baal cult which had been routed by Jehu was now restored. It is against this background that the wrathful outbursts of Amos and Hosea must be understood. These prophets saw no salvation unless the moral and social decay into which the country had been plunged were halted.

While the upper classes gained in wealth, the poor fell into disastrous social decline. Amos, in his splendid tirades, came on the scene as an eloquent social reformer. The King and his supporters, Amos warned, had broken the Covenant with God: "They sold the righteous for money and the needy for the price of a pair of sandals." In the name of God, Amos portrayed the moral peril of a society in which the powerful held the poor under a heavy yoke.

The same warnings were uttered also by Hosea, an Israelite contemporary of Amos. Only if Israel turned back to God could the catastrophe be averted: "Return, O Israel, to the Lord your God. For you have stumbled in your iniquity."

The warnings of Amos and Hosea were to be confirmed. The dynasty of Jehu ended, as it began, in a wave of bloodshed.

Six kings were to follow Jeroboam II on the throne, one of them lasting for no more than a month. Anarchy at home was aggravated by the new menace from abroad. Assyria stood ready to strike. Not even a hastily conceived alliance with Phoenicia, Damascus, and Egypt could avert the danger. The war raged and Israel was slowly dismembered. The first province to fall was Gilead. Its population was deported. Civil war was flaming up again as Hoshea, the last of the Israelite kings, ascended the throne in 732. His Assyrian adversary, Shalmaneser V, besieged Samaria for three years. The next Assyrian king, Sargon II, broke Samaria's resistance and occupied the city in 721, thus ending the independence of the Northern Kingdom once and for all. On the inscriptions he left behind for posterity Sargon boasted of his conquest of the "wide land of Beth Omri" and of the "27,290 Israelites" he led into captivity.

This deportation has given rise to a double misconception: first, that there were ten tribes in northern Israel at the time of its destruction; and second, that these ten tribes were "lost," only to reappear elsewhere in the world. Time and time again, people all over the world have claimed descent from these "Ten Lost Tribes." But there were not, in fact, ten distinct tribes in Israel at the time of Sargon, the Assyrian. The exiles were lost as an entity. They were absorbed wherever they were transplanted. Only a few of the descendants of the Israelite exiles remained true to their God and managed, nearly 150 years later, to join with the exiles of Judah. The foreign settlers in Israel intermarried with the native popula-

Bas-relief showing Jews being exiled from Lachish. The siege and surrender of the fortified town was the highwater mark of the Babylonian invasion of Judea directed by King Sennacherib.

tion and partially absorbed its traditions. Thus a new race arose, to be known after the capital, Samaria, as the Samaritans. Without political independence, they could not, either spiritually or physically, be identified with the Hebrews, whose place they had taken. Their development led to the rise of an anti-Judean group among the Samaritans which was to resist the restoration of Jerusalem and the Temple when the Persians came into power in a later century.

The political independence and the spiritual identity of the Northern Kingdom now belonged to the past. It was in Judah alone that the national consciousness was henceforth embodied. Samaria became an Assyrian province, administered by Assyrian officers. Foreign settlers were transferred to its soil. The political and spiritual identity of the ten tribes became lost forever.

Judah under Assyrian Tutelage

With the Northern Kingdom annexed by Assyria, Judah found itself drawn more and more into the power struggles of the ancient world. Since the reign of Ahaz, its illusory independence had been bought from Assyria by tribute. Judah's geographic isolation, which had hitherto offered her some sort of protection, was likewise lost. Now she stood like "a tree with withered branches, feeling the Assyrian ax. . . ." Jerusalem lay barely thirty miles from the Assyrian garrison at Samaria. While Assyria and Egypt vied for supremacy over Palestine and Syria, Judah's situation became critical. It faced a crucial choice—to remain subdued forever or to take advantage of the rivalry between Egypt and Assyria in order to throw off the foreign yoke.

In 705 there came a propitious moment for an attempt at liberation by the subject peoples of Assyria. After the murder of Sargon II and the accession of his son, Sennacherib, Nineveh was beset by internal strife. Merodach-Baladan, a Babylonian, led a revolt in alliance with the kings of Sidon and Ashdod, and later with Hezekiah of Jerusalem.

Archers and spear throwers storm up the assault ladders in breaching an ancient walled city, probably Samaria. From an Assyrian bas-relief.

The prophets issued stern warnings against any involvement. "Take heed and be calm," said Isaiah, "and let not your heart be faint because of these two tails of smoking firebrands." He was referring to Pekah of Israel and Rezin of Aram who were destroyed in their rebellion against Assyrian power. But the prophets' warnings went unheeded. For the next hundred and twenty years the history of Judah was a struggle for national survival, first against the might of Assyria and, when Assyria fell, against the

two rivals for her inheritance: New Babylon and Egypt.

Judah found a determined king in Hezekiah. He entered into an alliance with Babylon, where a Chaldean dynasty had risen to power. He hoped that the united forces of Judah and Babylon would be able to deal a blow to Assyria. The Egyptians, too, tried to stem the Assyrian advance, but were defeated at Ekron.

In 701, the Assyrians swept through Judah, destroying all its fortresses and laying siege to the capital. Hezekiah was forced to capitulate to the superior forces of Sennacherib. The Bible tells us that Jerusalem was saved only by a plague which broke out among the Assyrian soldiers. "That night, the angel of the Lord went forth and struck 185,000 in the camp of Assyria. . . . And Sennacherib, King of Assyria, departed and went and returned to Nineveh." Other histories ascribe the sudden easing of the siege to the recall of troops to quell a rebellion which had meanwhile broken out in Babylon.

With the anti-Assyrian league disrupted, Judah could continue to exist only by Assyrian grace. For some time, peace reigned in the land, and, with it, a spiritual and religious reform led by Isaiah.

Reaction set in under Manasseh, the ruler of Judah for fifty-five years. From the beginning he was a subject vassal of Assyria. Palestine was constantly overrun by Assyrian troops on the move toward Egypt. The vassal peoples had to provide soldiers and money for each Assyrian campaign. As dependence on Assyria grew, foreign influences became more entrenched. Respect had to be paid to the overlord's gods. Manasseh persecuted the Judean reformers and allowed the cult of Ashtar to pollute the Temple itself. The Biblical writer remembers him "for the evil that he did in the eyes of the Lord."

Great changes occurred under Josiah (640–609). They were made possible by a shift in external conditions. Weakened by invasions from the north, Assyria crumbled before New Babylon and Egypt. Josiah used this respite to lend his support to important religious reforms. The discovery in the Temple of the "Mosaic Code" (which may have been the Book of Deuteronomy) excited and sustained a new religious enthusiasm. This Code, containing the social and moral ordinances of Moses, shows many signs of having been produced after the fall of Samaria. Now it was proclaimed to be law, reminding the Hebrews constantly that they were a holy people called to a unique destiny.

Josiah was at first supported in his reforms by Jeremiah, but the prophet later dissociated himself from the reforms when he saw that they had had no deep effect on the population.

Josiah died in battle, trying to intercept an Egyptian invasion after the fall of Assyria. A few months later, his son and successor was taken prisoner and carried in chains to the Valley of the Nile. His brother, Jehoiakim, was enthroned by the Egyptians as their satellite and proconsul.

The crushing defeat of Egypt by Babylonia at Carchemish in 605 inaugurated a dark period of isolation for Judah. She had neither allies nor protectors. Babylon was alive to her weakness. An army was sent into Judah and the country was quickly subdued. But as soon as the Babylonians relaxed their vigil, Jehoiakim revolted. The Babylonian reply was sharp. Jerusalem was besieged. Though the capital showed unexpected resistance, it fell after three months. Jehoiakim was killed in the siege. He was succeeded by his son Jehoiachin, who was soon led into captivity. For ten more years a puppet ruler, Zedekiah, was left on the throne of Judah. He summoned up enough courage to start another revolt; and this time the fury of Babylon was expressed with greater brutality. All the fortresses of Judea were razed to the ground. The siege of Jerusalem lasted for almost two years, after which the crushing superiority of the Babylonian armies forced capitulation. In 586 B.C.E. the Temple was burned. "Then they took the king and brought him to the king of Babylonia to Riblah and they gave judgment upon him. And they slew the sons of Zedekiah before his eyes and bound him in fetters and took him to Babylon." The Judean leadership was deported en masse to the land of the conquerors.

History seemed to have come full circle. The descendants of Abraham had left the shores of the Euphrates at the dawn of history. They now returned as prisoners and deportees. Judah was peaceful but desolate.

*T*HE PROPHETIC movement is the most original and potent expression of Hebrew thought. It was essentially religious in character; but it so transcended ritualistic and conventional morality as to become a durable philosophy of individual and social conduct.

The prophetic writings were compiled over a period of 250 years comprising the fall of the Kingdoms of Israel and Judah. The last phases of major prophetic writing barely outlive the fall of Jerusalem and the destruction of the Temple. This last blow was more than a political defeat: it had all the signs of an irrevocable historic judgment.

For generations, the prophets had been predicting the collapse of the Hebrew state. Consequently, when the disaster did finally come, the people were at least spared the bitter indignation which grows from incomprehensible catastrophe. The prophets had provided answers to the question of their fate. Their theme was that God had destroyed His own creation. But if the dire threats of the prophets had proved true, did not this also encourage belief in their message of ultimate comfort and redemption? So long as chastisement was humbly borne and repentance sincerely felt, there was still hope for the future. The people of Israel, politically decimated, went on living by its faith, sustained by prophetic promise. Israel was seemingly ended, but Judaism, as a religion transcending the soil of Palestine, had begun.

The prophetic writings that have come down to us are held to be those of the prophets themselves, transmitted orally by contemporary disciples. In order to evaluate the inner meaning of this literature, we must consider whether later editors, or disciples, were responsible only for the narrative framework and arrangement of the books, or whether they had a hand in their actual composition. Was the written prophecy altered so as to match new circumstances and reflect later ideas? The view of Yehezkel Kaufmann is that "a purposeful, continuous, large-scale revising of ancient traditions is nowhere in evidence. It is clear that the transmitters considered it their duty to preserve the text of the prophecies as they received them."

"I was no prophet, neither was I a prophet's son," says Amos, the first among the literary prophets. He claims no other intellectual denomination: ". . . I was a herdsman and a dresser of trees." The inference is that his words proceeded from revelation, not from any educated art. Indeed the classical prophets were visionaries. They are sometimes described as miracle workers, but magic was not their true genius. They were moved by an individual call, and came, often reluctantly, to a people who had not sought them. Their message was heavy with criticism and reproof. Considering themselves to be links in a chain of divine messengers that began with Moses, they did not seek to innovate. They founded their legitimacy on their fidelity to ancient values. They constantly appealed to the early covenant between God and His people. Like most reformers, they pretended to desire a restoration of the past, but what they asked, in fact, was nothing less than the radical transformation of a previous faith. In Kaufmann's words: "They did not so much repudiate the popular religion as rise above it."

If classical prophecy is to be taken as a distinct unit in Hebrew thought, it is important to remember that it covers almost three centuries of hectic and violent experience. The political and social circumstances in which the prophets lived were marked by sharp diversity. And the literary prophet would never transgress his human condition. He regards himself as chosen by God as messenger to His people. But this does not make him feel more than human. He craves no superiority. He allows himself to be shaken by anger and moved by passion. He can yield to prejudice or predilection. He has moments of weakness and hesitation. He can even sink into despair. Strongly individual, he proclaims ideas which reflect his own philosophy and temperament. The prophetic books are works of personal creativity. It is therefore artificial to seek an ordered spiritual continuity leading successively from one prophet to his "successor." But in spite of all the diversities which mark its particular phases and expressions, prophetic thought has an underlying consistent unity. It also has a significance far transcending the temporal factors that helped to create it.

The obvious common principle shared by all the representatives of Hebrew thought is the basic conception of "One God, sole creator and judge of the world, a non-mythological, non-magical deity—a supreme will, unfettered by fate or compulsion." The social and political implication of this conception had already been probed by such earlier prophets as Samuel, Nathan, and Elijah. Nathan's parable of the poor man and the ewe lamb (II Samuel 12:1–5) has remained one of the most expressive symbols of spoliation; Elijah's "Have you murdered and also taken possession?" (I Kings 21:19) is a concise masterpiece of social criticism. Nathan might be considered as the "ideological ancestor" of all who have ever challenged the institution of monarchy by appealing to its arbitrariness. But neither Nathan nor Elijah was a theoretician. Their indignation was directed against specific facts and incidents. And Samuel, despite his inner conviction, actually founded the monarchy against which he warned. The early prophets were not capable of generalizing their experiences or of elevating them to the level of principle.

Classical prophecy, on the other hand, was to involve an entire reconsideration of human relations. It was concerned not with contingent events but with the very structure of human and social nature. Because it is independent of any particular historic context, classical prophecy is invested with a power which can never fade.

The Moral Imperative

The prophets were not the first to demand morality. Good and evil were existing notions before they came upon the scene. But they were certainly the first to define the essence of these concepts, independently of any ritual or dictated behavior. According to them, the essence of God's demand of man is not cultic but moral: Human goodness is the realization of the will of God on earth. The cult in itself has no intrinsic or transcendent value.

God's admonition to His people "I hate, I despise your feasts..." (Amos 5:21) must have seemed strange to the prophet's audience. God, after all, was supposed to be grateful for the sacrifices offered to Him. Amos' demand put the whole cult in a new light: God is in no way dependent on it, since cult is only one manifestation of His grace to man. Its only sense is symbolic: it is useful if it inspires a knowledge of God. But where "there is no loyalty . . . no knowledge of God in the land . . ." (Hosea 4:1), the cult, separated from its inner purpose, becomes a profanation of God's name.

> For I desire righteousness (*hesed*), not sacrifice,
> And knowledge of God more than burnt offerings.
>
> HOSEA 6:6

The Hebrew word *hesed* has no single equivalent; it connotes piety, goodness, love, grace. It means the natural instinct that makes a man use goodness without constraint. Not only does God prefer *hesed* to burnt offerings; it is, in fact, all that is really required from man:

> It hath been told thee, O man, what is good,
> And what the Lord doth require of thee:
> Only to do justly, and to love mercy,
> And to walk humbly with thy God.
>
> MICAH 6:8

Hence the vehement attacks on idolatry in its variant expressions. "To have turned away from God" does not necessarily mean adoration of foreign deities. It is often used to qualify the impure way in which men worship God. Since the people have not resisted the allurement of heathen cultic rites and have submitted to the "spirit of harlotry" (Hosea 5:4), God will not accept their worship.

"Harlotry, wine and new wine take away the heart. . . ." A man governed by appetites can no longer know God. Harlotry and drunkenness are incompatible with kindness and humility.

Previously, idolatry had been considered a sinful path to be eschewed specifically by Israel, to whom God had made known the meaning of true devotion. Isaiah is the first to envisage idolatry as a human failing not forbidden to Israel alone. This marks the beginning of prophetic universalism. The connection between idolatry and national pride is still to be found, but the roles of cause and effect are inversed. Now idolatry is conceived as a result of human pride. "The wisdom through which man is creative and can control nature has become his stumbling block. Trusting in his power, he makes himself gods. In adoring them, he worships himself."

> Their land also is full of idols;
> Everyone worshippeth the work of his own hands,
> That which his own fingers have made.
>
> ISAIAH 2:8

Not only does idolatry blot out God. It nourishes man's ambition
to domineer over his fellow man. Idolatry, therefore, is the source
of all social and moral evil in the world. Isaiah is fascinated by
the human aspiration to achieve ever greater heights, as symbolized
by the Tower of Babel, high walls, or fortifications. This ambition expresses the vain quest for domination. Consequently, the
end of idolatry will be heralded by "the fall of towers," when all
that is proud and lofty is lowered:

> For the Lord of hosts hath a day
> Upon all that is proud and lofty,
> And upon all that is lifted up, and it shall be brought low.
> And upon all the cedars of Lebanon
> That are high and lifted up,
> And upon all the oaks of Bashan;
> And upon all the high mountains,
> And upon all the hills that are lifted up;
> And upon every lofty tower,
> And upon every fortified wall.

ISAIAH 2:12–15

Social and Political Justice

The more urgently this morality was required, the less could it be
left to the individual as a matter of personal option. For the first
time in history, morality is referred to as a decisive factor in
national life. The most vehement reproaches of the prophets deal
with social corruption. But they no longer limit themselves to mere
denunciations, as Nathan and Elijah had done. The earlier
prophets regarded David and Ahab as solely responsible for the
crimes which they had committed, and chastisement was to visit
them alone. From now on, the nation as a whole was to be held
accountable, and was threatened with nothing other than the loss
of its very existence.

Israel and Judah are to be judged for "selling the righteous for
silver" (Amos 2:6).

> Hear the word of the Lord, ye rulers of Sodom; give ear unto the
> law of our God, ye people of Gomorrah.
>
> To what purpose is the multitude of your sacrifices unto Me?
> saith the Lord: I am full of the burnt offerings of rams, and the
> fat of fed beasts; and I delight not in the blood of bullocks, or of
> lambs, or of he goats.

ISAIAH 1:10–11

And when ye spread forth your hands, I will hide Mine eyes from you: yea, when ye make many prayers, I will not hear: your hands are full of blood. Wash you, make you clean; put away the evil of your doings from before Mine eyes; cease to do evil; learn to do well; seek judgment, relieve the oppressed, judge the fatherless, plead for the widow.

ISAIAH I:15–17

There is a constant stress on the culpability of the ruling class.

Hear, I pray you, ye heads of Jacob
And princes of the House of Israel:
Is it not for you to know justice?
Who hate the good and love the evil;
Who rob their skin from off them,
And their flesh from off their bones;
Who also eat the flesh of my people,
And flay their skin from off them,
And break their bones;
Yea, they chop them in pieces as that which is in a pot,
And as flesh within the cauldron.

MICAH 3:1–3

Therefore shall Zion for your sake be plowed as a field,
And Jerusalem shall become heaps,
And the mountain of the house as the high places of a forest.

MICAH 3:12

The oppressors are often identified with the new non-patriarchal class of royal officials, established by the monarch. Hosea even goes so far as to denounce monarchy itself as a rebellion against God:

It is thy destruction, O Israel
That thou art against Me, against thy help.
Ho, now, thy king,
That he may have thee in all thy cities!
And thy judges, of whom thou saidst:
'Give me a king and princes!'
I give thee a king in Mine anger
And take him away in My wrath.

HOSEA 13:9–11

Samuel, in his early moment of truth, would surely have approved of such passionate speech.

The political attitudes of the prophets are intimately connected with their ethical conceptions. The salient principle is their utter condemnation of militarism as the worst expression of heathen pride. Assyria, the military power incarnate, will be punished— but not for its deeds:

> Wherefore it shall come to pass, that when the Lord hath performed His whole work upon Mount Zion and on Jerusalem, I will punish the fruit of the arrogant heart of the king of Assyria, and the glory of his haughty looks.

> For he hath said:
> 'By the strength of my hand I have done it,
> And by my wisdom, for I am prudent;
> In that I have removed the bounds of the peoples,
> And have robbed their treasures,
> And have brought down as one mighty the inhabitants.
>
> ISAIAH 10:12–13

If Israel's trust in military power is a moral sin, it also represents a religious crime since it implies mistrust of God:

> Woe to the rebellious children, saith the Lord,
> That take counsel, but not of Me;
> And that form projects, but not of My spirit,
> That may add sin to sin;
> That walk to go down into Egypt,
> And have not asked at My mouth;
> To take refuge in the stronghold of Pharaoh,
> And to take shelter in the shadow of Egypt!
>
> ISAIAH 30:1–2

Israel should, rather, have sought its salvation through serene and resigned confidence in God:

> For thus said the Lord God, the Holy One of Israel:
> 'In sitting still and rest shall ye be saved,
> In quietness and in confidence shall be your strength;
> And ye would not.
> But ye said: 'No, for we will flee upon horses';
> Therefore shall ye flee;
> And 'we will ride upon the swift';
> Therefore shall they that pursue you be swift.'
>
> ISAIAH 30:15–16

Prophecy also involves political criticism. In seeking to oppose Assyria through a coalition with Egypt, Israel commits exactly the same sin for which Assyria is to be punished. Thus the fight for independence becomes a sign of defiance to God. Subjection, on

the contrary, becomes a token of contrition and repentance. Paradoxically, total surrender remains the only way to salvation:

> Thus saith the Lord, the God of hosts, the God of Israel:
> 'If thou wilt go forth unto the king of Babylon's princes, then thy soul shall live, and this city shall not be burned with fire; and thou shalt live, thou and thy house.'
>
> JEREMIAH 38:17

Such an attitude in the days of the mighty empires of Assyria and Babylon doubtless represents one of the highest summits that religious and moral idealism can ever attain. And yet, one cannot help wondering why the messengers of God lacked the slightest feeling of common patriotism. Could their philosophy, however elevated, have stifled all sense of national honor? It seems that in the last resort it did not. In the supreme crisis, while Judah is invaded and Ravshakeh orders the city's gates to be opened, Isaiah—and Isaiah alone—bids the king to resist, in complete contradiction to the policy of resignation which he had previously been advocating. Holy Jerusalem could not submit to heathen Assyria.

> The virgin daughter of Zion despises and mocks you
> The daughter of Jerusalem nods her head after you.
> Whom have you taunted and blasphemed?
> Against whom have you raised your voice
> And lifted your eyes aloft?
> Against the Holy One of Israel!
>
> ISAIAH 37:22–23

The ruins of ancient Babylon, capital city of the once mighty Babylonian Empire, whose towering ziggurats and terraced gardens were the wonders of the ancient world. Where once the gate of Ishtar proclaimed Babylon's barbaric splendors, now there is only rubble and silence.

Circumstances and his own temperament, on the other hand, made such fierce optimism impossible for Jeremiah. He never retracts from his call to surrender; but his lamentation is sufficient warrant of his love for Israel. He had tried to intercede in their favor, but God had said to him, "Do not favor this people," and there was no withstanding the word of God. He could only curse the day he was born.

Even extremists in the acceptance of fate like Hosea and Micah could not resign themelves to their people's utter destruction:

> How shall I give thee up, Ephraim?
> How shall I deliver thee, Israel?
> How shall I make thee as Admah?
> How shall I set thee as Zeboim?
> My heart is turned within me,
> My repentings are kindled together.
>
> HOSEA 11:8

For even if Israel is unworthy, God will forgive the "remnant of His inheritance." The people will be redeemed for the sake of the Patriarchs:

> Thou wilt show faithfulness to Jacob, mercy to Abraham,
> As Thou hast sworn unto our fathers from the days of old.
>
> MICAH 7:20

The End of Days

The idea of ultimate redemption is central to the prophetic idea. Psychologically it appears as the expression of the prophets' unwillingness to admit Israel's definitive doom, but this does not mean that their thoughts and aspirations were devoid of national consciousness. In their critical way, the prophets of national doom were animated by a national spirit that would not be satisfied by Israel's mere survival. Their eschatology is based on the idea of Israel's supremacy. This is not, to be sure, a common supremacy of might and power. Israel is to rule the world not by the force of arms but by its spirit alone. The "elected people" has been charged with a mission: it is through Israel that mankind will learn to "know God and to follow His commandments."

However elevated their conceptions might have been, the prophets were no naive utopians. The higher their ideal, the clearer was their consciousness of its unattainability. But even if the aim could not be reached, it could, nevertheless, indicate a direction of conduct. Fulfillment, if ever, would come in the "end of days."

Having thus made the necessary concession to reality, the prophet gives full vent to his imaginative thought. In the remote future, Israel will be governed by a righteous king:

> And the spirit of the Lord shall rest upon him, the spirit of wisdom and understanding, the spirit of counsel and might, the spirit of knowledge and of the fear of the Lord;
>
> And shall make him of quick understanding in the fear of the Lord, and he shall not judge after the sight of his eyes, neither reprove after the hearing of his ears;
>
> But with righteousness shall he judge the poor, and reprove with equity for the meek of the earth; and he shall smite the earth with the rod of his mouth, and with the breath of his lips shall he slay the wicked. And righteousness shall be the girdle of his loins, and faithfulness the girdle of his reins.
>
> ISAIAH 11:2–5

It is not only to mankind that God's ultimate grace is assured.

The animal world, as well, shall be reformed and the age-old hostility among men and animals shall cease:

> The wolf shall lie down with the lamb
> The leopard shall couch with the kid
> ... And a little child shall lead them.
> ... The suckling shall play at the den of the asp
> ... They shall not hurt or destroy in all My holy mountain,
> For the land will be full of knowledge of the Lord
> As the waters cover the sea.
>
> ISAIAH 11:6–9

This is the predestined climax of the vision of the "end of days," when

> ... The mountain of the Lord's house shall be established
>   as the top of the mountains,
> And shall be exalted above the hills;
> And all the nations shall flow unto it.
>
> ISAIAH 2:2

Nor is this merely a site of worship; rather it is the place from which justice and law will go out to all mankind:

> For out of Zion shall go forth the law
> And the word of the Lord from Jerusalem.
>
> ISAIAH 2:3

Here we reach the ideological core of prophetical eschatology. At the climax of history, mankind is reunited, all men and nations are to share the divine grace which heretofore had been promised to Israel alone. Equal before God's justice, all the peoples of the world will equally share His grace at the "end of days." Then God will say, "Blessed be My people Egypt, and Assyria My handiwork, and Israel My possession" (Isaiah 19:25).

It is probable that such a prospect did not evoke enthusiasm in an Israel oppressed by Assyria and betrayed by Egypt. But the prophetic message does not court popularity. Beyond its political implications, Isaiah's vision of the "end of days" lifts the curtain on a horizon of universal fraternity, when people shall not fight each other, when

> ... They shall beat their swords into plowshares,
> And their spears into pruning hooks;
> Nation shall not lift up sword against nation,
> Neither shall they learn war any more.
>
> ISAIAH 2:4

In this respect, the role of Israel as the depositary of true religion is almost self-evident: the freeing of mankind from the idolatry which obstructs its salvation. For as Isaiah understood, there can be no redemption for man unless he conquers self-deification. He must abandon the worship of his own creations, and liberate himself from his lust for power, avarice, domination, and the cult of the state. There can be no redemption until man recognizes his moral obligations as transcendent and divine. No form of government, no level of material well-being, will save man. He will be redeemed only when "towers fall, and Jerusalem triumphs over Babylon."

What is at stake, finally, is not only intelligence but feeling. Man has to change his heart. Salvation, the prophets tell us, is preconditioned by repentance. The redeeming act of God waits upon man's initiative.

6 ❦ *Exile and Return*

*I*SRAEL'S history assumes a unique quality with the Babylonian captivity. Many peoples have preserved their nationality on their own soil, even under foreign conquest. But never before had any people been able to maintain its identity and spiritual distinctiveness in exile for thousands of years with sufficient vitality to ensure an ultimate rebirth. The singularity of Judaism lay in this extraordinary power to flourish in Diaspora. In Babylon, to be sure, there was much assimilation. The source of collective destiny was not always held firm against erosion. There were many who, in Ezekiel's words, served "gods of wood and stone." But the main nucleus stayed intact. It remained separate and unique. Indeed, what seemed by all previous and subsequent logic to be the condition of national disappearance became, instead, the hour of reassessment. The Jewish people had sprung from Israel; "Judaism," as a system of ideas and a way of life, was born in the Babylonian Diaspora.

There is no precise way of knowing how many went into exile. There were waves of deportation between the capture of Jehoiachin and the murder of Gedaliah, the Jewish governor appointed by the Babylonians after the fall of the Temple in 586. But there is compelling evidence to prove that the cream of Judean society was exiled. The political and military leaders, the priests, the prosperous artisans and the skilled workmen, were banished to Baby-

lonia. They settled in cohesive groups in central Mesopotamia and in the city of Babylon itself. Jehoiachin, the king, though imprisoned, was treated with regal deference. He was to be Nebuchadnezzar's pensioner "all the days of his life." When his patron died in 562 B.C.E., Jehoiachin was even released from detention. As long as he lived he embodied a royal legitimacy and kept the hope of restoration strong in Jewish hearts.

The captives from Judah now found themselves in the most brilliant civilization of the ancient Near East. They were not the only foreign group in Babylonia. The Chaldean empire was a cosmopolitan society, its capital a world metropolis. For Babylon surpassed all the ancient cities of the Orient. It was greater than Thebes, Memphis, and Ur, more imposing than Nineveh.

It was thus against many allurements and temptations that the Jews in Babylon defended their separateness and identity. Surrounded by foreign peoples, exposed to the grandiose temples and shrines of foreign gods, the Judean captives might well have believed themselves to have been deserted by their own God. But while they took part in the economic and political life of pagan society, they resisted the influences of pagan religion. Other captives, drawn from pagan nations, could easily adopt the local cults; the Israelites knew that their unique monotheistic belief stood to be preserved or lost, according to the strength or weakness of their own fidelity.

Thus, with extinction threatening them, they drew closer to their prophetic vocation. Their faith assumed the quality of a democratic possession: it embraced an entire ethnic community.

The tension between identity and assimilation was to dominate the nation's history for many centuries. It was never completely resolved either in the first Diaspora or in those that followed. Assimilation or restoration? The dilemma posed in Babylon became the central preoccupation of Jews in many lands and in many ages. The scales seemed heavily laden for assimilation. The influences of the new Babylonian environment were strong. And there were vast transformations at work in the outside world as well. The sixth century was one of the great historic eras. The neo-Babylonian Empire, founded on the ruins of imperial Assyria, had fallen an easy prey to Cyrus, who had also subdued Media and Lydia (Asia Minor). The boundaries of the Persian Empire, which swallowed New Babylon, were soon extended from India and Central Asia to Egypt and the Balkan peninsula. Within a single empire the Indo-Iranian cultures confronted the ancient civilizations of the Fertile

In Isaiah, the Lord's words called Assyria "the rod of Mine anger." Here, a winged Assyrian demon with the head of an eagle plucks grapes from vine.

Crescent, Egypt and Phoenicia and the Greek culture of Asia Minor. In the history of religious thought no century can boast of a more distinguished galaxy of names than Confucius, Lao-tse, Buddha, Pythagoras, Deutero-Isaiah, Jeremiah, Ezekiel, and, to go by the era of his greatest influence, Zoroaster.

It is not difficult to imagine what an overwhelming impression these sudden and turbulent movements must have made upon clear-sighted men in the Asiatic world. Certainly the almost simultaneous expansion of both Parsism and Judaism from Egypt to Iran brought about as deep a spiritual upheaval in the minds of all western Asiatic peoples as did Persia's military victories in the political sphere. "A race which did not acknowledge a plurality of gods," writes Sidney Smith, "the men of Israel and Judah had been scattered over many provinces by the Assyrians and Nebuchadnezzar. Peoples who would not worship figures of gods in human shape, the Medes and Persians, were impinging on the civilized peoples of western Asia from the east. . . . Some effort at reform and clarification of the polytheistic chaos was necessary."

To these bewildering influences we must add the despair of Judeans as they brooded over the destruction of their land. Many believed that the gods of Babylon had defeated the God of Israel. The prophet Jeremiah exhorted them to make peace with their new destiny. "Build ye houses and dwell in them; and plant gardens, and eat the fruit of them . . . that ye may be increased there and not diminished. And seek the peace of the city whither I have caused you to be carried away captives."

But there was also another prophetic idea at work. Ezekiel, who had been carried off among the exiles to Babylon, became its voice. He promised that exile would be temporary. With splendid eloquence he defended the hope for a return. But meanwhile, life had to be adjusted and reorganized to preserve national identity and unity. In its efforts to ward off assimilation, Babylonian Jewry emphasized the preservation of ancient traditions and of literary and religious continuity. A new literary creativity came to birth. The main corpus of the Torah (Pentateuch), whose major components had long since been in existence, were collected and codified. Most modern scholars are of the opinion that the historical part of the Bible, from Genesis to Kings, must have been written down during this period of exile. The composition of Lamentations and the Psalms also belongs to this date. All this work was carried out by the scribes and the priests who were the spiritual leaders of the exiles and their communities.

The exile had cut the people off from worship and sacrifice at their Temple. The national faith was no longer incarnate in physical institutions or rituals. Perhaps for this very reason, its central creed became intensely spiritual and abstract. Jerusalem and the Temple were idealized. The return to Zion and the rebuilding of the Temple became the ultimate longing of those from whom God had withdrawn His grace. The grief which had afflicted the people through the destruction of the Temple had to be assuaged and repaired if God's honor was to be redeemed. The longing for Zion was not born out of material hardship. The Jews in Babylon were a thrifty and resourceful folk whose living standards soon surpassed what they had known in Judea. When it finally came about, the return of the exiles to Jerusalem, like Abraham's original migration to Canaan, illustrated the sacrifice of material welfare to an obsessive idea.

Judah after the Fall

The land which the captives had left behind disappeared from the attention of chroniclers for fifty years. Indeed, there was little to record but devastation and anguish. The ravaged country had no sources of strength from which to draw renewal or vitality. The Temple was burnt and Jerusalem deserted. The Babylonian governor established his residence in Mizpah. Nebuchadnezzar had removed the compliant governor Gedaliah from the capital to the presumed security of Mizpah. But a fanatic patriot reached Gedaliah in his city of asylum and put him to death. The assassin was a descendant of the House of David, Johanan ben Kerach. From now on, Judah was to be administered from Samaria.

Babylonia did not resettle Judah with foreign elements as the Assyrians had done in northern Israel. But peoples from Moab and Edom whose kingdoms were destroyed by Nebuchadnezzar penetrated the Judean hill country to settle permanently in its southern parts. Gilead and Galilee, left alone by the occupying power, continued to maintain sizable Jewish populations. So did parts of the northern Negev. Egypt after 586 B.C.E. no longer played any part in the affairs of Palestine—at least until the emergence of the Ptolemies. Judah was beyond recovery unless it were to receive an infusion of strength from one direction—the exiles in Babylonia, where Jewish life had its center of gravity. But Babylonia as a whole was doomed. It was destined to occupy only an interlude between the Assyrian and Persian empires. Persia's ascendancy dawned in 559 when Cyrus the Great came to the throne. He shook off Median suzerainty and set out on a campaign of swift conquests. He was followed in this course by his successors Cambyses and Darius, who extended Persian suzerainty as far as Carthage and the Peloponnesian peninsula, where Greece finally stemmed the tide of Persia's westward expansion. Cyrus consolidated his Asian holdings by defeating the Lydians (549). By 539 he had dealt a death blow to Babylonia. For two hundred years Persia was to remain the center of the ancient world, unchallenged until Alexander the Great came upon the scene. The dynasty that created the Persian Empire continued to rule during the entire period of its dominance.

Of all the despotic rulers of antiquity, the Persians were the most liberal. They had a talent for administration and showed tolerance for the various ethnic groups living in their midst. The diverse civilizations which had fallen under their dominion were allowed to survive in national and spiritual freedom. Though religion was a central element in Persian culture, no attempt was made to impose the Persian cult on new subjects of the realm.

The Return to Zion

With the fall of Babylonia, Palestine and Syria became part of the Persian Empire, and remained in this condition until Persia was conquered by Alexander the Great in 332. There is no archaeological evidence to throw light on the two hundred years of Persian rule in Palestine.

Judah became part of one of the twenty administrative satrapies into which Persia divided the land. The Greek historian Herodotus recounts that the fifth satrapy included Phoenicia, Syria, Palestine, and Cyprus. In his writings, the word "Palestine" appears for the first time as a collective name, having been used before only for the area occupied by the Philistines. (The Greek invaders made their first contact with the coastal areas and applied their name to the whole of the country.)

Cyrus, who ascended the Persian throne in 559, was to play a large role in Jewish history. Under his aegis the prophetic vision of a return to Zion was to be fulfilled. No sooner had he annexed Jerusalem, than he issued his decree of return:

> Thus says Cyrus, king of the Persians: "The Lord God of heaven, who has made me a king of the whole world, has charged me to build him a house in Jerusalem, which is in Judah. Therefore,

Seed of Cyrus the Great, Darius and Xerxes, father and son, great kings of Persia, pictured in regal power on a Persepolis relief. After the Babylonian captivity, the Persians supported restoration of a Jewish State.

whoever among his people so desires, let him go up to Jerusalem
and rebuild the house of the Lord God of Israel. And whoever
remains where he now sojourns, let him help with silver, and with
gold, and with goods, and with beasts, besides the freewill offerings
for the house of God in Jerusalem."

EZRA 1:2-4

Babylonian Jewry did not rise as one man to meet this challenge.
Only a minority went, not more than fifty thousand in the first
wave. But they were men of conviction and purpose, "whose spirit
God had aroused to rebuild the house of the Lord in Jerusalem."
"And those who stayed behind, strengthened their hands with vessels of silver, with gold, with cattle, and with other precious
things." The first restoration is connected with the leadership of
Zerubbabel, who was inspired by the prophets Haggai and Zecha-
riah to rebuild the Temple.

The country to which the Israelites returned was no longer a
land overflowing with milk and honey. It was, to the contrary, "a
land that eateth up the inhabitants thereof." The early years of the
restoration were disappointing. Frustrations crowded in upon the
returning exiles. The rebuilding of the Temple was a difficult enterprise, made even more difficult by the deliberate efforts of the
non-Jews who had settled in the land to obstruct the work. The
foundation was laid in the second year of the return, but the construction was not to be completed until twenty years later, in 516.
For sheer magnificence, it could not be compared with the edifice
built by Solomon, but the passage of time lent it a growing prestige, until it could be said with justice that "the glory of the latter
house was greater than of the first."

The Reforms of Ezra and Nehemiah

Events in Judah after the consecration of the Temple are shrouded
in darkness. Much more is known about the growing strength of
the community of Babylon, whose spiritual revival was to save the
mother country from decline and to elevate a corner of the Persian
Empire to a position of growing influence on the life of the Jewish
people and on the entire human story.

Throughout the exile, close ties had been maintained between
Jerusalem and the Diaspora. When news reached Babylonia of the
desperate conditions in which Judah was plunged, a wave of fraternal solidarity gripped Babylonian Jews. Two men put themselves
at the head of a movement to save Jerusalem from disintegration:
Nehemiah in 444 and Ezra in 397 came to Jerusalem where they

reorganized the national life so effectively that the province was able to weather storms from internal stress and external hostility.* Nehemiah gave the returning remnant a political status and an administration; Ezra reformed its spiritual life.

Nehemiah had already attained high office at the court of Artaxerxes I when he was given permission to visit Jerusalem. There he found a condition of stark distress. The people of Judah lived in perpetual fear of their neighbors in Samaria. Relations were strained between the returning exiles and the remnant that had stayed behind and inherited their property. Heavy taxation weighed cruelly on the impoverished people.

Nehemiah's first project was the rebuilding of the city walls of Jerusalem. There was fear that this might be considered a hostile act by Samaria. Thus the builders of the wall carried on the construction as "one hand worked and the other held the weapon." Next, people had to be settled in a town whose population was too small to ensure defense. Nehemiah remained in Judah for twelve years, during which time he strove hard to alleviate distress by social reforms. He then returned to Babylonia. Later he came back to Judah to find conditions steadily deteriorating again. He reached a strong conviction about the need for religious reforms.

Ezra, the inaugurator of the needed reforms, brought with him the Torah which had been written down by the scribes in Babylon. The essence of his reform was the imposition of a strict code to organize community life, preserve ethnic purity, and affirm the holiness of Israel's destiny.

The conditions of this law encouraged separatism. Both Nehemiah and Ezra fought against intermarriage, the former out of a zeal for ethnic purity, the latter by virtue of his vision of a unique people, "a kingdom of priests." The precedent was thereby set for a habit of voluntary segregation which was to shield the nation in centuries to come from the erosion of its identity.

Thus a Jewish community, living in what was a small province of the Persian Empire, was able to cultivate and develop its beliefs and values far away from the mainstream of civilization. It was to return to the center of history when Alexander the Great set foot on Asian soil.

---

* According to the Chronicler, Ezra came first (457) and Nehemiah followed him in 444, when they combined in joint leadership. However, it is improbable that they were contemporaries. According to the Scriptures, Nehemiah found a small population on his arrival, whereas Ezra found a numerous one. The Chronicler also reports that the city walls had been rebuilt by the time of Ezra's arrival.

*T*HEY HAVE filled the City with harbors and dockyards and walls and tributes instead of with righteousness and temperance." This was the verdict of Plato on the transition of Greece from glory to decline. The obsession with material progress is, at best, only a part of the explanation. There was never a time, even at the peak of its creativity, when Greek society was totally dominated by all the qualities of harmony and balance, symmetry and order, which its greatest minds articulated and pursued. The democratic principle was eroded by serfdom. A pervasive talent for division asserted itself in every ordeal. The greatness of Hellas lay not in the institutions which it built but in the ideas which it nourished. By the time that Greece and Israel met each other in history both peoples had already given mankind their most radiant gifts.

But if the Hellenistic age was a period of decay for Greece, it was to offer a new era of resurgence for the peoples of the Orient which Greece penetrated in the wake of Alexander's eastward sweep. Ancient cultures merged into the new civilization. Old nations gave up their identity in willing surrender to new ways of life and thought. One tradition alone held out against the tide. Neither the twilight of Greek splendor nor the dawn of Roman power could dazzle the Jews out of their tenacious self-assertion. The mystery of Jewish preservation finds potent expression in the refusal to accept assimilation to Greek and Roman culture.

When Alexander embarked on his career of swift conquest of Asia in 334 B.C.E., Judah was living securely under Persian rule.

It was a small province, remote from the coastal trade routes which linked Asia to Africa. Syrians, Phoenicians, and Samarians stood between Judah and the wider world, committing the Jews to political obscurity and mercantile backwardness. With Alexander's conquest of Judah in 332 B.C.E. a new epoch began. Henceforth Jewish history was to be caught up in currents broader and stronger than itself.

Alexander's military campaigns do not tell the full story of his achievement. He had an intense cultural vocation. He saw himself as the heir of a splendid legacy which he was destined to reanimate and to expand. The traditional view of Hellenism as an epoch of decline arose in later years, when the grace of Athenian culture could be compared with the prosaic and formalized products of Hellenistic art and literature. Those who actually lived in the age of Alexander had no such presentiment. The Greek world was elevated by a mood of self-confidence. The literary heritage was held in reverence, and Greek culture spread far and wide across the Mediterranean and the Near East. While economic and cultural decline afflicted the Greek mainland, the daughter cities of Hellas entered on a period of creativity which contrasted sharply with the languor and apathy of the mother country. For Alexander regarded Hellenism as a concept far transcending the Greek homeland. He married Persian wives, encouraged intermarriage, and induced the society around him to espouse attitudes of tolerance and fraternalism toward the peoples of the colonies. Hellenism was to be an impulse of the spirit, not an accident of birth.

Alexander became the patron of scientists, most of whom—like himself—were the pupils of Aristotle. Few of their original works have survived but their technological skill was expressed and preserved in the monuments which they left behind: the waterways, highways, amphitheaters, and new cities of the Alexandrian age.

In the wake of Alexander's conquests Greek cities arose everywhere across the East Mediterranean. The expansion continued after his death in 323 B.C.E. Thirty cities were founded in Palestine alone, with temples and altars, gymnasia and theaters. The Macedonian and Greek settlers of the new cities made the Middle East a versatile arena of Greek culture and Greek ways of life.

The Ptolemies in Judea After Alexander's death Palestine was ruled by two successive regimes. The Ptolemaic Empire in the south, with Egypt as its center, governed Palestine for over a century, from 301 B.C.E. to 198 B.C.E. The Seleucid Empire in the north, based in Babylonia, brought a more assertive and missionary Hellenism to Palestine when it forced Egypt to give it up in 198 B.C.E.

There was from the beginning a deep reciprocity of influence between the Jewish and pagan worlds. Judaism was the donor as well as the recipient of new insights and disciplines. The Greeks saw the Jews as a strange people, tenacious in their inherited peculiarities. But they also sensed their higher morality. They discovered a "nation of philosophers" constantly probing the mysteries of nature and man; a people governed by a priesthood and held together in allegiance to a law transmitted from God.

The God of the Jews—invisible, transcendent and remote—had a special attraction for the more philosophical and spiritual gentiles. There was a wave of conversion. Many of the new proselytes did not assume all the Mosaic obligations, and few were circumcised. But they accepted monotheism, observed the Sabbath and festivals, and abstained from the grosser sensualities and superstitions of paganism.

It is not surprising that the Spartans had particular affinities with the Jews. Sparta, more than any other Greek city-state, had been consolidated by traditions of law and communal spirit. The austerities and rigid precepts of Judaism were congenial to Spartan minds. There is a deep symbolism in the fact that when the Jewish High Priest, Jason, was ousted from Jerusalem, he fled to Sparta—a city where authority was held in respect.

There was, however, a sharp difference between the reactions of Judah and those of Alexandrian Jewry to the advance of Greece. Judah resisted the flood and eventually sought to turn it back by the Maccabean revolt. During the century of Ptolemaic domination, Hellenization remained at the margin of life in Judah. In the Greek cities which surrounded their land the Jews had abundant opportunities to learn the Greek manners and language. But the masses of the people remained unaffected. The upper classes alone were swept into the strong currents of the new culture. Two parties— the Hellenizers and the anti-Hellenizers—arose within Jewry and waged a struggle for the nation's soul.

Alexandrian Jewry It was in Egypt that the convergence of Jewish and Greek minds celebrated its highest creativity. Alexandrian Jewry produced an original culture, marked by Jewish and Hellenistic characteristics, which influenced the philosophy of the old world and, particularly,
The Hellenistic Period of early Christianity.

A coin graven with the imperial profile of Ptolemy II who freed the Judean slaves brought to Alexandria by Ptolemy I.

Jews had come to Alexandria soon after the foundation of the harbor city in 331 B.C.E. The core of their settlement was provided by Jewish captives from Judah who were forcibly transferred under Ptolemy I (323–263 B.C.E.). The males were settled in military fortresses. The old men and children became slaves. Recent research reveals that most of these slaves were set free under Ptolemy II Philadelphus (263–246 B.C.E.), an act which illustrates the sympathy which grew up between the Jewish community and the Ptolemaic court.

The Jews in Egypt under the Ptolemies had full religious and cultural autonomy. They were exempt from any duties conflicting with their religion. They were not required to render divine honors to the King. Hellenistic sovereigns saw the Jews as a reliable element in the population. Most Roman emperors were to follow the policy of Hellenistic kings in their insistence that Alexandria and other Greek cities allow the Jews to follow their religion and customs without interference.

Hellenism in orthodox Jerusalem's eyes meant idolatry, impiety, amorality, paganism. Greek literature and thought did not penetrate the main body of Jewish life. Not many Jews had knowledge of the Greek language. They shunned the theater and gymnasium, in which Greek social and intellectual activity was expressed, and the loftier elements in the Greek tradition lay beyond their experience. In resisting the forcible imposition of foreign culture they had the sensation of defending pious values against immorality.

It was different in the Diaspora. Here Hellenization had a deep impact on the Jew. Greek became the mother tongue of Jews who could study the writings of Greek philosophers and discover in them something akin to Hebrew ideals. Thus the inner conflict which tormented the Jew in the Diaspora in his contact with Hellenism was more acute than that of the Jews in Jerusalem, who looked on the new culture with sturdy skepticism. The encounter of Jew and Greek in the Diaspora gave birth to a rich and lively literature, inspired by the Greek spirit. Although Jewish writers defended their heritage against the superstitions of Olympian religion, they held themselves in all other respects to be true and proud exponents of Hellenic culture. They were Hellenes of the Jewish persuasion.

The mother country and the Diaspora reinforced each other. Judea's political position was enhanced by her "colonies." Conversely, the Diaspora looked to Jerusalem for political and moral reinforcement. Alexandria in Roman times had an estimated population of half a million, among whom the Jews were a small minority. But they occupied two of the five quarters of the city. Philo reports that "there were synagogues all over." The Jews had their own community organizations and juridical institutions, though in business they usually had recourse to existing Hellenistic law.

Though the Jews lived in separate quarters, they soon came under the spell of the Greek metropolis on Egyptian soil. For Alexandria was unique in its cultural energy. It had a museum and a university for literature and science. Its proudest possession was its library. Egypt, the country which had produced the papyrus on which books were written, became a book factory for the whole Mediterranean world. Scrolls containing the philosophies of Plato and Aristotle and the teachings of the Stoics came into the hands of young Jews whose language was Greek.

But while Jews enjoyed a broad autonomy, they could not attain full Alexandrian citizenship. This was available only to those who renounced their religion and worshiped the gods of the *polis*. Not many Jews seem to have been converted to paganism. They assimilated to Hellenism only in the non-religious aspects of their lives, preserving their inner sanctuary intact against corrosion by alien and pagan faiths.

Hellenization under the Seleucids

With the advent of Seleucid rule in 198 B.C.E. Hellenism became entrenched in Jewish territory itself. For the Seleucids refused to leave the Jews alone in their spiritual isolation. The ruling party in Jerusalem fawned on everything Greek and recoiled from most things Jewish. The orthodox resentment at this is expressed in the Book of Maccabees: "In those days there went out of Israel wicked men who persuaded many, saying: Let us make a covenant with the heathen round about us, for since we departed from them we have had much sorrow." The Jewish Hellenists strove to make Jerusalem a Greek *polis*, even to the point of tolerating pagan rites in Judea. When Antiochus IV Epiphanes took the throne at his brother's death he did not always have to force Hellenism on Jewish society. He found much congenial soil already prepared. A pattern had been established which was to recur in many later epochs of Jewish history. The upper classes espoused the foreign culture, while the simpler masses held tightly to the old inheritance.

Disregarding the traditional freedom of Judah in religious observance, Antiochus introduced pagan customs into Jerusalem and into the villages of Judah. He plundered the Temple in order to finance his military campaigns against Egypt. He had decided that Judah was to be treated like all other Seleucid provinces, and that the Jews must be forced out of their particularism.

Our own sources leave no doubt that Antiochus had the active help of the Jewish Hellenists. Jason, the High Priest, had achieved his office by bribing Antiochus. Outwardly, Jason was the guardian of the law. In fact, he collaborated with Antiochus, not only in providing him with funds, but also in fostering Greek customs, in accordance with the royal policy of spreading Hellenic culture throughout the Seleucid realm.

Jason proceeded to build a gymnasium in which young priests competed naked in athletic games. Soon they exchanged their priestly garb for the Greek. The Jewish zest for Hellenization sometimes surpassed the demands of the Seleucid king himself. But even Jason was not considered sufficiently energetic in promoting Hellenism. He was succeeded by Menelaus, who bribed himself into the High Priesthood. It is not surprising that the people turned in wrath against its leaders. There was a moment of hope when rumors of the death of Antiochus reached Jerusalem. But he had only suffered a local defeat which compelled him to withdraw his troops from Egyptian soil. He now turned his resentment and fury against the Jews. Marching at the head of a vast army into Judea, he slaughtered thousands of Jews, defiled the Temple, and outlawed the sacred observances of Jewish law.

The Maccabean Revolt

The Jews had known much travail in their history; but never before had they been forbidden to practice their faith. They now rose up in arms. The spark of rebellion was kindled in Modin, a small village south of Jerusalem, at the foot of the Judean mountains. Here the arrival of the king's envoys, bent on the enforcement of the pagan laws, was greeted by open revolt. Mattathias, a priest, and his five sons fled to the mountains, gathering the pious masses around them. In an astonishing surge of rebellious courage they foiled Antiochus' policy of forcible assimilation. Their achievement surpassed their highest ambition. Complete religious freedom was restored to Judea and an independent state with extended boundaries was established under their rule.

When Mattathias died in 167 B.C.E. his son Judah, called Maccabee (the Hammer), became the leader of the rebellion. He stands out across the mists of time as one of the great military

In a marble garden in
Ashkelon the headless
torso of Nike, Roman
goddess of victory, still
stands on the globe of
the world which rests
on the shoulders of Atlas.

figures of history—a resistance leader of indomitable force. Judah aroused simple peasants and led them in a guerrilla war against overwhelming might. It was, like many religious wars, a struggle of the few against the many. After three years of savage fighting Jerusalem was liberated and the Temple dedicated once more to the divine service. This event is commemorated in Jewish history as Hanukkah, the Feast of Lights. Beyond its immediate effects, it stands as a symbol of a nation's struggle to maintain its spiritual identity against superior force.

Peace with the enemy beyond the gates did not, however, put an end to internal strife. The Hellenizing parties succeeded in regaining the High Priesthood. They disavowed Judah and his followers, and even invited Syria to intervene in their behalf. Judah Maccabee, who had resisted the foreign tyrant, was slain in this internecine battle. Two other Hasmonean brothers, Jonathan and Simon, who shared Judah's military prowess, succeeded in transforming this family of rebels into a ruling dynasty.

At Simon's death in 135 B.C.E., his son John Hyrkanos ascended the throne. The Hasmoneans continued to rule for a century but with diminished glory. They had lost touch with popular will. The prizes which they sought were those that glittered in the outside world. The dynasty of national liberators petered out in a sorry succession of petty imperialists and despots. The Maccabees who had suffered and fought for national freedom were now a forgotten legend. The accession of John Hyrkanos (135–104 B.C.E.) inaugurated the age of expansion. His aggressive policy enlarged the borders of the country by annexing Transjordan, Samaria, and Idumea. Hyrkanos is responsible for a unique chapter in Jewish history; he forced the Idumeans to embrace Judaism. There is no other instance in all of history of Jews as the agents, rather than the victims, of forcible conversion. (The Jews were to suffer terrible vengeance for this act when Herod the Idumean later ascended the throne.) Hyrkanos assumed the dual role of Prince and High Priest; the government and the aristocracy were now ranged together against the people.

The Decline of the Hasmoneans

The successor of John Hyrkanos as King and High Priest was Aristobulus, who gained the throne after murdering his mother and elder brother. Though his reign lasted but one year he entered history through the sheer horror of his brutal acts. He was succeeded by his brother Alexander Jannai, whom he prudently had kept in prison. Alexander Jannai reigned for twenty-seven years. He too was notorious for his power and cruelty. He waged one war after another, constantly enlarging his territory but giving its citizens no rest. War was to him not a reluctant necessity but a consuming passion, for which the people had to supply money and men. By favoring the party of the Sadducees he alienated the people. The Pharisees revolted openly against him. In despair they invited the Syrian king to support them against their own master. In this civil war Alexander Jannai was driven out of Judea whither he was able to return after six years only with the help of the Pharisees. Once safely in his palace again, he had hundreds of Pharisaic leaders put to death. Thus, after only three generations, the descendants of the great Hasmoneans had wrecked both the structure which their ancestors had built, and the ideals which had inspired it.

After the death of Alexander Jannai, his widow, Salomé Alexandra, became Queen. Her nine-year rule marks the only tranquil period during eighty years of Hasmonean strife. Under the benign influence of her brother, Shimon ben Shetah, she restored the position of the Pharisees, and invited Judah ben Tabbai, together with other fugitives from Alexandria, to reorganize the system of education. Salomé Alexandra was the last independent ruler of Judah. Her gentle spirit arrested, but could not turn back, the tide of internal strife. The hatred between Pharisees and Sadducees continued after her death in 67. Her two sons, Hyrkanos and Aristobulus, fought over the succession. Hyrkanos sought the assistance of Antipater, an Idumean, in order to attack his brother in Jerusalem, who was also in need of external help.

Thus, when Rome appeared on the scene of Jewish history, the nation's fortunes had reached a low ebb. It had lost its inner cohesion. Its lofty visions had been corroded by sensuality, and its mind was centered on ambitions of power and conquest which it lacked the strength to fulfill or sustain.

Pharisees and Sadducees

We have seen that the political history of Judah during the Greek and Roman epoch was constantly intersected by movements of religious controversy. At the beginning of the exile, spiritual development was in the hands of the priests and the scribes. During the Maccabean revolt their ways parted. After the Maccabean victory they emerge as two conflicting sects. From the priestly circle came the Sadducees. From the scribes the Pharisees emerged.

The difference between Pharisees and Sadducees can best be understood in terms of their social positions and their attitude toward the law. The mass of the nation was inclined to Pharisaism, whose cardinal principle was the strict application of the law to every sphere of life in the interest of national preservation. They were ready to abandon political power for the sake of spiritual glory. Their name itself expresses the idea of "renunciation." As expounders of the law the Pharisees became the trustees of the nation's culture. They were more inclined to impose duties than to concede rights to their followers. But they responded to the popular instinct and were held in honor.

The Sadducees represented the priestly class and the aristocracy. They attempted to Hellenize Judah in the days of Antiochus Epiphanes, although they were not the only Hellenizers. On religious issues they dissociated themselves from Pharisaism. They all but ignored the development of the Oral Law and insisted on rigid application of the canonized Law alone. Although they were always a minority their political power at times was great. As priests they were guardians of the Temple treasury, and their affluence determined their social prejudice.

Under the Hasmoneans the schism between the two parties had sharpened, with successive rulers favoring one or the other party. Under Alexander Jannai the conflict erupted into nothing less than civil war.

The religious fervor of the Sadducees centered on the Temple and its sacrifices. The Pharisees did not reject the Temple or the privileges of the priestly class. Much emphasis had been attached to ritual forms during the exile and the Maccabean revolt. But the Pharisaic teachers sought to save them from petrifaction by giving them the spirit of popular institutions. They introduced a new folk festival (*Simḥat Bet Ha-shoeva*—Water Procession Festival). They popularized the Passover sacrifice as well as the pilgrimage to Jerusalem. They thought that Judaism, both in Palestine and in the Diaspora, required something more vital than the ritualistic requirements of Priesthood, Temple, and sacrifices. Pharisaism revealed itself as an astonishingly expansive force making for flexibility and evolution. In Hellenistic as well as in Babylonian Jewry Pharisaism dominated the popular scene, while the movement of the Sadducees remained restricted to Palestine. The Sadducees' effort to ignore the evolution of the Oral Law must have

The "Thanksgiving Scroll," one of the Dead Sea Scrolls, discovered by Bedouins in the caves of the Wadi Qumran.

The gnarled stony configuration of the Qumran caves from whose depths the ancient scrolls which have revolutionized modern Biblical scholarship were salvaged.

alienated the Jews in the Egyptian, Syrian, and Babylonian communities for whom the accepted folkways were the essence of Judaism itself. The Sadducees did not survive the destruction of the Temple.

One of the lesser factions of the Pharisees was that of the Zealots, who were active in guerrilla warfare against Rome. They believed in armed uprising as a divine command, aimed at the expulsion of the Romans. Pharisaic leaders denounced this policy. For them no armed clash could decide the struggle with this mighty empire, which could be resisted by the power of the spirit alone. There were no theological differences between Zealots and Pharisees; but they were sharply at odds in their appraisal of the political possibilities.

The Essenes, on the other hand, were a wing of Pharisaic Judaism which rationalized political weakness and poverty as though they were intrinsic virtues. This sect lived mostly in segregated communities, earning a meager subsistence from cattle-raising and simple crafts. In its concentration on ethics and its preoccupation with social justice, it abandoned the world in order to devote itself to religious observances. The recent discovery of the Dead Sea Scrolls in the caves of Wadi Qumran have brought to light many fragments of the writings of this sect. Some of the Essenes lived rigidly disciplined lives in communities which may have served as a model for the monastic orders of early Christianity.

The Septuagint and Philo Jewish creativity during the Hellenistic period has left imposing monuments. Most of that literature, however, remained unknown to the Jews of Palestine. The books written by Hellenistic Jewry were preserved by the Christian Church. They were not included in the Jewish Bible and their clandestine status is expressed in the word by which they are known, Apocrypha, the hidden books.

The most important spiritual event in Hellenistic Jewry was the translation of the Old Testament into Greek. This translation, known as the Septuagint, was the product of a group in Alexandria, helped by scholars from Palestine, who began their task during the third century. Legend has it that seventy translators were enclosed in seventy different chambers, and that they all emerged with an exactly identical version. It is not agreeable to question such an attractive belief, but scientific truth leads us to believe that the work of translation was long, arduous, and highly contentious. It

lasted for a hundred years, starting with the Pentateuch and the

Prophets. As a literary model the translation is of little merit. It is mechanically literal, lacks fluency, and shows excessive regard for the Greek reader out of respect to pagan sensitivity. In an effort to make the text fully comprehensible to the Greek reader, general terms and ideas were often replaced by purely local and national concepts. Yet no work of translation has ever had such a potent effect. Without a Greek version of the Old Testament the early Christian missionaries would not have been able to convert Greek-speaking gentiles, and Christianity would never have become a world religion.

The synthesis between Jewish tradition and Greek philosophical thought is most brilliantly represented in Philo of Alexandria. He lived in the twilight between the old and the new era. His life coincided with the reign of Herod and Agrippa in Israel and he is a younger contemporary of Hillel. He belonged to one of the most distinguished families of Alexandria. It is certain that during his lifetime he visited Jerusalem as the guest of Agrippa. He is a combination of a statesman and a philosopher. His intensely searching mind was brought to bear on the task of establishing a bridge between Hebrew monotheism and Greek paganism. He maintained that all philosophical thought went back to Mosaic Law through which God had revealed His will. Torah was in his view but another name for "wisdom," and this "wisdom" (*hochma*) and *sophia,* or Greek science, were the same. For many centuries before and since Philo, efforts were made to vindicate Hebrew thought by proving that it was similar to something else. Philo held that the true Jewish philosopher must first apply himself to outside culture, and, with that training, attempt to probe the more sublime philosophy of the Divine Law.

Philo thus embodies the extreme Hellenic development of Judaism. He held that between faith and philosophy there is no conflict. But he did not convince the Jews of his age, and few gentiles seem to have yielded to his advocacy to the point of accepting the Mosaic Law as the true Natural Law, and Judaism as the universal religion. A modern historian has described him as "a man of vast knowledge and noble intentions, a great and useless figure. . . . The bridge he had built was not used by those for whom it was intended, but by the Christians when they came to develop their dogma." The thought of Philo became the starting point of medieval Christian philosophy; for later generations of Jews, he was unknown. For Christian scholarship, however, he was to become and remain a significant figure.

8 ❧ Under Roman Dominion

*T*HE HISTORY of the Roman Empire in the east begins with the defeat of Carthage in the second Punic war. The process of consolidation lasted for a century and a half during which Carthage in the west and Corinth in the east were sacked. Pompey's conquests and the establishment of Roman rule in Asia Minor and Syria were the culminating stages in Rome's supremacy. Egypt alone of the Hellenistic kingdoms retained some measure of independence until 30 B.C.E.

No Mediterranean country could successfully hope to challenge the dominant power of Rome, which had grown from a city-state to an empire greater than that of Alexander. Rome imposed a political unity of which Alexander had only dreamed. This indeed was its most glittering achievement. The Greek historian Polybius, in his universal history, covering the years 220–145, wrote:

> I cannot believe that anyone could be so dull as not to wish to know how the Romans in less than fifty-three years succeeded in subjugating nearly the whole inhabited world to their sole government—an achievement unexampled in history.

While Rome conquered the Hellenistic Empire, the culture of Greece conquered Rome. The moral, cultural, and intellectual life of Rome was dominated by a superior civilization. Greek became the language of the educated classes. Roman writers produced comedy and tragedy in Greek for Roman audiences. Roman writers wrote the history of their own nation in Greek. The Greek style in architecture and art was followed everywhere. Public and private building were faithful to the Greek model. Greek sculptures and paintings were imported and imitated. Physicians, surgeons, and teachers were recruited from Greece. No less profound was the impact of Greek ideas on Roman religion and thought. Stoicism appealed to the Roman mind and temperament. The Greek gods commanded reverence in Rome.

Economic conditions under Roman dominion underwent great transformations. The economy of Italy had been mainly agricultural. Now the peasants had become landless or were uprooted by constant wars. Italy was flooded with slave workers. The provincial administration enriched itself by pillaging the occupied countries. It invested its savings in land at home, leading to the creation of large holdings which left the small peasants landless and even jobless, since slave labor was easily available. Thus a proletariat converged on the capital city, its rebellious instincts held in check only by "bread and circuses."

The municipal constitution of Rome was incapable of solving the acute problems of the vast territories which had come under Roman sway. The provinces, therefore, became the prey of governors, who ruled in virtual independence, sustained by their command of great armies. In this atmosphere, dictatorship flourished. The most spectacular of the new autocrats was Caesar, who became dictator for life and was worshiped as a god. For Rome herself the immediate results of victory were class wars, corruption, and civil strife. By these the Republic was destroyed. Caesar was assassinated in the name of republican liberty, and the struggle for his political inheritance began. For some time the Empire was shared by Anthony and Octavian, but it was only a matter of time before they too clashed. By 29 B.C.E. Octavian had made himself the sole master of the Empire. He still lacked the title of emperor but as *princeps* and first senator his sway was unchallenged. He became known as Augustus, and the principate which he established, a kind of monarchy under the cloak of republican forms, was to endure for two centuries, until the death of Marcus Aurelius in 180 C.E. Order and security came to the entire Mediterranean world.

Alexander had united the eastern Mediterranean with western Asia; Rome added the western Mediterranean. Roman institutions and Hellenistic ideas fused into the structure and cultural life of the Empire. That Empire had been initially divided into two parts

—the Hellenistic East and the Roman West. The first was an amalgam of Oriental nationalities and religions, united by the general diffusion of Greek speech and culture. The second was a collection of Celtics, Berber tribes, and Italians, imbued with Latin speech and pervaded by Latin traditions.

This division led first to the split of the Empire into western and eastern parts, and later to the schism of Christianity between the eastern and western churches.

The Herodian
Period

In Palestine, Roman intervention had been decisive in the rivalry between the two sons of Salomé Alexandra. Rome supported Hyrkanos as High Priest and rejected Aristobulus, who was exiled to Rome with his two sons. Pompey exhibited them in his triumphal parade through the Roman forum. But, Aristobulus soon escaped and reached Judea again. There he assembled an army which retook Jerusalem. He defended the city against the Romans for three years until he was captured, sent to Rome again and this time poisoned. After yet another futile attempt to usurp the throne against the Roman will—this time led by Antigones, the son of Aristobulus—Rome decided to give the crown to a trusted emissary: Herod, the son of Antipater the Idumean, became King of Judea, a decision of fatal significance.

Herod was born to command. At the age of fifteen he had fought Jewish rebels in Galilee. Ruthless in war and impervious in civil government, he ascended the throne with thousands of murdered victims lying easily on his conscience. While he ruled there was nobody he would not fight—the Hasmoneans, the aristocrats, and, above all, the people, who were unwilling to accept an Idumean and a friend of Rome as their master. Though married to a Maccabean princess, he considered the Hasmonean family to be his enemy. He first disposed of Hyrkanos, the High Priest. Then he had his mother-in-law and other members of the dynasty executed. Finally he put his wife to death. Afraid of all opposition, he imagined himself surrounded by treason. He even murdered the two sons born to him by his wife Mariamne. The Emperor Augustus said of him: "One would rather be Herod's swine than his son," not too far-fetched an appraisal.

A deep gulf separated Herod from his people. They resented the pagan customs which he brought to Jerusalem. They were revolted by the circus and gladiatorial games. They abhorred his disrespect

for animal and human life. Totally uneducated, Herod posed as a champion of Hellenistic culture, and for this duplicity too, he was hated.

The longer Herod's reign lasted, the more savage became his brutalities. His distrust for the people led him to hire foreign mercenaries for his army. He filled the country with fortresses directed not against an external enemy, but against the people whom he ruled. His success lay in his foreign relations. He was trusted by the Emperor Augustus who allowed him to enlarge his territories. He created new cities at Sebaste, the Royal City, and at Caesarea, which he named after his patron, Caesar Augustus. His munificence was famous throughout the empire. He constructed huge buildings in foreign cities. His passion for construction led him to pave the streets of Antioch with marble blocks two and a half miles long, adorned with colonnades of equal length. All this was paid for by the taxes squeezed from his Palestinian subjects. Not even the magnificent Temple which he started to build in 19 B.C.E. could appease his impoverished citizens. In deference to the Romans, Herod had had a Roman eagle placed over the principal gate. This was torn down by the Zealots when they heard false rumors of Herod's death. As punishment, forty-two men were burned alive. In addition to Hellenistic cities Herod also built theaters, gymnasia, and, in the pagan cities, temples to pagan gods. He thus enraged his Jewish subjects, who clung to their customs and beliefs and refused to be impressed by the sophisticated glories of Greece.

After Herod's death in 4 B.C.E. the country was ruled by Roman procurators, although Herod's sons continued to wield a measure of power as tetrarchs or princes in the provinces. There was to be one short interval during which Palestine came under a Jewish king, Agrippa I, who ruled from 41 to 44.

Herod had been known as one of Rome's richest vassals. But the very splendor of his reign brought the people of Palestine to ruin. He had heavily taxed the poor, and expropriated the rich to such a degree that a delegation came to Augustus to complain of his confiscations. Rome's colonial policy always favored the local aristocracy, and Herod's alienation from the Jewish aristocrats may well have hastened the decision to replace the vassal kings by direct procuratorial control. Another factor, surely, was the reign of Herod's son Archelaus, who was openly known as "The Fool" and who so offended both Jewish and Roman sensibilities that he was finally sent by Augustus into exile in Gaul.

Hewn stone blocks rest on the Mediterranean shore in the old Roman harbor of Caesarea, founded by Herod the Great in 22 B.C.E. and named in honor of Augustus Caesar.

Lacking any positive ties with the ruling power, the distressed people looked for guidance to the religious academies. The heads of two schools during Herod's reign, Shammai and Hillel, had a profound influence on the development of Judaism. Abundant legend surrounds that famous pair of sages. Shammai, a brilliant scholar, represented the more conservative school. Hillel, his counterpart, was poor but universally loved. He was born in Babylonia but had come to Palestine in search of learning. It was there that the best schools were still to be found. He represented the Pharisaic outlook, maintaining that the Written Law alone did not represent the whole of Judaism. Hillel insisted that scholars in all ages were entitled to search the Torah and apply a rational logic to its interpretation. He is famous for his interpretation of "Judaism in a nutshell" which he distilled into the single sentence: "Do not unto others what you would not have done unto you." In contrast to the narrow interpretations of Shammai, Hillel strove to ease hardship in law by mitigating its provisions in the name of welfare and humanity. He opened his academy to all who wished to study, rich or poor, humble or prominent. The impact of Shammai and Hillel on their age was so deep that the schools of thought which evolved from their academies were known henceforth as *Bet Hillel* and *Bet Shammai*.

Rome and Jerusalem

With the banishment of Archelaus and the abolition of his monarchy, Judah became a Roman province, governed by an imperial procurator with judicial authority. The procurator commanded a small body of troops and resided not in Jerusalem but at Caesarea. In making this arrangement Augustus illustrated once again his leniency toward the Jews, to all of whom, in Jerusalem and in the Diaspora alike, he guaranteed the maintenance of the privileges granted by Julius Caesar: freedom of worship, exemption from military service, the right to send the annual Temple tax to Jerusalem, and the coinage of money without the head of the emperor or any other image.

But the procurators were not as tactful as their emperor. Relations between the representative of Rome and the Jews became tense. The governors changed frequently, for the emperor wished to limit their powers and curb their greed. This did not ease the hardships of the local population. Each procurator tried to squeeze out his loot in a shorter period of office. There is a famous saying about Varus, governor of Syria: "Poor he entered rich Syria; and rich he left poor Syria."

The oppressive procurators were a constant source of unrest. Conspicuous among them was Pontius Pilate, who ruled from 26 to 36. His brutality exceeded that of the others. He held the religious scruples of the Jews in special contempt and provoked their anger by bringing banners inscribed with the emperor's head into the Temple itself. Caligula, the mad emperor who followed Augustus, had wished to have his statue put up at the Temple. For forty days the Jews, revolted by this blasphemy, laid siege to the governor's residence, until, luckily, news came from Rome of the assassination of the madman.

Relations between Romans and Jews now grew so strained that men were executed at the smallest sign of insurrection. This violent persecution drove the resistance groups, known as Zealots, to fatal extremes. Bands of *Sicarii,* or dagger-bearers, terrorized the Romans and intimidated reluctant and moderate elements among the Jews. In 66 C.E. the despotic rule of the procurator Florus led to an insurrection in Caesarea and the outbreak of the Great Jewish War.

Florus, according to the historian Josephus, was so wicked that he made all his predecessors seem public benefactors. There was no limit to his zest for plunder. It was evident that the smallest spark would start a conflagration. The Jews were insulted by the privileges granted to their gentile neighbors in Caesarea, who tried to interfere with their Sabbath services and sacrificed a bird at the synagogue entrance. Florus refused to settle the disturbance, although he had previously accepted a bribe in advance of his arbitration. This treachery so angered the Jews that they passed baskets around to collect money for "poor" Florus. The procurator swore to avenge this treason. He held a court martial and several Jews were crucified. Then Florus attempted to rob the Temple treasury. His men slew without mercy.

Indignation now burst all bounds. The small nation had resolved to fight the greatest power on earth. The Jewish leaders were moderate men who had tried every resource to contain the insurrection. They received no help from either Agrippa or Florus, and the Zealots got the upper hand. By refusing the customary sacrifice on behalf of the Emperor Nero, Eleazar, the leader of the Zealots, declared overt rebellion against Rome.

Rome did not underestimate her opponent. She appointed one of her ablest generals, Vespasian, to command the war against the Jews. The Romans used the best instruments of warfare and applied their keenest strategy to the Jewish campaigns. They built ramparts in order to storm fortresses and constructed walls around whole cities in order to starve their inhabitants into submission. On the Jewish side there was little war material and a great deal of famine and hatred. Nevertheless, the Jewish resistance lasted seven years.

The first stage of the war was enacted in Galilee. Joseph ben Mattathias (Josephus Flavius) was made commander of the defense in Galilee. It was an incongruous choice. One city after another surrendered to Rome almost without resistance. Josephus himself defected to the enemy in 67. The hero of this province, Johanan from Gush-Halav, escaped with his band of Zealots and reached Jerusalem. Their arrival in the city plunged Jerusalem into civil war. With the help of volunteers from Idumea, Johanan became the master of Jerusalem. Many of the aristocracy and the Pharisaic leadership who opposed the war were killed.

Vespasian decided to wait and let the Jews destroy themselves through civil war in Jerusalem itself. It was not until the spring of 68 that he resumed his operations. Perea was soon conquered. At this moment news of Nero's suicide made him hasten back to Rome. The war was now interrupted for a year, as various factions jockeyed for power in Rome.

Vespasian was proclaimed Emperor, and his son Titus resumed the war in 69. In a short time the whole countryside was subdued, and the siege of Jerusalem began. Three leaders headed the defense of the city: Johanan, Shimon ben Giora, and Eleazar ben Shimon. This was not a unified command. It had no war material adequate to deal with the superior Roman legions. Josephus has described the operations in great detail. The city was surrounded by three walls. Inside the defenders suffered from famine and exhaustion. The first wall fell in May of the year 70. The defenders held out for three months until the gates were captured on the ninth day of Av. A last battle was fought in the Temple courts and the Sanctuary went up in flames. Johanan and Shimon escaped to Herod's palace, where they withstood another siege for five more months. When this last bastion fell, they were captured.

Masada was now the last fortress remaining in the hands of the Jews. On this granite rock in the Judean desert, overlooking the Dead Sea, a desperate defense was maintained for over two years.

Aerial view of Masada, the fortress on the west bank of the Dead Sea, where the Zealots made their last heroic stand, fighting the Romans to the death.

When the Romans finally captured the stronghold, they found that its 960 defenders had committed suicide. It was the first day of Passover. Remembering their slavery in Egypt, the Jews had preferred death to renewed captivity. Only two women and five children remained alive to tell the story of this last act of heroism. Excavations recently undertaken at Masada have given modern man new contact with this heroic age. From the top of Masada one can still discern the remains of the Roman encampments which laid siege to the fortress.

The war was now over. "Judea Capta" was inscribed on the coins minted to celebrate Titus' victory. Thousands had been killed. Thousands more were seized as captives and sold as slaves. In Rome Titus was given the honors due to a hero, as he entered the capital in triumph. The loot from the Temple and the prisoners from Jerusalem were exhibited. An arch was erected in the Forum, showing trophies from the Temple carved in stone. The Arch of Titus, as it came to be known, depicted the ravages of the defeat on the conquered. Yet the arch is more significant as a reminder of Jewish resistance than of Roman victory.

In its war against Rome, Judea had hoped that the Jews of the Diaspora, at least in the non-Roman world, would come to its help. The Jews in Palestine were already conscious of the power which their kinsmen exercised throughout the Mediterranean world. In most countries they were a favored minority. It was only in Palestine that the Romans subordinated the Jews to the Greeks.

In Palestine itself the people were deeply divided: The Sadducees were either pro-Roman or so intensely concerned with the preservation of the status quo that they had no heart for the revolt. The Pharisaic leadership too was more deeply preoccupied with religion than with political problems. They also may have thought that a Jewish-Roman war might seriously jeopardize the interests of world Jewry. Yet despite the enormous disparity of forces, the war continued intermittently for seven years, sustained by the devotion of the leaders and the sacrifice of their followers.

The sandals, skull and plaited hair of a Judean woman unearthed in recent diggings at Masada.

There are two conflicting sources regarding the responsibility for the destruction of the Temple. Josephus, who is a highly prejudiced historian, maintains that Titus had given orders to save the Temple, but was disobeyed by his soldiers. The other source, Julianus, who was one of the members of the Roman war council, reports that Titus had announced his policy for the destruction of the Temple. Whatever the truth, the name of Titus has become inseparable from the great catastrophe of Jewish history.

Joseph ben Mattathias was born in 37 C.E. of a priestly family in Jerusalem. Educated by Sadducees and Pharisees alike, he earned an early reputation for his learning. The elite of Jerusalem would turn to him for advice and interpretation of the Law. In 64 he was sent to Rome to intervene on behalf of Jewish prisoners. He succeeded in obtaining their release with the sympathetic help of Poppaea Sabina, the wife of the Emperor Nero.

When he returned to Judea he found the country seething with unrest. He was appointed leader of the defense in Galilee. In this he was bitterly opposed by the more fervent Zealots who had grouped around Johanan of Gush-Halav (Gishala). Josephus was not cast in the heroic mold. Besieged by the Romans in Jotapata he tried to negotiate surrender. When he failed he was forced to fight with inferior forces. When the stronghold fell, many of his comrades committed suicide, rather than be captured by the Romans. But Josephus quietly slipped out of the mountains and surrendered to Vespasian.

Jewish history has few renegades. Josephus entered its annals as a traitor. But his reputation for inconstancy was mitigated by his literary achievement. He left two major works of historic importance: *Jewish Antiquities*, a history of the Jews from the Creation to the Roman War; and *The Jewish War*, an account of the Jewish struggle against the Romans. Though written with a clear apologetic bias, the latter is an unrivaled source for this period of Jewish history. Josephus was also the author of *Against Apion*, a polemical book which constitutes the first detailed exposition and defense of Judaism as a religion.

The Bar Kochba Revolt

Twice after the great war the Jews were to engage again in battle with Rome, both times with disastrous consequences. Under Trajan, rebellions broke out in Alexandria, Cyprus, and Cyrene. The Jews paid a heavy penalty in suffering and death. But far more vivid and memorable was the rebellion in Palestine, led by Bar Kochba, in the reign of the Emperor Hadrian.

Josephus tells us that the Great War had passed without leaving deep scars in most of Palestine. The fall of Jerusalem appears as an episode rather than as the close of an epoch in Jewish history. Many cities had opened their gates to the Roman soldiers and were thereby saved from destruction. In a short time the country had returned to normality. Jerusalem, before the fall of the Temple, was not only the spiritual center; it was also the economic and commercial heart of the country. It had suffered fearfully in the war. Now it had to renounce its status as a *polis* as well as its internal autonomy.

The whole of Judea became a province under a general who had the tenth Roman legion under his command. The land belonged to the Roman government which distributed it at will to discharged soldiers. This conformed with the government's policy of settling foreigners in Judea. The Sanhedrin and the local courts were for a short time deprived of their privileges. The Jews now settled their cases in Caesarea. They built a new spiritual center in Yavneh. But they considered this a period of transition and continued to hope for the restoration of the Sanctuary in Jerusalem. They refused to accept the destruction of the Temple as a final or irrevocable fact.

In 118 Hadrian ascended to the throne of the empire. He sought to pacify the embittered Jewish masses by holding out vague promises to rebuild their holy city and, perhaps, to reconstruct the Temple itself. But it soon became clear that such a plan would conflict with Hadrian's policy of achieving greater cultural homogeneity in his empire. He therefore decided to rebuild Jerusalem not as a Jewish center but as a Greek city, to be called Aelia Capitolina.

This caused fierce resentment. Rabbi Akiva, the country's spiritual leader, who was known as a moderate, tried to calm the embittered masses and to negotiate with the emperor. The talks were protracted but Hadrian was not to be moved. Preparations went forward for building Jerusalem in the Greek pattern. The day had come for the ploughing of the building line, a Roman custom which traditionally marked the beginning of urban development and heralded Hadrian's intransigence.

For the Jews this was a bad omen. A new rebellion flared up. Its leader was Shimon bar Kozeba, a descendant of the family of David. His lineage entitled him to be considered by many as the Messiah. Even Rabbi Akiva followed him, together with many other martyrs, on his sacred war. It was Akiva himself who changed his name to Bar Kochba, "Son of the Star."

Many legends have come down to us about Bar Kochba. They extol his physical strength, his military genius, and his personal magnetism which enabled him to lead masses of volunteers in guerrilla warfare. These legends have now acquired historic authenticity. Valuable evidence was discovered during excavations in

A shekel struck by Bar Kochba during the abortive second Jewish revolt (135 C.E.) decorated with a likeness of Herod's temple.

Minted during the reign of Vespasian, this coin engraved with Judea Capta, a stalwart Roman legionary and a mourning Judean woman, celebrates the Roman defeat of the Jews.

1960–61 in caves of the Judean desert. Aside from pottery and glass, a bundle of papyrus rolls were found, proving to be letters in Hebrew, Aramaic, and Greek, signed by "Bar Koseba Ha-nasi of Israel." Coins found from the Bar Kochba period bear inscriptions like "Redemption of Zion," "Freedom for Israel," or "Shimon, Prince (Nasi) of Israel."

In the first stage of the rebellion Jerusalem was captured by the Jews. Sacrifices were reintroduced, even though the Temple did not exist. In that year, Jews in their thousands made a pilgrimage to Jerusalem and coins were struck with the inscription "Eleazar, High Priest." The Sanhedrin under Rabbi Tarfon and Rabbi Akiva was briefly revived. The flame of Jewish independence flickered anew.

The onslaught came in the summer of 134. Sextus Severus had been called from Britain to head the tenth legion. But the Emperor Hadrian felt sufficiently anxious to order that the campaign be conducted from Gerasa in Transjordan. With the fall of Jerusalem Bar Kochba transferred his resistance to Bethar, some eight miles to the south. Fortifications were hurriedly improvised. They would not withstand the Roman attack. As at Masada the Romans built ramps leading to the top of the hill and forced their way into the fort. According to Jewish tradition Bethar fell on the ninth of Av, the anniversary of the destruction of the Temple, after a war which had lasted for three and a half years. Bar Kochba was among the dead. Akiva and many of his fellow rabbis were martyred by Hadrian's lieutenants.

Jewish independence was now finally crushed. But Bar Kochba's resistance was to live on as a powerful historic legend, stirring heroic hopes and proud memories in Jewish hearts.

9 🎗 *The Rise of Christianity*

*A*T THE birth of Christianity, Jewish history had already crossed the boundaries of Palestine. Jews had settled in almost all the countries of the civilized world. Their communities extended from Italy and Carthage in the West to Mesopotamia in the East, from the Black Sea in the North to Ethiopia in the South. About four million Jews lived within the Roman Empire outside Palestine. There were at least a million more in Babylonia. Palestine had a population of about three million, including half a million Samaritans, Greeks, and Nabateans. Even before the destruction of the Second Temple, there were twice as many Jews in the Diaspora as in Palestine. The name Palestine itself entered common usage during the Greco-Roman period. In the Bible it was used to designate the country of the Philistines, a coastal stretch adjoining the Sharon Valley. The Romans, in conquering the land in 63 B.C.E., took the name of the province of Judah for the whole of the land. The Talmud, in referring to Palestine, speaks of it simply as "The Land," a term which has endured in Jewish terminology to this day.

As a result of the territorial conquests in the Hasmonean period, the country now comprised, aside from Judah, the provinces of Galilee, Transjordan, and Idumea. The Samaritans lived apart as a closed religious and ethnic group.

The populations of the various provinces were marked by deep contrasts. There was an intense Jewish vitality among the inhabitants of Judah. The province basked in the great distinction of Jerusalem and the Temple. For nearly ten centuries Jerusalem had been the holy center of the Jews. The whole Diaspora looked upon it as the "center of the world." In comparison with the other capitals of the Roman Empire, it was a humble place. But the modesty of its scale and amenities was transcended by its historic pride and significance.

The Temple outshone all the splendid edifices and palaces which had been built in Jerusalem during Roman rule. First built by Solomon and destroyed by Nebuchadnezzar, rededicated more modestly by Ezra and Nehemiah, it arose in new splendor during the reign of Herod, even though its construction was not completed until shortly before its destruction by Titus.

Jerusalem's population, estimated at 120,000, was intermittently swollen by masses of pilgrims who at times outnumbered the local population. The Temple and the Court provided permanent employment. Jerusalem was the seat of the High Priest and the Sanhedrin, while rich landowners and well-to-do merchants and craftsmen found it attractive for settlement. There was a thriving business in luxuries, including precious stones and expensive cloths.

The people of Galilee, on the other hand, had only joined the Commonwealth during the Hasmonean period. Their region was the main center of the common people (*am ha-aretz*), who took liberties with the Law, in which they were not well versed. They remained permanently wedded to ancient superstition. There were, as yet, no great centers of learning in Galilee. It boasted no large cities or famous teachers. Its inhabitants could not compare in scholarship with the population that lived close to the splendor of the Temple. Many dispossessed and landless could be found wandering from village to village. From these downtrodden Jews came Jesus of Nazareth.

The current language was Aramaic, spoken in a different dialect from that of Babylonia. The people of Judah despised the Galileans for their peculiar accent. Hebrew still remained in use as the language of the Scriptures and of the learned class.

The economy was based on agriculture. Wheat and barley were produced in great quantities, mainly in Galilee. But the crops of the orchard and the vineyard were even more abundant. Palestinian oil, figs and dates were highly prized in all the countries of the Mediterranean.

Commerce lay mainly in the hands of Greeks, from whom the

Jews were learning mercantile arts. Josephus Flavius said of the Jews of his day, ". . . we are not a commercial people; we live in a country without a seaboard and have no inclination to trade."

Under Hasmonean rule, some coastal cities such as Ashkelon were temporarily captured and Israel renewed its contact with the sea. The Emperor Titus, on occupying Palestine, had a coin struck with the inscription "Judea Navalis."

The Hasmoneans had built a strong economy in Palestine. Herod slowly destroyed it. Much of his building program took place outside the Jewish territory, so that its benefits accrued to neighboring provinces. A grave economic crisis beset the country during the close of the century. This became even more severe after earthquakes and floods. Crops were destroyed and famine raged. The tax burden became unbearable.

Internal Government

The civilian Jewish authority was the Council of Elders, or Sanhedrin, composed of seventy men. Though there is no trace of this institution for the first thousand years of Jewish history, its origin goes back to Moses, of whom God had requested "seventy men from the Elders of Israel." From the Hellenistic period, the Sanhedrin comprise the state administrative and judicial organs.

The High Priests of the Maccabean and post-Maccabean period were not only religious leaders. They were also ruling princes. Their position was strengthened by lifelong heredity. But their status was weakened under the Roman governors who appointed and dismissed them at will. There were no fewer than eighteen High Priests during the Herodian-Roman period.

The priestly caste was important so long as the Temple stood. Its members had the exclusive right to bring sacrifices and their personal purity was ensured by the meticulous laws which governed their daily lives. Their social position was enhanced by the fact that they shared the wealth of the Temple and of the sacrifices. They also received special remunerations for services performed outside their regular duties.

Jewish Demography

There are many estimates but no reliable figures concerning Jewish population during the Roman period. In the Hellenistic age, the Jews had become dispersed over the whole Greek world. As early as 140 B.C.E. the author of the Sibylline Oracles testified "that the whole land and seas are full of Jews." Strabo, a contemporary of Herod, says, "It would have been difficult to find a single place in the world where there are no Jews." And Josephus added, "There are no people in the world among whom part of our brethren is not to be found." Philo speaks of the "wide expansion of the Jews throughout the world" and of Jerusalem as "the center of the scattered nation."

The population of the Greco-Roman world during the first century B.C.E. is estimated at 60–70 million. Of these Egypt had a population of approximately seven and a half million, Alexandria about 500,000, two-fifths of whom were Jews. Another source puts the population of Alexandria in 38 B.C.E. at one million or more, of whom no less than two-fifths were Jews.

Palestine, before the destruction of the Temple in 70 C.E., had a population of about three million Jews. One million at least lived in each of the countries of Egypt, Syria, Asia Minor, and Babylonia, so that Diaspora Jewry heavily outnumbered that of Palestine.

All in all, a total Jewish population of eight million is not improbable.

In the Eastern Roman Empire, the Jews constituted about 20 per cent of the population, so that every fifth "Hellenistic" inhabitant of the Eastern Mediterranean was a Jew. In the West, the figure was one in ten. At no time in history, before or since, have Jews formed so large a part of the known population of the civilized Occidental world.

The Rise of Christianity

The century between the conquest of Jerusalem by Pompey and the end of the governate of Pontius Pilate (39 C.E.) was marked by external peace and internal strife. Judah was ruled by puppet princes who succeeded each other through assassination and war. The number of victims of civil war has been estimated at 200,000.

Turning away in despair from the political chaos, many people sought refuge in religious speculation. Sects multiplied. Religious discussion was dominated by a belief in the "approaching end of the days" and the imminence of the Messiah. The temporary reign of the "children of darkness" was to be followed by the rule of the "sons of light." The belief in the early coming of the redeemer was stimulated by despair and nourished by ecstatic hope.

The air was heavy with volcanic foreboding when Jesus of Nazareth appeared. Jesus was a Pharisaic Jew. He lived among the common people of Galilee and was the spokesman of their ideas. Galilee was the stronghold of a robust Jewish patriotism, which found resonance in the teachings of Jesus insofar as they conformed with those of the ancient prophets. He never considered himself a universal prophet outside the Jewish context. It cannot even be said that he was indifferent to the external forms of religion. He meticulously kept Jewish laws, made a pilgrimage to Jerusalem on Passover, ate unleavened bread, and uttered a blessing when he drank wine. He was a Jew in word and deed.

Jesus articulated the ideas and manners of the masses. Even his attacks on the hypocritical leaders were not unprecedented. He himself declared in the Sermon on the Mount that he "had not come to destroy the Law but to fulfill it." Nourished by the ideas of Pharisaic Judaism, he stressed the Messianic hope, predicting its fulfillment in his own time. The terms, "Messiah" and "King of the Jews," were used by him in their spiritual significance. But in the atmosphere of the time they resounded like a call to revolution. The Roman authorities saw Jesus' activities as tokens of subversion. His arrest, trial, and execution reflected the intolerance of an insecure regime which had experienced many a Jewish revolt arising out of religious fervor.

After his death, a small circle of Jesus' followers began to spread his teachings among the Jews of Palestine. It was not until the moral crusade of Paul that this teaching spread among the gentile population in the form of a new religion.

Saul of Tarsus became Paul in the New Testament. In contrast to Jesus, he was an intellectual, deeply influenced by Greco-Roman culture. His missionary genius transformed a despised and hunted creed into a world religion. Wherever the Apostle traveled, he denounced the evils of pagan society. In the passion of his moral zeal, Paul developed and crystallized the beliefs which made him the intellectual founder of Christianity.

The Jew had come, through the Torah, to a comprehension of God. To Paul, Christ was the incarnation of the Law, and even its substitute. Jesus had sacrificed himself in order to emancipate man from the burden of the Law. He was an intermediary between God and man. The principle of Christ as mediator became the cornerstone of the new faith, as Paul denounced the original Jewish Law as burdensome to Jew and Gentile alike.

Gradually the Jewish Christians were won over in increasing numbers to his views. As the new faith broke more and more sharply with the old institutions and the old prohibitions against deification, a final split became inevitable. In time, Christianity, in contact with the Roman world, grew more and more distinct from the parent Jewish faith.

If the Bible had not been translated into Greek, there would have been few converts among the Greek-speaking gentiles, and Christianity would hardly have become a world religion in the course of three centuries. The Septuagint had kindled a flame of religious yearning among the Hellenic population of the Empire. We have seen that the Jewish Diaspora was deeply rooted from the first century onward throughout the Hellenistic Middle East. The dispersion gave strong impetus to Christian teaching. The oldest Christian communities, established by the immediate followers of Jesus, consisted of Aramaic-speaking Jews of Palestine and Greek-speaking Jews of Cyrene, Alexandria, Syria, and Cilicia. When the Apostle Stephen was stoned in Jerusalem, his colleagues went to Phoenicia and Antioch, preaching the word to Jews of a more tolerant and less orthodox disposition.

The Jewish Character of Christian Thought

Early Christianity is closer to Judaism than the adherents of either religion have usually wished to admit. Both Christian theologians and Orthodox Jews have underestimated the original Judeo-Christian affinity. It was only gradually that Christianity severed its connection with the Jewish community and became transformed into a gentile religion.

The story of Israel has immense historic significance for all Christians. Besides Jesus himself, Judaism gave Christianity the One, the living God. It contributed a Sacred Book—its own Testament—and thereby paved the way for the New Testament. It passed on a historic tradition that made life purposeful and history full of meaning. The gospels are a record of Jewish life in Judea and in Galilee in the early decades of the first century. The actors in the drama are Jews living in their own land. Historians must in all objectivity include Christianity among the decisive achievements of the Jewish mind. Hebrew concepts and ethics permeate the faith and civilization which, with mysterious power, have dominated two millennia of human history.

The early Christians, when they set out to convert the gentiles, took the Old Testament as their text. In this they had an inestimable advantage over their rivals: no other religion in the empire possessed a Book charged with such vitality and eloquence. Israel had given to Christianity the prophets of truth and righteousness as well as the belief in the Messiah. No other people had conceived such a potent myth. The Messianic faith is the seed of progress planted by Judaism in human history, the only idea capable of counteracting the chronic pessimism of Helleno-Roman culture.

The most significant feature of the Jewish heritage was its view of history. Other ancient peoples have believed in a golden age, but they have always located it in the past, at the beginning of history. Israel alone looked forward to a golden age in the future and interpreted history as a meaningful and progressive movement toward Messianic consummation. Thus Jewish thought marked a revolt against previous religions. Never before had a people conceived a vision of human destiny as something sharply different from the natural process, with its inexorable succession of birth, life, and decay. Man had broken loose from the servitude of inevitability and predestination. He was a sentient being, endowed with the hazard of choice.

10 ⚜ New Centers of Diaspora

A DISTINCTION should be made between two terms—Exile, which means a compulsory banishment, and Diaspora, which signifies a voluntary scattering. Both have been part of Jewish existence from earliest history. Exile became Diaspora when the Jews adjusted themselves to their new environment. The first captivity, *Galut Jehoiachin*, gave rise to feelings of great bitterness among the people exiled to Babylonia: they incessantly called on those left behind to deliver them. On the other hand, Jeremiah urged them to meet their fate with resignation: ". . . Build ye houses and dwell in them; and plant gardens and eat the fruit of them; take ye wives and beget sons and daughters . . . that ye may be increased there, and not diminished. And seek the peace of the city whither I have caused you to be carried away captives . . ." (Jeremiah 29:5–7).

The Diaspora is almost as old as the Jewish people itself. There were Jewish settlements outside Palestine in the days of the Kings. Jewish traders went to Egypt to buy horses, and to Damascus to establish bazaars. Other settlements arose from the captivity of the Ten Tribes in 722 B.C.E., and the exile of Judah to Egypt and Babylonia in 586. Some Jewish captives of Nebuchadnezzar escaped to Egypt and settled in the town of Taphnis. The prophet Jeremiah was one of these. Jewish slaves were sold to the Ionian Islands during the reign of Jehoshafat in the middle of the ninth century, and the Jewish military colony of Elephantine in Upper Egypt dates from the seventh or sixth century B.C.E. The Jews exiled to Babylonia spread far and wide, especially during the Hellenistic period. In the days of the Roman Empire, about four and a half million Jews lived outside Palestine.

The early migrations from Palestine were mainly brought about by catastrophe. The exiles were victims of foreign invasion and were regarded by their conquerors as part of the booty. But there were also Jews who were induced to settle abroad by hope of commercial success. In time, overpopulation became a primary cause of emigration. In the words of Philo: "No one country can support the Jews because they are so numerous." Even before the Hasmonean expansion Judea was too small to contain the entire Jewish nation. By Philo's time, the Jews lived in the whole of Palestine and spilled out beyond its borders.

The last armed resistance of the Jews against the Roman yoke took place in 132–135 C.E. under Bar Kochba. The country was ravaged by war. Most of the cities and villages in Judah were either destroyed or abandoned. Some tenacious farmers continued to cling to their soil, but most of the survivors fled to Galilee, where the wounds inflicted by the war were quickly healed.

Of the seventy-five known villages in Judah, not one was left with any sign of Jewish life after the fall of Bethar. The Jewish community was reduced to about 800,000, half of whom now settled in Galilee, where only eight settlements had been destroyed, leaving fifty-six at the end of the revolt. The biggest cities were Tiberias and Zippori, while smaller ones existed at Shafr'am and Bet Shearim.

The Romans erased the name of Judah from official usage, choosing deliberately to call the country Palestine. Jerusalem, already a city closed to Jews, was renamed Aelia Capitolina; Roman soldiers guarded it assiduously against any Jew who might dare come to weep at the ruins of the Temple. The Temple Mount was sown with salt. All that remained was the Western Wall, the ancient retaining wall at the foot of Mount Moriah. Five hundred thousand Jews died or were sold as slaves in the final act of Roman oppression.

The destruction of a great part of the population was followed by the ruthless suppression of its intellectual life. A series of laws

*An important center of learning and the seat of
the Sanhedrin during the time of Judah Ha-Nasi,
Bet Shearim has been carefully excavated to reveal a
synagogue and numerous tombs.*

deprived the Jews of every vestige of their religion: circumcision, keeping the Sabbath, or any observance of Jewish law was forbidden by decree. Giving or receiving Rabbinical ordination (*semichah*) was punishable by death. The authorities were well aware that the conferment of spiritual authority would revive a sense of community. Any study of Jewish lore was made punishable by torture and death. The pages of Jewish history in this dark period are full of the names of martyrs who were killed for the infringement of Hadrian's decree. (Rabbi Judah ben Bava was put to death for ordaining six pupils at Usha. They survived to become leaders in a new academy.) But the spark of Jewish identity was not easily quenched.

The Schools   Under Antoninus Pius (138–161), Hadrian's successor, a more liberal atmosphere prevailed. Most of the anti-Jewish laws were repealed. In consequence, many of the exiles returned, among them a group of disciples ordained by Rabbi Akiva.

   The fall of Bethar had ended the political independence of the Jewish people, but its spiritual life now flourished with a new intensity. The revival had begun long before, with Johanan ben Zakkai. During the siege of Jerusalem he had remained in the beleaguered city until the end. Anticipating its fate, he resolved to ensure Israel's survival by saving its spiritual integrity. The chain of tradition must not be broken. He had himself carried out of the city in a coffin, as though for burial, and when discovered and brought before the Roman general, he had but one request: "Yavneh and its sages." Vespasian agreed to let the old man have the crumbling walls of his school. He could not have been expected to realize that he was allowing the seed of Jewish revival to be planted anew. In making his request, Johanan was not primarily concerned with the lives of a few dozen old sages. His concern was to give a new lease of survival to the spirit which these men embodied. His act became symbolic of Jewish priorities for generations to come. Learning was held to be the essence of national survival for a people which lacked the normal conditions of collective identity. Spiritual strength would, when circumstances allowed, give birth to a capacity for active revolt. This idea was soon to be tested. It was Rabbi Akiva and his students who gave fervor and spirit to the Bar Kochba revolt. Alert now to the decisive role of the academies in keeping political energy alive, the
New Centers of Diaspora   Roman authorities moved to suppress the schools.

When Yavneh eventually fell, the center of gravity shifted to Galilee, where the disciples of Rabbi Akiva set up the nucleus of a new school at Usha. A new Sanhedrin was chosen, with Rabbi Shimon ben Gamliel at its head. He was known by the new title of *Nasi*. His dogmatism was tempered by social empiricism. He said, "It is not fitting to impose laws on the people, unless it is certain that the majority are able to endure them."

The Roman administration, in its efforts to pacify the country, collaborated with this new Patriarch. Thus the foundation was laid for the development of the Palestinian Patriarchate which was to guide its destiny for several generations.

Rabbinical policy sought means for adapting Jewish life to the changed conditions. It was necessary to consolidate a population decimated by wars, emigration, and religious conversions. The old national institutions had to be replaced by a new focus of loyalty. The memory of the Temple and the glory of Israel were somehow to be stirred into life.

Soon enough the Greek cities of the Galilee underwent a change. They became centers of study which attracted scholars and students from all parts of the land. A public invitation was issued to "anyone who had studied to come and teach, and anyone who had not studied to come and learn."

Rabbi Shimon ben Yochai opened an academy in Tekoa near Safed, Rabbi Yosi ben Halafta at Zippori, Rabbi Nathan and Rabbi Johanan bar Nappacha founded schools elsewhere. These groups gave new impetus to Jewish life. The teachers were all very poor. They had to earn their livelihood as craftsmen or Torah scribes. Rabbi Meir is the most vivid personality of this group. He was a favorite pupil of Rabbi Akiva. His birthplace is said to have been in Asia Minor, and he was believed to have descended from a branch of the family of Emperor Nero which had converted to Judaism. His fame lay in his intimate knowledge of Hebrew. He once wrote the whole Book of Esther from memory without a single mistake.

Meir was also famous for his fables, hundreds of which have been passed on to us. They have something of the lucidity of La Fontaine. "He who touches Meir's staff becomes wise," said the people of Zippori. He was considerably more learned than Rabbi Shimon, the *Nasi*, but also much younger, and therefore less respected. He reacted to this situation by saying, "Look not to the vessel but to its contents. Many a new vessel contains old wine, but many old casks are empty."

The loss of the Temple had been a traumatic experience for the Jewish people, and insistent efforts were made to perpetuate its memory. The Rabbis introduced the custom of marking all events by the date of the destruction. Jews in Palestine and abroad continued to pay the tithe. Pilgrimages to Jerusalem were maintained long after the Temple's loss. These took place not only on Tisha b'Av (Ninth of Av) but also on each of the three pilgrimage holidays (Pesach, Shavuot, and Sukkot). Prayer became a substitute for sacrifice, and rituals were adopted to reinforce the symbolic link between the Temple and the synagogue. These included the *lulav* ceremony on each day of the week-long Sukkot festival; the blowing of the *shofar* on Rosh Hashanah; and the observation of the year of release (*Shemitah*). A revision of the Haggadah was made to include reference to the Passover sacrifice at the Temple and prayers for the restoration of Jerusalem.

The next step was to reestablish Palestinian spiritual controls over Diaspora Jewry. Emigration from Palestine had reached alarming proportions, and the Rabbis strove mightily to stem it. A characteristic passage in the *Tosefta*, evidently originating from discussions in the post-Hadrianic period, reads:

> A man should live in Palestine, even in a city with a gentile majority, rather than abroad in a wholly Jewish city. Living in Israel is the equivalent of fulfilling all the commandments in the Torah, and he who is buried in Palestine, is like unto one who is buried under the altar. . . .

The unification of the Jewish world demanded the regulation of a single Jewish calendar, fixing the celebration of the new moon and the ensuing holidays. Another important bond was secured by reviving Hebrew as the national language. When Jerusalem fell, the vast majority of Jews spoke either Aramaic or Greek. Now Aramaic was barred from higher schools and synagogues. Rabbi Meir placed the speaking of Hebrew on the same level as residence in the Holy Land, as a condition of Jewish piety. In the synagogue, too, prayers remained predominantly Hebrew.

The Assembly at Usha was important because it established a national institution whose authority was recognized even by its spiritual opponents. Thus Rabbi Shimon ben Gamliel succeeded in laying the foundation for the Patriarchate of his son Judah who raised the prestige of the office to its peak. Judah achieved a position unparalleled by any of the *Nesi'im* and became known in Jewish history simply as "Rabbi." His early life was spent at Usha. His later sojourn at Bet Shearim gave lasting fame to that city, which he had to leave for Zippori at the end of his life for reasons of health.. His household was little less than royal, and even the maidservant therein spoke Hebrew. His activity covers almost half a century (170–217) and his great achievement is completing codification of the *halakhah* (Oral Law) in the form of the Mishnah, the epoch's great literary and legal document.

Side by side with the Written Law (Torah), there had existed for centuries a vast amount of Oral Law which was handed down by memory from generation to generation. This law interpreted individual cases of human behavior in terms of Biblical precept, the general issue in each case revolving around the question of what a man should do or should not do in order to carry out the spirit and ordinances of the Torah in every detail. Thus there had accumulated, in addition to the written code, a vast body of "case law," handed down in the schools by word of mouth. It was Rabbi Akiva who began to reduce this chaotic mass to a semblance of order. He sought justification in the Biblical text for every act which extended life beyond Biblical experience. His pupil, Rabbi Meir, revised and elaborated the work of his master, without committing anything to writing. The final redaction was undertaken under Judah Ha-Nasi with whose name the codification of the Mishnah is preeminently linked. In his work Judah drew on some thirteen previous collections, containing traditions handed down in the names of a hundred and fifty scholars. These traditions were collected and scrutinized, supplemented, and, where necessary, rearranged. The division by subjects was perfected. The whole was arranged in six Orders (Seeds, Feasts, Women, Damages, Hallowed Things, Cleanliness). Each of these six Orders was further divided into Tractates, Chapters, and Clauses. The language employed was a pure and vigorous Hebrew for which the Patriarch had a predilection. Those Rabbis who had collaborated in its production, from Hillel and his predecessors down to Judah himself, became known by the Aramaic name of *Tannaim* (teachers).

The Talmud and
Its Development

New Centers of Diaspora

As long as Rome flourished, Palestine's hegemony in the Jewish world was unchallenged. But the economic and social decline of the Roman Empire marked a concomitant decline in the Palestinian center. As a result of war the Jewish population had decreased.

Bet Shearim catacombs with the ritual candelabrum carved in stone.

Although there was no further interference with religious customs after the Hadrianic decrees were abrogated by Antoninus Pius, the Jews nevertheless led a segregated life; only secondarily did they consider themselves citizens of the Roman Empire. Christian missionary activities led to mounting friction with the gentile environment. The tax burden had become almost unbearable. The situation of the Jews deteriorated further when Christianity became a state religion and the rule of the Church fathers was established throughout the Empire. There was no room for both the Jewish Patriarch in Tiberias and the Bishop in Jerusalem.

This tension moved many Jews to emigrate. There had been mass emigration to Syria and Babylonia after 70 C.E. In Persia, the Sassanian monarchs who ascended the throne in 226 encouraged immigration since the new citizens brought technical skills for industrial projects and commercial undertakings. Under Shapur II, who reigned in the middle of the third century, 86,000 Jewish families moved from Armenia to the Iranian provinces. From Palestine, the main stream of emigration turned eastward toward Babylonia.

Jewish history in Babylonia had begun with the first captivity under Nebuchadnezzar. The community which had settled there never lost its national identity or severed its link with the mother country. Babylonian Jews paid their dues to the Temple, made pilgrimages to Jerusalem, and sent their sons to the Palestinian academies. Great scholars of Babylonia, of whom the most renowned was Hillel, found Jerusalem a congenial place for study.

By the end of the third century, however, community life and religious organization in Babylonia far surpassed conditions in the mother country. Jewish life in Babylonia was completely autonomous. Some cities, such as Nehardea—known as the "Jerusalem of Babylon"—were entirely Jewish.

At the head of the Jewish community stood the *Rosh Ha-golah* (Exilarch), whose authority was greater than that of the Patriarch. His writ transcended the religious domain: he was the supreme judge in criminal cases, and he wielded executive power in the country's economic life. Under the Sassanian dynasty he represented the Jews before the king, and in that capacity he ranked high among the imperial councilors. There seems to have been an unbroken continuity of exilarchic regime since the ancient exile of Jehoiachin, a line which was to extend a little beyond the year 1000 without interruption.

As in Palestine, the majority of Babylonian Jews possessed a highly developed agriculture, enriched by the abundant waters of the Tigris and Euphrates. Irrigation canals were dug and maintained under government supervision. Agricultural activity was so important that the courts interrupted their sessions during the months of the high season. The Jewish population contributed to the success of Babylonia's economy, earning particular fame by the transplantation of the olive tree from Palestine.

The status of the exilarchate did not depend solely on the powers conferred on it by the central government. Its fate was closely linked with the influence of the scholarly class which was then rising to leadership in the Jewish community. As in Palestine, the power of the rabbinate grew with the development of the academies. But as the Palestinian centers of learning declined, those of Babylonia grew in importance. By the end of the third century Babylonia was academically independent and materially predominant in Jewish life.

The central text of study was the Mishnah of Judah, the *Nasi*. Babylonian scholars had found that many explanations in the Mishnah referred exclusively to Palestinian traditions, and that too little consideration was shown to conditions in Babylonia. Therefore they felt they had the right to follow their own path and to elaborate on the work of their Palestinian colleagues. It was thus that the famous academies of Sura and Pumbedita arose. They were dedicated under Rav and Samuel in the third century. If there was any difference between them, it lay in their relations with Palestine during their early years. Pumbedita, the heiress of Nehardea, which was destroyed in 259, carried on the old tradition of native Babylonian Jewish learning. Pumbedita was headed by Mar Samuel, a pupil of Judah Ha-Nasi who favored independence from the Palestinian method. Rav, on the other hand, founded his academy in Sura "where there had been no Torah before." He transplanted much Palestinian learning and adopted many Palestinian customs which he too had studied at the school of Judah and brought to the new circumstances.

For some time, the schools of Palestine and Babylonia worked concurrently on the Mishnah. But after the victory of the Christian Church in the Roman Empire, Palestinian Jewry fell into decline and its scholarship was enfeebled. The most extensive research of the Mishnah took place under generations of teachers called *Amoraim*. They discovered that the Mishnah did not contain all the available legal material, and certainly not the additional *halakhot* (laws) which had meanwhile accumulated. Their task was to collect all these additions, codify them, and give them the stamp of finality. Thus there arose the compilation of legal exegesis called the *Gemara*. Mishnah and Gemara together form the Talmud, that immense commentary on Jewish life.

The Palestinian and Babylonian academies carried on their research independently, although an exchange of ideas took place through mutual visits of the Rabbis. The Palestinian Talmud—also known as the Jerusalem Talmud—was begun by Johanan bar Nappacha (199–279) when he was head of the academy of Tiberias. It was finished by the middle of the fourth century, under adverse political conditions. In comparison to the Babylonian Talmud it has many shortcomings. It is incomplete and lacks continuity. However, it is an important source of information on Palestine Jewry and therefore of great historic significance.

The Babylonian Talmud is not so much a book as a literary monument. It reflects nearly ten centuries of Jewish life in Palestine and Babylonia. It is the record of Jewish intellectual and religious creativity. The word of the Bible is its starting point, but it wanders far afield from there into a world of sagas and legends, tales and poems, allegories, ethical reflections and historical reminiscences. Of the two and a half million words of the Talmud, fully a third are devoted to *Midrashim*, or homilies. These belong to the *Aggadah*, the narrative, or non-legal part of Rabbinical literature which reflects the personal opinions of the teachers and scholars. *Aggadah* digresses endlessly and charmingly from its starting point and breaks the tedium of *halakhic* debate by flight into history and folklore, astronomy and medicine.

Legal problems in the Talmud are dealt with by dialectical exposition, through a form of reasoning called *pilpul* which exposes both the truth and its opposite, examines all the arguments for and against in order to arrive at a logical reason for the application of a given law. This form of dialectic has sharpened the tradition of rationality in Jewish life.

The compilation of the Talmud was not completed until the end of the fifth century. But the chief work is ascribed to Rav Ashi (352–427), who for fifty years was head of the academy at Sura. During the sixth and seventh centuries the Talmud was enlarged by the school of the *Sevoraim* (reasoners), who were the successors to the *Amoraim*. It was then interpreted by later scholars, whose contribution to its elucidation is inestimable.

Only one complete manuscript of the Talmud exists. It is in the

*Capitals and pediments at the second-century
Capernaum synagogue with intricate carvings that
include one of the Holy Ark (at the right).*

Museum of Munich and was written in the middle of the four-teenth century. One of the main reasons for the absence of any other surviving manuscripts is the fact that, since the Talmud contained the main teachings of the Jewish religion, it was considered to be the core of Jewish resistance to conversion to Christianity, and was often consigned to the flames by medieval Christian authorities.

If the Bible was the Book Eternal, the Talmud was a daily companion. Prosaic, homely, practical, and replete with countless answers to human needs, to the men in the ghetto it was a reservoir of national life, the faithful mirror of an ancestral civilization in Babylonia and in Judea. In the face of outward hostility and of enforced segregation, the Jews of the Middle Ages were thrown inward on independent sources of memory and experience. Hostility helped to rally them around the traditions of their forefathers. They were aided in the cultivation of their separate identity by the regulations collected in Talmudic literature, which henceforth governed their life. The Talmud offered an open door to a full, vivid, bustling world of Jewish experience.

Triumph of the Church

The Emperor Constantine, after his conversion to Christianity in 313, decided to establish a new capital in the East: Constantinople. He sought also to preserve Rome but succeeded instead in founding the Byzantine Empire. The curtain slowly came down on Rome. The dying Empire gave birth to the Papacy, which now took over the responsibilities of the state. Christianity was declared a state religion under Theodosius. The transfer of the capital from Rome to Byzantium was of great political importance. It led to the break-up of the Roman Empire and to the split of the Church into eastern and western parts.

The "Peace of Constantine," as Herbert J. Muller has called the Edict of Milan of 313, ushered in a long period of intolerance. From now on, Christianity was to impose itself by force. Toynbee, inexplicably, speaks of "the way of gentleness" which marked the triumph of the Church in contrast to the "moral offense of attempting to impose religion by political force," such as was the practice of Islam. Muller, however, points out that it was Christianity which introduced Toynbee's "moral offense" into history as a deliberate and sustained policy.

New Centers of Diaspora

120

The century-and-a-half preceding the spread of Islam were marked by a political and economic decline, accompanied by a pessimistic outlook which gained ground among Christians and pagans alike. The Jews had to bear insult and degradation. They bore the stigma of a "nefarious" sect and a "sacrilegious congregation." Until they could assume their important role under the mighty Islamic Empire, they were to suffer some of their greatest agonies under Persia and Byzantium, and amidst the newer civilizations slowly emerging from the smoldering ruins of Western Rome. From the sixth century on, Jews were systematically harried from place to place. They were either forced into baptism or uprooted from the soil. Though they had no political home, they continued to represent an entity and were treated as such.

The western part of the Roman Empire could not resist the onslaught of the German tribes and disintegrated completely. Rome was first sacked by the Visigoths (Western Goths) in 410; the last Western emperor was ousted in 476.

Palestine, at the end of the fourth century, had become a predominantly Christian country. After the completion of the Palestinian Talmud, most information on life in Palestine is derived from Christian sources.* The densest Jewish settlement was in the northern part, but even there the Jews did not represent more than 10 or 15 per cent of the population. Disillusioned, many started to emigrate, though Hieronymus (St. Jerome) writes that the Jews "grow like worms."

The fact that Palestine had become a Christian country now attracted many Christian pilgrims to whom, ironically, the Jews served as guides, especially at those shrines mentioned in the Old Testament. On the other hand, the Christians also began to remove from Palestinian soil the relics of their early saints and of Biblical prophets and figures.** They also built churches over the burial places of prophets and saints. This was the time when Jews lived as aliens in their own land. Only on the ninth of Av were they allowed to enter their Holy City. Sometimes they had the good fortune to find a Roman soldier who, for a bribe, would let them weep a little longer at the ruins of the Temple. Hieronymus de-

---

* Tell-tale evidence can also be pieced together from the many remnants of ancient synagogues from the 2nd–6th centuries, excavated in recent years in Israel: Capernaum, Bar-Am, Nirim, Bet Alpha, Gadera, and others.

** In 395 the remains of Joseph were transferred from Shechem to Constantinople; those of the prophet Samuel were exhumed in 406.

A mosaic floor depicting the signs of the Zodiac at the Bet Alpha synagogue in Israel.

scribes the sight of the mourning people: ". . . women whose strength had left them because of old age; they are unkempt and their clothes are torn, they look pale and weep. While the men blow the *shofar* on the ashes of the Temple, the Roman soldiers ask for more money, before they agree to their desire to weep for a while longer. All this happens under the golden crosses of the Church of Burial, and of the crosses of Mount Olive."

Thus Jerusalem was forbidden to the Jews, who once again fell into the old lament: "How does the city sit solitary, that was full of people."

The frequent wars between Byzantium and Persia were intensified under the reign of the Emperor Heraclius. Initially, the Persians conquered large territories, including Palestine. Jerusalem was captured by the Persians in 614. Many Jews had fought in the Persian armies against Byzantium, and in gratitude, the Persians handed over to the Jews the administration of the city. Steps were now taken to reintroduce the cult and to rebuild the Temple. But this interlude lasted for only three years, after which time all hopes for the reestablishment of Jewish rule collapsed: the Persians were defeated and Jerusalem returned to the Christians. Jews were forbidden to dwell within a radius of three miles of the city.

By this time, however, Byzantium was so weakened by endless wars that it was no match for the fierce Arab armies advancing from the deserts in the south. The age of Islam was about to begin.

*T*HE BEGINNING of the seventh century found Jews inhabiting most areas of Europe. In few European lands, however, were they permitted to live unmolested for more than decades at a time. With the spread of Catholic Christianity, and the increasing influence of the Church on governments, one Jewish community after another underwent the fate of exile or enforced baptism. The story of Jewish survival in Christian Europe is for centuries punctuated by this oppressive rhythm of rejection and expropriation.

The Jews had first arrived in Europe in the wake of the conquering Roman Legions; it was thus that they came to northern Italy, the Franco-German realm, and Spain, countries where other peoples, among them Phoenician and Syrian traders, had already settled. For the convenience of synagogue worship and community life, the Jews tended to settle in groups and to occupy separate urban quarters—a pattern followed by virtually all foreign groups in the great cities of the Roman Empire. Jews were to be found in all professions, but the majority of them, having begun their life in the Diaspora as slaves, were engaged in the humbler occupations, including agriculture (in Italy, tilling the land was principally a slave occupation).

Under the Edict of Caracalla (212), all Jews residing in the Roman Empire had been granted citizenship. This status remained initially unaffected even when Italy and Western Europe were overrun by the barbarian invaders. Most barbarian kings continued to adhere, in their dealing with the Jewish population, to the edicts embodied in the Theodosian Code. This code, promulgated in 438, was designed to stipulate the precise limits of Jewish civil rights in the Empire. Among other restrictive measures, it forbade Jews from marrying Christians, from holding Christian slaves, and from building new synagogues. To be sure, the code also provided for the protection of Jewish rights in other areas, but its main impact was to furnish a legal basis for later restrictive measures executed and enforced by the Church. Under this later legislation Jews would be defined as ethnic aliens and religious infidels, until—stripped of their civil rights and made subject to special restrictions—they would enter the ghetto, that peculiarly medieval institution which men in all ages have fastened upon as the very instrument and symbol of social degradation.

With the adoption of Catholicism by the Ostrogoths in Italy, the Visigoths in Spain, and the Franks and Burgundians in France, the Jews became the target of Christian zeal. Although they were still, officially, members of a "permitted religion"—a *religio licita* —it became increasingly difficult for the Jews to navigate successfully through the turbulent waters of the newly converted, and newly fanatic, European nations. The Theodosian Code applied to all countries under the influence of the Church, but its interpretation depended very much on the whim of the individual sovereign. Spain was especially harsh: the Church Councils of Toledo insisted venomously that all anti-Jewish regulations be strictly enforced. As relations with the Christians deteriorated, the Jews of Spain, in a last attempt to prove their innocence, tried to show that their ancestors had left Palestine long before the time of Christ, and hence could have had no part in the crucifixion. Needless to say, arguments of this kind—whether rational or spurious—were of no avail. The oppressive measures reached a climax of sorts in 613, when King Sisebut demanded that all the Jews of Spain accept baptism; it was the first time such a decree had affected an entire country, and it formed a sinister adumbration to the tragedy that was to befall Spanish Jewry eight hundred years later. Hundreds succumbed to the pressure, and converted. Yet, despite these mass conversions, and despite the severe punishments meted out to those who later "relapsed" to Judaism, whole communities managed to survive. Neither the political force of kings nor the religious zeal of bishops sufficed to ensure compliance with persecution.

A 7th-century Burgundian sarcophagus in Bourges showing Daniel in the lions' den.

The same may be said of France, where the Merovingians, following the example of Sisebut, demanded baptism or expulsion of their Jews in 629. The mass conversions which ensued left an easily identifiable group of "converted Jews" who were regarded as full-fledged Jews neither by themselves nor by their neighbors, and who seized the first opportunity to drop all pretense of conversion. Many Jews who had accepted baptism at sword's point reverted to Judaism as soon as the immediate danger passed, or as soon as a new king ascended the throne. Indeed, when one considers the unremitting intensity of the persecution, it is astonishing that so many Jews clung to their own values; nothing less than an unshakable conviction of moral and religious superiority could have enabled them to survive the relentless waves of terror and forced conversion which, in the seventh century, led to the almost total devastation of Spanish Jewry.

The effect of this prolonged persecution was a steady decline in the number of Jews in Christian countries—this, despite the fact that geographically Jews were to be found in more countries than ever before. It is of course true that this period also witnessed a general economic decline, but no small role in the decimation of Jewry was played by the Catholic Church. In Palestine, only a small remnant was left; in Egypt, the decline was appalling. There may have been three million Jews during the period of the Second Temple; by the beginning of the seventh century, in what then remained of the Roman Empire, that figure had dwindled to not more than half a million.

The record of baptism and expulsion was accomplished in these lands by a process the goal of which was to transform the Jews into an alien and disenfranchised people. Frequent persecutions took their toll in the debilitation of the social and economic structure of the Jewish community. Excluded from the economy at large, Jews were forced to abandon the pursuit of agriculture— an occupation which would have linked them physically to the soil of Europe—and to take up trade. In this role, for which the fact of Jewish dispersion fitted them materially, they would achieve a universal and unenviable prominence in centuries to come and become a natural target of abuse.

In concluding this brief survey of the Jewish world at the beginning of the seventh century, we must take note of the large Jewish community in Babylonia. Sassanian rule had on the whole been kind to this community. Despite occasional acts of violence (two of the Exilarchs were put to death), the situation in Babylonia was better than that in most Christian countries. Babylonian Jewry constituted the greatest reservoir of Jewish spiritual and physical strength at this time. But it exercised little influence on the distant Jewish communities of Europe. Soon, however, even this state of affairs would change, when the advent of Islam and of Arabic rule would radically alter the geographical and political map of the Byzantine Empire and the entire Mediterranean world.

The Rise of Islam

From time immemorial, Arabia—the birthplace of the Semitic peoples—has been a land of nomads. Up until the seventh century, it may be said that life in this arid land underwent little change. From time to time, bands of nomads drifted north, east, and west, into the civilized areas of Egypt, the Mediterranean coast, and Mesopotamia. Various empires in various epochs claimed a rather tenuous hegemony over the Arabian peninsula. By and large, however, the land itself, as well as the people in it, was little affected by these shifts in temporal conditions. The few patches of fertile ground along the coastal strips supported a scanty agricultural population. Across the desert wandered the nomads, with their sheep, cattle, and camels. Commerce was effected by means of caravans which maintained some contact among the scattered Arab peoples.

The two chief towns of Arabia were Mecca and Medina (Yathrib). Mecca at the beginning of the seventh century may have had some twenty or tweny-five thousand inhabitants; it was populated mainly by Bedouins. But even at that time Mecca was more than a trading center. It was the site of the *Kaaba*—a small temple of black stone, the cornerstone of which was a meteorite—and as such a center of religious pilgrimage. Medina at that time was a smaller city, founded, it is said, by Jews who had originally come there from Yemen. Until 525, the princes of Medina had for centuries professed Judaism as their religion.

Indeed, long after 525, the Jews of northwest Arabia formed a numerous and powerful community. Several oases and cities lay entirely in their hands. They were said to have introduced the palm tree into the region, and thus to have been responsible for the cultivation and profitable marketing of dates. Their relations with their neighbors, many of whom found themselves attracted to Judaism, were generally cordial. Jewish folklore and customs had become an integral element in the over-all environment.

It was against this background that the career of Mohammed unfolded. Born in Mecca in 570 C.E. in humble circumstances, Mohammed, according to legend, rose from a camel-driver to become first the leader of a caravan, and then the leader of the whole Arab people. While on his caravan routes, he came into contact with many Jews and Christians, and was intrigued by their religious beliefs. For some time Mohammed had felt himself possessed of prophetic power—a power whose supernatural provenance was attested by occasional visitations from heaven. Mohammed conceived of himself as uniting in his person two distinct religious functions: that of the *nabi*, or prophet, and that of the *rasul*, or apostle. The basis of his doctrine was simple: there was one God alone (in this Mohammed adopted the Jewish conception of unity as opposed to the Christian doctrine of Trinity); and there should be one community of believers. He began to preach these beliefs and secretly to convert those with whom he came into contact. His earliest followers were slaves and people of humble origin; the prosperous and the well-to-do, suspicious of his motives, shunned him. Indeed, so intense was their opposition to Mohammed, whom they believed to be a threat to their prestige and power, that his status in Mecca soon became endangered and increasingly precarious.

In 622, fearing for his life, Mohammed fled with a few close followers to Medina. The date of this flight—known in Arabic as the *hejira*—marks the beginning of the Moslem calendar. In Medina, Mohammed's position among his fellow Arabs was assured. But he met with unexpected resistance from the Jews. Because of the similarity of his new religion to Judaism, Mohammed had counted on the sympathy of Arabian Jews. More than that, he had fully expected them to embrace Islam without hesitation. He had failed, however, to recognize two factors: first, the high degree of cultural and historical awareness which existed among the Jews of Arabia, and which was in good measure responsible for their attitude of disdain toward this self-styled "prophet" and his crude, unlettered disciples; second, the prominent social and political status of Arabian Jews, which made it unnecessary for them to entertain thoughts of conversion as a means of social advancement. Angered by their opposition and jealous of their financial success, Mohammed conceived a hatred for Jews that was in ensuing years to have grave consequences for many Jewish communities.

To propagate the new religion of Islam, Mohammed then selected a novel method. Most of his converts were won on the field of battle, where the vanquished—principally members of trading caravans from Mecca—were given the alternatives of conversion or death. So impressive was Mohammed's display of military powers that many Arabs became convinced of the divinity of his mission. Another tool of conversion used effectively by Mohammed was the imposition of special taxes on those of his victims who refused initially to accept him as a prophet. With the passage of time, Mohammed became powerful enough to be finally granted permission to make a pilgrimage to Mecca. That city thereafter became a Moslem center, and the *Kaaba* a principal Moslem shrine.

By 632, the year of Mohammed's death at the age of 61, Islam already embraced the whole of Arabia and part of Western Asia and North Africa. These vast territories had been subjugated by relatively small armies, whose phenomenal success may be accounted for by the help and sympathy they received almost everywhere from the local population, which invariably welcomed the soldiers of Allah with open arms. The native culture of these places had become degenerate and lifeless. Christians and Jews who refused to surrender to the new religion could buy their freedom by paying a tribute, and they were then accorded the status of *dhimmi*, protected infidels. But they were a minority. A millennium of Greek and Roman domination had left most people in the conquered territories ready for change, and the Arabs were considered closer in spirit than their Christian predecessors. The same may be said of those who lived in the decaying Sassanian Empire. Within an astonishingly brief period the new religion of Islam had become an Arab Empire; by absorbing much of Persian and Byzantine culture, it would shortly become a civilization. The Sassanians capitulated in 637, Syria and Mesopotamia fell soon thereafter. In 639 Alexandria was laid siege to by Omar, the successor of Mohammed, and was conquered the following year. From their new capital of Damascus, where the first mosque was established, the Arabs swept over all of Northern Africa, and thence to cross into Spain in 711. The advance of the Mohammedan armies was checked in the east only by the Byzantine Empire, and in the west only by France.

The vast territories of the Arab Empire were consolidated by the Umayyads, Mohammed's immediate successors and the first Moslem dynasty. For nearly a century the Umayyad family single-handedly ruled from its center in Damascus. Following an internal revolt in 747, a new Moslem power, the Abbasids, succeeded in establishing hegemony over all the eastern sections of the Arab Empire. From its new seat in Baghdad, the Abbasid dynasty ruled Eastern Islam for five hundred years, until the invasion of the Mongols in 1250. Spain and North Africa, meanwhile, remained under Umayyad suzerainty. One member of the Umayyad family—Abd-el-Rahman—had successfully escaped to Spain during the internal strife for power. Having been declared Sultan of Spain, he took up arms against Charlemagne, who had an alliance with the Abbasids, and drove him out of Spain. One of the heroes of this war was Roland. Spain under Abd-el-Rahman was the first province to detach itself from the recognized centers of Islam. A new seat of government was established in Cordoba, which became the capital of Western Islam, and a dazzling center of high culture. Abd-el-Rahman III (912–961), who declared himself Caliph, founded a university in Cordoba and was responsible for a florescence of civilized activity in the political, economic, and intellectual spheres that left an imprint on Spanish culture for centuries to come. Among the principal beneficiaries and catalysts of this surge of activity were the Jews of Spain, who were to bring a rich contribution to the culture of the Moslem Golden Age.

Jewish Elements in Islamic Thought

So numerous, and indeed so striking, are the elements of Jewish origin in Islamic thought that we can only assume a deep familiarity with Judaism on the part of the early Moslems, not excluding Mohammed himself. It is clear that the Jews of Arabia maintained an active community, with synagogues, schools, and open lines of communication to the Jews of Palestine and Babylonia. Nor was this community a young one. There were Jews in Arabia as early as the period of the Hasmoneans, and their number was augmented substantially after the defeat of Bar Kochba in 135 C.E. Thus, by the time of Mohammed the Jews were a well-entrenched part of Arabian society, particularly in Yemen. There is no doubt that Judaism made a lively impression upon the Arab mind, and that many of its fundamental themes may be heard to resonate in the theology of Islam.

Examples of this influence abound. Like the Jew, the Moslem affirms the unity of God, and the immediacy of man's ability to approach Him. Like the Jew, too, the Moslem believes in the immortality of the soul; in personal liability for deeds committed on earth; in the primacy of justice; in the giving of alms (Hebrew:

tzedakah) as an act of righteousness rather than as an act of self-conscious philanthropy. The Jewish calendar, the Jewish concept of the Sabbath, the Jewish attitude toward food—all these things were taken over into Islam, albeit with qualifications. And aside from such basic tenets, Islam also resembles Judaism in many of its customs; the habit of facing in a particular direction during prayer and the practice of washing the hands before devotions are but two such instances of marked similarity. Indeed, a thorough examination of the Koran will reveal a quantity of Jewish influences that testifies eloquently to the indebtedness of Moslem religious thought to the genius of the Hebrew mind. It was the genius of the Arab mind, however, that welded these disparate elements of sacred thought, even as it welded the most varied peoples, from the most diverse lands and backgrounds, into a single, coherent body.

Jews Under Moslem Dominion

Under Moslem rule, world Jewry entered into a new period of physical and intellectual expansion. In almost diametric contrast to the Persians, whose religion had all but disintegrated under the impact of Islam, and to the Eastern Christians, most of whom had surrendered their faith to the new dispensation, the Jews not only retained their ancestral creed but gained new strength in the lands of the Moslem conquest. This remarkable burst of vigor, moreover, characterized the Jewish communities of the West no less than those of the East.

Let us examine first the large Jewish enclave of Babylonia. Baghdad, the new capital, and the seat of the Jewish Exilarch, attracted many Jewish settlers. According to the historian Salo Baron, it was in fact a Jewish mathematician and astrologer, one Masha'allah, who collaborated in drawing up the measurements for the new metropolis, which had "6000 streets on the west and 4000 streets on the east side, within a perimeter of nearly twenty miles." So numerous was the Jewish community of Baghdad that even as late as the twelfth century, after civil war and famine had taken a considerable toll in lives and property, the traveler Benjamin of Tudela found 40,000 Jews there, and these 40,000 still supported and maintained twenty-eight synagogues and ten academies of higher learning.

The rejuvenation of the Palestine community under Moslem rule

وقطع جمع كلمه فضالوا النا خرج من بلادك فضال النبي علیه السلم ان لا ابدان كم قطلو كم وظلمسكم لكن ان خرجم مرحوب
ماولادكم وتركون اموالكم وسلا حكم وسلبكم فرضوابذلك وكانوا الحربون سيوتهم بايديهم والبی المومنین وكانت ماده محامه نفسمه
عه سوقا فاقعد هم عن حوالی المدینه وكان مستولی الخراج محمد بن سلمه فصوا ماولاد مسم ونسا هم وستمایه محمل محمل الی خیبر لا هـ كان قرب

*A miniature of Mohammed and his followers who
brought Islam to the Middle East and united the Arabs.
Believing himself the anointed prophet of a true
Arabian religion, he thought both Jews and Christians
would flock to his banner. When they did not, he
turned violently against both. Mohammed's revelations
were collected and written down in the Koran.*

was equally swift. Oppressed and numerically decimated by its Byzantine sovereigns, the community in Palestine now rose to such heights that it seemed ready to regain its authority over world Jewry, which had for years looked to the *geonim* of Babylonia for leadership. Despite the old Hadrianic law prohibiting Jews from living in Jerusalem—a law perpetuated by the Christians and in theory by the Moslems—the number of Jews in that city now grew rapidly. Negotiations with the Caliph yielded permission for seventy families to return to the Holy City, and in time this initial group was augmented by large numbers of "Mourners for Zion," who clustered around the Western Wall, the last visible remnant of the Temple. Jerusalem's Jewish population was supported by donations from Jews everywhere, who saw in the rebirth of this community and the re-establishment there of the old Rabbinic academy, tangible evidence of their people's unbreakable ties with its homeland. The community of Jerusalem continued in existence until the year 1099, when it was mercilessly destroyed by the invading Crusaders.

Jerusalem was not the only city to experience a renaissance under the Moslems. Tiberias, which throughout the Byzantine period had maintained continuous authority over the settlements of Galilee, and indeed over all of Palestine, now surrendered its academy to Jerusalem. It remained, however, a foremost intellectual center in the fields of Hebrew poetry, exegesis, and linguistic studies. Through their efforts in these fields the citizens of Tiberias were responsible for preserving the Hebrew language in all its purity of syntax and pronunciation. Still other centers of learning were Gaza, Ashkelon, and Haifa. The city of Ramleh became for a while the residence of the Caliph, and thus also the administrative capital of Palestine.

A similar story of rebirth may be narrated with regard to the Jewish communities of Syria. Following the evacuation of large numbers of Christians, waves of Jewish settlers flowed into the towns of Tripolis, Tyre, and Aleppo, which were regarded as part of the Holy Land. In Syria proper, Damascus must be singled out as a uniquely important center of Jewish life and learning, especially after the Seljuk occupation of Jerusalem in 1071.

We turn next to Egypt, where once again we encounter a recovery of former glory and an increase in economic strength. Cairo, the equal of Baghdad in refinement and culture, became after the establishment of Fatimid authority in 969 a world center of science and Jewish learning. In their opposition to all things emanating from Baghdad, the Fatimid rulers guaranteed independence to all religious leaders in Cairo as well as in such provinces of the Fatimid Empire as Syria and Palestine. The granting of freedom enabled the Jewish communities of these lands to consolidate their affairs and to confer with one another on pressing issues of communal concern. Throughout this period Cairo (Fustat) exercised an influence far beyond the boundaries of Egypt, serving as a focal link between Eastern and Western Jewry. Its *genizah*, or storehouse of outworn Hebrew books, uncovered in the early part of the present century by Solomon Schechter, has yielded not only valuable local records but numerous transcripts of important communications, the originals of which had been sent from Syria and Palestine to Fustat, whence they were forwarded to their ultimate destinations.

Second only in prominence to Cairo was Alexandria, another city boasting importance in international trade. Alexandria's strategic geographical position made its Jewish community the frequent target of demands to ransom Jewish captives taken by Moslem raiders on the high seas. One of the few surviving holograph manuscripts of Maimonides is a request for funds to redeem such Jewish captives from Moslem hands.

To the west of Egypt there existed numerous other well-established Jewish communities. Kairuwan, near the site of the ancient civilization of Carthage, had a fully developed Jewish community by the time the Fatimids rose to power (909), a community strong enough to throw off the tutelage of the academies of the East. While it still voluntarily supported the Babylonian academies, the community of Kairuwan was led by eminent scholars of its own, sages who corresponded with the *geonim* of Sura and Pumbedita on terms of equality. There were also settlements of considerable size in neighboring Tripolitania and in Morocco. One of them, Fez, became a major center of Jewish culture, and Jews were among the founders of Marakesh (1062).

The social position of Jews in Moslem lands was determined by inconsistent discriminatory legislation, and it naturally varied from one locality to the next. In general, Moslem legislation aimed at establishing the social superiority of the true believers over the *dhimmi* (infidels). A single authoritative code of discriminatory legislation against Jews and Christians had in fact existed since the time of Omar I, but its strictures were rarely enforced in their entirety. Among its provisions was the stipulation that all non-Moslem religious groups were to pay a special tax to the govern-

Tunisian synagogue of Hara Srira with characteristic and graceful Moorish architecture.

ment. In addition, the construction of new churches or synagogues was forbidden, and no existing church or synagogue was permitted to stand higher than a neighboring mosque. Infidels were required to ride on mules or donkeys rather than on horses, and were prohibited from carrying weapons. Intermarriage was naturally forbidden, and conversion was allowed only from a non-Moslem faith to Islam.

In practice, however, these prohibitions were applied selectively. Jews were not required to live in ghettos, and were free to maintain their own communal institutions. Thus, Jewish courts exercised full judicial power over the community, and no recourse was necessary to Arab courts. As for the special taxes, these were levied per capita on Jews and Christians alike. For the most part Jewish communities were able to function with relative autonomy in the execution of their internal affairs.

Similarly, the laws concerning the special colors by which garments of "unbelievers" were to be distinguished from those of Moslems were frequently ignored, although in other cases they were not only enforced but carried to absurd extremes. One Fatimid Caliph, for instance, ordered the Jews to wear five-pound balls around their necks, in commemoration of the calf's head which their ancestors had once worshiped. Another decree prescribed that each Jew should wear a yellow badge on his headgear and hang a silver coin from his neck inscribed with the word, *dhimmi*. Distinguishing marks for women included shoes of two different colors, one red and one black, with a bell to announce their arrival. All such laws were aimed at lowering the social esteem of the infidels, who lived surrounded by an atmosphere of cultivated contempt. In the words of an eleventh-century writer:

> Cruel men and women were hired to oppress the Jews, male and female, and to heap upon them all manner of curse, shame, and contumely. And the gentiles used to ridicule Jews, the mob and children often assaulting Jews in all the streets of Baghdad.

It must be said that Jewish leadership did not object to the severity of Moslem segregationist legislation. It too was interested in preventing a removal of the barriers between the faiths, and did everything in its power to maintain a segregated situation without jeopardizing the physical safety of the community. Thus, to keep the Jewish quarter free from outside intrusion, Jewish law forbade the selling of a house to gentiles, and all social communication between the religious groups was discouraged.

No amount of legislation, however, could prevent a certain degree of fraternization. Jews and gentiles were brought together by common business interests or by simple curiosity. This was especially true of the higher strata in society. As Jews rose to important positions in the fields of finance, medicine, and scholarship, they frequently tended to associate with their non-Jewish colleagues socially as well as professionally. Arab respect for Jewish expertise often overcame legal and social barriers. The following, for example, is the poetic tribute paid to Maimonides by a Moslem physician:

> Galen's art heals only the body
> But Abu-Irman's [Moses'] the body and the soul.
> His knowledge made him the physician of the century.
> He could cure with his wisdom the disease of ignorance.
> If the moon would submit to his art,
> He would free her from her spots at the time of full moon,
> Would relieve her of her monthly ailments
> And at the time of her conjunction, save her from waning.

One index of inter-faith mingling is the adoption of Arabic names by Jews—this, despite the Covenant of Omar which forbade such use of Arabic family names by infidels. "Ibn," "Abu," and "el" regularly appear as components of Jewish names, together with elements of Hebrew or even purely Arabic origin. But nowhere was the discrepancy between law and life more apparent than in the Moslem practice of appointing Jews to public office. In Byzantium and Persia, the Jew had been barred from all administrative posts. Arab caliphs and governors, however, freely enlisted the services of Jews in their administrations, and depended heavily on their expert advice in matters of finance and international diplomacy. The trustworthiness of these civil servants was perhaps best expressed by a ninth-century vizier of Baghdad:

> Not because of any sympathy on my part for Judaism or Christianity did I take the unbelievers into civil service, but because I found them to be more faithfully attached to the dynasty than Moslems.

The rise of the Fatimid Empire and of Moslem Spain saw a concomitant increase in the number of Jewish counselors attached as political and even as military advisers to Arab courts. The diplomatic and linguistic abilities of these courtiers enabled them to rise quickly in Arab administrations, and their services soon became indispensable to the smooth functioning of the Moslem Empire.

In the two mutually exclusive sections of the Mediterranean world
—Romance- or Greek-speaking Christendom and Arabic-speaking
Islam—the Jew alone had a foot in both camps; he alone could
move from country to country with relative ease; he alone was
master of a tongue which could carry him about everywhere; and
he alone had reliable contacts and agents among his coreligionists
in all major centers of trade. It was in this period, moreover, that
Moslem expansion brought the great Jewish populations of Mesopotamia, for the first time, under the same rule and into the same
intellectual orbit as the farthest outposts of Europe to the West.
The Jewish courtier, whose career, due to the vicissitudes of power
and the swiftly changing moods of his employer, was often as
short-lived as it was brilliant, served to unite by his talents these
farflung corners of the Islamic and Christian worlds.

The Jews in
Mesopotamia
At the beginning of the Moslem period most Jews still lived
in Babylonia. These Jews had suffered severe setbacks under the
late Sassanian rulers. Many of them had been pushed off the soil;
academies had been forced to close; the threat of persecution was
constant. Nevertheless, the situation in Babylonia was incomparably
better than that in the lands under Christian domination. And when
large masses of Jewry became united under the aegis of the Moslem Empire, Babylonian Jewry was once again able to claim pre-
eminence. Its direct influence on other Jewish communities now
extended from India to Spain.

In regaining its former status, the Babylonian community was
aided by the policies of the Moslem Caliphate, which for reasons
of stability and control had decided to retain all pre-existing
Jewish institutions and even to strengthen their authority. The
Exilarch became again the spiritual leader of all Jews in the Empire, and was also granted occasional temporal powers. Exilarchic
appointments were made from families claiming unbroken descent
from King David. The Exilarch had a seat in the chief imperial
councils; when the center of Arab government shifted to Baghdad,
the Exilarchate went with it.

The new Moslem rulers in the East extended to the Jews freedom
of religion, freedom of settlement, freedom of occupation, and
freedom of movement. Jews now entered high positions in government and were especially prominent in the economic sector. As
"unbelievers" they were of course denied the right to serve in the

army or to hold public office, but many important administrative posts became open to them.

As Jews rose into significant economic positions and gained a measure of political power, the authority of the Exilarch declined. Now attaining to parity was the scholarly class, which in the eighth century achieved control over the Jewish community. As in the Talmudic period, the distinguished teachers of the academies now exercised broad communal controls. Their prestige was further enhanced by the fact that the Babylonian Talmud had been designated as the authoritative law by all Jewry.

The two foremost schools were those of Sura and Pumbedita, the heads of which were given the distinguished title of *Gaon*. Revenue for the upkeep of these academies was donated by Jewish communities from near and far. For centuries, the schools enjoyed world-wide prestige and influence, far beyond the boundaries of the Moslem Empire. They served as academies of learning, each of them with a substantial enrollment of students, who hailed from all over the Arab-speaking world. But they also took the place of the ancient Sanhedrin, functioning as a Court of Appeals for communities as far away as Kairuwan, and taking responsibility for the appointment of local judges. The most effective measure of government instituted by the academies was the *ḥerem* (ban of excommunication). Theoretically it was introduced to take the place of capital punishment, and indeed this new form of punishment constituted a death sentence from the social point of view; no person placed under *ḥerem* could live within the boundaries of the organized community. (A tenth-century poet compared the lot of such an outcast with that of a leper.) This threat of total exclusion from the community was but rarely applied; its effectiveness lay in the acknowledgment by all concerned of its terrible finality. Because there was common agreement on this point, the *ḥerem* was to prove an essential element in the preservation and development of Jewish institutions under Islam.

The rivalry between the two academies lasted as long as did the institution of the *Gaonate* itself. Their authority began to decline only in the tenth century, with the general deterioration of Babylonian life. By this time, however, Egyptian and Spanish Jewry were ready to assume leadership; the crucial task of transmission had been accomplished. A large body of material existed in the form known as Responsa literature, which consists of the questions addressed to the scholars of the academies on matters of law, theology, historical problems, and communal affairs, together with

their answers and advice. For three centuries these questions had been directed to the sages of the East, and their answers had gone out to the communities of the West. Now the West had its own scholars, and its own academies: the chain of tradition, reinforced by strong new links, would continue unbroken.

In the eighth century, a movement of revolt against Talmudic law began that was to threaten for some time the unity of Jewish religious observance, and to lead to a schism within Judaism. This movement, known as Karaism, was to last for four centuries. The violent controversies which it provoked led to the formation of various sects that split Judaism into several camps. The first clash occurred in Mesopotamia during the period of the *geonim*, and was initiated by the founder of Karaism, Anan ben David.

In 761, Anan ben David, a nephew of the Babylonian Exilarch, was prevented by the *geonim* from succeeding his uncle because of his anti-Talmudic tendencies. He was obliged to leave the country and settle in Palestine, where he built his own synagogue in Jerusalem as a stronghold from which to wage his war against Rabbinic Judaism. Anan reproached the Talmudists with having corrupted Judaism, with having added too many complex interpretations to the pristine purity of the Torah, and with having disregarded many of its commandments. The catchword of his new sect was "Search the Torah thoroughly, and lean not upon my opinion." Fragments of the volumes in which Anan expounded his fundamentalist religious views have survived, so the origins of Karaism remain therefore very much in obscurity. We do know, however, that the hostility of Karaism to Talmudic Judaism resulted in an increase rather than in a lessening of the individual's religious duties; many observances which had long been abolished were now reinstituted, often without regard to the changes necessitated by the passage of time. The most important alterations introduced by the Karaites related to the observance of the Sabbath and festivals, and to marriage and dietary laws. Anan abolished the fixed calendar which had been established in the middle of the fourth century. He introduced the Karaite custom of quenching all flame at the inception of the Sabbath and of spending the Sabbath eve in darkness and cold. As his opponents rightly affirmed, the result of his call to return to Scripture was the promulgation of a new Talmud, far stricter and more rigid than the "old." But the most disastrous effect of his preaching was the severance of the living link between the Biblical past and the present. Unlike Talmudic Judaism, Karaism represented not the natural spiritual evolution of a people but a wholly artificial and unnatural creation.

The movement which started with Anan was consolidated by Benjamin Nehawendi, who gave the sect the name *B'nei Mikra*— children of the Bible. This phase of the Karaite movement closed with Daniel el-Kumsi, in whose time it came under the fierce attack of Saadiah Gaon (882–942), the head of the academy at Sura and a scholar of immense erudition and intellectual acumen. Saadiah's definitive critical assault on Karaism was to have a lasting, debilitative effect on the movement. Despite periodic revivals in later centuries, Karaism after Saadiah may be said to have lost its essential élan.

One "positive" outcome of this schism within Judaism was a rekindling of interest in the close study of Scripture. An effort was made by both parties to the debate to establish a single authentic text of the Torah. The Rabbis had long before taken the lead in determining the correct spelling and vocalization of every word in the Holy Scriptures, as well as the proper notations for chanting the verses. This scholarly work, known as *Masorah* (tradition), was carried out primarily in Palestine. Since that time all Hebrew Bibles have been produced in the manner established under the *Masorah*.

Since the abolition of the Exilarchate in Palestine, Babylonia had assumed the leadership of world Jewry. Yet Palestine had nevertheless remained an independent focus of Jewish life. The glories of the past and the undying hopes for future redemption had tied the destiny of the entire Jewish people to the Land of Promise. External developments could weaken but never sever this attachment. The *geonim* themselves, the leaders of the Talmudic academies in Babylonia, could not escape the spiritual impact of this unrelenting attachment. The inalienable claim of the Jewish people to its ancestral land is illustrated in legal terms by an ordinance originating in Babylonia which justified the implementation of a complicated legal fiction by the following statement:

> The land may have been occupied [by gentiles] for many generations, but we have the old legal maxim that [ownership of] land is never lost by illegal seizure, and hence Israel still holds title to it.

Yet another example of the Jews' unshakable ties to Palestine may be seen in the following Rabbinical statement regarding the prayer for rain:

> Even if men of eastern lands and those banished [to the islands of the sea] require moisture during the Tammuz season, they must not pray for rain except when the land of Israel needs it, too.

For if one were to permit them to pray whenever they need precipitation, even during the summer, they might believe that they are living in a country of their own. But they ought to look upon themselves as living in a hostelry [temporary shelter], while their heart turns to the land of Israel. Prayers for rain must come, therefore, in their stated time.

Such sentiments were not the product of mere nostalgia, nor did they spring from idle Rabbinic fancy, without basis in historical reality. They expressed, rather, the common intention of Jews everywhere: to assert, through law and ritual, their continuity as a sovereign people, tied to a single homeland by divine authority and by human right.

The Jews in Moslem Spain

From the year 711, when the Moslem general Tarik first set foot in Visigothic Spain, until the establishment of Umayyad rule in 756, Spain was in a state of civil war. The first major city attacked by the invaders was Cordoba. When the walled town was finally captured, the Jews were the only ones to welcome the Moslems as liberators from oppressive Christian rule; in gratitude, the Moslem conquerors entrusted them with guarding the city. As town after town was captured, Jews were given the guard wherever they were present in sufficient numbers. From the beginning they became a trusted minority in Moslem Spain.

Because of their favored position it is not surprising that Jewish refugees, many of whom had fled from Spain to North Africa long ago, followed the victorious Arabs back into Andalusia. Slowly, Jewish life began to rise again out of the ruins of Visigothic domination. The new era of tolerance and prosperity began formally in the year 756, with the establishment of the Caliphate of Abd-el-Rahman I, a descendant of the Umayyads. Cordoba now became independent of Baghdad, and before long Spain became the wealthiest and most civilized country in Europe. Cordoba was transformed into a center of high culture, a university town boasting a library of some 400,000 manuscript volumes. In the breadth of its intellectual activities, in knowledge and learning, Cordoba far surpassed the finest centers of Christian Europe.

The cultural enlightenment of Moslem Spain went hand in hand with political tolerance. During the reign of Abd-el-Rahman III many Jews attained prominent positions in the administration of the state. Foremost among them was Hasdai ibn Shaprut (915–

970), who rose from court physician to become chief adviser to the Caliph in financial and diplomatic affairs. Like many Jewish courtiers after him, Hasdai combined the highest integrity and loyalty to his Moslem employers with a keen devotion to his own people. In his many contacts with foreign missions he collected information about Jews in distant lands. Hasdai may have been the first to receive information about the Jewish kingdom of the Khazars on the shores of the Volga and the Black Sea. Desirous to establish contact with these Jews, he sent an emissary to the Khazar kingdom by way of Constantinople. The emissary, however, owing to the hazards of the journey, failed to reach his destination. Some time later Hasdai entrusted two Jewish members of a delegation from the "King of the Gebalim" (Bulgars) to carry a letter to the King of the Khazars "via Bulgaria and the Russian-Land." This letter, written in Hebrew and beginning with the phrase, "we the remnant of Israel in exile," is a remarkable document. In it, Hasdai portrays the situation of the Jews under the Caliphate in Cordoba. He explains to the Khazar king the nature of his own activity at court, where he receives the various embassies of foreign governments and determines policy with regard to international trade. Nevertheless, he states, despite his exalted position, he would gladly resign from the court of Cordoba to serve the king of an independent Jewish state.

Hasdai was unfortunately never to achieve his desire. The kingdom of the Khazars was destroyed by the Russians in 969, a year before Hasdai's death.

During Hasdai's time, the Jewish communities of the West began to gain ascendancy over the Eastern centers. As youthful Cordoba replaced aging Baghdad in the Arab world at large, the more vital elements in Jewry also shifted to Cordoba. Within a relatively short time that city became famous for its rabbis, who both lectured at the academies and directed the social and religious affairs of the community. Instead of traveling eastward, young Jewish scholars from Spain and North Africa studied the Talmud at the academy of Cordoba, and in due time they were joined there by students from the East as well. The masters of these students were known throughout the educated Jewish world for their expertise as grammarians and lexicographers—disciplines in which they made a decisive contribution to the general renaissance of Hebrew letters in Spain.

The astonishing cultural and economic florescence of Cordoba lasted for almost exactly a century. It was put to an end in a series

of wars with invading Berber tribesmen who succeeded finally in destroying the capital and in forcing many Jews to seek refuge in other parts of the country.

After the dissolution of the Caliphate, Moslem Spain broke up into little princedoms. Thenceforth, Spanish Jews lived in the Emirates of Granada, Seville, Saragossa, etc. Of all these princedoms it was Granada that inherited the illustrious traditions of Cordoba; from now on, its name too was linked inextricably with the history of the Jews in Moslem Spain. Arab chroniclers tell us that the city was "compact with Jews"; "who ever did not see their splendor in Granada, their good fortune and their glory, never saw true glory—for they were great with wisdom and piety." High in the annals of Granada's Jewish glory is placed the figure of Samuel ibn Nagrela, the Prince (*Ha-Nagid*)—courtier, poet, and warrior —who guided the destiny of Granada until it reached the summit of its glory and power.

Born in Cordoba in 993, Samuel was a trained Talmudist, grammarian, mathematician, and philosopher, and the master of seven languages. After the sack of his native city, he fled to Malaga whence he was summoned to a high position at the royal court in Granada. Finally, as vizier of Granada, and on numerous occasions field commander of its armed forces, Samuel led this state to unsurpassed heights of material power and wealth. Nor did Samuel in his glory neglect the Jewish community, of which he had been made principal guardian. Not only did he provide amply for the educational and philanthropic needs of the Jews in Spain; he was especially solicitous of, and generous to, the Jewish settlement in Palestine. Like Hasdai before him, and Yehudah Ha-Levi after him, Samuel Ha-Nagid stood in a relationship of tension toward his adopted state. Entranced by the beauties of Spain, he never relinquished the dream of Jewish independence on Jewish soil; at the same time, he devoted his most ardent efforts to the perpetuation and development of that culture in which he lived, and to the state which had bestowed upon him rank and responsibility.

But Granada was to follow the fate of Cordoba. Dynastic wars, which erupted during the viziership of Samuel's son Yehosef, and resulted in the young man's assassination, again caused many Jews to flee. We find the next great concentration in Seville, where Jews were courtiers, physicians, astronomers, and viziers to Moorish kings until the middle of the twelfth century, when once again invading armies of fanatic Almohades forced upon them the alternatives of conversion or flight.

Arab-Jewish baths in Palma de Mallorca, the Spanish Balearics.

Toledo had a golden age of its own which outlasted the Moorish domination. Jewish legend attests to the presence of Jews in Toledo long before the coming of the Goths, and even claims a Jewish origin for the city. The Hebrew poet Al-Harizi speaks of at least a dozen synagogues, "beautiful as nowhere else." For its learning, its piety, and its splendor, Toledo was called the "New Jerusalem." Two of its synagogues have remained to this day, to sustain Al-Harizi's boast. Even now, after centuries of abuse, they are "as nowhere else." The financial genius of Toledo was Samuel Ha-Levi Abulafia, who as a monument to his riches left the great synagogue of El Transito. He himself, in an episode characteristic of the times, was tortured to death by his master, King Pedro the Cruel, whose booty from this betrayal of his guiltless adviser included 70,000 gold doublets, 4,000 silver marks, 20 boxes of jewels and costly garments, and 80 Moorish slaves. History's final irony is that Samuel's mansion and synagogue are shown to visitors today as a historic Jewish monument.

In the area of spiritual achievements, the name of Toledo is linked to those of the philosopher-poets Yehudah Ha-Levi and Abraham ibn Ezra, and the chronicler Abraham ibn Daud, all of whom were born in that famous city and spent their rich creative lives there.

When Toledo was captured in 1085 by Alfonse VI of Castille, the Moslems requested reinforcements from North Africa. They came in the form of fanatical Berber tribes known as the al-Moravides, who were not content with defeating the Christians but declared holy war on the Jews as well. For several decades the Jews suffered severely; many communities were forced into conversion, foremost among them the wealthy Jewry of Lucena. This performance was repeated—after a brief period of relaxation—when the Almohades crossed the straits of Gibraltar in 1146, once again to enforce a stern policy of repression against non-Muslim religions. This time, not a single professing Jew was left in the south of Andalusia.

Against this background of periodic invasion and repression, interrupted by years of tolerance and understanding, there took place one of the most astonishing outbursts of spiritual activity in the annals of Jewish history. No other Jewry has ever risen with such rapidity to such lofty administrative status as that attained by the Jewish statesmen and financiers of Andalusia. Never before, and perhaps never since, has a single community left upon Western civilization such an indelible impression of its achievements in scicnce, literature, and philosophy. The nature and scope of that achievement is described below; here it must suffice to remark that Jewish experience on the soil of Moslem Spain in the medieval period, an experience of enlightenment and opportunity, of suppression and trauma, brilliantly illustrates both the finest and the most tragic aspects of Diaspora history.

The Khazars The story of the Khazars in their relation to Judaism represents an underestimated dimension of that experience. It is a story which has attracted the curiosity of scholars ever since it became known to the Western world with the translation of Yehudah Ha-Levi's *Kuzari* into Latin in 1660. The *Kuzari* consists of an imagined philosophical dialogue between the king of the Khazars and a rabbi; to it is appended the exchange of letters between Hasdai ibn Shaprut and Joseph, the Khazar king. From this and other sources, notably the reports of Arabs and Jews from tenth-century Constantinople, the following picture emerges: During a mass migration in the fifth century a Turkish tribe, known as the Khazars, settled on the Caspian Sea. From there its members expanded westward to the Black Sea to form an "empire of the steppe," a continental bridge crossed by wandering merchants, and also a buffer state in the eighth-century wars between Byzantium and the expanding Islamic powers. Caught on the teeter-totter between Islam and Christianity, the rulers of the Khazars apparently converted to Judaism at the end of the eighth century, although the majority of the population appears to have remained either Christian or Moslem.

There had, of course, been ancient Jewish settlers in this region, whose number had increased with the streams of migrants fleeing Byzantine and Sassanian intolerance. As elsewhere, the Jews had engaged in various pioneering pursuits. They taught their rather primitive neighbors more advanced ways of cultivating the soil and means of exchanging goods among themselves and with foreign nations. They probably also taught their neighbors the art of writing. A tenth-century Arab author states that "the Khazars use the Hebrew script." It is therefore only natural to expect a certain degree of religious influence as well. Finally, about the year 740, according to a not altogether implausible tale, Bulan, king of the Khazars, after listening to representatives of the various religious systems, decided to adopt Judaism.

The Age of Islam It appears that the rulers of the Khazar kingdom retained their

Jewish faith to the very end. But, separated from the great centers of learning, they evidently suffered from their ignorance of Talmudic law. Nevertheless, in the dispute between Karaites and Rabbinites the Khazars supported the latter. The real tragedy of the Khazars, however, began in the tenth century, with the decay of the Abbasid Empire and the rise of Byzantium; the Khazar kingdom was now rendered superfluous as a buffer state. Constantinople offered it as bait to the Russians, who promptly seized the opportunity to invade it. Despite defeat and occupation, the Khazars continued as a nominally Jewish state until the invasion of the Mongols in the middle of the thirteenth century. It seems that descendants of the Khazars had in the meantime reached Western Europe, where their presence gave rise to romantic tales about the Ten Lost Tribes. It is likely too that some Khazar progeny reached the various Slavic lands where they helped to build the great Jewish centers of Eastern Europe.

This is all that is known of the facts. What the account omits, however, is an assessment of the impact on Jewry elsewhere of this seemingly fabulous story of an independent Jewish kingdom. We know the fascination this concept held for men like Hasdai ibn Shaprut and Yehudah Ha-Levi, Jewish courtiers who, at least as a class, held in their hands the reins of considerable power. Yet this power, though held by Jews, and susceptible of exploitation for the benefit of fellow-Jews, was finally a thing of little consequence. The real dream, the only dream which vindicated history and confirmed the metaphysical longings of the Jewish people as a whole, might have lain for these courtiers in the emblematic tale of the Jewish Khazars. Spain, although attractive beyond desire, remained in the end Spain—the property and inheritance of a people not Jewish. It was perhaps inevitable that after completing his great philosophical work, a work dominated by the figure of a king ruling over an independent Jewish nation, Yehudah Ha-Levi abandoned Moslem Spain and set out alone for the Holy Land.

Jewish Culture in the Moslem Period

The Age of Islam

Four hundred years before the European Renaissance, the lands of the Arab Empire experienced a remarkable rebirth of culture that in intensity and scope, as well as in the sheer quantity of its achievement, equaled, if it did not surpass, any similar period in human history. In philosophy and science, in theology, literature, and linguistics, an astonishing range of talent and innovative genius was applied to the verbalization of man's quest to know, and to the expression of man's thirst to enjoy. No small part in this renaissance was played by the Jews of the Moslem world. Dispersed among the people of East and West, the Jews served as an international educational bridge. There was marked cooperation between Arabs and Jews in scientific and philosophical studies. By translating important Arabic works into Hebrew, Jews acted as the transmitters of Arabic culture to Christian Europe, where other Jews translated the Hebrew into Latin.

Just as Jewish philosophers in Alexandria had written their works in Greek, so the scientists and philosophers of the Spanish age wrote in Arabic. Hebrew—which now experienced a great revival was reserved for works of literary and poetic imagination, whether of a religious or secular nature. The Jews in the Diaspora had always been bilingual, but not until the Arab period did the greatest creative minds of Jewry alternatively use two linguistic media in their writings with equal facility. Great masters of Hebrew poetry, like Solomon ibn Gabirol or Yehudah Ha-Levi, wrote their philosophical works in Arabic with perfect ease.

This period also saw a renewal of interest in the comparative study of languages. Great strides were made by Jewish scholars in the field of lexicography. The first to compile a regular dictionary of terms was Semah bar Paltoi, in Mesopotamia, who restricted his work to Talmudic vocabulary. Spanish philologists went far beyond this modest beginning. Menahem ben Saruk, a protégé of Hasdai ibn Shaprut in Cordoba, published a pure Hebrew dictionary to the Bible as well as a number of studies in the structure of the Hebrew language. Similar works on the Talmud followed; the Talmudic dictionary—or *Arukh*—of Nathan ben Yehiel of Rome (ca. 1030–1106) remained unsurpassed until the nineteenth century which brought more sophisticated philological efforts.

In literature, the "people of the book," as the Jews had long been called by their Arab neighbors, made vast new strides. A veritable literary revolution took place at this time, a revolution which reached its apogee in Spain, where a new class of courtier-poets, writing in Hebrew, created a body of writing unexcelled in the range of its emotions and in the daring of its forms. This was truly the "Golden Age" of Hebrew literature.

All these poets—their number is large—turned for inspiration to two sources: to the landscape and environment of their new home, Spain, and to the Bible, the wellspring of Hebrew poetic genius. Almost for the first time since the Jewish people had left its own land, Jewish poets began to celebrate, in language sharply reminiscent of such monuments of Biblical literature as the Song of Songs, the beauties of nature and the sweet allurements of human love. In language both exuberant and refined, in brilliantly polished metrical forms, these many aristocrats of courtly life created an enduring body of verse in which the concerns and emotions of an entire people, at a particularly rich moment in its history, find abiding expression.

It would constitute a distortion, however, to imply that the Hebrew poetry of medieval Spain was all celebration and panegyric, or all fancy and playfulness. There is much personal anguish in this verse, as well as, in the religious poetry, a sense of national urgency and a longing for redemption. Indeed, the greatest and most prolific of the Spanish poets combine in their work all these elements in profuse abundance. The unquestioned accolade of greatness has been bestowed by history primarily upon four poets of this period: Samuel ibn Nagrela (993–1056), vizier to the king of Granada, poet, patron of poets and model of courtly excellence; Solomon ibn Gabirol of Malaga and Saragossa (1021?–1058?), neo-Platonic philosopher, perhaps the most talented, if not the most accomplished, of the Spanish-Hebrew poets; Moses ibn Ezra of Granada (1055?–1138?), master poet and aesthetic theorist; and Yehudah Ha-Levi of Toledo (1075–1141), protégé of Moses ibn Ezra, philosopher, poet of exquisite sensibility, and a man of the most extraordinary talent and integrity. These four, together with their students, colleagues, and friends, bequeathed a various and multiform collection of verse to later generations—high in artistic standards and often of breathtaking lyrical beauty, an enduring testimony to the creative possibilities which inhere in favorable cultural conditions and in a society governed by the ethic of tolerance.

Yehudah Ha-Levi,
Poet and
Philosopher

Yehudah Ha-Levi, the prodigy of the literary salons of Andalusia, began to write verse at an early age. His skill was uncanny in adapting the forms of Arabian love ballads to Hebraic content. These amatory verses, which it was the custom to recite aloud before the company at court, turned ingeniously from lyric to panegyric, and ended with elaborate tributes to the host or patron. Ha-Levi possessed an innate gift of mirth and wit which he parried with incredible agility. But in later years a slowly perceptible shift took place in his poetry, as love of man became replaced by love of God.

Surrendering himself utterly to the theme of the national-religious spirit, Yehudah composed some of the most overpowering verse in the history of Jewish literature. His plaintive *Songs of Exile* and the electrifying "Ode to Zion" give voice to the profoundest longings of his people; learned and recited by heart for generations after his death, indeed to this very day, these poems of lofty feeling and all-embracing love strike to the very core of the Hebrew spirit. Many of Yehudah's poems have been permanently incorporated into the synagogue liturgy, and his "Ode to Zion" is chanted during the emotion-charged services of the Ninth of Av.

Yehudah Ha-Levi's philosophical thought is of a piece with his poetry. For him, the metaphysical ideas of the rationalist, Aristotelian tradition are subservient to the realities of Jewish consciousness —a consciousness based on God's absolutely free and spontaneous revelation of Himself to His chosen people.

Yehudah's great philosophical work was the *Kuzari*, subtitled a "Book of Arguments & Demonstration in Aid of the Despised Faith." In this work, which was originally written in Arabic, Ha-Levi sought to demonstrate the superiority of Judaism over Christianity and Islam. The form of the book, as we have seen, is that of a Platonic dialogue between a Jewish scholar and a king of the Khazars who had recently embraced Judaism.

In the *Kuzari,* Yehudah Ha-Levi concedes that philosophy, or reason alone, is indeed capable of adducing proofs for the existence of a god, a ruler, an organizer of the world; but he asserts that philosophy alone cannot lead one to the unsullied truths of religion, which stresses the existence of a close relationship between God and man. Such a relationship, essentially personal, can derive only from actual experience, from inner illumination, from revelation of a highly intense kind.

Now, precisely this sort of revelation, but one involving an entire nation, was vouchsafed to Israel at Sinai. For Yehudah, this Sinaitic revelation is the one unassailable foundation of all religious knowledge, and it confirms the supremacy of the truth and the faith of Israel. At Sinai, Israel, the people of revelation and of prophecy, was divinely selected, just as certain individuals in the course of history have become endowed with the divine faculty to prophesy. This divine faculty (*Inyan Elohi*) had first been implanted in Adam, the direct creation of God's hand, who transmitted it, by heredity, through an unbroken chain of chosen individual descendants. From Jacob's sons, it passed on to the entire community. Thus, every Jew possesses this potential gift, and is capable of the

highest religious attainments. It is a faculty subject to the influence of careful nurture (the commandments of the Torah, particularly in their purely ritual aspect, channel and foster these spiritual energies) and physical environment (prophecy is attainable only in the Holy Land, "whose air makes one wise"). By its peculiar structure and beauty of expression, the Hebrew language is the medium best suited for the communication of the prophetic spirit.

The *Kuzari,* despite its fierce nationalism, does not lose sight of universal values. Yehudah maintains that in the Messianic Age all peoples will attain the same degree of spiritual perfection as that originally bestowed upon Israel. According to him, Israel may be compared to the heart; it supplies the body, or world, with its moral life blood, but is also the organ most vulnerable to external depredations. In the Messianic Age, however, the truth enshrined in Israel's message of moral integrity and uncompromising social justice will course out through the arteries of all nations, and then shall dawn the epoch of universal peace.

It is natural that a thinker as preoccupied as was Yehudah with the concepts of election and of national destiny should have given special consideration to the problem of *Galut,* or Diaspora. When he finally set out for Palestine, thereby personally enacting his philosophical program of redemption, Yehudah did so not as a romantic dreamer, but as one who had analyzed an actual political situation and come to a well-reasoned conclusion which led inevitably to migration to the Holy Land. "The son of the maidservant pursues us with hate; we turn pleading to Esau, and he tears us like wild beasts," he wrote. To the practical politicians, seeking places of refuge for the Jews driven out by the Christian conquerors from the north, he retorts: "Have we in the East or in the West a place on which to rest our hope?" His trust was in the Land of Israel. No Jew before him, since the Babylonian exile, had expressed such ardent longing for the "home and mother earth" of the Jewish people from so profound a historical vision.

Yehudah Ha-Levi's passionate love of Zion drove him finally to abandon his home, his family, and his friends, and to set out via Egypt for Jerusalem. The details of his sea voyage and his warm reception in the Jewish communities of Egypt are known to us from the poetry Yehudah wrote on this trip and from correspondence by him and his Egyptian hosts. We do not know for certain, however, whether he ever reached Jerusalem; according to a poignant and long-standing legend, he was trampled to death by an Arab horseman as he stood transfixed and in tears before the Western Wall.

In Spanish Toledo the gracefully arched Moorish architecture reveals neither that it was once the Shushan synagogue nor that it also served as a church. It is now a museum.

An illumination from a 15th-century Italian manuscript of
Maimonides' Mishneh Torah *depicts the* Avodah,
or Temple service, and portrays the methods of ritual slaughter.

With the figure of Rabbi Moses ben Maimon we reach the very apex of the Moslem period. The most profound intellect of his time, Maimonides is justly famous not only for his unique and intrinsic genius but for his influence on later European philosophy; indeed, until the eighteenth century, it was through the works of Maimonides that the thought of post-Biblical Hebraism reached the non-Jewish world.

Maimonides was born in Cordoba in 1135; when he was still a boy, his family, along with many non-Moslems, fled Spain after it succumbed to the rule of the fanatical Almohades. The family lived in Fez for a while, then emigrated to Palestine, and finally settled in Fustat (old Cairo) where the great philosopher died in 1204.

Like so many Jews of his time, Maimonides was an eminent physician, court doctor to the royal family of Saladin. He wrote a number of well-known medical works which demonstrate his deep knowledge of natural science (astronomy, mathematics, and physics), and by which he was principally known to generations of medical students after him. Despite his fragile health, Maimonides also took an active part in world Jewish affairs, and frequently was turned to by Jewish communities all over the Mediterranean world for advice on matters of Jewish law and ethics, as well as on questions of belief. So universal was his fame, and so revered his memory, that he was honored after death by the saying, "From Moses to Moses, there arose none like Moses."

The most comprehensive of Maimonides' philosophical works is the *Guide for the Perplexed,* an attempt to establish the compatibility of Judaism with Aristotelianism. Maimonides' copious and scrupulously accurate citations from philosophers preceding him have also made it a pre-eminent source of information regarding medieval Arabic theology and philosophy. The *Guide* was translated from the original Arabic into many European languages, and thus served not only to lay the foundations of subsequent Jewish philosophy but also to provide philosophical impetus to Latin Christianity in the Middle Ages. Among Christian thinkers, St. Thomas Aquinas was especially influenced by Maimonides; among Jews, perhaps his most illustrious student in later centuries was Baruch Spinoza.

A great admirer of Aristotle, Maimonides was prepared to be guided by reason in all things, provided only that the most vital and absolute doctrines of Biblical thought remained whole and intact. This assured and demonstrated, Maimonides proceeded to set forth in the *Guide* the most comprehensive and systematic anal-

ysis of the theological tenets of Judaism ever undertaken by any thinker. The monument of erudition and insight which resulted from this labor of many years stands to this day.

But if Maimonides is known best to non-Jews as the author of the *Guide for the Perplexed,* among his own people his fame for a long time rested on his great code of Talmudic law, the *Mishneh Torah.* This work is a systematic arrangement, topic by topic, of the whole of Jewish law. Maimonides' intention in the *Mishneh Torah* was to present a work at once comprehensive and accessible to the laymen. "Everyone who will read it, after the Written Law," he stated, "will know from it the whole of the Oral Law and will not have to study any other intermediate book." Maimonides' Code is a supreme example of the disciplined power of the rationalist mind. Devoid of personal judgments or opinions, it provides the reader with a clear and organized summary of Jewish law in accordance with the recognized principles of the *halakhah.* Essentially, Maimonides' approach to the formulation and application of the law is a humanistic one: "The ritual law has been given to man and not man to the ritual law." Thus, he believes that some laws are adaptable according to necessity, "in order to bring back the multitudes to faith and save them from religious laxity." While it would be too much to deduce from this humanistic approach an attitude of unrestrained progressivism, it is possible to conjecture that Maimonides would, to a certain degree, have found justified some of the steps taken by progressive movements in Judaism over the past century-and-a-half in order to insure the active participation of the greatest number in the life of the community. For all the discipline he imposed on himself in the composition of his works, he was not, in matters of communal concern, a man of doctrinal rigidity. And this flexibility, too, must be acknowledged as one of the finer human qualities of his powerful and original spirit. Such a combination of virtues is rare indeed: one might say that it was as a philosopher and as a codifier of law that Maimonides also realized his calling as a physician—solicitous of his people's health, mindful of their needs, eager at all times to relieve their suffering.

The End of the Golden Experiment

The Arab world would never recapture the unity of political idealism and religious zeal which had once characterized the great centers of Spain and North Africa. The increasing fragmentation of purpose and disintegration of social norms, which would end in the Christian Reconquest, was accompanied in the two centuries after Maimonides' death by an arbitrary and frantic policy of discrimination toward Jews and other non-Moslems, as—in a pattern familiar to students of Jewish history—Arab leaders, in an hysteria of recrimination, began to blame others for the inexorably widening fissures in the wall of their own self-assurance. While it lasted, the golden age of Arab-Jewish relations witnessed an astonishing symbiosis of talents and intentions. The dammed-up waters of Jewish creativity, let free at last, poured forth in torrents to enrich not only the native soil of Jewish literature, religion, and philosophy, but the arid ground of European civilization as it emerged from the Dark Ages. As statesmen and financiers, as scientists, translators, and developers of international trade, the Jews left an incalculable impact on the Mediterranean world. It was through their intermediary efforts that the fallow and uncultivated fields of Europe in the later Middle Ages received the irrigating waters so necessary for the growth of true culture. By that time, however, caught between the sirocco of Arab fanaticism and the tidal wave of Christian expansion, these healthful and infusing waters had once again been forced underground; unseen, their presence would for centuries go unacknowledged.

And yet the fact remains: for at least two centuries, under Arab tutelage and with grudging Arab condescension, the Jewish communities of Spain and North Africa witnessed a florescence in all areas of creative activity never before achieved in the Diaspora, and unequaled thereafter until the experience of nineteenth-century Germany and Austria and twentieth-century America. This florescence, this symbiosis, lasted precisely as long as it was allowed to last, until the Arab peoples, deflected from the pursuit of social justice by an age-old propensity to fanaticism, blinded to the possibilities of fertile coexistence by a craving for absolute power, reverted in baffled fury to the sterile tactics of suppression and persecution—to the doom not only of the Jews living in their lands, but of themselves. The end of the golden experiment in Arab-Jewish symbiosis marked also the end of Arab power in Europe. The lesson here is a sad one, perhaps sadder than usual for a people accustomed to periods of tolerance followed by periods of persecution and intolerance. For never under Christian domination has the Jewish spirit attained the heights of cultural expression it had once realized under Arab rule.

The Jews in Europe to 1492

B Y THE tenth century, Europe had become the major ground of Jewish history, and would continue so for the next thousand years. At the beginning of this millennium there were not more than one and a half million Jews in the world. Of these, a strong nucleus still existed in Mesopotamia, Syria, even in distant India. Though Palestine had declined in importance, the number of Jews there was constantly being replenished by a stream of pious immigrants. During the twelfth century, for instance, three hundred rabbis and scholars went to Acre from a single town in France.

By the end of the fifteenth century, when Jews had been excluded from the whole of Western Europe, with the exception of some parts of Germany and Italy, where political disunity prevented the formation of a single policy of discrimination, the largest concentrations were to be found in the two great eastern empires of the age: in Poland, new home of the Ashkenazim, or Northern Jews, and in Turkey, where the Sephardim, or Spanish Jews, lived. Available records tell innumerable stories pertaining to the inception of each of the new communities which sprang to life in the Middle Ages. In many cases, Jews were invited to settle in a town by the bishop or secular ruler, who might have entertained the hope that the presence of Jews would aid the commercial development of his domain. Such, for instance, were the origins of the Jewish community of Mainz (Mayence), whose Jews were called from Lucca by Charlemagne. The nucleus of the community was a family by the name of Kalonymos.

Jews arrived in Northern Europe mainly as merchants and craftsmen. For some time now, both in Babylonia and in Palestine, they had held a steadily declining share in agricultural life; the decline may be traced to an unfair tax system, but also to a general depreciation in the status of agriculture as a profession—a depreciation inspired by official Moslem disdain for field labor. In Europe, however, there were still other reasons for the general absence of Jews from the land. Visigothic legislation, for one thing, had deprived all Jews of their landholdings. Moreover, the Church demanded that both Jews and their employees refrain from working the fields on Sundays. Now, Jews also did not work on the Sabbath, and this enforced two-day-a-week stoppage often resulted in serious crop damage. Added to this were the constant threat of loss of land in periods of expulsion and the exigencies of Jewish religious observance, which made habitation in close Jewish settlements extremely desirable. All these factors help us to understand why so many Jews left the age-old pursuit of agriculture in favor of trade and mercantilism. Nevertheless, and especially in newly settled countries, the Jewish pioneering spirit still was attracted to agriculture. In Christian Spain, Jews were to be found engaged in the cultivation of orchards and vineyards which lay close to the protection afforded by medieval towns. Jews also pioneered in industries connected with agriculture, such as the production of flour, the manufacture of wine-presses, and the development of spinning and weaving establishments.

In trade, so long as no guild restrictions prohibited their participation, Jews were to be found in virtually every conceivable field of endeavor. In fact, some industries, which had been imported by Jews to the West, became typical and almost wholly-owned Jewish trades, as for example dyeing, silk-weaving, embroidery (Jewish artisans fabricated the costly royal robes for the coronation of the Hapsburg emperors), silver- and gold-smithery, and glass-blowing (as early as the seventh century there existed in France a process known as "Jewish glass").

Jewish mercantile evolution was equally swift, and soon outstripped the pace of local gentiles. The rapidity of this development went hand in hand with growing Jewish expertise in the area of international trade. The Western world had already begun to show an ardent desire for the luxuries of the Orient. Although Moslems were great travelers, they rarely ventured into hostile

Christian countries, and free trade between Europe and Asia and Africa had therefore been paralyzed for long years. The need for a mediating class between the Moslem and Christian worlds was met and filled by the Jew, who took over the role which in the fifth and sixth centuries had belonged to the Syrians. The Jew's efficacy as an intermediary was greatly enhanced by his ability to communicate with his coreligionists all over the world by means of a common language—Hebrew. The holy tongue now became in effect a vernacular, adapted by necessity to very practical purposes; in the ninth century it had already become the principal international language used in commercial transactions between Paris and Baghdad or Cairo. By virtue of a common faith and common social habits, Jews from Western lands were able to join hands with their fellow Jews in the remote countries of the East.

The basic uniformity of Jewish law was another important factor which gave the Jew an advantage over his gentile competitor in the development of commercial relations. The judges of a Jewish court in Cairo knew that their decisions would be accepted by the Jewish authorities in Aden or Marseilles. As business contracts were drawn up in a uniform legal terminology, contracting parties could obtain full justice in any city large enough to sustain a Jewish community. Nor may we disregard, finally, the fraternal feelings which existed among Jews in the various lands. Jewish merchant-travelers felt secure under the protection of Jewish communal leaders. They set out on their travels equipped with letters of introduction which would assure them a cordial reception and hospitality in the most remote communities. In case of shipwreck or piracy, they were assisted or ransomed by their nearest coreligionists.

Jewish pre-eminence in foreign commerce became jeopardized in due course when the Italian city-states arose as seafaring merchant centers; in addition to commercial talent, the Italians had at their disposal superior armament which they used as protection against brigands and pirates, and often as a means of pressuring natives to exchange goods. A similar preponderance of heavily armed merchants along the Northern routes was established by the formation of the Hanseatic League. With these Italian and Hanseatic merchant marines the Jews could no longer compete; by the time of the Renaissance the Jews were largely phased out of their role as the main international traders.

Perhaps the most notorious of Jewish occupations in the Middle Ages, and certainly the most unjustly maligned, was money-lending. The Islamic prohibition against usury, and similar canon laws of the medieval Church, had the effect of relegating money-lending, as an occupation, to the "infidels." Previously, under the Roman and Byzantine Empires, loans at low rates of interest had been legal, and the Jews did not play any special role in the credit system. Not until the Islamic expansion, when money-lending became entrusted to the *dhimmi,* did Jews enter this profession on a larger scale, although even then it never became a major independent occupation, but rather was connected in most cases with banking and trade.

In Christian Europe, as the Western Churches progressively sharpened their opposition to money-lending by Christians, a vacuum was created which the Jews were invited to fill. They soon had a virtual monopoly in this profession, although many Christian individuals and institutions, including some churches and monasteries, engaged in it also (indeed, until the twelfth century the clergy belonged among the most important groups of money-lenders). Jews arriving from more advanced countries often had cash available—either from the liquidation of their landholdings or as a result of their commercial activities. In addition, the Jews were permitted to engage in money-lending openly—whereas the Church had to find subterfuges—and were protected by the local rulers. As time progressed, kings and emperors also became vitally interested in the Jewish money trade.

By the thirteenth century, but not before, money-lending became the pre-eminent occupation of the Jews in France; still later it became that of the German Jews as well. Yet it must be borne in mind that Jews were never the sole suppliers of credit. Christian merchants continued to lend money, as did foreigners in general, and the Flemings and Lombards in particular. The fact remains, however, that the secular authorities especially encouraged the Jews in this profession, firstly because Lombards and ecclesiastical bankers held aloof from the laity as risky clients, and secondly because the richer the individual Jew became, the greater were the taxes and other spoils accruing to the state. The towns of Augsburg and Regensburg justified their protection of the Jews on the grounds that they "were useful citizens and indispensable to the ɔmmon man." It was thus that Jews were often granted a monopoly in the trade and were on occasion, as in the case of Silesia under Henry IV, forbidden any other occupation.

The newly established Jewish communities of Western Europe guided their internal affairs in accordance with Talmudic civil law, which they were at particular pains to adapt to their new conditions. The communities of Spain and Italy, because of their spiritual proximity to the Jews of Babylonia, maintained close contact with the *geonim* throughout the tenth and eleventh centuries, as long as the Babylonian academies continued in active existence. For the French and German communities, the problem was more complicated. It is, however, clear that they, too, addressed numerous inquiries to the heads of the schools in Babylonia—many such communications have been preserved—and that they were helped by emissaries from the East who visited the new communities with the aim of collecting contributions for their academies. These fund collectors were often scholars of note, who on occasion could be persuaded to stay in the new communities in Europe. Thus the seed was planted for a new flowering of Jewish scholarship in Italy, Spain, France, and Germany.

While still in their numerical infancy, the Jewish communities of France and Germany produced a major scholar and teacher: Rabbi Gershom of Mayence. His work laid the foundation for the communal organization of German and French Jewry in centuries to come. Given the title *Meor Ha-Golah*, "Light of the Exile," Rabbi Gershom headed the first Talmudic academy in Mayence. The esteem in which he was held is indicated by the fact that a number of regulations promulgated by him were immediately accepted by all European Jewry. Under pain of excommunication Rabbi Gershom prohibited polygamy, made it obligatory for a husband seeking a divorce to seek his wife's consent, and forbade the reading of mail addressed to others.

Communal self-determination was facilitated in Europe by the penchant for segregated living which characterized medieval society in general; that Jews wished to live apart from the rest of the population was thus pretty much taken for granted, although it was also a major goal of Rabbinic law to prevent any undue infiltration of gentile ways of life into the community. The Jews themselves often welcomed the assignment of segregated quarters as a distinct favor, particularly if these quarters—or *juderias*, as they were known in Spain—were located in fortified places. In 1084, Bishop Rudiger of Speyer even considered the establishment of such a separate Jewish quarter, surrounded by a wall, as a means of attracting Jews and hence of enhancing the city's prestige and trade relations. These quarters by no means constituted ghettos, in the strict meaning of the term. Numbers of Jews were always to be found living outside them, and non-Jews frequently established residence within the Jewish quarter. Legislation enforcing segregation was yet to come; when it did, it was invariably a sign that the natural social barriers had become so weak as to threaten the status of the majority. But before 1200, the majority of Jews in almost every town voluntarily congregated in a separate sector of their own, where they could more fully enjoy the educational and religious facilities and the amenities of life offered by a spiritually and socially homogeneous group.

Within the Jewish quarter, law reigned supreme. Here the communal administrators and judiciary had the full confidence of their constituents. Government was carried out along lines hallowed by ancient custom and reinforced by legal sanctions, the ultimately divine origin of which was acknowledged by everyone. Behind this protective wall of law and custom, more than behind actual physical walls, the drama of Jewish life was enacted. Enclosed in a spiritual fortress, the Jews felt greater kinship toward their most distant coreligionists than toward the nearest gentile townsman, whose problems and behavior they were often unable to understand, and for whose culture, family, and social life they had little sympathy.

The Jews in France, Germany, England, Italy

From the tenth and eleventh centuries on, there exists evidence of firmly established Jewish communities in every town of importance in France and Germany. Thereafter, the record of habitation is continuous. There is, moreover, documented evidence of previous settlement in these lands, as far back as the era of the Carolingian Empire, whose borders stretched from the English Channel and the Atlantic Ocean to the Adriatic Sea, and from the Oder to the Ebro. A Jew by the name of Isaac was a member of a delegation sent by Charlemagne to Harun el-Rashid—and the only member to return, bringing with him the first elephant ever seen in Europe. It was under Charlemagne's regime that the first Jews were brought to Mayence (Mainz), and at this time Jews were also to be found in Cologne, Aachen, and other towns of the Rhineland. The first records of the presence of Jews in Metz date from 888, in Magdeburg from 965, in Worms from 960, and in Speyer from 1084.

The usual process of settlement was this: Jews were invited, or allowed, to settle in a town because it was felt they would be of value to the economic development of the area. Once they were accepted, their legal status was regulated by capitular legislation,

Prague's Altneuschul, spiritual center of Bohemian Jewry since 1568. The dormer clock has Hebrew letters and its hands move counterclockwise; the tower clock has Roman numerals and runs clockwise.

which granted them certain rights and imposed upon them certain restrictions. The early charters granted to Jews were colored deeply by feudal concepts and terminology. In return for protection, the Jew was bound to the court by an oath of fidelity, and, of course, was required to make regular payment to the overlord. Almost all such charters contained the phrase: ". . . to live quietly under Our tutelage and protection and faithfully to serve Our court." In this feudal relationship, the Jews' direct dependence on royal power became the mainstay of the entire legal structure which defined their status. So long as the charter was drawn between the Jews and the king or emperor, the Jewish community was on the whole secure. When feudal power was delegated to barons or bishops, however, the position of the Jews was endangered. Thus, in 973, when the city of Merseburg was remitted by the emperor, "everything included in the walls of Merseburg, with Jews and merchants," was handed over with it.

The physical expansion of French and German Jewry kept pace with the general development of these two countries. Every new town of significance had its contingent of Jews. In the travel-diary of Petahiah of Regensburg we find that the line of Jewish settlement followed the main trade routes along the rivers and overland roads. Mainz, for example, was an important point of departure for trade caravans to Eastern Europe and Asia. Despite occasional infringements of their rights or blatant persecution, Jews were in general accepted everywhere for their abilities in trade and commerce; in the land-bound feudal economy, they performed an indispensable role.

Until the eleventh century, relations between Jews and gentiles in these countries were comparatively quiet and amicable. A number of communities developed a flourishing intellectual life and supported Talmudic academies; the greatest scholars of the ages were Gershom of Mainz; the prolific genius of Biblical and Talmudic commentary, Rashi of Troyes; and the grandsons of Rashi, Samuel ben Meir and Rabbenu Tam. Then, in the twelfth and thirteenth centuries, as the nationalist states began to evolve in Germany (under Frederick II) and France (under Philip Augustus), Jews once again fell victim to the intolerances of the medieval world. For France and Germany, this was the era of the expansion of indigenous trade and industry, of the rise of towns and the building of spectacular cathedrals; the Jew, having prepared the way for this effort, having in one sense made it possible, was now no longer needed, and hence no longer wanted. The status of the

A German woodcut of 1509 shows Jews taking the formal oath of fealty to the royal court.

Jews was henceforth determined by the Church of Rome and its representatives, whose double-edged policy was to insist on the one hand on tolerance and moderation, and on the other to persuade Jews of their moral and spiritual inferiority, and to induce them to convert.

In the British Isles, the history of sustained Jewish settlement is contained in the two centuries between the Norman conquest in 1066 and the expulsion edict of 1290. The decline of English Jewry was as rapid as its rise was meteoric. Jews were called into the country to fill an urgent economic need—the development of the money market. They were transformed in England into a class of royal usurers, whose main function it was to provide credit for both political and economic ventures. The total Jewish population of England was always small; in 1200 the community numbered about twenty-five hundred families. But although Jews constituted but one tenth of one per cent of the population, their contribution to the royal income in ordinary taxation was estimated at about 3000 pounds, or approximately one seventh of the total revenue. Most English Jews had originated in France, with a minority deriving from Spain, Italy, and Morocco. Among themselves, they spoke Norman French. As on the continent, they were considered "serfs of the royal chamber" and were allowed considerable autonomy in the conduct of their affairs. Their life differed little from that of the larger Jewish agglomerations on the continent. In all, they were probably the least important Jewry in Western Europe, both numerically and culturally. At the time of the expulsion they numbered about 16,000 souls, living scattered all over the country. Their brief history is a microcosmic image of the saga of Jewish survival in medieval Europe, with all its constituent elements: initial encouragement, followed by degradation, persecution, and finally expulsion. Although Edward I did allow them to take movable possessions with them, their real property, needless to say, went to the Crown.

In Italy, the principal Jewish communities, until the thirteenth century, lay to the south of Rome, where by virtue of location and timing they were able to provide an important link in the transmission of Jewish learning from East to West. During the Moslem era they experienced a renaissance of cultural activity similar to, although of lesser degree than, the "Golden Age" of Spain. Palermo, at that time the capital of Italy, was almost wholly an Arabic city, and as in Spain the Jews were allowed to take part in the general economic and intellectual life. Their prosperity continued for a while even under Norman domination; but with the ascendancy of the Hohenstaufen rulers after 1187, the Jews of southern Italy gradually found themselves forced into the prevailing mold: they too became "serfs" of the Imperial Chamber. However, the somewhat more lenient atmosphere of Italy allowed for the continued flowering of Hebrew literature and science, so that at least culturally South Italian Jews were able to view the two centuries of Norman and Hohenstaufen rule as a rather circumscribed extension of their "golden age" under the Moslem regime.

The communities to the north of the Papal States were for the most part small. The most important of these northern communities was Lucca, famous for is academy of learning. Venice had not yet allowed Jews to settle within her borders.

Relationship to Church and State

The Jews of Christian Europe during the Middle Ages were regarded as a distinct racial and religious group which should not be subject to the same laws as the Christians; hence the special charters given to the Jews which assured them the protection of "life and limb" and left them the right to govern themselves in communal and religious matters. These charters were originally issued with a view toward attracting wealthy Jews to migrate into a given area which was in need of economic development and money; most of them contained detailed provisions encouraging Jews to engage in money-lending. From Germany, the practice of granting charters soon spread to all other European countries. Yet even with such charters, the Jews were not always secure. It sometimes happened that an emergency situation, or simple greed for money, would impel a granting sovereign to confiscate Jewish wealth and property, and not infrequently these acts would be followed by the expulsion of the local Jewish community.

As for the Church, the spread of Christian heresies at the end of the twelfth century had compelled it to reassert its power and to strengthen its organization. In time, punitive actions against heretics were extended to include Jews as well. The Fourth Lateran Council, convened in 1215 by Pope Innocent III, issued a number of decrees directly affecting the Jews of Europe. According to the Council, the anti-Jewish laws enacted by the Christianized Roman Empire and the Church were to be observed scrupulously; the repression of Jews was to serve as an edifying example to vacillating Christians. The general tendency of legislation passed at the Lat-

A post-Byzantine icon reveals one result of Pope Innocent III's Fourth Lateran Council: Jews wearing the mandatory marks of discrimination, the round badge and hat.

eran Council was to segregate Jews socially even more than had been the case in the past. (The waves of expulsion from Western Europe in the course of the next three centuries were the direct result of this new social isolation effectuated by Innocent.) Old regulations forbidding Jews authority over Christians were to be reinforced. No Jew was to be appointed to any office by any prince under pain of excommunication. Jews were to remain in their homes with shutters closed on Easter, and a special tax was to be paid annually on that day. Jews and Christians were now expressly forbidden to dwell together, and all unbelievers were henceforth to be distinguished by a special badge. The way to the ghetto was being prepared.

Despite the fact that the entire code did not secure immediate enforcement, its very promulgation marked a turning point in Jewish history. The code hung over the heads of European Jewry as a constant threat, suspended by the fragile thread of expediency and temperament. Whenever the forces of reaction triumphed in a state, whenever the Church felt endangered from within or without, the code was likely to be invoked. Fanatics and pietists clamored incessantly, with some success, for its rigid enforcement. The protective Papal Bulls which had been issued in the past now remained to a large degree a theoretical defense only, ineffective in the realm of practical politics.

One important area of friction between Jews and Christians lay in the interpretation of the Bible, a text which both faiths held in common but about whose meaning they differed radically. The Church claimed to represent the fulfillment of all Biblical promises. On the other hand, all Biblical threats and denunciations against the Jews were considered to apply in their original force. Jewish defense against repeated accusations of inferiority proved of little avail. It was constantly being dunned at the Jews that they represented an accursed people, an enemy of the human race. The effect of this unceasing, incendiary harangue was on the one hand to inflame mob passions, often with devastating results, and on the other to debilitate the spirit of resistance among Jews.

Another target of assault was the "blasphemies" of the Talmud. Jews were sometimes forced into public disputations, presided over by kings and bishops, to defend their traditional literature. The Jews almost always "lost," and the Talmud was not infrequently condemned and burnt. The most spectacular of such book-burnings, involving twenty-four wagonloads of Talmudic manuscripts, took place in Paris in the year 1240. Continued official condemnation of the Talmud resulted finally in a prohibition against studying these volumes altogether, and this in turn led to the cessation of Rabbinic studies in, among other places, northern France, where Talmudic academies had flourished since the days of Rashi of Troyes. Such, then, were the extremes to which Christianity was led by its fear and hatred of those who had asked not to be special, but only to be different.

The Crusades   In the eleventh century the entire Western world came under the influence of the Church in Rome. After the final rupture with the Byzantine Christians, Pope Gregory VII (1073–1085) had cleansed the Church of vice and corruption. His successor, Urban II, took it upon himself to divert Western Europe from internal wars, to find a fitting outlet for the immense energy of the Normans, and at the same time to deliver a final blow to the Byzantine Church by extending the power of Rome to Turkey, Syria, and Palestine. All these aims were to coalesce in the grand design of the Crusades.

Throughout the eleventh century complaints had reached Rome concerning the harassment by the native Moslems of Christian pilgrims to Palestine. The Caliph Al-Hakim had gone so far as to murder Christians and destroy their most sacred monuments in Palestine. Christian traders, moreover, were being constantly attacked by Arab pirates, and Christian trading stations in Moslem countries sacked by marauding Arab bands. Thus, when the Byzantine Emperor requested intervention, he found the Church ready to undertake a universal war against the Moslems. All feuding among Christians was to cease until the infidel had been swept back and the site of the Holy Sepulchre returned to Christian hands.

This was the rallying cry of the Crusades, a cry that went out not only to knights and princes, but, through the preaching of Peter the Hermit, to the common man as well. Barefoot, clad in a coarse garment, riding on a donkey and bearing a huge cross, Peter traveled throughout France and Germany, haranguing vast crowds in church and marketplace with tales of the wanton destruction of the holy places by the Seljuk Turks.

The motives that lay behind the Crusades were many. There was, first of all, genuine religious zeal, mixed with the desire to revitalize the spiritual faith of the common man. Second, the Latin Church saw the Crusades as an opportunity to subdue the Byzantine Church. There was also an overriding economic motive. The

A French mid-thirteenth-century miniaturist in La Bible Moralisée *paints a Jewish-Christian "debate." On the right, the monks are modest and composed; on the left, the Jews, phylacteries on their arms, stand adamant. The crowned figure between is probably French King Saint Louis who presided over just such a debate.*

presence of the Seljuks and Fatimids had erected an impassable barrier which blocked the eastward trade from Genoa and Venice that up till now had flowed through Baghdad and Aleppo, or through Egypt. These channels had to be forced open again if Eastern trade was not to be controlled or monopolized altogether by Constantinople.

All these factors came together and resulted in Pope Urban's call for a Crusade. The response was overwhelming. From all over Europe men flocked to the standard of the Holy War against the infidels. Some were impelled by a thirst for adventure; others were hired by the prospect of realizing great wealth; still others came to escape a burden of debt at home, or to gain the remission of sins promised by the Pope to all participants. The First Crusade, lacking organization and leadership, was truly a popular uprising, with all the attendant cruelties and excesses which characterize a lawless mob. When the first two advance parties reached Hungary, on the road eastward, they committed such atrocities that the local population, driven to fury, destroyed them totally. A third horde inaugurated its trek with a wholesale pogrom against the Jews of the Rhineland. It too was destroyed in Hungary. The next two waves, under Peter the Hermit, succeeded in reaching Constantinople, to the astonishment and dismay of the Byzantine Emperor Alexius. After looting the city they crossed the Bosporus, to be massacred by the Seljuks (1096). Such was the first manifestation of "the popular will" in modern European history.

As might be expected, one of the principal victims of the "people's Crusade" was the Jews. Tempted by Jewish wealth, the Crusaders suddenly found it unnecessary to go forth to kill God's enemies in the Holy Land when the Jewish infidel lay so close at hand. "Kill a Jew and save your soul" became the shortcut taken by many a zealous Crusader. The massacre began in Rouen: property was looted, houses burned. Even baptized Jews had difficulty escaping alive. The attack spread through northern France to the Rhineland, where the promises of protection made to the Jews by bishops and townsmen were swiftly broken in the face of the advancing mobs. The Jewish communities of Metz, Speyer, Mayence, Troyes, and other towns were destroyed. A small number of Jews accepted baptism to remain alive; the majority refused, and died.

The following year, 1097, saw a renewal of the First Crusade, this time by organized forces. The Crusaders took diverse routes from France, Normandy, Flanders, England, Italy, and Sicily. After crossing the Bosporus, they more or less followed the route originally taken by Alexander the Great. They captured Nicea, laid siege to Antioch, and defeated a great army of Seljuks near Mosul. One smaller force, under Godfrey of Bouillon, went on to Jerusalem. After a month's siege, the city was captured on July 15, 1099. The slaughter that day was terrible. At nightfall the Crusaders came together at the Holy Sepulchre to declare the establishment of a Latin kingdom in Jerusalem. The Jewish population of the Holy City was herded into the synagogues and burned alive.

Christian domination of the Holy Land was first challenged by a powerful Seljuk atabeg (ruler) who recaptured some of the territory under Christian control, including the fortress of Edessa near Mosul, which was the outpost of Christianity in the East. Thereupon, a Second Crusade (1147) was declared by the German Emperor Conrad III and King Louis VII of France. This was a far less glamorous undertaking, sabotaged from the beginning by the refusal of the Italian republics to sacrifice their maritime interests in the East in order to come to the help of the Franks. The Crusade was stemmed in Egypt, which was defended by Saladin—then an army officer—who had given orders to set fire to Fustat rather than let it fall into the hands of the Christians.

Following the victory, Saladin felt strong enough to attempt a *jihad* against Christendom. In 1187 he recaptured Jerusalem, and thus set the scene for the Third Crusade, a Crusade openly undertaken as a war of the Cross against the Crescent. The finest of European knighthood, imbued as much by romantic and knightly ideals as by religious hatred, set out in 1189 under the leadership of Richard the Lion-Heart. This Crusade, too, ended in failure. Jerusalem remained in the hands of the Moslems, although the Christians did regain possession of the Palestine sea coast.

The privileges of a Crusader participating in Richard's campaign, like those of Crusaders on the Second Crusade, included a moratorium on all debts owed to Jews. Physical assaults on Jews in France and Germany were fewer in number than previously. But in England the Jews suffered much physical violence. Before the inception of the Third Crusade an unfounded rumor spread that Richard had ordered an attack on the Jews; the riots which consequently broke out were stopped only by a proclamation, signed by Richard, forbidding the molestation of Jews. This proclamation remained an effective hindrance until Richard departed for Palestine, when fresh outbreaks occurred. The worst was in York in 1190, where the Jews took refuge in the royal castle. There they held out for several days; finally, rather than surrender to the mob, they com-

At Acre the 13th-century
Crusaders' Wall, brick
and mortar at the edge
of the blue
Mediterranean, still
defends the ancient city
against invasion from
the sea.

mitted suicide. Those few who had not submitted to self-slaughter
were killed anyway by the crowd.

Physical traces of Crusader rule in Palestine exist to this day.
From Acre to Ashkelon a chain of thick walls was erected to defend the coastal strongholds; Crusader towers still stand in Ramleh
and Caesarea. All together, the rule of the Crusaders lasted for
two hundred years. During this time Acre became the Jewish center
in Palestine, for the Christians had renewed the prohibition against
Jewish habitation in Jerusalem, with the exception of a few families who had obtained the special permission of the Christian
mayor (or King of Jerusalem, as he had entitled himself). At one
time, three hundred scholars from France came to settle in Palestine; when the Holy City was recaptured by the Moslems, many
were allowed to resettle there. The Crusaders were finally driven
out of the Holy Land by the Egyptian Mamelukes in 1291.

The Crusades were responsible for the murder of tens of thousands of European Jews and the destruction of many Jewish communities. Loss of capital drove the Jews deeper than ever into the
business of money-lending, but this time into consumer's rather
than producer's loans. Unable to obtain such loans, the lower
classes conceived an even deeper hatred for Jews than that instilled
in them by the Church. But the Jews had no choice. The opening
of trade-routes to the East had created vast new opportunities for
Christian merchants, and the Jews were deprived of most of their
foreign trade.

The Crusades inaugurated an epoch of acute suspicion and
rivalry in Europe, which was to prevail throughout the rest of the
Middle Ages. By the end of the Crusades, Europe had been transformed from a relatively open to a closed society—a society only
too eager to exclude those upon whom, ironically, it had already
wrought its most terrible devastation.

Persecutions and Expulsions

The discriminatory doctrines and regulations of the Church possessed a self-fulfilling capacity, in that the daily existence of the
Jew, as it was defined and circumscribed by these regulations, only
tended to confirm the Church's contention that he had been rejected by God. A *cordon sanitaire* had been thrown about him to
prevent the infection of Christian souls. Social relations were reduced to a minimum, the common man having been forbidden to
discuss matters of faith with Jews. The decrees of the Lateran

Councils, demanding that Jews be distinguished by badge and dress, encased every Jew in a personal ghetto long before the communal ghetto was to complete the humiliation.

In the hands of the ordinary cleric and layman, the decrees issued by the various Councils and Synods became an additional weapon in the existing arsenal of superstitions and greed. The very fact that such legislation had been passed—regardless of its actual content—served to justify the most outrageous acts of cruelty on the part of the masses and the lower clergy. To the Lateran Councils must be laid the blame for the anti-Semitic epidemics that swept Europe in the thirteenth and fourteenth centuries—outbursts predicated on allegations which the higher clergy knew to be false, but for which they had already paved the way. Once these outbursts had been set in motion, nothing the Pope or the bishops might say could impede their awful consequence. Indeed, the princes of the Church frequently remained silent, and by so doing lent an air of complicity to the unrestrained fury of the mob. Papal Bulls decrying the slaughter of Jews were of no avail; under torture, Jews would make detailed confessions to crimes they had never committed, and thereby justify the behavior of their persecutors. Besides, upon the death of the "culprit," all debts and mortgages held by him were automatically cancelled; the spoils were divided among his Christian accusers.

The Jews soon became a universal sounding-board of religious tension, registering, often with their lives, the fluctuations of sentiment in the world at large. False accusations of crime, often initiated by apostates from Judaism—the traditional harbingers of hatred—were frequently levied against them. That the Jews as a whole adamantly refused to be baptized only served to intensify the rancor of their accusers. One of the most virulent, and most fantastical, of the charges made against Jews was that of ritual murder. The pattern was as follows: A Christian would disappear, and the Jews would be accused of having crucified him in mockery of the martyrdom of Jesus and of having used his blood for Jewish ritual purposes. It was alleged either that the blood was distributed among the community, or, in the more elaborate versions of this indictment, that it served as a necessary ingredient in the preparation of Passover *matzah*. The "guilty" Jews were then massacred, their property confiscated, and the proceeds allocated to the local church. Not a few parishes attained sudden wealth from such procedures.

In our current, "enlightened" condition, we may strive to understand the psychological mechanism of these blood accusations by reminding ourselves that in the medieval world magic and witchcraft were part of the ordinary baggage of society. The particularly potent concept of blood, combined with deep ignorance and fear of the "other" person, all served to perpetuate these accusations. Yet the blood libel survived the Middle Ages to appear again and again in the midst of the most advanced societies. In the nineteenth century its specter was raised in the Orthodox Christian world, and it lay behind the celebrated trial in 1913 of Mendel Beilis. Subsequently it was revived by the Nazis, and as late as the 1960s it was repeated in Communist newspapers in the Moslem republics of the Soviet Union. It has, in short—as lies repeated at sufficient intervals—sometimes become an integral part of the legend of the Jew in the non-Jewish mind; under conditions of severe social stress, it is always likely to re-emerge.

Even in the Middle Ages, public declarations by the Emperor Frederick II and by Pope Innocent IV, denying the validity of these blood charges, had no effect. The libel was immortalized in literature by the lovable prioress in Geoffrey Chaucer's *Canterbury Tales*. Chaucer drew material for his tale from the story of William of Norwich—one of the earliest cases of blood accusation in Europe. In 1144, in Norwich, England, a boy, William, had been found dead. The Jews were accused of having murdered him for religious purposes, and were tortured until they confessed to the deed. It is substantially this pattern which recurred in the later English episode of Hugh of Lincoln, as well as in subsequent instances of blood libel on the continent.

Another accusation commonly leveled against Jews was that of having desecrated the Host, a wafer of unleavened bread which in the celebration of the Mass is transformed, according to the Catholic doctrine of transsubstantiation, into the body of Christ. The allegation was that the Jews, anxious to torture and destroy this representation of Jesus, would steal the holy wafers and stick pins into them, or plunge them into boiling water, or pound them in a mortar. On such occasions blood was believed to have flowed from the wafer, or other miracles to have taken place. For this offense, the accused Jews were killed. In 1298, the Jews of Rottingen were accused of profaning a Host in this manner, and the ensuing outbreak against the Jews spread throughout all of Bavaria and Austria. A total of one hundred forty communities were pillaged. In 1336, similar accusations provoked a wave of violence which extended from the Rhine to Bohemia and Moravia.

A bronze figurine from the Halberstadt Cathedral, decked out in 13-century Jewish garb, is shown stoning the first Christian martyr, Stephen.

In 1321, a story arose that the lepers of Europe—who at that time were treated less humanely than animals—had begun to spread their disease by poisoning wells. The Jews were accused of encouraging them in this deed, even of abetting them with money. Several Jewish communities were plundered and many Jews were tortured and killed, their property confiscated by local authorities. This accusation was revived in even greater force in 1348, when the Black Death smote country after country in Europe. Possibly because of the more advanced state of their medical knowledge, and because of their segregated and, on the whole, more hygienic living conditions, proportionately fewer Jews died from this plague than Christians. But because of this fact the Jews were also accused of being in league with the Devil in instigating the Black Death. Entire Jewish communities were burned and thousands of Jews perished in retribution for a disease which destroyed fully one quarter of the population of Europe.

There were other accusations as well. In Vienna Jews were blamed for a drought, and were also alleged to have materially aided the Hussite armies in their rebellion against the Catholics in Bohemia. These accusations resulted in a familiar pattern of massacres. In 1241, when the Mongol invasion spread across the German lands, it was rumored that among the invaders were descendants of the Ten Lost Tribes of Israel; thus the Jews were also held responsible for the ravages of the Mongol hordes.

Expulsions of Jews were common in this period. They proved to be an efficient way for a ruler or a bishop to replenish the empty coffers of his treasury, since all Jewish property was confiscated by the local sovereign upon expulsion. It often occurred, moreover, that after an initial expulsion the Jews were recalled to a country when their talents became needed again, only to be expelled once more after they had revitalized the economy and thereby fulfilled the purpose for which they had been recalled.

The history of German and French Jews in this period, for instance, is one of successive expulsions and recalls. Between 1182 and 1321 the Jews of France were expelled and recalled four times. In 1322 they were expelled again, and for forty years there was not a single Jew on French soil. In 1361, when King John II was captured by England, the Jews were invited back to France in order to raise the enormous ransom needed to redeem the king. In 1394, they were again expelled from the country.

Equally tragic was the fate of the Jews of Provence, an area that boasted one of the happiest and culturally most productive

Jewish communities in Christian Europe. As late as the thirteenth century its Jews were still permitted to own property and engage in trade. The Jewish physicians of Provence were famous throughout Europe, and its Jewish financiers were called upon to assist in the administration of Toulouse. Yet it was this very liberality of spirit and cultural openness that was to prove the ruin of Provence. Sufficiently advanced to see the faults and corruption of Church organization, a protesting group of Provencal Christians denied the Catholic Church and established its own. These dissenters, known as the Albigenses, became the victims of a vigorous crusade waged from 1208 to 1215 by Pope Innocent III, whose wrath flamed out not only at the heretics within his Church, but against the Jews of Provence as well. By the time the vanquished Provence fell to Rome, the Jews of Christian Europe had lost their final outpost of cultural opportunity.

And finally, the fate that overtook the Jews of Spain, was a tragedy more spectacular in scope and effect than anywhere else in Europe. Nowhere else had Jews risen to such heights, or become such an integral part of the population, and nowhere else did an expulsion of such dramatic and large-scale proportions take place as in Spain in 1492.

Throughout the second half of the eleventh century, Spanish Jewry had gradually been transferring its center of activity to northern Spain and Portugal. While the provinces south of the Pyrenees were one by one reconquered by Christian princes, the Jews in these localities remained more or less in their former condition. Internal and external struggles continued to characterize the northern Christian courts as much as they had those of the southern Moslem provinces, and Jews were hence often considered by the Crown to be its most reliable allies. They were, furthermore, useful in developing newly acquired backward and depopulated areas. Their experience in agriculture and industry in the southern parts of the peninsula became readily available to the north, which now received many refugees fleeing the invading Almoravides and Almohades.

At first the Jews served the Christians as they had the Moslems, as statesmen, counselors, and physicians. Their knowledge of Arabic stood them in good stead in their positions as official Court ambassadors to Moslem lands. Jewish savants played a major role in intellectual activity, especially as astronomers and devisers of nautical instruments. Slowly, however, the favored status of the Jews incited the resentment of the Church. After the death of

מקנת כספי הצעיר חיים לבית הלוי

נכתב הספר הזה שישבו ארבעה ועשרים
ספרי הקדש על יד המשכיל ר אברהם טאליה נע
במדינת טליטולה אשר בספרד ונשלם בירח ניסן
שנת חמשת אלפים ומאתים וחמשים ושתים
לבריאת עולם להחכם השלם ר
נרו בן החבר הנכבד כר זל הא יזכהו ר
להגותבו הוא וזרעו וזרע זרעו עד עולם ובשבעה
בקשא בא מרח שנה הנזכרת יצאו מבוהלים ונרושים
בדבר המלך גלות ירושלם אשר בספרד וסימניך ר
בוא יבא ברנה נושא אלומותיו ואניחיים חיים
כתב זוני בוקיצה המסורת והפלונתות שנת נזר אלהיו
יגל ראשו לפרט במדינת קוסטנטינה ישעיקרב

Alfonso VI in 1109, serious anti-Jewish riots broke out in Toledo and spread from there to other communities. The Church, afraid that Christians might imitate Jewish ways of life, demanded strict implementation of Lateran laws segregating Christians from Jews. Application of these laws, however, remained for a time more or less dependent upon the will of the ruling secular power. As was frequently the case in the Middle Ages, the Church was unrelentingly doctrinaire in its pronouncements, but local sovereigns were equally adamant in their opportunism.

As elsewhere in Europe, Spanish Jews were regarded as serfs of their Christian rulers, their rights having been set forth by the Crown in charters. Inside their own quarters (*juderia*) they enjoyed complete autonomy, but the fortunes of the Jewish communities as a whole varied with the ascent and death of the various rulers of Aragon and Castile. By the end of the thirteenth century, as the Reconquest was virtually concluded, Spanish rulers began to adjust their treatment of the Jews to the prevailing mood of Christian Europe. Jews were now eliminated from public service. Although in the thirteenth century the position of Spanish Jewry was superior to that of the Jews in other parts of Europe, this arrangement was nevertheless insecure, and was liable to erupt at any point from the pressure of internal strife, foreign wars, or the inroads of the Church, which worked in subtle and always indirect ways to persuade the secular powers of the wisdom of expulsion or physical extermination of the Jews—policies which the Church as a body never explicitly advocated, and which it pretended officially to abhor.

In 1391 Ferrand Martinez, the Archdeacon of Ecija, instigated a wave of outrages against Jews which spread through all the cities of Castile and Aragon. Some communities were almost completely annihilated; others were sacked or burned. The persecution differed in kind from that in other parts of Europe: here, Jews en masse were forced to decide between baptism and death. Pressure was brought to bear by depriving Jews of all civic and economic rights. Faced with this threat, many surrendered to what appeared inevitable anyway, and converted. Often the wealthy and influential members of the community, who were accustomed to their own affluence, and whose morale had perhaps been undermined by the long period of ease, were the first to be baptized. Whatever the reason, a uniquely large number of Jews converted at this time. (In Toledo over four thousand converts were made in a single day when a priest broke into synagogues demanding death or baptism.) Of the neophytes, some returned to Judaism when the danger passed, but the majority did not. Some of them even became sincere Christians, and occasionally—as in the case of Pablo de Santa Maria (formerly Rabbi Solomon Halevy), who became Bishop of Burgos—rose to high ecclesiastical office. Indeed, Pablo confirmed the pattern of Jewish apostates. Under his guidance, fresh anti-Jewish attacks broke out. Another ex-Jew, Joshua Lorki, took part in a public disputation held at Tortosa in 1414 which resulted in the condemnation of the Talmud.

All these anti-Jewish activities came to a head in the year 1479, when the Crowns of Castile and Aragon were united in the persons of Ferdinand and Isabella, the Catholic sovereigns. For them, the immediate expulsion of non-believers was essential. Determined to rule a truly "Catholic" country, free of heresy and disbelief, Ferdinand and Isabella ordered the expulsion of all Jews from Spain in 1492. The last Jews left Spain on August 2, the ninth of Av, a day of Jewish mourning and the day on which Columbus set sail from Cadiz on his expedition to the New World.

Thus, by the end of the fifteenth century, Jews had been effectively excluded from the whole of Western Europe, with the exception of some parts of Germany and Italy, where political disunity prevented the adoption of any single policy with regard to the Jewish population. But in any country which had achieved national consolidation during this period, and which fell under the unilateral influence of the Catholic Church, the story is the same: appalling degradation, torture, slaughter, and expulsion. Henceforth Jews were to be concentrated overwhelmingly in the two great Eastern empires: Poland, which held the Ashkenazim (Northern European Jews), and the Ottoman Empire, where lived the Sephardim (Jews of Spanish or Latin origin). Elsewhere in Europe, the legend of the "wandering Jew" had been realized in fact; it had, indeed, been willed by a hostile world into existence.

The Marranos Crypto-Judaism—the practice of Jews who hide their Judaism from the outside world—is as ancient as persecution itself. It became a widespread phenomenon, however, only with the advent of a politically forceful Christian Church. In theory, Christianity forbade conversion by force, although in practice, faced with the alternatives of "death or baptism," one would be hard put to differentiate *Jews in Europe to 1492* between coerced and voluntary conversion. The Church, at any

rate, regarded such conversions by threat as freely undertaken, and history records many instances of mass baptism under these circumstances. But as the conversions were in most cases insincere, their victims tended to revert whenever possible to the practice of their ancestral faith. Gershom of Mayence prohibited the unkind treatment of those forced converts who returned to the Jewish fold, and a special prayer in synagogues was composed to implore divine protection for all the House of Israel, including, in medieval parlance, the "forced ones." As far as the Jewish community was concerned, then, forced conversion was not considered by law to be the same as voluntary apostacy.

The insincerity of the forced convert's belief, and, obversely, the tenacity of his crypto-Jewish faith, are attested by the fact that knowledge and practice of Judaism seldom expired with the death of the original convert, but were passed on from generation to generation. This was so especially, although not exclusively, in Spain and Portugal. At the close of the thirteenth century, Angevin rulers in Naples forcibly converted Jews who under the name of "Neofiti" had retained a crypto-Jewish existence for over three centuries. Their secret fidelity to Judaism was one reason for the establishment of an Inquisition in Naples in the sixteenth century. There were similar cases in the Moslem world: for instance, the Daggatun of the Sahara. In Persia there were the Jedidim and in Bokhara the Tschola. It is known that in Spain there were cases of crypto-Judaism in Roman times.

Outwardly, these Marranos, as they were known in Spanish, were Christians; inwardly they were Jews. Their disbelief in the dogmas of the Church was notorious. They kept traditional Jewish ceremonies; some would eat only kosher meat; usually they married exclusively among themselves; they consorted with ex-coreligionists and sometimes furtively attended synagogue. Worst of all in the eyes of the Church, they transmitted their disbelief to their children.

With the removal of religious disabilities upon conversion, all walks of life became officially open to the Marranos. In Spain, they were in every profession: law, government, the army, the universities, the Church itself. In time, they all but dominated Spanish life. Within a few generations almost every aristocratic family had some Jewish blood in it. The revival of vernacular literature at the court of Juan II in Aragon was in large part due to the genius of persons of Jewish blood. Fernando de Rojas, considered one of the great classical writers of the Spanish tongue, was of Jewish descent. Such persons were usually called "New Christians," to distinguish them from those who were born Christian. Popularly they were known as "Marranos"—an old Spanish term dating to the early Middle Ages and meaning "swine." The term expresses all the contempt which the ordinary Spaniard felt for the insincere neophytes by whom he had rapidly become surrounded.

As the fifteenth century advanced it became clear that these mass conversions had created a disturbingly hypocritical element in Christianity. In addition, by now a new generation had been baptized at infancy and was considered fully Christian. The Church was in a difficult position. "Spontaneous baptism" had transformed a considerable proportion of the Jews from infidels outside the Church to heretics within it. These doubtful Christians were rightly regarded as a greater menace than avowed Jews.

The populace too had become enraged by these hypocrites who had gained a monopoly in important financial positions. As tax farmers for the Crown, they became synonymous with royal oppression. Nor was the Spanish nobility itself remiss in its detestation of the *conversos,* who had achieved high positions in the administration. In 1449, Marrano tax-gatherers, out to collect a forced loan for the defense of Toledo, were turned upon by the mob. Later, a decree was passed declaring *conversos* unfit to hold office or to bear testimony against Christians. Pope Nicholas V condemned those responsible for this statute, but in 1467 it was reenacted. Trouble broke out in many other towns of Spain; this time it was impossible to save oneself by conversion.

In 1464, at the Concordat of Medina del Campo, it was decided to establish an inquiry into the conduct of the New Christians. In 1478, after some *conversos* were found celebrating a Passover ceremony, three persons were empowered by the Church with complete jurisdiction over heretics. This constituted the formal establishment of the Inquisition. Matters began to move forward in 1480.

The city of Seville was one of the main centers of *conversos.* Under the leadership of Diego de Susan, a wealthy merchant, the New Christians decided to resist the Inquisition. But the beautiful daughter of Diego disclosed the secret to her Christian lover, who thereupon revealed it to the Inquisitors. With a positive weapon in their hands, the Inquisitors now moved against the *conversos* of Seville. Wealthy and honorable citizens were arrested, tried, and condemned to death.

Early in 1481 the first *Auto de fé* took place in Seville; six men and women were burned alive. On the second occasion Diego himself was executed. A permanent pyre was now constructed just outside the city walls for these executions by burning. Many Marranos fled to neighboring territories, but were remanded by the nobility at the urging of the authorities. Their property was confiscated, most of the proceeds going to the Crown. The public burning of secret Jews continued with regularity, and soon became popular spectacles. At each of these public judgments the sentences of the accused were pronounced, and punishment—which included flogging, imprisonment, banishment, or death by burning—was carried out. A list was circulated detailing the 37 signs by which one could recognize a Judaizer. The promise of free pardon for full confession encouraged widespread denunciations. Jews, particularly former synagogue officials, were enlisted, at pain of excommunication, to expose all they knew. At least 2000 of these "spectacles" took place in the peninsula and its dependencies, and in all some 400,000 persons were tried by the Inquisition in Spain and Portugal during the three and a half centuries of its existence; of these, about 30,000 were put to death. It was not until the eighteenth century that the activity of the Inquisition began to diminish, and by that time it had done its work so effectively that victims were difficult to find. The institution was finally abolished in 1834.

After the expulsion from Spain in 1492 many Jews had found their way to Portugal where the wealthy among them were gladly admitted and others were allowed, upon payment, to remain for a temporary period of eight months. In 1496, however, King Manoel II of Portugal, wishing to marry the daughter of Ferdinand and Isabella, was able to obtain consent only on condition that he rid his country of Jews. By 1497 no known Jews remained in Portugal. Manoel, who had wanted the Jews to remain, tried initially to baptize them. Knowing the extreme love Jews had for their children, he issued orders that all Jewish children between the ages of four and fourteen be baptized. But his plan failed. The children were baptized, but their parents did not follow suit. The sight of children being dragged to the baptismal font, terrible and heart-breaking though it was, could not sway the adults into breaking, of their own free will, a cardinal tenet of Judaism. Yet another attempt was made to convert the Jews on their way out of the country. They were ordered to pass through the capital, where they were herded into the palace and urged again to convert. At this point, many gave in. A few, however, led by Simon of Miami, chief rabbi of Portugal, resisted. Simon died for his efforts; many of his followers were transported to Africa, a pathetic relic of the once renowned Portuguese community.

Thus, there was no real exile from Portugal, only a mass conversion. The Portuguese *conversos* proved more tenacious than the Spaniards; having been converted by force, they still regarded themselves as Jews. Since the Inquisition did not begin operations in Portugal until fifty years after the expulsion, these *conversos* had more time than their Spanish brethren to acclimate themselves to a crypto-Jewish existence.

Following the expulsion edict of 1496, these New Portuguese Christians were granted twenty years immunity for religious offenses. No legislation was to be passed against them as a separate race. Many Marranos now left the country to be able to practice their Judaism elsewhere. But in 1499 Manoel forbade any New Christian from leaving without royal permission. In 1506, a terrible massacre of New Christians occurred after it was alleged that one of their number had laughed at a "miracle" which had been caused by an inordinately luminous crucifix. The king, mindful of his need for Jewish talent, punished the principal instigators of the disorders against them.

In 1536, the Inquisition was introduced into Portugal. Despite Manoel's earlier decree that the *conversos* were not to be treated as a separate entity, the Inquisition fastened upon them as a distinct body. Family after distinguished family was exposed, and incidents of martyrdom were not uncommon. A young Franciscan friar, Frei Diogo da Assumpiao, proclaimed his belief in Judaism so vehemently that he was burned. One of the greatest martyrs was Don Lope de Vera, who actually had no Jewish blood in him. He had studied Hebrew and was attracted to Judaism. Denounced by his brother, he declared to the Inquisitors that he wished to become a Jew. In his cell he circumcised himself and changed his name to Judah the Believer. He was burned alive. When being led to his death he is said to have recited Hebrew prayers.

Until the sixteenth century, the Marranos retained some knowledge of Hebrew. As time passed, however, transmission of the Jewish heritage became more and more a matter of oral instruction, handed down from one generation to the next. The Marrano creed was summed up in one sentence: "Salvation is possible through the Law of Moses, not through the Law of Christ." Intended as a confession of the Jewish faith, this sentence employs the language and conceptions of Catholic theology, and hence typifies the Marrano predicament: a fierce desire to remain Jewish, but an inevitable vulnerability to the influences of the environment. Restoration to the "Land of Promise" occupied an important place in Marrano hopes and prayers. Children of New Christians were usually informed of Judaism at Bar Mitzvah age. Babies were not circumcised, however, as this deed, if discovered, would be tantamount to the death sentence. Often women became the spiritual leaders of Marrano communities. Acquaintance with Hebrew was rare, and prayers were recited in the local vernacular. Usually no books were used in services. In worship Jewish and Christian practices were often intermingled; for instance, the Marranos kneeled rather than stood in prayer, and prayers were often not chanted but recited. Most abstained from pork. The Sabbath was kept, as was Passover and the Day of Atonement. More regard was generally paid to fasting than to feasting; where the one was private and could be concealed, the other tended to be public, and hence incriminating. Nevertheless, the festival of Purim was very popular, probably because the story of Esther appeared to resemble that of the Marranos themselves; "telling not her race nor her birth," Esther yet remained faithful to the religion of her fathers in an alien environment. Marranos often observed Jewish mourning practices scrupulously, and a Jewish wedding would be held privately after the compulsory Catholic ceremony. Biblical names were frequently used in secret. Thus, despite the elements of syncretism that crept into their observance, the Marranos held on fiercely to the faith of their fathers—or that part of it which they were able to remember and reconstruct. Without books, without schools, without leadership, and above all in constant danger of being discovered, they held on —at what cost it is impossible to compute, but to what end it would be blasphemy to question.

It was only natural under these circumstances that many *conversos* should seek to leave their countries of origin. Indeed, despite legislation prohibiting New Christians from emigrating, many fled from Spain and Portugal by pretending to be going on religious pilgrimages. They fled everywhere—to the Levant, to Italy, Holland, England. Often special consideration was made for these Marranos in their new homes. João Migues, a Marrano refugee to Turkey, for a time was virtually ruler of the Turkish Empire. Alvaro Mendes was another who became powerful and important at the Turkish court.

In Italy, the city of Ferrara became a center of Marrano emigration. There the first Spanish translations of the Bible were produced for the Marranos. In Venice many Marranos joined the ghetto and lived freely as Jews. Pisa actually issued an invitation to Marrano Jews; within a few years of their arrival, that city, through their efforts, had become one of the most important ports in Italy.

The story in France is similar: so welcome were Marranos there that in 1624 the loyalty of the "Portuguese Merchants" was singled out for official praise. In 1730 they were formally recognized as Jews. Indeed, everywhere they went the Marranos played an important economic and commercial role. As the English author, Joseph Addison, wrote: "They are, indeed, so disseminated through all the trading parts of the world, that they are become the instruments by which the most distant nations communicate with one another, and by which mankind are knit together in a general correspondence." The Marranos were accepted in these countries as persons of a different faith rather than as members of a different people. They had equal rights, and their political emancipation was guaranteed by the government.

Judaized New Christians were at one time forbidden to enter the Low Countries. In 1565, however, fresh immigration began, and early in the seventeenth century a Jewish congregation with an enrollment of over four hundred families was formally established in Amsterdam. The former Marranos soon gained control of a large part of Dutch maritime commerce and constituted 25 per cent of the capital of the East India Company. Their official languages were Spanish and Portuguese. The standard of education in the community's school was very high. In 1627, Menasseh ben Israel established the first local Jewish printing press, and for the next two hundred years Amsterdam was the center of the Jewish book trade. Rembrandt van Rijn, living amidst them in the Jodenbreestraat, found in these fugitives an ideal subject for his brush. Despite an influx of Polish (Ashkenazi) Jews in 1648, Amsterdam remained for some time the spiritual center of the Sephardic Marranos and was called the "Dutch Jerusalem."

The Marrano community in England was quite small, but it included some prominent members. Oliver Cromwell patronized a settlement of Marranos because he felt they could assist in establishing London as a center of European commerce. Indeed, Menasseh ben Israel had paid a famous call on the Protector to plead the cause of his brethren. In 1664 a formal charter was issued to protect this community, which soon took its place beside Venice, Amsterdam, Hamburg, and Leghorn as an important Sephardi center. Freedom of worship was granted in 1673. The Anglo-Jewish community received almost equal treatment with the rest of the population, although no Jew could hold office because of the requisite Christian oath. England was able to maintain this largess

The district of the silversmiths on Palma de Mallorca is still inhabited by the people thought to be descendants of the Marranos.

because Jewish settlement on the island, ever since the expulsion of 1290, had never officially been condoned, and therefore could not officially be suppressed. Although they were by no means universally loved, the English Jews were conveniently tolerated; for the Protestant English, it was simply a matter of looking in the other direction. In 1701, the first synagogue since 1290 was constructed. As elsewhere, the Marranos in England proved capable physicians, financiers, and merchants. Their official language was Spanish or Portuguese. By 1755 the pure "Sephardi" community had become diluted by the advent of refugees from other countries, but credit for the re-establishment of English Jewry still lies firmly with the Marrano settlers.

We turn finally to the New World. "In the same month in which Their Majesties issued the edict that all Jews should be driven out of the Kingdom and its territories—in that same month they gave me the order to undertake with sufficient men my expedition of discovery to the Indies." Jewish involvement with the expedition of Columbus goes deeper, however, than the mere coincidence of dates mentioned by Columbus himself in this report to his patrons. The enterprise, in fact, was largely a Marrano one, both in inspiration and in financing, and there are even grounds for believing that Columbus was of a New Christian family. The expedition was made possible by a loan raised by Luis de Santangel, a financier of Marrano extraction. Gabriel Sanchez, the High-Treasurer of Aragon, of full Jewish descent, was a great patron of the expedition. It was to these two that Columbus issued his famous letter announcing his new discoveries. Many of his shipboard personnel were also of Jewish blood; the most famous of them was Luis de Torres, who was baptized just before sailing and was the first European to set foot in the new land. The Marranos soon realized the possibilities of the New World. By the sixteenth century they were masters of colonial commerce and most imports and exports passed through their hands. It is said that sugar-cane was first introduced to Brazil by the Marranos, and in 1640 the number of Jewish inhabitants in that country was alleged to be higher than that of Christians. In Surinam, under Dutch rule, the Jewish settlement also flourished, and the status of Jews in local affairs was considerable. So deeply had the Marranos penetrated life in the New World that an Inquisition was established as early as the sixteenth century to free the land from Jews and heretics. Numerous Judaizers suffered at the hands of the Tribunal, particularly in Mexico, where nine were burned at an *Auto de fé* in 1596.

The number of Marranos in the world today is very small. Indeed, for a long time it appeared that the Inquisition had blotted out all traces of Judaism in Spain and Portugal. But in 1917, a Polish Jew by the name of Scwarz, living in Lisbon, gathered information to disprove this contention. Scwarz discovered colonies of Marranos who even after the abolition of the Inquisition continued to practice their Judaism furtively. They still adhered to the basic Jewish beliefs and married only among themselves. Knowledge of Hebrew had all but disappeared, although the word *Adonai* (the Lord) was still remembered. Unknown to Jews elsewhere, these Marranos lived mainly in the villages of Portugal, where they were able to practice their secret religion without excessive fear of discovery. Today, the Marranos of Spain and Portugal are mainly of the lower middle class, and many are uneducated. Their Jewish consciousness has slowly been revived in the last half-century, due to the frequent visits of scholars and to the activity begun about the same time as Scwarz's discoveries by Barros Basto, a descendant of a New Christian family, who organized a formal congregation and established a synagogue for his community. In addition, a Portuguese Marrano committee was formed in London under the auspices of the *Alliance Israélite Universelle*, the Anglo-Jewish Association, and the Spanish and Portuguese community. Today, these Marrano communities are slowly being drained as the young men go off to the cities or marry outside the faith. A few have even gone to Israel to join their brethren once again. It does not seem likely that the Marranos of Spain and Portugal will survive the Age of Technology. But that they have survived to this day must be accounted one of the more wondrous achievements of an indomitable collective will. By this alone, one might say, a people's history has been vindicated.

13 ❧ New Centers of Jewish Settlement

OR FIFTEEN hundred years, world Jewry had been moving west-ward. At the beginning of the sixteenth century, following the brutal and traumatic expulsion from Spain and Portugal, this trend was suddenly reversed. Over 300,000 Jews, unwanted in the West, now sought shelter in new homes. Many of them went East, in the direction, once more, of their ancestral homeland. The Levant was now to assume central importance in the developing history of the Jewish people.

The arrival of large numbers of Jewish refugees in the countries of the Levant was to have an electrifying effect on these somnolent communities. Egypt, North Africa, Syria, and Palestine had all been experiencing a general population decline over the preceding centuries. In the thirteenth century the Mamelukes had inherited the old Fatimid Empire. The Mameluke regime, based on military strength and economic power, drained the citizens of strength and the land of resources; as a result of this ruthless policy, population figures declined to less than half of what they had been under the Fatimids. The population of Egypt, to take but one example, dwindled from four million to two million in this period. Naturally, Jewish population figures in these countries followed the general downward trend under the Mamelukes; many Jews, indeed, emigrated to Europe, only to return with their Western coreligionists after the waves of European expulsions.

Jews had already begun to flee to the Orient after the pogrom of Toledo in 1391. In 1430 refugees from Spain made their way to Adrianople and to the communities of North Africa, which their presence awakened to new life. The stream of refugees swelled in 1453, when the Ottoman Sultanate captured Constantinople and opened its doors to immigrants. After 1492 the numbers again rose to new heights. As in North Africa, in a short time Jews were to rise to prominence in the general and in the Jewish life of the countries of the Levant.

The Turks were essentially a military and agricultural people, and the trade of the Empire was left almost entirely in the hands of Jews, Armenians, and Greeks. Within decades of their arrival, Jews largely had control of international trade throughout the eastern part of the Mediterranean. Constantinople—the same city which in the year 330, as capital of Byzantium, had inaugurated the career of Jewish suffering over the next millennium—now became a place of refuge. At one of the most tragic moments in Jewish history, the Ottoman Empire offered asylum and hope to the shattered exiles from Spain: some 100,000 Jews and Marranos found shelter in Turkey, the first communities being established in Constantinople and Salonica. Among the newcomers were persons of high rank who immediately rose to important positions in the Ottoman Empire, like Joseph Hamon of Granada, who became physician to Sultan Selim I. As had been the case in Moslem North Africa and Spain, the relationship of the Sultanate to the whole of Christian Europe was one of hostility; among the foreign citizens living in the Ottoman Empire the Jews were the only ones of a different faith whose integrity and trustworthiness could be counted upon with some confidence.

In addition to the refugees from the Iberian peninsula, many Jews escaping from the religious wars and the religious zeal of the Reformation also sought the relative freedom of Turkish rule. By the middle of the sixteenth century, the Jews had become an important economic factor in Turkey, and had entered into a "Golden Age" of their own (having been granted the usual autonomy within their own community) which lasted until the death of Selim II in 1574. Many individuals rose to stations of importance and influence as physicians, financiers, and statesmen. With worldwide connections, their influence at the Court of the Sultans often enabled them to come to the help of their more unfortunate brethren in other countries. The most celebrated case of such intervention was that undertaken by Solomon ben Nathan Ashkenazi, who pre-

vented the expulsion of the Jews from Venice. Since the Spanish and Portuguese Jews of Turkey were skilled in the art of cannon manufacture, Ashkenazi was able to threaten Venice with the loss of Turkish support in its maritime ambitions should any harm befall his coreligionists in the Italian city. So powerful was Ashkenazi's influence that he succeeded in having the expulsion edict canceled.

The expansion of the Turkish Empire also saw the conquest of Palestine in 1517. The Ottomans found in the country a paltry total of 1176 households; the economy was at the brink of ruin. In a short time a great influx of refugees changed this picture drastically. The largest Jewish population was concentrated in the town of Safed in Galilee, where refugees from Jewish communities all over the Diaspora lived in their own quarters, named Castile, Aragon, Hungary, Italy, Germany, and so forth. Jerusalem was the second largest city, and Gaza, Hebron, Acre, and Tiberias also experienced revivals. Under Ottoman rule a period of prosperity began. Safed was the home of a thriving cloth and dyeing industry and became a transit market for the agricultural produce of the colonies in Galilee whose wares were then shipped to Damascus. Safed's prominence declined somewhat after the Turkish conquest of Cyprus in 1571, when new settlers, among them Jews from Safed, were compelled to move from Palestine to develop the economy of this new possession. This compulsory movement of settlers affected particularly the rich dyeing merchants of Safed.

But first and foremost, Safed achieved its importance as a city of learning. Scholars and rabbis who had previously been reckoned among the greatest luminaries of Spain, Portugal, and Sicily established themselves there in large numbers. Successive waves of persecution over the past centuries had caused a subtle shift in Jewish religious thought from a this-worldly to an other-worldly preoccupation; battered into shock by terrestrial events, many rabbis had turned to the compensatory rewards of mystical contemplation. In this search for ultimate meaning they relied heavily on the Zohar, the Book of Splendor, chiefly a mystical commentary on the Pentateuch. This work was ascribed to Rabbi Shimon ben Yochai, a *tanna* of the second century, who had lived and died in Safed; in all likelihood, however, it is the work of a medieval Spanish rabbi, Moses de Leon, a mystic and Kabbalist.

Safed in the sixteenth century was a center of renowned mystics, among them the *Ari the Holy* (Rabbi Isaac Luria), and his disciple Hayim Vital. Many Jews were driven to Palestine by an inner, messianic longing and by a mystical belief that the revival

Safed, the ancient Zephat of the Bible, has from the Middle Ages onward been a center of Jewish learning and scholarship. Seat of the Kabbalists, it was also the place where Joseph Karo wrote the Shulḥan Arukh.

of the homeland as a spiritual center of sanctity was a necessary precondition of universal redemption. The mystics of Safed strove not only to understand and systematize the mysterious workings of the Infinite, but to use their knowledge in order to redeem the world below, to usher in the era of universal peace. Thus, in the trauma of exile, these rabbis and scholars sought to find a comprehensible pattern, a clue to the workings of the Divine Will. Nor was this the preoccupation of the mystics alone. Another great scholar of Safed, Rabbi Joseph Karo (1488–1575), sought to unify the scattered remnants of Judaism through his monumental code of religious practice, the *Shulḥan Arukh* ("Prepared Table"), whose four volumes lay down detailed instruction on every aspect of life. To this day the *Shulḥan Arukh,* together with the commentaries which have grown up around it, remains the standard reference work on Orthodox Jewish observance.

Turkish Jewry   The Jews in Turkey formed a variegated and flamboyant element in the larger society, which looked upon their feverish activity with a mixture of admiration, wonderment, and scorn. We are fortunate in having a first-hand report on Turkish Jewry from the German diary of a sixteenth-century Bohemian public servant, some excerpts from which appear below:

> . . . In Turkey you will find in every town innumerable Jews of all countries and languages. And every Jewish group sticks together in accordance with its language. And whenever Jews have been expelled in any land they all come together in Turkey as thick as vermin; speak German, Italian, Spanish, Portuguese, French, Czechish, Polish, Greek, Turkish, Suriac, Chaldean, and other languages besides these. . . .

> The Jews are allowed to travel and to do business anywhere they wish in Turkey, Egypt, Missr (that is, Cairo), Alexandria, Aleppo, Armenia, Tataria, Babylonia as far as Persia, Roussen, Poland and Hungary. There is no spot in the world which hasn't some of its Jews in Constantinople, and there are no wares which the Jews do not carry about and trade in. Just as soon as a foreign ship comes in from Alexandria, Kaffa [now Feodosia in the Crimea], Venice and other places, the Jews are the first to clamber over the side. . . .

> There are all sorts of artisans among the Jews who make a living selling their products publicly, for in Turkey every man is

free to carry on his trade at home, in a shop, or on the streets. Whether he is skilled or not, knows little or much, no one has a word to say if he only pays his tax to the sultan and his rent for his shop. [Unlike the Christian lands, there were no limitations on Jews in Turkey in the practice of the crafts and commerce.] . . .

There are two cloth-shearers among the Jews and some among the Greeks, too. The Jews of Constantinople also have a printing press and print many rare books. They have goldsmiths, lapidaries, painters, tailors, butchers, druggists, physicians, surgeons, cloth-weavers, wound-surgeons, barbers, mirror-makers, dyers . . . silk-workers, goldwashers, refiners of ores, assayers, engravers. . . .

The sultan has never used any but a certain Jewish physician [Moses Hamon, d. about 1554] who probably rendered good service to him and the court. He was allowed to build a large stone house of three or four stories in the Jewish quarter. He died while we were at Constantinople. His son [Joseph] is also said to be a physician. He now has his father's position; is said to have a prescription to cure a bellyache. . . .

The Jews do not allow any of their own to go about begging. They have collectors who go about from house to house to collect into a common chest for the poor. This is used to support the poor and the hospital.

(From J. R. Marcus: *The Jew in the Medieval World*)

The two outstanding personalities among the immigrants to Turkey were Gracia Mendes and her nephew, Joseph Nasi, to whom she gave her daughter Reyna in marriage. The Mendes family was reported to be fabulously wealthy. They fled Portugal to Antwerp, Venice, and Ferrara before settling finally in Constantinople, where Gracia Mendes established her extensive business and took benevolent care of the needy Jews of the region. Her nephew Joseph soon became a valuable adviser to Suleiman the Magnificent, whom he was able to serve brilliantly through his world-wide diplomatic and commercial connections. In gratitude, the Sultan made over to Joseph, in perpetuity, the district of Tiberias in Palestine, which was to be transformed into an exclusive haven for Jewish refugees.

Upon acceding to his father's throne, Prince Selim II further rewarded Joseph by naming him Duke of Naxos and of a number of other islands on the Cyclades. At his gorgeous palace near Constantinople, Joseph received ambassadors from all over the Mediterranean world who came to sue for peace or to make common cause with Turkey. True to his people, Joseph took special interest in the welfare of the Jews in Europe, and was particularly assiduous in executing his plan for the resettlement of refugees in Tiberias. He had the city rebuilt with the intention of starting a manufacturing center in Palestine, as a practical measure to employ Jews and build up the economy of the country. Mulberry trees were planted for the raising of silkworms, and cloth was brought in from Venice. The Duke invited Jews to settle in this new colony, and many heeded his call, particularly those from the Papal States in Italy, who had been hardest hit by the restrictive and oppressive measures of Paul IV and Pius V. These first shiploads of emigrants, however, were seized in transit by Maltese pirates and sold into slavery. Too much occupied with his political schemes at home, Joseph was unable to give the colony at Tiberias the attention it needed, and the experiment failed. It must be reckoned, however, as one of the first practical plans for the resettlement of Jews in their homeland, and a forerunner of the schemes later put into effect by nineteenth-century Zionists. Indeed, Joseph in many ways resembled the greatest of all Zionists, Theodor Herzl: at home in the capitals of Europe, respected by non-Jews for his political skill and social grace, agitated by a dream of Jewish independence for which he was uniquely qualified to enlist the help and admiration of the nations.

The Beginnings of East-European Jewry

East-European Jewry, at least until the end of the eighteenth century, was located principally in what are today the Crimea, the Ukraine, White Russia (Byelorussia), Poland, and Lithuania. To this region Jewish settlers had been migrating since the last days of the Second Temple. The process of settlement began in the south of Russia, on the shores of the Black and the Azov Seas, where one of the most ancient communities in Europe was established. Many inscriptions, partly or entirely of Jewish content, have been found here, the oldest dating from the first century C.E. Those Jews who in ancient times settled north of the Black Sea were the first to bring monotheism to Eastern Europe. Monotheism in its Christian form spread only after the decline of the Roman Empire.

For six hundred years, despite contact between the littoral cities and the steppe provinces, Jews lived only along the northern corner of the Black Sea. In the seventh century, the Khazars took control of the steppe area between the Caspian and the Black Seas, and the

New Centers of Jewish Settlement

Jews now spread eastward to the center of the Khazar state. About the end of the tenth century, when, as we have already seen, Khazaria collapsed, defeated by the Russian Prince Sviatoslav, the Jewish settlement of the Caspian shore disappeared through assimilation and migrations.

The center of Jewish settlement in the East now became transferred to Kiev, the capital city of the Russian principality. By the tenth century Kiev was the political and cultural center of the southeastern Russian principalities and by the eleventh century it had become an urban commercial center as well. It boasted a permanent Jewish community, enjoying complete freedom of trade and commerce. To be sure, this community suffered severely in the political upheavals of the early twelfth century, but it was not forced to remove itself from Kiev; its population was in fact augmented after the Crusades, when immigrants from Germany also found their way to Kiev.

The Jews played a role in the flourishing foreign trade of Kiev, which for a time served as intermediary between Russia and Byzantium. At the end of the eleventh century, with the rise of the Italian cities and the eastward expansion of Christendom brought about by the Crusades, Kiev was forced to look for a new clientele. It was now that trade with the German states increased, and once again the Jew played an important part in blazing the new routes from Regensburg or Prague to Kiev via Poland or Hungary. The Jewish merchants were known in Hebrew as *holchei Russia* (Russian itinerants) or *holchei derachim al Russia* (Russian wayfarers). They traveled in caravans, often armed for safety. According to one source, these caravans included Jewish partners and non-Jewish mercenaries. The *holchei Russia* engaged in export from Germany, serving as agents for the manufacturers, and in import from Russia (where they were their own independent manufacturers).

Economic ties led inevitably to cultural ones. On occasion, a scholar would accompany the caravans from Germany, or Russian Jews would travel westward to study at the German *yeshivot*. Until the twelfth century there were also ties with Babylonia; Rabbi Moses of Kiev is known to have corresponded on *halakhic* matters with the principal of the *yeshivah* in Babylonia. On the whole, however, the culture of Russian Jewry was rather low at this time; indeed, Kiev was the only community which had a rabbi.

In the mid-thirteenth century the invading Mongols took possession of the Crimea, which they held until it fell to Turkish domination at the end of the fifteenth century. The Turkish con-

שבט

חֲמָתְךָ עַל הַגּוֹיִם
אֲשֶׁר לֹא יְדָעוּךָ וְעַל
הַמַּמְלָכוֹת אֲשֶׁר
בְּשִׁמְךָ לֹא
קָרָאוּ

סְפוֹךְ עֲלֵיהֶם זַעְמֶךָ וַחֲרוֹן
אַפְּךָ יַשִּׂיג גַּם תִּרְדֹּף בְּאַף
וְתַשְׁמִידֵם מִתַּחַת שְׁמֵי יְ־

quest resulted in closer commercial relations between the Jewish centers in the Crimea and those in the Levant.

While the Jewish colonies on the shores of the Black Sea and in southern Russia were formed mainly by immigrants from the Orient, Jewish settlement in Poland was due to newcomers from Western Europe—from the lands of German culture and "Latin faith." Jewish commercial caravans on the Regensburg-Kiev route left their first trace of settlement in Cracow, the principal Polish station on that route. Other permanent settlements sprang up in western Poland and Silesia. The propagation of Latin Christianity in Poland after 966 placed that country under the control of German emperors and German bishops, and the increased influx of German settlers was followed by one of Jewish merchants and settlers. A sparsely populated land, Poland had been largely ruined from continual invasions. Settlers were now encouraged to go there and help rebuild the economy, and among those who heeded the call were the Jews of Western Europe, who followed the path of the German pioneers. These Jews took with them from the West their traditions of communal organization and religious life; the German gentile brought with him his tradition of religious intolerance and political disenfranchisement for Jews.

At the end of the fourteenth century Poland and Lithuania united in a Federation. By this time Polish Jewry had become so entrenched a factor in the economy that the state was bound to deal with it formally. Charters were issued, and the Jews were given legal autonomy based on the privileges they had been granted in Central Europe, except for a few Karaite communities, whose autonomy was based on the Magdeburg Law. The basic principle was that the Jews were "servants of the treasury." In exchange for protecting their lives and property, the prince could do with them what he liked.

Jews were soon exposed to economic and class strife and religious antagonism, imported into Poland by the immigrants from Germany. As the Polish rulers found it necessary to encourage economic activity on the part of Jews for the benefit of the country, they were forced to enact laws to shield the Jews from the insults of their Christian neighbors. The most important statute defining the rights of the Jews was promulgated under Boleslav the Pious in 1264. This charter has a noteworthy preamble:

> The deeds of men, when unconfirmed by the voice of witnesses or by written documents, are bound to pass away swiftly and disappear from memory. Because of this we make it known to our

A 16th-century woodcut of a Haggadah from Mantua, Italy, showing Elijah entering Jerusalem. The words are from Psalm 79, "Pour out Thy wrath upon the nations that know Thee not, And upon the kingdoms that call not upon Thy name."

contemporaries as well as to our descendants, that the Jews, who have established themselves over the length and breadth of our country, have received from us the following statutes and privileges. . . .

Among the more important clauses in this charter are those guaranteeing the inviolability of Jewish persons and property and forbidding the harassment of Jewish merchants on the road, the extortion from Jews of higher duties than those paid by Christians, the destruction of Jewish cemeteries, or the defacing of synagogues.

While the temporal powers of the state, guided by the economic needs of the country, endeavored to establish Jewish life in Poland on rational civic foundations, the ecclesiastical authorities made every possible effort, just as they did in Western Europe, to detach the Jews from the general life of the country. Jews were segregated from the Christian population and reduced to the position of a despised caste. As had happened before, Jewish life in medieval Poland was at the mercy of two, often diametrically opposed, powers: the secular administration, moved by economic considerations, accorded the Jews the elementary rights of citizenship, while the Church, prompted by religious intolerance, endeavored to exclude them from civil life. The Catholic Synod of Breslau (1266) adopted a constitution, similar to the Laws of the Fourth Lateran Council, which resolved:

> In view of the fact that Poland is a new plantation on the soil of Christianity, there is reason to fear that her Christian population will fall an easy prey to the influence of the superstitions and evil habits of the Jews living among them, the more so as the Christian religion took root in the hearts of the faithful of these countries at a later date and in a more feeble manner. For these reasons we must strictly enjoin that the Jews shall not live side by side with the Christians but shall live apart in some section of the city or village.

In Lithuania, by the time of its federation with Poland, there were already a number of important Jewish communities, such as Brest, Grodno, Troki, Lutzk, and Vladimir. Between 1388 and 1430 the Jews of these communities received charters similar in content to the statutes of Boleslav and of Casimir the Great, who had reaffirmed the charter of Boleslav in 1334. In these enactments the Lithuanian sovereign demonstrated an enlightened concern for the development of a peaceful relationship between Christians and Jews and for the inner welfare of the Jewish community. The Jews enjoyed autonomy in internal affairs, as far as religion and prop-

A 15th-century miniature shows delegates from five Rhenish provinces—their shields below—paying tribute to Jupiter Vindex in Trier. From The Chronicle of Heinrich von den Beeck.

erty were concerned. They were guaranteed inviolability of person and property and the free pursuit of commerce and trade on terms equal to those granted to Christians. The taxes which they had to pay were not especially excessive. On the whole, their position was more favorable than that of the Jews in Poland.

Nevertheless, despite the existence of such charters in both Poland and Lithuania, anti-Jewish outbreaks characterized the early history of the Jewish communities in the region. The outbreaks were generally instigated by townsfolk resentful of Jewish competition, and were fostered by the tradition of hostility maintained by the Church and the masses alike. The threat of expulsion loomed over Poland's Jews as early as the fifteenth century, and in 1496 they were temporarily banished from the principality of Lithuania, in an action which may have been stimulated by the example of Spain. Widespread expulsions from Warsaw (in 1483), and later from Cracow (in 1491), set the pattern for future banishments from one city or another of the Federation.

Yet in the face of the growing opposition of the burgher class, and the hostility of the Church, the Jewish population of Poland and Lithuania advanced steadily in the fifteenth and sixteenth centuries. Jews were to be found in every branch of wholesale and retail trade, in export and import, in money-lending, in medicine, and in industry. But their economic rise did not go unopposed. From time to time restrictions were placed on their activity whenever it appeared to threaten the non-Jewish burghers. At the beginning of the sixteenth century, for instance, profit-taking was fixed by law at 8 per cent for Poles, 3½ per cent for Jews. Similarly, in 1538 tax-farming was taken out of the hands of Jews. Despite all these repressive efforts the Jews continued to retain a marked economic superiority until, at the beginning of the seventeenth century, religious excesses under the direction of the Jesuits combined with economic restrictions to drive the Jews from the towns into the country. There they became middlemen for the sale of agricultural produce, until this activity too was forbidden, and 60,000 Jewish families were left destitute.

It is estimated that by the middle of the seventeenth century half a million Jews were living in Poland, spread over hundreds of communities. Jews were able to live and maneuver in Poland partly because they fitted into the intervening space between two opposing interests within the Polish economy, that of the burghers and that of the nobility. The noblemen demanded free enterprise, in order to promote their newly-organized agricultural estates to the best advantage, and in this they opposed the burghers who maintained monopolized privileges in the economy. Between the two, by exercising considerable tact and agility, the Jew could manage to survive, and even to climb over the economic barriers placed before him.

The Council of
the Four Lands The Jews had come to Poland with their own system of autonomous laws. The basis of the well-organized community was the *kehillah,* which bound the individuals dwelling together within a given city into an association with its own regulations, its own synagogue and cemetery, its own rabbis and religious judges, and all the other services required by an organized community. The governing body of the *kehillah* was the *kahal,* a committee elected by the more prominent members of the community. The main community expenditures went for welfare, health, and education. The officers of the *kahal* were unpaid. They saw to it that each man lived within his means and that each man was taxed according to his ability to pay. In raising the taxes demanded by the Crown, the wealthy and middle classes covered the payments for the poor.

The *Vaad Ha'aratzot* (Council of *kehillot*) dealt with matters both internal and external with which the *kehillah* would not cope, or with matters concerning all Jews in a given province. During the sixteenth century such regional organizations were established throughout the country; the over-all supervisory became known as the Council of the Four Lands (*Vaad Arba Aratzot*). The four countries were Great Poland, Little Poland, Russian Poland—or Volhynia—and Lithuania. The Council grew out of meetings held at the great fairs at Lublin and Yaroslav, where communal leaders and judges dealt respectively with organizational and administrative problems and with legal and religious questions affecting the general welfare. As recognition grew of a community of interests among the Jews of the various provinces, these "fair councils" merged into a permanent organization of provincial councils. The Council of the Four Lands was the supreme legislative and executive body of Polish Jewry. It rendered legal decisions and promulgated regulations binding on all communities represented at the Council. The officials of the Council were also *shtadlanim*—men who had access to the gentile authorities—or trustees who farmed

New Centers of
Jewish Settlement

211

the royal revenues collectable from the Jewish population. The moral authority of the Council was recognized outside the borders of Poland as well, throughout the Ashkenazi cultural sphere and even beyond.

From 1648 on, a series of catastrophes inundated Poland and brought disaster upon the Jewish communities. The years 1648–1649 saw a Tatar invasion, led by the Cossack hetman Bogdan Chmielnitzki, which laid waste large sections of southern and eastern Poland and resulted in unspeakable massacres of Polish Jews. In 1654 the Muscovites invaded the northeastern section and in 1655 the Swedes destroyed the west. The Tatars and Muscovites fought against "nobility, clergy, and Jews." Jews were expelled, or banished into the Russian interior (many having been forcibly converted or sold as slaves), or simply slaughtered. At least 100,000 perished. Great numbers fled the country for Hungary, Turkey, Holland, and Germany.

The Development of the Ghetto

In medieval Europe Jews were placed outside the main currents of political, social, and cultural life. They formed a class apart, denied any rights of citizenship. The total effect of the medieval scheme was to segregate the Jew completely from his environment. Politically, socially, intellectually, he was to be cut off from all contact with the non-Jewish world around him. This isolation was symbolized by the institution of the ghetto—a term which dates from the year 1516, when the Venetian Republic ordered the segregation of the Jews in a special quarter, formerly known as the "Ghetto Nuovo," or New Foundry.

Yet if the individual languished in his confinement, Jewish group life thrived. A pattern of community organization evolved in the ghetto which was almost uniform throughout all the towns of Europe. Indeed, long before the Church had enacted compulsory segregation, Jews had developed a self-protective tendency to live in separate quarters. The need for internal discipline in order to maintain the purity of the Jewish faith and to allow the free development of a uniquely Jewish society, as well as the need for an institution providing mutual aid against a hostile world, made the ghetto a convenience, if not an inevitability, even before it became a compulsion.

New Centers of Jewish Settlement

In early medieval records the Jewish quarters which existed in every important town were called *Vici Judaeorum*—"Jewries"—a name which reappeared in all modern tongues as *Juderia, Juiverie* or, simply, *Judengasse* (in Germany and Austria) or *Jodenstraat* (in Holland), or *Giudecca* (in Italy). In Rome the Jews had occupied a section near the Tiber from earliest times. In early medieval cities Jewish settlers and merchants usually sought protection in the fortified sections of the city, near the residence of the representative of the Crown or the Church. (A street just off the famous Cathedral of Rouen is still called *rue des Juifs.*) This quarter could be closed off by massive doors bolted from within. For the ghetto was initially intended as much to keep enemies out as to keep Jews in. This precaution was particularly useful at Easter time, when no Jew dared show his face outside the ghetto walls, for fear of blood accusations.

Since the original area of the ghetto was rarely increased, Jews came to live in appalling conditions of overcrowding. Their houses could grow only vertically, and often came to tower over the rest of the city. Overcrowding led to another important development. Since Jews were not allowed to own real estate, a system had to be devised to prevent dispossession of tenants through the greed of landlords. On the basis of the ancient law of *ḥazakah*—proprietary right—the tenant was protected from the threat of eviction resulting from overbidding. Nobody was permitted to bring about the expropriation of a tenant, or to offer the landlord a higher rental fee than that paid by the present occupant.

Not everywhere were the laws of the ghetto enforced with equal rigidity. But in its general configurations the life of the Jewish community was similar throughout Europe, whether particular Jewry was sealed off by a bolted gate or not. In Venice, Prague, and Frankfort, the pattern was the same. Ghettos may have varied widely in physical appearance, but there was little difference in the mode of life as it unfolded in the ghettos of Italy, Germany, Austria, and Bohemia.

"Build a fence around the Torah," the ancient Rabbis enjoined; and this is precisely what the Jews of the ghetto did. Talmudic law, by which life in the ghetto was regulated, received its fullest application in this period. The same discipline of legal and moral integrity which had proved so adequate a defense against Rome in the days of Johanan ben Zakkai was now employed against the heirs of Rome, the Holy Roman Empire and the Catholic Church.

By and large, the Jew was left alone with his fence and with the garden of life and law which he tended within it. The Church at the time was burning Christians for secretly embracing the mere

In Poland synagogues were modelled on fortresses for communal protection against persecution and pogrom. Here, the rare and beautifully designed late 18th-century wooden synagogue at Wolpa.

shadow of such disbelief as the Jew preached openly and unmolested in his synagogues. The state raised armies to crush unbelievers at home and abroad, while it shielded the Christ-denying servants of its treasury. So long as the Jews were able to exploit this paradox by remaining, in effect, invisible, they were allowed to survive. When their activity appeared to threaten either one or the other of the two powers which suffered them to live, the results were catastrophic. Such, for a number of centuries, was the price of Jewish survival.

Within the ghetto, the synagogue was the hub and nucleus of communal life, together with the schools connected to it. Indeed, intensive education, at all levels, was the distinctive and controlling feature of Jewish life. It was not an abstract, academic truth which scholars of the ghetto sought in their studies; they lived by the teachings they pored over in the academy. Talmudism, as the Jew felt it, meant a preoccupation with existential reality, not a denial of it. The thousands of communal regulations issued by the great medieval rabbis represented the fruits of an ongoing adjustment of legal norms and precepts to the conditions surrounding the Jew in his new world.

Aside from synagogues and schools, the Jews had their own courts and administrative offices. Occasionally they even achieved the dignity of a town hall. They had communal baths, bakeries, slaughter-houses, inns, cemeteries, and even prisons, administered by their own elected authorities. The government of the community was vested in a body of *parnasim* (leaders), usually numbering twelve in the larger centers. One of these, as a rule the rabbi, was recognized by the secular authorities as the responsible head of the Jewry, often called Jew's Bishop in Germany. Indeed, the *Judengasse* was a republic unto itself: a training ground in self-government that prepared generations of Jews in the intricacies of civil government and in the prideful execution of democratic order.

Into the ghetto the Jew had taken his own language, a South-German vernacular of the thirteenth century. He spiced it with Hebrew words and he translated into it, especially for the women-folk, not only Scriptures, prayers, and moral writings, but folk tales and anecdotes; a specimen of this latter type of literature, the *Maase-Buch,* survived down to our own time in the Polish *shtetl.* The Yiddish language was carried by the Jews into their exiles in Poland and Hungary, Russia and Bohemia; its spread was only halted by the equally stubborn Ladino dialect spoken by the Spanish Jews in the Mediterranean countries.

Today the Prague ghetto has become a museum piece, a microcosmic relic not only of the heritage of its own inhabitants through forty generations, but of other Jewish communities of Bohemia and Moravia where life flourished up until the Second World War. A collection of religious treasures and other Jewish memorabilia—a collection begun by the Nazis with the plunder taken from numerous Czech Jewish communities—stands now in Prague as mutely eloquent testimony to the rich life of a host of communities which are no more, and to the barbarous movement which destroyed them.

The old Prague ghetto, known as a "City and Mother in Israel," was one of the most celebrated settlements in the Diaspora. Its reputation for distinction rested on its famous scholars and its architectural monuments, as well as on the fact that it had been left in relative peace by the rulers and people of Prague.

The ghetto's best known monument is the Old-New Synagogue, built in the second half of the thirteenth century. The synagogue and its adjacent Jewish Town Hall became the symbol of this famous Jewish community. The synagogue and the old Jewish cemetery still stand; the cemetery in particular, with its intricately sculpted gravestones, provides a wealth of information about life among the Jews of Prague. Among the many luminaries buried there is David Gans (1541–1613), an astronomer and mathematician and one of the first Jewish historiographers of the modern age. Rabbi Judah Loew, the miracle-worker of Prague, is also buried in this cemetery; until World War II, troubled Jews would make pilgrimages to his grave with requests for his intercession.

The history of the Prague ghetto may be said to have begun about the year 900, when the Jews in the city had increased so greatly in number that they were granted a large site on the right bank of the Vlatava, known as the Old Town of Prague. (Historical evidence indicates that there existed a Jewish settlement in Prague prior to this date.) The Bohemian kings profited nicely from the Jewish colonists, who founded a tradition of commercial astuteness in Prague famous even beyond the borders of Bohemia. Until the twelfth century the Jews lived in Prague in freedom. Then, in 1150, the Jewish Town was attacked by a sect just exiled from Bohemia. The Jews resisted: "the Jewish butchers rushed out with their choppers and drove the attackers from the town." As a reward for having defended royal property, the Jews were granted the privilege of adding the double-tailed Bohemian lion to their emblem. They were also allowed to fortify their town with bastions

The brooding tumbledown jostling intimacy of the gravestones in the Prague cemetery where the bones of the great Rabbi Judah Loew ben Bezalel, putative creator of the Golem, rest among his compatriots of the Czech Jewish community.

as protection against similar attacks. The Jewish Town now took on the shape of a fortified ghetto.

In 1349, when the plague reached Bohemia and spread through Central and Eastern Europe, the Jews in Prague were protected by Charles IV, the Holy Roman Emperor, as his personal servants, and so escaped the ravages their brethren suffered elsewhere. The University of Prague, known as Charles University, was founded in the house of Charles IV's Jewish treasurer, Lazar. It was one of the first European universities to admit Jewish students and to grant doctor's degrees to Jews. Even under the anti-Semitic rule of the Hapsburg Empress Maria Theresa (1717–1780), Christians and Jews continued to study there side by side. The first Jew to be awarded the degree of Medical Science was Beer Joss—the event, which occurred in 1788, was celebrated as a holiday throughout the Prague ghetto. Many Jews subsequently served as lecturers and professors at this university, which was among the first to open the gates of its knowledge to Jewish students.

It was in April 1389, on the last day of Passover, that the first pogrom occurred in the Jewish city. Sand had been thrown at a priest walking down a street, and as the story passed from mouth to mouth, it became each time a little more distorted and a little more horrifying. The Jews proved an admirable target against which to unleash pent-up emotions. Into the Jewish Town raged the mob, murdering innocent men, women, and children, and plundering the homes. Over four thousand were massacred; those who survived formed a dispirited and broken group which for years lived in poverty and misery.

In 1594, Rabbi Judah Loew, originally of Moravia, became Chief Rabbi of Prague at the age of eighty. Rabbi Loew is the renowned creator of the Prague *golem*—an automaton which came to life when a piece of paper inscribed with the Divine Name was placed in its mouth. The *golem* remained the servant of its creator so long as the paper remained in its mouth, but became a monster of destruction or an inert mass when the Ineffable Name was removed. Rabbi Judah Loew's *golem,* aptly enough, worked only on weekdays and rested on the Sabbath. Whenever an injustice was committed against the Jews of Prague, the *golem* intervened on their behalf, and so came to be known as the staunch defender of the Prague ghetto. It was this magical being which allegedly relieved the Jews from their hardships during the period of the Counter-Reformation, when the Jesuits attempted to convert them to Catholicism.

Mordechai Maisl (1528–1601), a mayor of the Jewish Town, is

The Frankfurt Judengasse *in Germany about 1870.*

another well-known figure in Prague's history. Maisl was a very wealthy financier, benevolent and generous, who put his heart and enormous energy into renovating the Jewish Town. He had the whole quarter paved at his expense, founded a hospital and Talmudic High School on his own land, and built a synagogue. He also had the Town Hall rebuilt after it was destroyed by fire.

In 1648 the Jews were again called to the patriotic defense of Prague, this time against the onslaught of the Swedish General Koenigsmark and his invading armies. In return for their help the Jews were granted the right to live in any of the imperial cities and royal towns of Bohemia, and the right to participate in all trades except armament. As a visible symbol of appreciation the Jewish Town received a large red flag with a six-pointed star and a Swedish helmet in the center. This flag became the official banner of the Jewish Town.

But such moments were not destined to last. In 1689, the ghetto was leveled by a fire in which hundreds were burned to death. Not until 1704 was the ghetto rebuilt. In 1744, the Empress Maria Theresa issued a tragic order of expulsion for the Jews of Prague. In response, the Ashkenazi community of London, in one of the first interventions of philanthropy in Jewish history, sought an interview with King George II to plead for their brethren. Moved by this plea, the King ordered his ambassador in Vienna to speak with the Queen-Empress about the matter. Others, too, protested and in 1749 the order was rescinded in return for a promise to pay new and even higher taxes. But less than half the community's original Jews returned in 1749. After their return Maria Theresa issued an order "for all Jews without beards," including women, to wear the yellow badge. This humiliating edict was repealed in 1781 by the Emperor Joseph.

In 1848 all discriminatory legislation against the Jews of Prague was removed, and a year later they were granted equality by Franz Joseph—a momentous event in the history of the Prague ghetto. In 1852, the ghetto itself was officially abolished. The social and legal barriers between the Jews and other inhabitants of Prague had at last been removed.

Jews in Holland

New Centers of Jewish Settlement

Large-scale immigration of Jews into Holland began immediately after 1579, when the Union of Utrecht, which marked the termination of the revolt of Protestant Holland against the Spanish Crown, proclaimed freedom of conscience throughout the Dutch states. The majority of those who rallied early to this declaration of tolerance were Marranos, seeking refuge from the Spanish and Portuguese Inquisition. Story has it that the first to arrive in Holland was the Marrano family of Mayor Rodrigues, which set sail in its own boat from Portugal together with a few other refugees. At sea, the party was captured by an English captain, who was finally induced to allow the refugees to continue on course. They arrived in Emden; the rabbi of this German-Jewish community, Moses Uri, persuaded them to go on to Amsterdam.

The Emden rabbi, having followed the group to Amsterdam, began to instruct them in Judaism, and soon they were all received back into their ancient faith. Ironically, these Marranos were at first suspected by the Protestant Dutch of being Papists in disguise: on the Day of Atonement, 1596, officials of the town fell upon the small congregation and arrested Moses Uri and his son as traitors. The error, however, was quickly explained; the Jews were now granted the right to profess their religion openly, and in 1598 to build a synagogue. News of favorable treatment encouraged other Jews to settle in Holland; Amsterdam soon boasted a community of four hundred families and a number of Hebrew printing presses, the presence of which marked the beginning of a tradition that made the town a foremost center of Jewish book trade for hundreds of years.

Throughout the seventeenth century the economic activities of the Jews in Holland were extensive and productive; their share in the financial operations of the country was far out of proportion to their numbers. A committee of forty-one, for instance, appointed by the Amsterdam Stock Exchange, had thirty-seven Jewish members, and fully a quarter of the stockholders in the Dutch East India Company were Jews. So efficacious were Jewish merchants in promoting Dutch maritime trade that various other European monarchs began to invite Jewish settlers to perform similar functions in their own domains, much to the anger and spirited opposition of gentile merchants.

The spiritual life of Dutch Jewry was anchored in traditionalism. Religious discipline in the ghetto was rigorously maintained and social solidarity enforced; the type of person who inhabited this world has been immortalized in Rembrandt's portraits of ghetto Jews. Yet the ghetto spawned its measure of secularist spirits too, among them the brilliant and iconoclastic philosopher, Baruch Spinoza, who evidently posed a threat of such magnitude to the

A sensitive Rembrandt portrait of a
patriarchal Amsterdam Jew.

cohesiveness of the Amsterdam community that in 1656 he was excommunicated from its midst by the rabbinate. Spinoza had received his education at the *yeshivah* in Amsterdam, but had become involved with various Christian notables in philosophical discussions. Although in his opinion remaining a Jew, Spinoza preached a gospel that was strictly heretical; he opposed rabbinical authority and the claims made in behalf of revelation, maintaining that the state must ensure freedom of thought. Unsure of itself, the Amsterdam community could not afford the luxury of so powerful a dissenter as Spinoza. His thought went largely ignored by Jewish philosophers, entering rather into the mainstream of European philosophy, upon which it had an immense and long-lasting effect. For it is from Spinoza that modern philosophy may be said to have taken its start, just as it is with Spinoza that medieval philosophy may be said to have come to an end.

Jewish life in Holland remained relatively stable for the next century and a half. In 1795, Holland became the Batavian Republic, and equality for all citizens, including Jews—who now numbered about 50,000—was guaranteed. Jews were now invited to take part in the elections to the first Batavian National Assembly, and although none was returned, a precedent of equality had thus been established which continued through the subsequent period of Dutch monarchic rule.

Jews in England

The unofficial readmission of Jews to England had its origins under the reign of Oliver Cromwell. At this time, Christian millenarian expectations and a reawakening of interest in the Old Testament sparked by the Puritan movement conjoined to initiate a new attitude of tolerance toward the Jews, who, it was believed, must be allowed to settle in the British Isles to fulfill the condition of total dispersion necessary for universal redemption. Jewish settlers soon found a niche in the economic life of London and other cities. By the end of the seventeenth century they occupied important posts in the East India Company and had twelve seats on the London Stock Exchange. Prosperous Jewish merchants and financiers were accepted into English society.

No small role in the drama of the readmission of Jews to England was played by the prolific and talented *diplomat extraordinaire*, Menasseh ben Israel of Amsterdam. Menasseh was the scion of a Marrano family that had settled in Amsterdam. Although not profoundly learned, he possessed a fertile and imaginative grasp of the issues which agitated his contemporaries, and in the position of communal leader, teacher, printer, and publisher, he swiftly gained a reputation in the gentile world as the very type and model of the best in Jewry. Among his admirers was Rembrandt, who in one of his most famous portraits caught the features of this colorful rabbi for all posterity.

Aside from his other gifts, Menasseh was bountifully endowed with a talent for letter-writing—in excellent Latin, Spanish, and English—that was to serve him in outstandingly good stead in his international campaign for the readmission of the Jews to England. Following is the epistolary crown of Menasseh ben Israel's political career, the letter written to Oliver Cromwell in September 1655 that was to prove incalculably influential in the Protector's decision to readmit the Jews to England's shore.

> These are the boons and the favors which I, Menasseh ben Israel, in the name of my Hebrew nation, beseech of your most serene Highness, and may God prosper you and give you much success in all your undertakings. Such is the wish and desire of your humble servant.
>
> I. The first thing which I ask of your Highness is that our Hebrew nation be received and admitted into this mighty republic under the protection and care of your Highness like the citizens themselves, and for greater security in the future I entreat your Highness, if it is agreeable to you, to order all your commanders and generals to defend us on all occasions.
>
> II. That it please your Highness to allow us public synagogues, not only in England, but also in all other conquered places which are under the power of your Highness, and to allow us to exercise our religion in all details as we should.
>
> III. That we should be allowed to have a plot or cemetery outside the city for burying our dead without being molested by anyone.
>
> IV. That it be allowed us to trade freely in all sorts of merchandise just like every one else.
>
> V. That (in order that those who come in shall do so for the benefit of the citizens and live without doing harm or causing trouble to any one) your most serene Highness should appoint a person of prominence to inform himself of those who enter and to receive their passports. He should be informed of those who arrive and should oblige them to take an oath to be faithful to your Highness in this country.
>
> VI. And in order that the justices of the peace should not at all be bothered with litigation and quarrels which may arise among

those of our nation, we ask that your most serene Highness grant the liberty to the rabbi of associating with himself two Jewish clergymen in order to adjust and to judge all the disputes at law in conformity with the Mosaic code, with the privilege, nevertheless, of appealing a sentence to the civil judges. The sum to which the party will have been condemned must first be deposited, however [before the appeal from the Jewish court to the state court is made].

VII. That if, peradventure, there should be any laws against our Jewish nation, then first and before all things they should be revoked so that by this means it should be possible for us to live with greater security, under the safeguard and protection of your most serene Highness.

If your most serene Highness grants us these things we will always be most attached to you and under obligations to pray to God for the prosperity of your Highness and of your illustrious and most sage Council. May it be His will to grant much success to all the undertakings of your most serene Highness. Amen.

(From J. R. Marcus: *The Jew in the Medieval World*)

Jews in the Renaissance and Reformation

The Italian cities most directly affected by the new birth of humanistic studies in the fourteenth and fifteenth centuries were Rome, Florence, Milan, Genoa, and Venice—cities whose Jewish communities were also caught up in the intellectual ferment of the Renaissance. The cities of Italy had but recently received a great influx of Jews fleeing from the Spanish Inquisition or from persecution in Northern Europe. Unable to compete with the rising class of Italian merchants and international traders, many Jews turned to money-lending and banking, professions in which their skill was recognized and rewarded.

The story of the Jews in the Renaissance is a story of individuals. For the most part, the Jewish community as a whole remained untouched by the winds of change that swept the intellectual world in this period. Many individual Jews, however, found in the more open social climate an opportunity to exercise their unique talents as cultural intermediaries, as well as to cultivate their newly receptive Christian neighbors. Jews, for instance, were sought as teachers of Hebrew and of Kabbalah—subjects to which the Italian humanists were particularly attracted. One such Jew was Elijah Levita (1468–1549), who taught Hebrew to Cardinal Egidio in exchange for instruction in Greek. Similar teaching positions were held by Jews in Florence, Sienna, Mantua, Padua, and in Venice. The re-

New Centers of Jewish Settlement

vival of Hebrew studies in the Italian Renaissance was such that Hebrew tutors were busy all over Italy. A knowledge of Hebrew was needed both for a correct interpretation of the Bible and for philosophical studies. The great religious reformers of the age Erasmus, Calvin, Reuchlin, and Luther, all were students of Hebrew. In 1488 a chair for Hebrew was established at the University of Bologna; other Italian universities soon followed suit, as Christian Hebraists flocked to study the Holy Tongue from Jewish scholars and teachers.

Hand in hand with the study of Hebrew went a renewed interest in ancient Hebrew manuscripts. Pope Sixtus IV, who built the Sistine Chapel of the Vatican, acquired a magnificent collection of Hebrew manuscripts for the Vatican Library. This collection was augmented by Pope Nicholas V with the help of Gianozzo Manetti, a Florentine scholar and statesman, who had learned Hebrew from a servant.

The Renaissance humanists, along with their interest in the literary splendor of ancient Greece, were fascinated by the Arab inheritors of the Greek philosophical tradition, notably Averroes and Avicenna. The works of these great representatives of Arabic thought were made available to European intellectuals through a circuitous route, for the barrier dividing the Moslem and the Christian worlds was not merely a religious one, but a cultural and linguistic one as well: the learned world that wrote and thought in Latin had had no contact with the world that wrote and thought in Arabic. Here again the Jews, who alone had an intellectual foothold in both of these worlds, played an important role. Jews had already translated into Hebrew many of the scientific texts studied by Arabs, and thus had access to intellectual resources of which most erudite Christian scholars were completely unaware. By retranslating these works into Latin, Jewish linguists and scholars contributed enormously to the broadening of European cultural horizons and to the education of many individual thinkers.

Apart from the few Jews who were employed as teachers of Hebrew at the Italian universities, the record of Jewish admittance to institutions of higher learning during the Renaissance is a poor one. From most universities Jews were simply excluded, although there were exceptions to this rule, notably at Padua, where the first Jew to receive a doctorate was graduated in 1409. Nevertheless, the level of education among Jews was high, as it had always been, and Jews who were themselves not university-trained were on occasion offered instructorships at Italian universities. Such was the

A poetic portrait of the entrance to the Cracow ghetto in Poland embodies the feeling of a hundred East-European ghettos where Jews lived their daily round and Judaism thrived.

case, for instance, with Don Judah Abarbanel, known as Leone Ebreo, who was the scion of a famous Spanish-Jewish family and the author of the well-known neo-Platonic philosophical treatise, *Dialoghi di Amore.*

The invention of the printing press was another of the revolutionary advances made in the Renaissance, and its impact was soon felt in the Jewish world. The first section of the Old Testament to be printed in Hebrew was the Book of Psalms, which appeared in 1477. In 1488, the first complete Bible in Hebrew appeared under the imprint of the Soncino family, which was responsible for the production of some of the finest incunabula printed in Italy at this time. The most famous name connected with Hebrew printing is that of Daniel Bomberg, a non-Jew who was born in Antwerp and opened his press in Venice. Bomberg issued three different editions of the Hebrew Bible with commentaries, the first printed edition of the Babylonian Talmud (1523–1525), as well as Midrashim and philosophical and liturgical works. In Venice, which soon became the capital of the Hebrew publishing world, some of the most eminent Jewish personalities of the Renaissance—among them the colorful Rabbi Judah Leon Modena—oversaw the editing and proofreading of many a pioneer edition of printed Hebrew texts.

As the humanist spirit spread through Europe, new chairs of Hebrew studies were established along the Italian pattern at universities elsewhere. Elijah Levita, the self-same tutor to Cardinal Egidio in Rome, was invited to occupy one such chair at the University of Paris, but declined on the grounds that his coreligionists were excluded from residing within the city limits. In England chairs for the study of Hebrew were established at Cambridge in 1540 (under Henry VIII) and in London (by the Merchant Taylors) in 1561.

In Germany, it appeared for a short time that the fresh breeze of humanism would dispel the heritage of blood and tears that had been the lot of the Jews in that country, and that a measure of freedom and more humane treatment would finally be granted them. This was the eve of the Reformation, and the era of the famous Pfefferkorn-Reuchlin case. Johann von Reuchlin was the most distinguished humanist in Germany. In his research into the ancient world he had become an ardent student of Hebrew literature. In 1494 he wrote a dialogue, *De Mirifico Verbo,* wherein he praised the beauties of Hebrew, "the language in which God, angels, and men spoke together," and followed this eulogy with one of the first Hebrew grammars and dictionaries. The Church did not observe this enthusiastic study with equanimity. For some time the humanists had been under suspicion by the watchful Dominicans of engaging in a potentially heretical enterprise. To protect the unity of the Church and deter the critical study of Scripture, the Dominicans turned to Johann Pfefferkorn, a baptized Jew, whom they encouraged to publish inflammatory pamphlets against the Talmud, exposing its contents as blasphemies against Christ, the Virgin, and the Apostles. Pfefferkorn won the ear of the Emperor Maximilian, who ordered the seizure and examination of all Hebrew books in Germany, and the destruction of those hostile to the true faith. Upon representations of leaders of the Jewish community, the whole matter was placed in charge of a commission, which was to decide "if the burning of Jewish literature were godly, laudable, and beneficial to the Christian faith." Both Pfefferkorn and Reuchlin served on this commission. In 1510 Reuchlin rendered his opinion. He maintained that Hebrew commentaries on the Bible could be of service to Christians. Kabbalistic writings, he found, supported and elucidated Christian doctrine. Prayer books must not be molested since Church and State recognized the right of the Jews to practice their cult. As to the Talmud, he confessed he had never read it and knew practically nothing about it. But, he added, the same could be said for many others who nevertheless condemned it. Finally, he proposed that every German university should establish courses in Hebrew: in this way Christians would gain a better understanding of Christianity and could more easily persuade the Jews of its truth.

But the battle did not end here. The Church sought backing for its repressive attitude in all theological quarters in Europe. In 1513, both parties appealed to the Pope, Leo X—a known humanist, but a canny politician. As pressure from the Dominicans mounted, and cries were heard for the general expulsion of the Jews, the Emperor Maximilian finally ordered the entire project dropped. In 1520 the Pope rendered a formal verdict against Reuchlin.

The Church, meanwhile, was faced with secession from within. Growing demands for reform, backed by the humanists, had culminated in 1517 in Martin Luther's notorious gesture of defiance at Wittenberg. At the height of his struggle with Catholicism, Luther advocated more tolerant treatment of Jews. He reminded Christendom that to no other people had God shown so much favor as when he had entrusted to the Jews the Holy Word. In 1523, with the publication of Luther's pamphlet, "That Jesus Was

Born a Jew," it suddenly seemed that the Reformation might indeed bring about a return to Christianity as a religion of love. But Luther, like Mohammed before him, was only acting out of hopes of converting the Jews to the new faith. When it became clear that the latter were not about to abandon their ancestral religion, and that his missionary overtures, like those of his Moslem predecessor, were futile efforts, Luther turned upon this stiff-necked people with all the virulence and fanaticism of a Dominican friar. In his later inveighings against the Jews every accusation of the Catholic Church, from ritual murder to poisoning of the wells, was repeated word for word in scurrilous language. The Christian world was eventually to inherit a measure of freedom as a result of the Reformation; not so the Jews. Their search for freedom was to be longer and more arduous. Centuries were to pass before liberty would be granted at last to the people who had taught the meaning of liberty to the world—and from whom liberty had been longest withheld.

14 ❧ Mysticism and Messianism

NORMALLY, a people lives by its geography; the most enduring element in any national history is the ground which nature provides as a home. This is not so with the Jews; and yet they endured. Lacking a political homeland of their own, dispersed among the lands of the earth, they nevertheless took with them into the Diaspora a priceless cultural and religious heritage which ensured a community of spirit and a unity of purpose that were to sustain them despite the loss of their sovereignty. Their loyalty went forth not to temporal rulers, but to an idea, a way of life, a Book. When Israel went into dispersion, its culture already had a coherent character, shaped by the lofty themes and moral imperatives of the Bible. As this was a book of divine origin, its ultimate truth was immutable, although its precepts, as interpreted by the fertile and searching minds of the Talmudic age, might be adapted to new environments and to changing political conditions. From the Bible the Jew also drew his history, his science, his principles of ethics, his law. This body of writing provided the bedrock of all religious and ethical thought. Mined for its multiform layers of meaning, its strata of significance, it became, together with the volumes of interpretative commentary that rose up around it, a unique literary structure, a monument of thought and feeling upon which rested the full weight of a people's spiritual strivings over the long centuries of *galut*.

The story of these strivings has many chapters. Jewish cultural activity included the writing of legal exegesis and religious philosophy, of homiletics and poetry, of Biblical commentary and narrative fiction. In scope, it ranged all the way from sober rationalism to the unbridled heights and soaring rhetoric of mystical speculation.

As the persecutions of the Middle Ages increased in intensity, some Jews tended to withdraw more and more from reality, and to find solace in the contemplation of the great universal mysteries. The *geonic* period, which followed upon the completion of the Talmud, may be regarded as the classical age of Jewish mysticism. It was in this period that the *Book of Creation* appeared, a curious work ascribing supernatural power to the forms, sounds, position, and numerical value of the letters of the Hebrew alphabet. For those unsatisfied with traditional faith, or with the answers given to questions of belief by the exercise of reason, this book provided a wellspring of spiritual regeneration. It is one of the primary literary sources of the great body of Jewish mystical thought—the Kabbalah.

The generation of Maimonides, a philosopher who had exalted the works of Aristotle and who had striven to establish rational harmony from confusion, was followed by a generation that glorified the Kabbalah and wrote commentaries to the *Book of Creation*. A spiritual reaction swept over the Jews of Spain, a mystic flight that was to gather momentum among scholars who flocked to the banner of the occult sciences. Out of this spiritual uprising came the Zohar, the Book of Splendor, a work attributed to Rabbi Shimon ben Yochai but probably the work of a thirteenth-century rabbi, Moses de Leon. Written in the form of a commentary on the Five Books of Moses, the Song of Songs, Ruth, and Lamentations, the Zohar set out to reveal the hidden meaning of the Torah. It is the masterpiece and crowning achievement of the Kabbalah, providing centuries of scholars and devotees of the mystic arts with a veritable mine of covert allusions and magical formulae, as well as a systematic and detailed theosophy of mystical speculation.

False Messiahs   Bound up with the history of the Kabbalah is the history of Jewish messianic expectations. Diaspora Jewry was convinced not only that its faith was a true faith, but that its faith would be ultimately

Mysticism & Messianism   vindicated, that in due course the sufferings of the Jews, not merely as individuals, but as a people, would end, and that they would be restored to their ancient homeland. This notion posited a doctrine of the Messiah—a savior who would redeem God's people not in some otherworldly existence, but in this world: a deliverer who would usher in a truly golden age of peace. The messianic dream was born during the Babylonian captivity, as the heart of the nation yearned impatiently for a redeemer to restore the Children of Israel to Jerusalem and rebuild the Temple. The dream gained in intensity throughout the ensuing epochs, and reached its acme after the expulsion from Spain and the wave of persecutions in the sixteenth and seventeenth centuries that left the ground of Europe drenched with Jewish blood.

For Spain had been the glory of Jewish civilization in the Diaspora, and the expulsion from Spain was a trauma that rocked Jewish self-confidence everywhere. Exhausted by their terrible sufferings, the exiles took refuge from their world of darkness in the Kabbalah. It seemed that only the science of mysteries could unlock the riddle of their strange destiny. Never was the Jewish scene so crowded with dreamers, visionaries, adventurers, and apocalyptic prophets, as during the years which followed the expulsion from Spain. From the obscurity of the Orient came one of the most flamboyant of them all, David Reubeni. Probably of German origin, he pretended to be a prince from the country of Haybar, of which his brother Joseph was purportedly king. David's mission was to raise money and an army to liberate the Holy Land from the Turks—a purpose for which he set out to win the support of the secular and religious powers of the Western world. Pope Clement VII granted this visionary an audience, and supplied him with letters of introduction to the King of Portugal. In Portugal the unhappy "messiah" fell under suspicion of excessive chauvinism; accused of secret dealings with recently converted New Christians, he was arrested and thrown into prison. Later he was taken to Spain where he probably died in an *Auto de fé*.

Reubeni's cause was next taken up by his apostle, the Marrano Shlomo Molcho. Molcho settled in Safed, the center of practical Kabbalah, and proclaimed the year 5300 of the Creation (1540 C.E.) as the date of imminent redemption. By a curious coincidence, part of his prophecy was fulfilled. According to the Kabbalah, Catholic Babylon, i.e. Rome, was destined to perish before the arrival of the Messiah. Rome was indeed destroyed by King Charles V in 1527. But the Messiah failed to appear, and his self-appointed prophet, on an expedition to Italy, was arrested in Bologna and then burned at the stake in Mantua by the Inquisition.

Many were the false messiahs who made their appearances in subsequent years; all of them claimed to be forerunners of the true Messiah, son of David, and all of them wrought havoc on the already damaged soul of the people to whom they promised redemption. Jewish national existence at this time, despite individual variations from country to country, and despite brief periods of amelioration, may largely be described as a holding operation, a period in which Jews tried to catch their breath after the cataclysms of the Middle Ages and to consolidate their inner resources for the trials that lay ahead. In Spain and Portugal, the problem of the *conversos* remained acute. Occasionally, the horrors of the Inquisition could be bought off with immense sums of money, or the right to emigrate secured with an equally large payment. For most Marranos, day-to-day life was conducted under the constant threat of discovery and exposure. In Germany, Jews were continually on the move, looking for a greater degree of safety in the more thickly populated Jewish areas of Austria, Bohemia, and Silesia. From some provinces they were expelled altogether. The brief hope held out by the humanist movement, by Reuchlin and by the early phases of the Reformation, was soon dashed to pieces. In Italy, the ancient paradise of tolerance and freedom, the Counter-Reformation inaugurated a new era of persecution and intimidation of the Jewish population which culminated in the fanatical measures taken under Pope Paul IV. As Cardinal Caraffa he had seen the Talmud consigned to the flames, all copies discoverable being burned publicly in Rome on the Jewish New Year, 1553—an example later followed all over Italy. Upon his ascendancy in 1555 Paul issued a Bull *Cum Nimis Absurdum*—in which he renewed, down to the last detail, all the oppressive medieval legislation with regard to Jews. Pope Paul instituted the Roman ghetto and enforced its regulations strictly. He also withdrew letters of protection which had been granted by his predecessors to Marrano refugees; as a result of this act twenty-four men and one woman were burned publicly at the stake. The policies reinstated by Paul remained in force almost everywhere in Italy down to the nineteenth century.

In the East, as we have seen, disaster overtook the Jews in 1648, when a Cossack revolt against the Poles was extended to Jewish "infidels" as well. In the name of religion the most hideous barbarities were committed. Hundreds of Jewish communities were destroyed to the ground, their men slaughtered, their women raped, their civilization obliterated. In the town of Nemirov alone six thousand Jews were massacred in one day. As the bath of blood

A labyrinthine abstraction presenting the Ten Spheres through which God rules the world. From a Kabbalistic treatise by Moses Cordovero.

spread over all of Eastern Europe, the toll of death and mutilation mounted in a crescendo of horror. No sooner were Chmielnitzki's Cossacks suppressed than the Russian army invaded Lithuania from the East; from the West, the Swedish forces under Charles X invaded Poland. The Polish militia, once it had reconquered the territories taken by the Swedes, fell on the Jews with redoubled fury, adding the martyrs of Great and Little Poland to the tragic roll of the Ukraine, Volhynia, and Podolia. It is estimated that in the decade from 1648 to 1658 no less than one hundred thousand Jewish lives were taken in Eastern Europe—tribute to human depravity, and gruesome portent of tragedies to come.

It is little wonder that many pious Jews all over Europe looked upon this era of catastrophe as the "birth pangs of the Messiah"— a time out of which only redemption could issue. So hellish was present actuality that only a supernatural miracle seemed the appropriate response of a beneficent Deity to the sufferings of a faithful people. And indeed, collective craving did produce a redeemer, in whose person the unbearable tension of an existence strung between the poles of exile and redemption was temporarily resolved. This redeemer, in whom all Jewry took frenzied hope, was Shabbetai Zevi.

Born in Smyrna in 1626, Shabbetai Zevi was a man of extraordinarily magnetic character. Versed in the Talmud, he had given himself up in early youth to the study of the Kabbalah, and had derived from its mysteries the certain knowledge that he himself was the destined Messiah. On a Sabbath morning in 1648—a year fixed by Kabbalistic computation as the beginning of the era of salvation—he entered a synagogue and pronounced the Ineffable Name of God to signify the restoration of the Godhead to its perfect state. Although Shabbetai had by this time already won the confidence of a number of well-placed persons in Smyrna, he was excommunicated for this act of blasphemy by the disquieted local rabbis. He thereupon left his native city and traveled to Constantinople, Salonica, Cairo, and Jerusalem, gathering adherents and creating a network of believers. He also found on his travels a mouthpiece, in the person of Nathan of Gaza, who became Shabbetai's herald and prophet, courier and amanuensis.

In 1665 Shabbetai returned to Smyrna after an absence of eighteen years. This time he was universally acclaimed. His reputation had grown immensely in the intervening years—European Jewry trembled in anticipation of the year 1666, the year now proclaimed by the self-styled messiah (as well as by many Christian millenarians) as the advent of the era of salvation. Shabbetai now once again set out for Constantinople, where the first event of the messianic age, the dethronement of the Sultan, was to take place. In Constantinople, he was promptly arrested and imprisoned in the fortress of Gallipoli. To this place, which soon took on the appearance of a royal residence, flocked hundreds of his adherents from all corners of the globe. Hundreds of thousands in the meantime began to pack their belongings, waiting only for the signal which would start them on their journey to the Holy Land.

While his followers waited, and held their breath, Shabbetai was denounced to the Sultan by a Polish Kabbalist, who accused him of being a false messiah and a charlatan. The Turkish government set about to persuade its prisoner to adopt the Moslem faith; on September 16, 1666, with the greatest alacrity and in full pomp and ceremony, Shabbetai Zevi became Mohmet Effendi and vanished behind the walls of a seraglio.

An audible shudder of despair passed through the body of world Jewry at the news of Shabbetai's apostasy. The movement he had begun was transformed overnight from a popular to a sectarian one, whose members often met now in secret. His conversion was considered by these followers to be one of the "birth pangs of the Messiah." Later, Shabbetai would surely return, and redeem the faithful. Pockets of believers remained in the Turkish Empire, the Balkans, Italy and even in Lithuania. Southern Poland too remained for a long time under Sabbatian influence. But the balance of world Jewry, disappointed now beyond illusion, recoiled from the once frenetic urgency of its messianic dreams into an exhausted and wary silence. In a gesture of self-protection, the ghetto now drew the wall of law tighter and thicker about, to ensure survival and to safeguard against future outbreaks of mass delusion. The lesson of apocalyptic cravings had been learned. The Jewish heart, stirred almost to the breaking point, took refuge now in the stern certainties of Rabbinic law. Segregation became a deliberate principle, a reflex of self-defense, and as the gap between the Jewish and non-Jewish world widened, it became increasingly difficult for any individual to pass from one to the other.

Nevertheless, just at the time when the memory of Shabbetai Zevi was beginning to fade, another adventurer appeared on the scene to claim the crown of the prophet of Smyrna: this was Jacob Frank. Born in Podolia in 1726 as a Turkish subject, a man of poor education and mediocre gifts, Frank came forward with a new Kabbalistic theory of redemption which combined Christian, Moslem, and Jewish elements in a hodge-podge of ecstatic gnosticism. In Poland, Frank presented himself as a Shabbetai Zevi incarnate, and ordered his followers to address him as *Santo Senior*. He repudiated both the Bible and the Talmud, establishing in their stead a new covenant based on the revelations of the Zohar. Frank was finally expelled from Poland, and rabbis pronounced a ban on those of his followers who refused to repent. Henceforth the study of the Zohar was prohibited to any Jew under the age of thirty.

The inglorious end of the Frankist movement coincided with the beginning of the darkest period ever visited upon the Jews of Poland. It also heralded the beginnings of a new age of spiritual vigor, to be brought to splendid fruition in the movement known as Hasidism.

Hasidism   At the same time that Jewry in Western Europe began to be affected by new ideas of rationalism and enlightenment in the eighteenth and nineteenth centuries, East-European Jews were turning for solace to religion. The Jews of Poland during the first half of the eighteenth century went through a period of intolerable political and economic privation. Not only had their external security begun to collapse, they also found themselves in grave spiritual distress after the débacle of Shabbetai Zevi. At this crucial stage, as rabbinical Judaism tightened the "fence" around the Law in an effort to retain control over its shattered domain, a new approach to religion blossomed forth: Hasidism. It was no accident that the Hasidic movement appeared first in Podolia and Volhynia, the regions where Sabbatianism had been strongly entrenched and its influence felt for a long time. Nor was it coincidental that the Jews of these regions accorded the new movement an ecstatic welcome. Its doctrine of joy, optimism, and enthusiastic worship resonated deeply in hearts that had been brought low by the fearful events of the recent past.

The Hasidic movement began as a revolt of the "unlearned" against the strict rule of the rabbis. Its first leader, Israel ben Eliezer of Medziboz, known as the Baal Shem Tov (Master of the Good Name, abbreviated BESHT), was born in Podolia in 1700. In his youth, he is reputed to have been attracted less to Talmudic study than to the world of nature, the fields and forests of his native province. Withdrawing into a life of contemplation and Kabbalistic study, the Besht spent several years preparing for a career as a "maker of miracles." Self-styled miracle workers abounded at this time in Eastern Europe. But none of them matched this young man in the intense magnetism of his personality or in the fervor of his religious faith. Long periods of mystical introspection, punctuated by visions of unearthly perfection led the Besht to abandon the vocation of faith healer and to go forth to preach the message imparted to him by the heavenly forces. His word spread like wildfire through Poland. People came in the thousands to hear him speak, to savor his words, to receive his blessing, and to join him in frenzied prayer. Here was a man who inspired them with new hope and optimism. The Besht was not a philosopher; he left behind him no theological system. Rather, he affirmed the oldest of religious truths, and in so doing struck the deepest chords of faith in the hearts of his listeners. He regarded the essence of religion as lying apart from ritual and law; though he recognized the validity of ritual, he declared that ritual alone did not constitute faith. To him, religion meant the establishment of a living relationship with God. The most efficacious means of communion with God was prayer, but for the true Hasid this meant prayer whenever one desired to pray, prayer with whatsoever words, or melodies, came to one at the moment of prayer. It was not necessary, indeed it was possibly deleterious, to restrict one's devotions to certain fixed times of day. Prayer was a matter of the heart, not of the clock; a matter not of obligation, but of inward joy.

In its emphasis on the emotions as opposed to the intellect, Hasidism acted as an equalizing influence on East-European Jewry, which had hitherto been dominated by an upper class made up of the wealthy and learned. Emotion is not a commodity given to monopolization. At the courts of the great Hasidic rabbis, rich and poor, educated and uneducated, mingled together freely in an atmosphere of true populist egalitarianism. For all had come for the same purpose: spiritual replenishment in the presence of the rabbi, or *Zaddik*—the man who was, in the words of Martin Buber, the "just or perfect man in whom immortality . . . found mortal incarnation." The words of the *Zaddik* were beyond question, his actions beyond criticism. He had an absolute measure of authority no rabbinical scholar could achieve, an authority based on the conviction of his followers that he had direct contact with God, and was able to perform miracles. The *Zaddik* served as a model of Jewish religious perfection. His personality, his habits, his idiosyncrasies— all became the object of unswerving adoration on the part of his followers, who often devoted greater attention to the *Zaddik's* life

than to his teachings. As one Hasid put it, "I did not go to the Maggid of Meseritz to learn Torah from him but to watch him tie his bootstraps." Naturally, this form of devotion could be easily subverted into a mere personality cult, and some Hasidic courts in fact succumbed to this tendency. But in the case of the great *Zaddikim,* personal charisma went hand in hand with a noble integrity of faith and deeds.

After the death of the Besht in 1760 his disciples carried Hasidism into every corner of Poland. Much as traditional Judaism attacked this "heresy," it soon gained hundreds of thousands of adherents, and in time was embraced by the majority of East-European Jews, for whom it provided an avenue of emotional escape from the threatening political developments of the nineteenth century. Various Hasidic dynasties were founded by the immediate followers of the Besht who passed on their callings to their sons and sons-in-law.

Opposition to Hasidism came not only from Poland where the Council of the Four Lands had pronounced a ban on the movement in 1772 but also from Lithuania, then the stronghold of Talmudic learning. Lithuania had been spared the ravages of the Chmielnitzki massacres, and the consequent disintegration of Jewish morale; in its academies, Talmudic studies flourished. Vilna, the capital, had earned the title, "Jerusalem of Lithuania," and was dominated at the time by an intellectual and religious giant, Elijah, later to be known as the "Gaon of Vilna" (b. 1720). Elijah's reputation was based on more than Jewish knowledge alone. He was at home in the sciences, he was familiar with secular literature, and the profundity of his philosophical and religious views was matched only by his active concern with the applicability of these views to everyday life. Elijah led the opposition movement to Hasidism. For some time East-European Jewry was divided into two ideological camps, that of the Hasidim and that of the "Mitnagdim," or opponents. This was the time also when the Polish provinces of Volhynia and Podolia fell to Russia. The Russian government ultimately intervened in the religious dispute and granted the Hasidim the right to maintain synagogues and rabbis of their own. With the further passage of years, both sides relented from their extremism, the Hasidim recognizing the importance of the traditional order of things and the *Mitnagdim* becoming more tolerant of the one-time "heretics," the warmth and vital intensity of whose faith had perceptibly influenced the opposition camp. The advent of Hasidism answered a deeply felt need in Jewish religious life; it reinforced a

"Your old men shall dream dreams, Your young men shall see visions": In Safed, an old Orthodox Jew in traditional attire leads his grandson to the synagogue.

זאת צורת הרב מהורר
רפאל כהן
אב״ד ור״מ דשק אה״ו
תקנ״ט ל׳
Raphaël Cohn
Berühmter Ober Rabiner

poetical and human element that had become obscured by excessive concern with legalism and rationalism, and brought the oppressed Jewish masses back into living contact with the mainstream of Jewish values. Its effect lives on to this day, not only physically, in the enclaves of Hasidic observance which still dot the landscape of Jewish life in New York as in Jerusalem, in Kiev as in Buenos Aires, but in the spirit of creative religious feeling and ethical idealism which Hasidim bequeathed to all subsequent generations of Jews.

The Nature of Messianism

Hasidism may be said to represent the culmination of one strand of Jewish mysticism: the quest for individual salvation. In Hasidism, the emphasis is placed on the internalizing and psychologizing of the ancient Jewish notion of redemption; through ecstatic prayer, inwardness of devotion, adherence to a particular way of life, the Jew prepares himself for communion with God. There is, however, another aspect of Jewish mystical thought, and one more closely related to Jewish political yearnings. This is messianism, in which personal salvation becomes secondary to the goal of collective redemption, the salvation of an entire people and the achievement of universal peace.

A further distinction must be made—a distinction between the messianic expectation and the more explicit belief in a personal Messiah. The messianic expectation is, in essence, the prophetic hope for political freedom and moral redemption which is to be followed by earthly bliss for all peoples. The belief in the personal Messiah, on the other hand, involves us more directly in Jewish mysticism and theology, wherein the particular conditions of the Messiah's appearance, the traits of his character, and time sequence of his actions become of paramount importance.

A late 18th-century mezzotint of an Ashkenazi rabbi in traditional fur-trimmed robe and hat.

One of Israel's original gifts to the world is her belief in the messianic age, her "clear expectation," as Joseph Klausner has expressed it, "of the restoration of the good conditions of Paradise by which history might be consummated." Even the Greeks, the most original and civilized people in the ancient world, had no real messianic doctrine; the Jews alone harbored this dream of world-wide peace and justice. They alone among all the ancient peoples spoke not of a golden age in the past, but of a golden age in the future. They alone, therefore, could break through the deterministic view of history which was held by all other ancient peoples,

A 15th-century Haggadah illustration portrays the coming
of the Messiah, announced with a blast of the ram's horn.

עַל הַמִּגִּלְבוֹת אֲשֶׁר בְּשָׁמִיר לְאִקְרָאוֹ

and point away from fatalism to the bright possibilities of human progress. Such a view, to be sure, was re-enforced upon the Jewish people by its own history of oppression and suffering, which implanted in the Hebrew soul a terrible aching to be delivered from affliction. Moses, whose very name signifies one who brings out, or ransoms, was the "first deliverer"; his personality is stamped indelibly in the later history of Jewish messianism as redeemer, as lawgiver, as spiritual leader, and as forerunner of the Messiah who will appear at the "end of days." But it was also a view which encompassed all mankind, not only the Children of Israel. This is articulated with particular forcefulness by the prophets, who chastise the people of Israel for their shortcomings, for their failure to be that "light unto the nations" which will ensure illumination of the world with the message of justice, morality, and peace.

The days of the Messiah as conceived by the prophets and Rabbis will reveal themselves as follows: The sins of Israel will bring final retribution on the Day of Judgment. This retribution, in the form of wars, destruction, exile, humiliation, and cataclysmic change in the order of nature, will represent the "birth pangs of the Messiah." After the Day of Judgment will come repentance, which in turn will be followed by redemption. At the time of the redemption only a "remnant of Israel" will have survived—a small group of the upright, the blameless, and the humble among the sons of Israel. After the redemption Israel will gain political strength to equal that of other nations, but her spiritual strength will surpass that of other nations. Thus will Israel attain an exalted position among all peoples. Material prosperity (improvement and progress) as well as spiritual welfare (human perfection) will accompany the redemption.

This Rabbinic conception contains the basic elements of Jewish messianic thought. The political and national hope for the redemption of Israel from bondage and servitude is combined with the dream of universal peace, the vision of an age when Israel, through its own deliverance, will ultimately bring spiritual deliverance to all mankind.

15 ❧ *The Dawn of Emancipation*

ON THE eve of the French Revolution there were some 400,000 Jews in Western Europe; of these, fully 300,000 lived in Germany. Although these Jews had proved, and continued to prove, a valuable asset in the economic development of the European states, to most of them the gates to Western civilization were shut fast. The eighteenth century, to be sure, had seen an improvement in Jewish economic status, but the majority of Jews were still quite poor, still confined to ghetto areas and subjected to oppressive and degrading taxes. Yet an ever increasing minority was beginning to edge its way into the world beyond the ghetto, and the economic security won by these Jewish entrepreneurs provided a material basis for the political, social, and cultural emancipation that was eventually to follow. The political liberation of the Jewish people at the end of the eighteenth century did not come about overnight. It was, in essence, due to three factors: the genius of the Jewish financier; the obsolescence of the old corporate structures; and the growth of rational humanitarianism.

As Europe entered into its capitalist and mercantile era, it was discovered that the Jews, for a variety of reasons—their detachment from the soil, their long, enforced experience with money matters, their network of contacts in urban centers throughout Europe—were the most versatile element in trade and commerce. Those Jews who could thus be usefully employed received a special status: they were *schutzjuden,* or "protected Jews." In Germany, where this type predominated, the rights granted such a person varied in each of the three hundred principalities that had been created after the Peace of Westphalia. Sometimes the *schutzjuden* received their rights as individuals, sometimes in groups; sometimes their rights were hereditary, sometimes they passed only to the first-born son. It became abundantly clear in time that although every duke, every prince, and every king wished to have, indeed needed to have, his protected Jews, none wanted too many.

It was in this period also that the picturesque figure of the "Court Jew" made its first modern appearance. The Court Jew lived under the direct protection of a princely court and was freed from the medieval chains burdening other members of his race. He was free to trade, to travel, and to dress as he pleased. His primary obligation was to procure loans for his sovereign, supplies for the army, and, in general, to contribute to the treasury and to the jewel chests of his protector.

Naturally, many individual Jews became wealthy in the fulfillment of their functions. Some were even elevated into the ranks of nobility; the list of aristocrats who passed from the ghettos of Regensburg, Munich, and Prague, from the yeshivah to the courtly salon, is a long and impressive one. Erstwhile peddlers became international merchants and suppliers of luxuries, as their ancestors had been before them in the Middle Ages. They dealt in silks and laces, in arms and ammunition; they supplied silver and bullion to the mints and handled bills of exchange on an immense scale. Occasionally, it was but a step from being financial adviser to a ruler to becoming his political adviser as well. The career of Joseph Süss Oppenheimer, immortalized in fiction by Leon Feuchtwanger, illustrates this transition. Nevertheless, the profession of the *schutzjude* was sometimes a dangerous one, exposed as he was to pressures from Christian competitors or to the intrigues of other courtiers. On occasion, a brilliant career was liable to end in disgrace, in jail, or, as in the case of Süss, on the gallows.

By and large, however, the influence and prestige of the Court Jews was to have an ameliorating effect on the fortunes of Jews everywhere, and led to the opening of many doors which had been shut tight for centuries. The Court Jew often took it upon himself to plead the cause of his fellow Jews before the reigning powers, and to gain for them a measure of the freedom and self-respect which he himself possessed in abundance. Thus, despite restringent laws, the old Jewish communities of Europe grew, and new ones

Salomon Herz bey sitzer in Nahmen der aus
schuß

Joseph Lazarus Beßlay des beysitzers in Nahmen
den ausschuß

Alexander ... beysitzer in Nahmen
ausschuß

Zacharias Canstat beysitzer in Nahmen
ausschuß

... Juden Mayntz

Lehman gemein ... Juden Mayntz
Jacob Hackstein ... Schuldeßer

Salomon Mayer ... Jude Mayntz
... Baruch Schlesinger ... Mayntz

Getz Garnober Jude in Mayntz
... Jud Lawin Mayntz

were established. The state, as ever, was eager to exploit the services of its Jews. Disregarding the opposition of his citizens, the Great Elector Frederick William of Brandenburg decided that "The Jews and their commerce, far from being a detriment to the land, are a decided benefit," and he appointed Elias Cleves, Levi Berend of Bonn, and Israel Aaron of Berlin as his bankers. In keeping with the cynical utilitarianism of the age, it became general policy to tolerate the Jews in return for inflicting upon them heavy payments and restrictions. Christian Wilhelm von Dohm, writer, diplomat, aristocrat and publicist for Jewish emancipation, gave the following account of the legal position of the Jews in Europe in the second half of the eighteenth century:

> In almost all parts of Europe, the laws of the state aim to prevent as much as possible the influx of these unfortunate Asiatic refugees—the Jews. . . . Everywhere the Jew is denied the privilege of service to the state. He is not allowed to engage in agriculture, nor is he permitted to acquire property. The only branch of economic activity left for him in which to eke out a livelihood is petty trade. When a Jew has several sons, he has the privilege of having with him only one, since the oldest alone is allowed to marry and raise a family. The others he must send away. His daughters remain with him only if they are lucky enough to marry Jews of his own city who have the right to stay there. Very rarely is a Jewish father fortunate enough to live among his children and grandchildren, and to establish the welfare of his family on a permanent foundation.

The codes regulating the status of Jews in Prussia, issued by Frederick the Great in 1750, and the Edict of Toleration issued by Joseph the Second of Austria, aimed at keeping the number of Jews static, and at imposing on those allowed to reside in the country a considerable financial strain. Especially humiliating was the *Leibzoll*, a poll tax which Jews had to pay upon crossing a frontier or entering a city. In the "Reglement of Frederick the Great," Jews were divided into classes according to their value to the state, which had now taken the place of the ruler as the supreme embodiment of the will of the body politic. Outside of a mere handful of "general-privileged" Jews, who were granted all economic and residential rights and were not obligated by this code, Jews were classified as "regular-protected" and "special-protected"; the former had limited rights of residence and vocation, transferable to the eldest child only, while the latters' rights were non-transferable altogether. Other Jews, such as communal officials, younger children of "regular-protected" and all children of "special-protected" Jews, as well as all domestic servants, were only "tolerated."

So prominent was the role played by Jews in the economic life of Germany, and indeed so numerous were the Jews themselves in Germany at this time, that the conflict between pro- and anti-Jewish elements in the nation at large reached public proportions hitherto unheard of in the West. It became, in short, a debate, and one which assumed unprecedented dimensions. Winds of enlightenment had begun to blow from West of the Rhine. French rationalists were preaching ideas of tolerance and reason, and of a more humane social order. The first to react to these doctrines, strangely enough, were not the Jews of France but their more cultured coreligionists in Prussia, who were more alert than they to the new age, having taken full advantage of the special circumstances made available to them by Frederick the Great, the enlightened monarch, who not only fostered arts and sciences in the French fashion, but also attracted French philosophers and poets—among them Voltaire—to his court in Potsdam.

Thus it was in Germany that the idea of emancipation found its warmest early reception among Jews, just as it was in Berlin that this idea found its first clear formulator. Berlin was the center and cradle of Jewish enlightenment, and Moses Mendelssohn its father. Its Christian godfather was Mendelssohn's friend, Gotthold Ephraim Lessing. Lessing's was the first strong Christian voice in Germany to speak on behalf of the Jews, a voice that issued from one of the greatest personalities Germany produced in the eighteenth century. Lessing was a freethinker, a man who wished to exalt the stage to a pulpit and art to a religion. His first play, *Die Jüden*, was the earliest creative effort in modern times to portray the Jew in sympathetic terms. It was followed in later years, when Lessing came to know Mendelssohn, and to be profoundly impressed by the beauty of his character, by the celebrated drama, *Nathan der Weise*, which was programmatically not only a vindication of the Jews but an appeal to Christians to do justice to themselves by rendering final justice to the Jews. With the parable of the three rings Lessing pointed in this play to the fallibility of all faiths and to the absurdity of the claim that nobility of soul was a Christian monopoly. That *Nathan der Weise* was banned from the stage for many years is the most eloquent testimony to its power.

Lessing and Mendelssohn became firm friends and mutual ad-

A Paul-Christian Kirchner engraving, "Jewish Ceremonials" (1734), graphically illustrates the rites and rituals of cooking, baking and cleaning of that era.

The Augsburg Judengasse *in the 18th century.*

mirers. Each influenced the other, Lessing by arousing in Mendelssohn an interest in the arts and literature, and Mendelssohn by stimulating in Lessing an interest in abstract philosophical thought. Under Lessing's influence Mendelssohn began a systematic study of the German language, a pursuit uncommon in traditional Jewish circles, and was introduced to the intellectual world of Berlin, known at that time as the "coffee house of the learned."

The road taken by Mendelssohn to this happy juncture had been long and tortuous. He was born in 1729 in the ghetto of Dessau, the son of a poor Torah scribe. With rare luck, he was introduced by his teacher, David Fränkel, not only to the Bible and the Talmud, but to the philosophy of Maimonides. When Fränkel left Dessau to become Chief Rabbi of Berlin, the young Mendelssohn tramped after him and was admitted within the gates of the city after having paid his *Leibzoll*. There he encountered a prosperous Jewish community, already acquainted with secular literature. Fränkel again took him under his wing and soon the hunchbacked student became the protégé of several "privileged" Jews who provided him with books and helped him in his studies of German and Latin, philosophy and metaphysics. He first met Lessing at a chess game; friendship between these two great intellects arose almost instantaneously. Under Lessing's tutelage and with his encouragement, Mendelssohn began to write essays in philosophy and philosophical discourses, and to engage in general literary work. He translated works by Rousseau and became editor of various literary journals. In a competition sponsored by the Berlin Academy he even won a prize over Immanuel Kant. In recognition of his merits, Frederick the Great made him a "privileged Jew," by virtue of which he could no longer be forced to leave the Prussian capital.

Despite his fame as a philosopher, Mendelssohn's greatest achievement must be said to be his translation into German of the Pentateuch. This was a most crucial contribution to Jewish enlightenment, providing, as it did, a steppingstone to the German language and to a life beyond the ghetto. Banned by some rabbis, who diagnosed correctly, if fearfully, the effect it would engender in the reader, Mendelssohn's translation nevertheless made its way into many a ghetto home. It became the tool of an inner emancipation.

Mendelssohn himself, despite the freethinking attitudes of his friend Lessing, remained a pious Jew. He defended Judaism against charges of obscurantism as a rational and humane theology. But at the same time he realized the need to overcome the stifling effects of ghetto education and to prod the Jewish world into an increased awareness of the secular world outside. He found the key to these treasures in the study of the German language, which would open the door to European culture in general. Acquisition of this culture, Mendelssohn was sure, would bring the Jews full legal equality. In the spirit of *Haskalah*, or Enlightenment, a full-scale attack was therefore begun on the restrictions of Rabbinical Judaism, which were felt to be antithetical to true culture. Mendelssohn himself wrote that his Bible translation was "the first step to civilization, from which my nation has held itself so aloof. . . ." The very choice of the Pentateuch, rather than a book of Rabbinic literature, as the text to be translated, symbolized a desire to turn away from the "shroud" of tradition to the pristine, trans-cultural origins of monotheistic faith. The result was that truly pious Jews spurned not only Mendelssohn's de-Hebraized translation but restricted study of the Bible altogether.

Yet Mendelssohn was correct in believing that his translation of the Torah would touch off a quiet revolution in Jewish cultural life. Soon enough the Jews of Germany mastered the German language and German culture; and the fruits of that mastery were to be proved beneficial in later years both to German civilization as a whole, and to Jewish culture in particular.

On the eve of the French Revolution, then, the secular wonders on the other side of the ghetto, although still within reach only of "exception Jews," were nevertheless recognized and desired by many. To be sure, the great majority of Western Jews, living in the world of the ghetto and of Talmudic dialectics, were to some extent unaware of the currents of humanism that eddied through Western society. But the number of enlightened was growing. Intellectually as well as economically, by the time emancipation was granted most Jews were quite prepared for membership in Western society; indeed, in many ways they had far outstripped that very society in enlightenment. The question now would be one of reconciling the "two camps" in which most Western Jews simultaneously stood: the camp of Jewish values, and the camp of Western civilization. The internal conflict which agitated many Jews, who were faced by what appeared to them to be an irrevocable choice between one camp or the other, is to be seen as early as the middle of the eighteenth century in the career of a near-contemporary of Mendelssohn, Solomon Maimon.

Maimon was born in Lithuania in 1754. A child prodigy, he had mastered the Talmud by the age of eleven, at which age he was offered, but refused, the title of rabbi. He was married at fourteen, a father at fifteen. He taught himself to read German in a community where secular learning was deemed blasphemous. At the age of twenty-five Maimon left his wife and family and made his way to Königsberg in Prussia, where he earned a living for a while as a tutor but made himself generally disliked for his outspokenly critical remarks concerning Orthodox Judaism. He subsequently moved to Berlin, was expelled from that city by the Jewish authorities for his continued publicizing of heretical opinions, and moved again to Posen. After a brief and unsuccessful attempt at conversion, and an even less successful attempt at suicide, Maimon returned to Berlin, where he published his first book, *Essay on the Transcendental Philosophy*, and his career took a turn upward.

Though his work possesses much greater philosophical value than Mendelssohn's, Maimon was completely overshadowed in his day by his magnetic contemporary. Mendelssohn had the gift of winning followers both in the Jewish and in the Christian world by the sheer force of his personality, whereas Maimon's rare talents made him hated. But he is an extreme example of a type that was to become common in Europe in later years: a "rootless" wanderer, in both the physical and intellectual sense, familiar with many cultures and at home in none, profoundly incisive in critical intellect, profoundly uneasy in spirit. Men of this type, who, in the words of Moses Hadas, "did so much to enrich European culture and traditions, were Bohemians who lived outside the limits of Jewish society and still refused to become members of any other well defined community. Maimon was the first of them, as Heinrich Heine probably was the greatest." Such men embodied in their persons and careers the fretful ambivalence which beset the European Jew in the era of emancipation.

Emancipation of the Jews in France

From Germany the quest for emancipation was carried to France. Freedom for French Jews seemed never so close as when the revolutionaries of 1789 pressed forward to the realization of their battle cry, "Liberty, Equality, and Fraternity." But the Jews had to campaign actively for their liberation. In the forefront of the struggle stood Cerf Berr (1730–1793), one of the first French Jews to be influenced by the new spirit emanating from Mendelssohn and his circle in Germany. In his capacity of supplier to the French army, Cerf Berr was granted certain privileges, and he was in a position to demand others. He was, for instance, allowed to settle with his family in Strassburg, where no Jews had been permitted. Slowly he succeeded in encouraging more Jews to come to Strassburg, and obtained for them from Louis XVI all the rights and liberties of royal subjects. In a single-handed attempt at social rehabilitation, Cerf Berr established three factories in Strassburg and employed Jews in them almost exclusively; his aim was to remove Jews from petty trading and hence to remove what appeared to be the cause of resentment toward them on the part of the general population. In an effort to win over public sentiment, he energetically distributed copies of Christian Wilhelm von Dohm's "Apology" for the Jewish people throughout France.

Berr was not alone in his efforts. From other quarters too the French government was being petitioned to lighten the oppressive measures which weighed heavily and in particular upon the Jews of Alsace and Lorraine. A commission was established to put forth proposals on how to ameliorate the condition of the Jews in these regions. Count Mirabeau (1749–1791), inspired by a reading of Mendelssohn, pleaded the cause of the Jews in his pamphlet, "Upon Mendelssohn and the Political Reform of the Jews" (1787). Mirabeau, like Dohm, was deeply moved by the martyrdom of the Jewish people; like Dohm, too, he attributed their "failings" to the ill treatment they had received. "If you wish the Jews to become better men and useful citizens, then banish every humiliating distinction, open to them every avenue of gaining a livelihood. . . ." The Reglement of Frederick the Great he scornfully termed "a law worthy of a cannibal." "There is only one thing to be lamented," he wrote, "that so highly gifted a nation should so long have been kept in a state wherein it was impossible for its powers to develop, and every farsighted man must rejoice in the acquisition of useful fellow-citizens from among the Jews."

The Jewish question soon attained prominence in France. A prize was offered by the Royal Society of Science and Arts in Metz for the best essay addressing itself to the question: "Are there means to make the Jews happier and more useful in France?" The most effective answer to this question issued from the Abbé Henri Grégoire, who, like Mirabeau, sat in the National Assembly and proved one of the most ardent defenders and promoters of the rights of French Jews.

At the outbreak of the Revolution there were less than 50,000

An 18th-century engraving of a Rosh Hashanah Shofar blowing in a French synagogue.

Jews in France, 20,000 of them in Alsace. In Metz there lived 420 families, in Lorraine 180 families (these numbers were fixed by law); in Paris there were a mere 500 persons who had entered surreptitiously since 1740; Bordeaux had about 500 Jews, most of them of Marrano descent. The Jews of Bordeaux and Bayonne lived under the best conditions of all; those in Alsace under the worst. Among the Jews of the various provinces little contact was maintained; therefore, no united appeal for their emancipation came forth in the first few months of the Revolution. Other individual communities, however, sent in petitions begging for legal equality. In the National Assembly the Jewish question was repeatedly discussed, and a final decision repeatedly deferred. A resolution passed in 1790 stipulated that those Jews in France who were called Portuguese, Spaniards, or Avignonese (of Bordeaux and Bayonne) should enjoy full privileges as active citizens. Although this constituted only partial recognition of the Jews, it served as a ground-breaking precedent. Within time, another partial concession was granted: the high taxes which the Alsatian Jews had to pay for their protection were annulled. And then, on September 27, 1791, the National Assembly finally granted the Jews of France the right to take an oath of citizenship.

Despite formal recognition of equality before the law, however, French Jews continued to suffer from the entrenched biases of the population at large. This situation remained basically unchanged until Napoleon Bonaparte took it upon himself, in a characteristically grand gesture, to solve the unsolvable.

Napoleon and the Sanhedrin

Except for a brief encounter with the Jews of Palestine during his unsuccessful campaign in 1799, Napoleon had given very little consideration to the "Jewish problem" until his return from victory at Austerlitz (1806). Breaking his journey in Strasbourg, he was met by the angry citizens of Alsace, who presented him with petitions directed against their favorite object of resentment, the Jews. At the beginning of the revolution a large number of the possessions confiscated from the clergy and the nobility had been acquired by the peasants of Alsace. The latter, determined to keep these new properties, but lacking the funds to work them, had turned to the despised Jewish money-lenders. The taxes fixed by law were unusually high. Revolutionary times were difficult; money had been devaluated, and the peasants found themselves unable to liquidate their debts. They blamed the Jews for their impoverishment. Disturbed by the complaints of the Alsatians, Napoleon returned to Paris determined to impose rigorous restrictions on the Jewish usurers. It so happened that just at this time one of France's leading newspapers published an article maintaining that the emancipation of the Jews had been one of the grievous mistakes of the revolution. In the opinion of the French public, the Jews could never be true citizens unless and until they became Christians. Napoleon, genuinely impressed by this position, at first considered declaring a moratorium on all debts owed to Jewish money-lenders, then hit upon a much grander idea. Against those who spoke rashly of expelling the Jews he declared: "It would be a weakness to chase away the Jews; it would be a sign of strength to correct them." Napoleon then followed this grandiloquent statement not merely with a one-year moratorium on debts to Jewish money-lenders, but also with a call for the convening of a Jewish assembly of notables to "study ways of remedying the situation."

This assembly, which met in July 1806, was headed by the financier Abraham Furtado. Its members were received by a guard of honor, whose hospitable welcome was followed by an abusive opening speech by Count Molé, Napoleon's adviser on Jewish affairs. The count delivered a tirade denouncing the shameful practice of usury. Stunned, the delegates were next presented with the notorious twelve "imperial" questions, in which they were closely examined as to Jewish laws of marriage, and the nomination and jurisdiction of rabbis; they were also asked whether Jewish law prohibited entering into the professions, if it encouraged usury, and whether the Jews considered France their country and were willing to defend it. The answer to the last question was a spontaneous "until death"; the delegates gave the expected answers to the other questions as well, in general expressing with alacrity a desire to comply with Napoleon's dictum: "Sa majesté veut que vous soyez Français."

Pleased with this declaration of loyalty, Napoleon now sought to legitimize the delegates' representations by a body of religious authority. Nothing less than the restoration of the ancient Sanhedrin would do. Every congregation was to send its representatives, both religious and secular; the Sanhedrin would convert into doctrine the replies formulated by the Provisional Assembly. At this stage Napoleon wrote in a letter as follows: "I desire to take every means to ensure that the rights which were restored to the Jewish people be not illusory . . . to find for them a Jerusalem in France."

NAPOLÉON LE GRAND,

rétablit le culte des Israélites, le 30 Mai 1806.

"I desire to take every means to ensure that the rights which were restored to the Jewish people be not illusory . . . to find for them a Jerusalem in France." So Napoleon Bonaparte wrote in sponsoring the full rights and participation of Jews in French society.

Molé stated that the decisions taken by this Sanhedrin were to be placed side by side with the Talmud and were to acquire in the eyes of the Jews of all countries the greatest authority possible. "This body, which fell with the Temple, will appear to enlighten the whole world about the people it once governed; it will recall the true spirit of its law, and impart to it a dignified explanation to destroy all untrue interpretations."

The Sanhedrin finally gathered in Paris in February 1807, with great pomp and ceremony. In conformity with Napoleon's wish that it resemble as closely as possible the ancient Council, there were 71 deputies in this latter-day Sanhedrin, a *nasi* (president), an *av bet din* (vice-president), and a *ḥacham* (second vice-president). David Sinzheim, rabbi of Strassburg, was made president. In its first session the Sanhedrin ratified the decisions of the Assembly and gave them religious sanction. Except on the question of mixed marriages, the Sanhedrin yielded on every point. But it was this very issue to which Napoleon attached supreme importance. Finally, a compromise was worked out whereby civil marriages between Jews and non-Jews were declared permissible; although not sanctioned by the Jewish religion, they bore, the Sanhedrin proclaimed, no inherent stigma.

With the decisions of the Sanhedrin the Jews of France renounced rabbinical jurisdiction, corporate status, and the hope for a return to the Land of Israel. From now on, their destiny was to be linked inseparably with that of France. As Abraham Furtado declared: "We are no longer a nation within a nation. France is our country, Jews. Your obligations are outlined; your happiness is waiting." The Sanhedrin's renunciation of separate nationhood marked an important turning point in Jewish history, and set the tone of Western Jewish life for the next century and more.

Emancipation in Western Europe A full century was to pass before the movement which began at the time of Moses Mendelssohn achieved its goal of complete legal and political emancipation for the majority of Jews in Western Europe. (By contrast, it would take only sixty years for this edifice, built at such cost, to come roaring down overnight with the rise of the Nazis to power.) With the exceptions of France and Holland, where Jews enjoyed full rights as set forth in the Constitutions of 1791, the rest of Western European Jewry underwent an agonizing struggle for civil rights that lasted throughout much *Dawn of Emancipation* of the nineteenth century.

In May 1814, following the final defeat of Napoleon at Water-loo, France hastily signed a peace treaty with the victorious allies which relegated most problems resulting from the new situation to a Congress to be convened in Vienna the same year. One of the most important items on the agenda was the framing of a constitution for the federation of thirty-six German states, most of which had previously belonged to the Rheinbund created by Napoleon. The "Jewish question" was to be dealt with in this Constitution. Indeed, this was the first time in history that an international forum was to consider the Jewish problem in this way. To safeguard their interests against the strong reactionary sentiment in all these states, the Jews began lobbying unofficially at the Congress through the agency of representatives from Frankfurt and Hamburg. At work in Vienna were some of the greatest minds of the day: Hardenberg and Friedrich von Humboldt from Prussia, and the most influential and untiring advocate of Jewish emancipation, Metternich from Austria. However, only these two states, Prussia and Austria, were prepared to include full emancipatory rights for Jews in the Constitution. The smaller states had for some time been trying to undo whatever rights the Jews had already been granted under Napoleonic rule, or which they had bought outright for cash, as had been the case in Frankfurt in 1811. In that city, instead of paying the annual protection money, the Jews were given the option of redeeming their rights through the payment of a single lump sum twenty times the annual "fee." Since even the rich Frankfurt Jews did not have this much cash on hand, it was agreed that the debt could be paid in twenty yearly installments (plus 5 per cent interest, of course). The Jews of Frankfurt had already paid for three or four years when the city fathers decided to reverse their decision after the downfall of Napoleon. Similar regressive measures were being undertaken in many Hanseatic cities, and over a thousand Jewish communities, fearful of new danger, pinned their hopes on the deliberations at Vienna.

Various Jewish delegations were at work in Vienna. From Frankfurt came two Jewish representatives, Messrs. Gumpertz and Baruch, who arrived in the city disguised as merchants, so as not to arouse the suspicions of the official Frankfurt delegation. Their presence, however, was discovered within a very few days by the Austrian secret police, who handed the Vienna police commissioner a full dossier on these two "merchants." The commissioner added to the file a notation to the effect that the true purpose of their visit was probably "to engage in some secret Kabbalah." The two emissaries were on the point of expulsion when the imperial house intervened in their behalf, in gratitude for some service which Baruch's father had once rendered to the Empress Maria Theresa. From now on they were allowed to conduct their "business" openly, and with Metternich's help they received permission to stay in Vienna for the duration of the Congress.

The Jews of Hamburg and the other Hanseatic towns had entrusted their interests to a Christian lawyer, von Buchholz, who appeared as the spokesman for all of Germany's Jews in their quest for equal rights. But the most important advocate the Jews had was the delegate from Prussia, Wilhelm von Humboldt. This was a man familiar with the Jewish problem from his early days in Berlin, where he frequented the salon of Rachel Levin-Varnhagen, and sympathetic to the condition of a people that constituted, in his own words, "so peculiar a religious and world-historical phenomenon that not the worst minds have raised doubts as to whether its existence can be explained in a human way only. . . ." Boldly Humboldt recommended unrestricted equality as the only just, logical, and politically wise solution to the Jewish problem in Germany.

But the Congress was plunged into an atmosphere of bickering and bargaining. The longer the negotiations lasted, the louder became the voices of reaction. The delegates were besieged with petitions emanating from their home states and demanding a curtailment of the rights of the Jews; the petitions came mostly from the burgher class which feared and hated the Jews for their economic talents. The clause dealing with the Jewish question, which had been formulated rather liberally when the Congress first opened, was finally passed in a vague and indecisive form.

The article had two parts. Part I promised that the Federal Assembly would deal with the Jewish problem with a view toward arriving at a common solution for the whole of Germany. This part of the resolution was destined to remain a mere paper formality. For a long time the climate was simply too unfavorable to deal with the recommendation. Times had changed: instead of revolution, reaction set in. The spirit of cosmopolitan enlightenment was replaced by the new ideals of pan-German Christianity, a romantic return to the Middle Ages which once again excluded the Jews as an alien group.

Part II of the Article, in which Humboldt had sought to safeguard the existing rights, was also watered down at the last moment. The resolution arrived at had provided that "the rights already conceded the Jews *in* the several federated states will be

A remarkable drawing of a bourgeois Jewish woman from Hamburg in the early 19th century. On the Sabbath she carries her pompadour parasol and under her synagogue cloak wears the fashionable décolletage of the period.

continued," but at the intervention of the delegate from Bremen, the word "in" was changed to "by." Since only three of the federated states had actually conceded citizenship to the Jews (all other rights having been enacted by the French occupation), this seemingly insignificant textual change succeeded in nullifying the hard-won gains of many Jewish communities.

As things eventually happened, the Jews of Germany secured their economic and cultural rights long before the last traces of "Jewish disabilities" disappeared from the Constitutions of the several states which made up Germany after the Congress of Vienna. The struggle for full emancipation was carried on by poets and bankers, by politicians and rabbis. Like no other Western Jewish community, German Jewry had to cope with a new form of anti-Semitism that flared up in the wake of the romantic movement. Though they were quick to absorb German *Kultur*, they found social acceptance slow in coming, and feelings of insecurity led many German Jews to conversion. Among the most illustrious Jews to succumb to the pressure were Ludwig Boerne and Heinrich Heine. Though German culture, to a large extent, had been born in the salons run by Jewish patrons of the arts, both male and female, Jews still had to buy their "ticket of admission to European culture" at the baptismal font. A tragic ambivalence characterized the spiritual climate of German Jewry at the beginning of the nineteenth century. Fully one tenth of the Jewish population of the German states, between 1800 and 1810, took the escape route of baptism, among these four of the children of Moses Mendelssohn.

The romantic revival of the spirit of the Middle Ages in the early decades of the nineteenth century also saw a spate of anti-Jewish writings emanating from the halls of the German universities. German philosophers and writers almost without exception accepted and publicized the doctrines of pan-Germanism. Jews in Germany were relegated to a condition of sufferance. From some cities they were expelled altogether. In Austria, most Jews were assigned to the ghetto. Anti-Jewish riots, led by the "Hep-Hep" movement (the initials probably stand for *Hierosylema est perdita*—Jerusalem is fallen!), deeply wounded Jewish pride. Jews who had been born outside the ghetto were now once again considered an alien, Asiatic people; the gulf between Jew and German seemed unbridgeable.

One avenue now exploited by the Jews in their efforts to gain more humane treatment was that of economic pressure. Economic progress was considerable at this time, and many Jews used this new strength to influence favorably the fate of their coreligionists. The

Rothschilds, who now maintained banking houses in the leading capitals of Europe, consistently refused loans to governments oppressing Jews. From their prominent social and cultural position, they were also able to lobby discreetly but effectively to change public opinion with regard to their fellow-Jews. In so doing, they had the additional effect of inspiring Jewish leaders to stand up to the challenge of anti-Semitism, and to fight for their rights. This fight was sustained on two fronts: on the one hand, Jews wanted their political rights to be ensured; on the other hand, they proposed to emancipate themselves through an understanding of their own world—that is, through the study of Jewish history and literature. Thereby the Jew would earn self-respect and be enabled to take his rightful place in the political system without having recourse to conversion. Thus the "Science of Judaism" (*Wissenschaft des Judentums*) came into being, a revival of Jewish studies which was to become one of the outstanding historical contributions of the Jewish enlightenment. Two names in particular are associated with this movement: Gabriel Riesser and Leopold Zunz.

Riesser (1806–1860) was a lawyer by profession, but like so many of his fellow-Jews, he was unable to work in his chosen profession, having been rejected on religious grounds from the bar and from a chair at the university. His rejection drove him into the fight for equal rights. He began to expound his ideas in a journal which he called *Der Jude,* and in time succeeded in making the emancipation problem one of popular concern. It soon became a central plank in the platform of the German liberals.

Zunz, on the other hand, not only invented the term *Wissenschaft des Judentums,* but spent his life creating it. He saw Jews turning to Christianity in order to achieve emancipation because "they had nothing else to turn to." When Zunz began his labors, Jewish history was a sealed book. He preached the methods of scientific research and a thorough understanding of the Jewish past. His aim was to gain freedom through knowledge, and though his work may not have been complete, and may indeed have been motivated by an ambiguous attitude toward Jewish national experience, it stands as a valuable link in the historic chain of Jewish scholarship and learning.

In the meantime, times had changed again. The revolution of 1848, which began in France, set in motion a spirit of liberation in Prussia, Austria, Italy, and elsewhere. It was in this period that Jewish emancipation was largely achieved. In their quest for freedom, Jews now entered the political arena directly, and soon found

themselves taking a leading role, particularly in the liberal movements. In Austria, in Italy, in France (where two Jews became
members of the Cabinet), and in Prussia (where Gabriel Riesser
was elected one of the vice-presidents of the great constitutional
parliament), many Jews participated in the movement of liberation
both at the higher levels and in the popular uprisings and street
battles. Their blood was shed "in a common battle for freedom and
fatherland," in the hope that now, finally, the goal of full political
rights could be achieved.

Jews were also, however, to be found in the conservative camp,
as, for instance, Disraeli in England and Friedrich Julius Stahl, the
founder of the conservative party in Prussia.

The zest with which young Jews threw themselves into the struggle for liberal ideas provoked vile attacks from the opponents of
Jewish emancipation, and the Jews were blamed, in the judgment
of the London *Standard,* for "all the mischief now brooding on the
continent." The 1848 revolution became identified with Jewish
emancipation, and when it miscarried, as it soon did, Jewish rights
were again revoked.

*Haskalah in
Eastern Europe* Since the sixteenth century, when the Muscovy Tsardom set about
consolidating the independent Russian principalities into a unified
empire, it had been fixed Russian policy not to admit Jews into its
territory, even for temporary purposes. The sixteenth-century monarch Ivan the Terrible spoke of the Jews as "importers of poisonous
medicines and misleaders from the Christian Faith," and this hostile and superstitious attitude was reinforced in persistent discriminatory legislation against the Jews that remained unmodified even
by economic considerations. In the words of the Empress Elizabeth,
"I seek no gain at the hands of the enemies of Christ."

This situation remained basically unchanged until the partitions
of Poland in 1772, 1793, and 1795, when the number of Jews
within the Russian boundaries increased suddenly to a figure of
900,000. It was now no longer possible to solve the Jewish problem by simple banishment. Special legislation was issued relating
to the rights of Jews in fixed territories, these being the areas in
which Jews had been living at the time of partition, which became
known as the Jewish Pale. But even within the Pale, Jews were
singled out for discriminatory legislation through the imposition of
Dawn of Emancipation a double tax upon Jewish merchants and burghers. But the fresh

breeze of liberation blowing in Western Europe made itself felt in Russia too, and slowly the Jews of the Pale were brought within sight of relief. In 1802 the Tsar ordered the creation of a committee for the "Amelioration of the Jews." The presence of a few liberal members on the committee ensured passage of a decision to invite representatives of the Jewish communities as advisers on the needs of their people. Though the continuation of the Pale was reasserted, and Jewish self-government restricted in scope, Jews were to be allowed to send their children to schools of the empire and to engage in agriculture. After the Congress of Vienna (1815), however, Russia, like other countries in Europe, soon succumbed to reaction, and Jewish hopes for more liberal treatment, so precipitously raised, became doomed to disappointment.

Under Nicholas I the situation grew worse. Jews became subject to conscription into the dread military service; in fact, this was one of the main instruments of official anti-Jewish policy. Jewish communities were required to provide cantonists to the Russian army, an obligation which was abolished only after the Crimean Wars. The system of cantonists—or juvenile conscripts—imposed a military martyrdom on Jewish youth and terrorized the Jewish populace. According to the Law of 1827 Jewish youths between the ages of 12 and 18 were to be conscripted. They were to receive preparatory training in the cantonist battalions and then had to serve an additional twenty-five years, the regular term of military service. The Jewish community was held responsible for the supply of the assigned quotas, and special agents were appointed, the so-called *chappers,* to round up the requisite number of children. These *chappers* kept the Jewish population in a state of dread and terror. The initiated children were not only exposed to physical hardships but to spiritual torment; missionary activity among the cantonists— under direction of the Tsar—was carried out with utmost severity and the number of converts among the children was considerable. A whole literature of martyrology gives first-hand accounts of the tortures designed to induce conversions to Christianity among conscripted Jewish children.

In 1835, a new code of anti-Jewish legislation further restricted the territory of the Pale of Settlement: it now consisted of Lithuania, Volhynia and Podolia, White Russia (Vitebsk and Moghilev minus the villages), Little Russia, New Russia, the province of Kiev (without the capital), and the Baltic provinces (for older settlers only). Rural settlement in the twenty-five-mile zone along the western frontier was forbidden to newcomers.

An 18th-century silver filigree spice box from
Poland; a circumcision plate from the same
time and place carved with the Akédah,
Abraham with the knife poised, Isaac the
sacrifice, the ram in the thicket.

The culture of East-European Jewry in the nineteenth century was shaped by the twin forces of Haskalah, or enlightenment, on the one hand, and Hasidism on the other. In the central areas of the Pale in particular, the two camps were in violent opposition to one another. The pioneers of enlightenment found a more favorable climate in the extreme North (Lithuania) and South (Odessa). But if Haskalah failed to take root with the masses of the people, especially at first, one may find the root cause only secondarily in native Jewish opposition; one must look first to the extreme severity of Jewish life under the reigns of Alexander I and Nicholas I. Along with the Russian masses these two monarchs shared the traditional prejudices against and fear of the Jew and his religion. The Jew as a human being was practically unknown in Russia. He was seen only through the lenses of anti-Semitic distortion and caricature.

The progress of Haskalah in Eastern Europe may be traced geographically. The impulses generated in Berlin gradually radiated eastward to Austria, then to Poland, Lithuania, and then to the other centers of Jewry in Russia. Since conditions in these lands were very different from those in Germany, the course of enlightenment in Eastern Europe diverged considerably from its original conception. There was, first of all, a much denser concentration of Jewish masses in Eastern Europe, and the non-Jewish environment itself stood at a lower cultural level than that which obtained in the West. Thus, although the danger of rapid disintegration of Jewish identification was not altogether absent in Eastern Europe, by and large the chances of its rapid occurrence were sharply diminished. The Haskalah in the East was confronted by indigenous Jewish forces—mystic revivalism in the form of Hasidism on the one hand, and Talmudic reform of the type originated by the Gaon of Vilna on the other—which for some time kept the masses impervious to its doctrines. Moreover, prolific though its literary output was, Haskalah had not yet brought forth a personality of the charismatic caliber of either Elijah, the Gaon of Vilna, or the Baal Shem Tov.

The aim of the Haskalah movement may be stated simply: the creation of a new Jewish character, ready to take its place in the society at large. The *maskilim* (proponents of the Haskalah) set out to revolutionize the very bases of Jewish life, thought, and education. Up to this time education had been general but parochial. Every Russian Jew, even many of the women, could read the prayers and the Bible. In the ghettos of Russia, as everywhere else within European Jewry, learning was a universal pursuit. When Max Lilienthal, a German Jew, was called to Riga in 1840 to reform the Jewish system of education, he found a situation epitomized by the following scene:

> Soon a poorly clad couple entered, the man carrying in his arms a young boy of about six, wrapped in a *talit* [prayer shawl]. Both father and mother were weeping with joy, grateful to God who had preserved them that they might witness this beautiful and meaningful moment. Having extended a cordial welcome to the newcomers, the *melamed* [teacher] took the hero of the celebration into his arms and stood him upon a table. Afterwards, the boy was seated on a bench and was the first to receive cake, nuts, raisins, and dainties, of which the happy mother had brought along an apronful. The teacher then sat down near the youngster, placed a card with a printed alphabet before him and, taking a long pointer, began the first lesson by blessing his newly-initiated pupil that he may be raised for the study of the Torah, marriage, and good deeds.

We receive another glimpse into cultural life in a small Russian town during the time of Nicholas I from the autobiography of Abraham Paperna, a Hebrew writer of the Haskalah:

> Educational institutions in the modern sense of the word were conspicuous by their absence in our town. There was no government or public school of a secular character in Kopyl. The Christian population was without exception illiterate. The Jewish population, on the other hand, had an overabundance of schools, though of a special type. First, there were the *hadarim* [elementary classes]—about twenty of them. Kopyl had a population of about three thousand souls, Jews, White Russians, and Tatars. Jews constituted the minority. All Jewish male children from the ages of four to thirteen were taught in *heder*. Although education was not compulsory for girls, they, too, in most cases could read the prayers and the Pentateuch in Yiddish translation. A Jew of Kopyl spared nothing for the education of his children. It was not rare for a poor man to sell his last candlestick or his only pillow to pay the *melamed*. . . . With the single exception of Meerke the idiot, who was both stoker in the bathhouse and water-carrier, there were no ignoramuses in Kopyl. And even this moronic water-carrier somehow knew the prayers and could quite satisfactorily recite the blessings over the Torah.

Although the culture of Russian Jewry was religious, secular sciences were not completely foreign ground. The Gaon of Vilna, as we have seen, believed that all sciences were essential to a proper

*A typical old-fashioned heder, the Hebrew elementary
school of most East-European Jewish communities. There,
a "rebbe" or "melamed" taught boys to read and write,
introduced them to Torah and Talmud, and to the
traditions of their fathers.*

understanding of the Torah. But the Gaon differed from the *maskilim,* or "Enlighteners," in that he had no intention of removing the Jew from the ghetto life and an essentially Jewish existence; the study of secular subjects was permissible to make one a better Jew, but was not intended to make one a better Russian.

Haskalah in the East was influenced significantly both by the writings of the earlier German *maskilim* and by commercial and cultural intercourse. East-European Jewish scholars traveled abroad in quest of secular knowledge; Berlin, the residence of Mendelssohn, became the "Jerusalem of enlightenment." After the Congress of Vienna, trade between East and West had increased substantially, broadening the horizons of East-European Jewry. Galicia, an active commercial center situated between Prussia and Russia, received the "enlightenment" from Prussia and in turn transmitted it to backward Russia.

The prince of the Galician Haskalah was Nachman Krochmal. Born in Brody in 1785, the son of a well-to-do merchant, he pursued his studies in Zolkiew, at the home of his wealthy father-in-law. Without teachers or formalized instruction, in an atmosphere of uncompromising opposition to secular learning, Nachman Krochmal not only gained the most exact knowledge of medieval Jewish philosophy, but also made his way into the foreign worlds of German philosophy, linguistics, and science. Soon the town of Zolkiew assumed in Eastern Europe the status held by Berlin in the minds of Western *maskilim*. From Krochmal's outward appearance —out of loyalty to tradition he dressed in the manner of his brethren—it would have been difficult to guess the revolutionary thoughts brewing in the mind of this inconspicuous figure, who seemed a typical Jewish scholar. During his lifetime, Krochmal taught and wrote, but published nothing, for fear of being misunderstood. As he confessed in a letter to S. David Luzzatto,

> Fearing the Lord, I hesitate to teach things that are as coals on fire, for even unwitting error weighs, in truth, like wickedness. . . . I tremble before the wrath of the zealots who are poor in knowledge, entangled in the chains of malicious stupidity. . . .

In 1851, eleven years after Krochmal's death, Leopold Zunz published the fruit of Krochmal's lifetime of strenuous intellectual labor. It is called, aptly enough, "Guide to the Perplexed of the Time." In this work Krochmal speaks of Judaism as an eternal spirit, whose group-soul revivifies the physical Israel in every generation. In the range of its ideas, in the genius of its conception,

Krochmal's "Guide" constitutes a worthy successor to its Maimonidean model.

The early Russian *maskilim,* excited as they were by the ideas of German Haskalah, also became admirers of German culture, of German dress and decorum, of German scientific and academic research. A conscious attempt was made, Russian culture being still too undeveloped to attract emulation, to model oneself after the great figures of the German enlightenment. The "Russian Mendelssohn" was Isaac Baer Levinsohn (1788–1860). Descendant of a rich, mercantile family, he received a secular education in the Russian language in his birthplace, Kremenits, Podolia. He spent many years in Brody where he associated with the leading scholars of Galician Jewry, compiled a grammar of the Russian language in Hebrew, and taught Hebrew in one of the modern schools. His most important work, *Teudah be-Yisrael* (A Testimony in Israel), published in Vilna in 1828, attempted to prove to the Jews that the program of Haskalah was not in conflict with Jewish religion. This book had a profound influence on young Jewish Talmudists, many of whom began to form clubs for the study of Hebrew and Russian. Levinsohn's second book, *Bet Yehudah* (House of Judah) outlined a program of reform for Russian Jewry which became the official platform of the *maskilim.* The author suggested:

> 1. That modern schools be established for children of both sexes, and theological seminaries set up in the cities of Warsaw, Vilna, Odessa and Berdichev. In addition to Jewish studies, students should receive instruction in secular subjects.
>
> 2. That a chief rabbi and council be appointed to have charge of the spiritual life of Russian Jewry.
>
> 3. That competent preachers be obtained to instruct the people.
>
> 4. That at least a third of the people be encouraged to engage in agriculture.
>
> 5. That Jews be discouraged from ostentatious display and luxurious living.

Russian Haskalah, one can readily perceive, was marked by a definite middle-class outlook. Almost all the pioneering humanists came from wealthy merchant families or were professionals (Rapoport, Joseph Perl, Nachman Krochmal). Even the poor *maskilim* were generally patronized by wealthy merchants and so they, too, tended to reflect the middle-class ideas of their benefactors. The very demand for secular education resulted from the conditions and circumstances of the life of the merchant class. It was essential for wealthy businessmen who came into contact with educated capitalists elsewhere to know the German or Russian language, geography, and other secular subjects. *Maskilim* encouraged the Jewish masses to "productivize" themselves, to engage in more useful and dignified occupations, firstly because they were now a handicap to the expansion of the internal market, and secondly because in so doing they would be accepted on a more respected footing by their non-Jewish neighbors. The chagrin of the *maskilim* at the "unproductive" life of their coreligionists led them to the conviction that their program of enlightened secularism would, if put in effect, succeed in solving most of the cultural, economical, and political problems of Jewish life.

Acceptance of the progressive ideas of the *maskilim* was deterred by the policies of Alexander I and Nicholas I. These rulers hoped to break down the isolation of the Jews by introducing secular studies into the curriculum of Jewish schools and to improve their economic status by encouraging agricultural settlement of the land. But the result of their policies was an aggravation of the actual situation, which drove most Jews to cling more tenaciously than ever to their religious traditions and practices. During the reign of Alexander I, secular education was used as a means of strengthening the Christian faith and the authority of the state. It was therefore rejected by Jewish communal leaders. Justifiably, these leaders feared that modern education would make the Jew sensitive to his legal disabilities and consequently dissatisfied with his lot, and liable to desert his faith. The *maskilim* were the only ones who hailed the establishment of the Jewish government schools, but their enthusiasm had no effect on the mass of Russian Jewry. Resistance to these schools only increased when the government introduced the so-called "candle-tax" to support them.

The literature of the Haskalah may be divided into several stages. The first was the period of the "Science of Judaism," with its emphasis on the revival of Hebrew, analysis of Jewish history, literature and philosophy. Rapoport and Krochmal were the main exponents of this movement. The next stage (in the 1820s and 1830s) may be characterized as polemical-rationalist, aimed at destroying the intellectual limits of the Pale, its dogmatism and emphasis on detailed religious observance. The Galician *maskilim* appealed to the Jews to explore the world which lay outside the ghetto, to delve into European literature, natural science, and vocational training. The prose literature of this period satirized in exaggerated manner the life and personality-types which existed within

The famous Genizah (Hebrew for "hiding place")
of the old Ezra Synagogue in Cairo, Egypt, which
yielded up its store of ancient and sacred manuscripts
to Cambridge University Professor Solomon Schechter,
who examines them here in England in 1898.

the Pale. In the 1840s and 1850s, the third stage of Haskalah literature, the emphasis shifted from the condemnation of life within
the Pale to appreciation of the world outside. During this romantic
period Abraham Mapu and Baer Levinsohn rhapsodized over the
glorious past of the Jews—the agricultural life of ancient Judah
and the vital perfection of the Spanish Golden Age.

The positivists among the *maskilim* wanted action, practical reforms which would result in social and economic improvements.
Novels, poetry, and satire were replaced by Hebrew language journals, scientific essays and manuals pressing for educational and
vocational reforms. The poet laureate of the Russian Haskalah,
Judah Leib Gordon, and his contemporary, Moses Leib Lilienblum,
impressed upon the Jews the need to be "modern," to adopt Russian dress and manners, Russian literature and life. At the same
time, but in private, they were to retain their Jewishness; "be a
Jew in your tent and a man abroad," was Gordon's slogan—a
phrase that, as in the case of the German *maskilim* as well, was
packed with innuendoes of assimilation and self-hatred. As we
shall see, however, most Russian *maskilim,* unlike their German
predecessors, were saved from the folly of this cultural program by
a keener sense of history, and turned finally from the misguided
aim of total assimilation to the more realistic, and more radical,
solution of Zionism.

Born as a reaction to Hasidism, the Haskalah in Russia succeeded
in bringing forth a new concept of national renaissance. It aroused
among Russian Jews an aspiration to free inquiry and a love for
knowledge. Among religious Jews, it helped to convert objects of
mere traditionalism into objects of thought; it raised men from the
sphere of blind and unconditional belief into the sphere of doubt,
into a quest for true understanding. And although its main stress
was on general enlightenment and a vague liberalism, it initiated
a spirit of specifically Hebrew revival that was to have tremendous
repercussions in later Jewish history. It prepared the way not only
for modern Hebrew literature, but for that modern triumph of the
Hebrew spirit, *Hibbat Zion,* the love of Zion.

*The Legacy
of Emancipation*

Dawn of Emancipation

Among the many aspects of the ambiguous legacy bequeathed to
later generations by the German movement for enlightenment and
emancipation was what we have come to call the dilemma of the
modern Jew in Western society. As the first dawn of enlightenment

rose over the ghetto walls, many Jews, with the best of intentions, acceded with terrible swiftness to the demand—felt or explicit— that they sever the bonds which tied them to race and tradition. The declaration of moral inferiority which such a capitulation involved was often lightly undertaken. For a radical change had taken place in the psychology of the Jewish people. The Jew's protective shield against the contempt of the world had been shattered. He was offered emancipation, but on very specific terms: that he recognize the turpitude of his people's past history, and acknowledge the bright benevolence of the society which had hitherto exhibited toward him nothing but intolerance and contempt, but which now, in a spirit of charity and condescension, tendered its favors to him. For fear of losing this favor, and in abject gratitude to those who extended it to him, many a Jew accepted without question the interpretation of his people which the outside world had pleased itself to present. To move into that world, he shed the proud tradition of Jewish individuality and uniqueness, divested himself, by a conscious act of the will, even of the knowledge that it was from the wellsprings of his own people's past that Western society drew the standards it now, in a fit of self-gratulatory liberalism, deigned to apply also to him. The Jew had been stripped of all autonomous political status; he was now nothing but a member of a religion, of a sect among other sects, and of a particularly backward one at that. His own intellectual leaders had told him, in what must surely rank as an outstanding example of the human capacity for self-delusion, that he must strive to "be a Jew at home, and a man abroad." Never before had it occurred to this people that to be a Jew was something less than, or other than, to be human. Indeed, to past generations of Jews, to be Jewish was to participate in the very noblest of human experiments, to embody all that was meant by the word humanity. All that, now, was gone. In its place stood merely the craving to be accepted, to be a German, a Frenchman, a Pole, like anyone else, with residual ties to a faith now demeaned to the status of a "persuasion."

Gone too, along with the surrender of a unique Jewish past, was the aspiration for a unique and independent Jewish future. The new spirit of humility before Western culture, and the fear of being thought disloyal, led in the German reform movement to the eradication of Zion from the prayer book, the elimination of Hebrew as the language of worship, and in general the blotting out of all traces of nationalism from Jewish rites and festivals. All recollections of national glory were stricken from memory. In the hope of

winning the confidence of the European world, of showing themselves worthy of emancipation, many Jews shrank not even from
baptism, "the ticket of admission," as Heine called it, "to European
society," but underwent that Christian rite.

History was to teach the lesson of irony to the descendants of
that generation which sought to ignore historical experience, and
which in such tragic innocence misread the spirit of European
tolerance. It soon became clear that the efforts to "elevate" Judaism
in accordance with the prescriptions of the Berlin Haskalah, and
thus to win the respect of Europe, were doomed to collapse. The
few who saw through the deceit and cynicism of the period turned
to revolutionary movements of all kinds, or away from politics
altogether into a dream-world of utopian speculation. But decades
were to pass before an entirely new generation would discover and
acknowledge the basic contradictions in the Jewish attitude toward
enlightenment. By that time Judaism had gone through a profound
crisis of conscience, and the torch of authentic Jewish feeling had
passed from Western to Eastern Europe. "So long as the Jew denies
his nationality," Moses Hess would then declare, "because he has
not the self-denial to admit his solidarity with an unfortunate, despised, and persecuted people, his false attitude must become more
intolerable with every passing day." The rise of modern anti-Semitism would enforce the intolerable quality of Jewish life in Europe,
and the rise of modern Zionism would provide the first clear diagnosis of a situation which had become well-nigh hopeless, and the
first solution to a problem which had become all but insoluble.

16 ❧ Anti-Semitism and Migrations

ANTI-SEMITISM in the nineteenth century took a new form. It was supported by racist theories and used as an instrument of power by political parties. To be sure, religious distrust of the Jews was no new phenomenon. Jews had been persecuted through the ages for professing adherence to a different religion, one which they were not prepared to surrender even at the penalty of death. Religious superstitions had thrived in the Middle Ages, at a time when they were not out of context with the spirit of the age itself. But that they should persist in the nineteenth century, in an era of modern ideas, scientific advancements, industrialization, movements of national liberation—this was not, on the face of it, to be expected. The most persistent of these lingering superstitions was the Blood Libel, an ancient canard according to which Jews were ritual murderers, who collected the blood of Christians to use in the baking of Passover *matzot*. Nothing could obliterate from the minds of the ignorant peasants this image of the Jew as a "drinker of blood." Before 1840, fifteen such accusations against Jews were aired in Rumania, Poland, Russia, Italy, and Germany. In February 1840, a high-ranking Catholic priest disappeared and the blame was deliberately planted on the Jews.

The insistence of the Jews on their unique religious observances never failed to arouse fear and distrust among Christians, who were still inclined to look upon the Jews as deniers of the true faith.

This attitude was reflected sharply in the Mortara case of 1858. It involved a Jewish child born in Bologna, who at the age of one became desperately ill, and was baptized by his Catholic nurse lest he die a heathen. For seven years the nurse kept the baptism a secret, but then finally divulged the information to the Holy Office. The Papal authorities immediately kidnaped the child, determined that he be educated as a Christian and granted all the privileges of Christian citizenship. Despite the pressures placed on the Pope by most foreign governments, including even Catholic ones, all pleas that the child be surrendered were coldly rejected. American Jewry, still quite unorganized at the time, found itself vociferously demanding action, and doing so with a good deal of support from the American press and the American people. Moses Montefiore went personally to Rome to see the Pope, but was refused an audience. Mortara grew up, entered the Church, and died as a missionary priest in Belgium during World War II.

Such was the ambiguous climate of the nineteenth century, an era which had given the Jew much longed-for and sought-after liberty, the opportunity to become a citizen, to participate fully in the social, political and economic life around him, to assimilate into non-Jewish society, and, sometimes, to try to forget the differences and deep-seated prejudices which centuries of enforced separation had fostered in the minds of those around him. The Jews had plunged with abounding energy, enthusiasm, and natural ability and will to succeed into every field opened to them: commerce, industry, the professions, journalism. Within a generation, in Germany and elsewhere, they had moved from a condition of servitude to positions of influence. They took their responsibilities and obligations to society very seriously indeed.

Why, then, were they not accepted? Everywhere during this century, the presence of Jews was felt very keenly by non-Jews. Despite their insignificant numbers—in France they constituted less than one per cent of the total population, in Germany just over one per cent, in the Hapsburg Empire only slightly more—their participation in the fields open to them was exceptionally high, and their rapid rise to economic success was bitterly resented. World economy had been upset by industrialization and mechanization. The middle class now emerged with sufficient power to challenge the aristocratic landowners on an economic basis. Jews, with their long experience in trading and merchandising, felt at home in this new situation. Excited by the challenge posed to their talents, and having little to lose, they were prepared to take risks in speculation. The lower classes, who were excluded from the general rush for money, and the upper classes, who were being replaced by the ascendant bourgeoisie, deeply resented Jewish participation in the rising capitalist classes. The wealth of the Jewish bankers, though grossly exaggerated in the popular imagination, was particularly irksome. These bankers had risen quickly and effectively to international power and wealth, largely through the financial assistance they afforded to European dynasties in the petty wars of the nineteenth century. Now they had served their purpose and seemed superfluous. Why, then, should they still be tolerated?

In 1873, a sudden slump in the German stock market was blamed directly on Jewish financiers, despite the fact that very few Jews had been among the speculators. All financial scandals were assumed to be Jewish in origin, to be in fact part of a vast web, with the Rothschilds at the center, which was designed to bring about the exploitation and impoverishment of Christian Europe. Upon the failure of investments in the Panama Canal scheme, in which three Jews had become involved, but only after it was too late to rectify the damage, the anti-Semitic press splashed news of alleged Jewish corruption all over Europe.

In the economic world, then, Jews were feared more than their capitalist Christian counterparts, partly because of their religious and national isolation, partly because they had no regard for the dying feudal and ecclesiastical society of which they had never been part and which was then the object of much sentimental nostalgia. Similarly, in the arena of politics, the Jews were held in general disfavor. There was a millennium of lost ground to be made up once citizenship was recovered, and Jews had spared no pains in entering into the political struggles of the period, usually on the side of the liberal and progressive forces, from whom alone they could hope for emancipation and tolerance. Now, suddenly, the rise of political anti-Semitism in Germany crushed all hopes for freedom and assimilation. The new economic order had pitted the classes against each other in political battle. The stage was alive with conflicts—the dying aristocracy, the rising middle class, and the excluded lower class each struggling for political control. In this struggle, new bait had to be found to lure the populace to the support of one or another of the various parties. Who better than the Jews could serve this function—the apparent culprits of the new social and economic disorder, the "industrialist liberal secularists" against whom there was already a long tradition of religious prejudice? There existed no more effective way of branding

An engraving portrays the new bourgeoisie of Britain under the arcades of The Royal Exchange at the end of the 18th century. The man with the stick at the right has the beard and dress of a foreign-born Ashkenazi Jew of the time.

the new institutions of society as undesirable than to label them "Jewish." Indeed, there was the added advantage that this maneuver helped to bind together many diverse groups and interests, each with its own particular grievance, into a single bloc.

Finally, as the concept of nationalism gathered strength and appeal in the nineteenth century, more and more the Jews were singled out as an international people, identified and grouped together by a religion, a language, and a body of writing, a people who professed loyalty to the country in which they were domiciled, but who yearned for their ancient home. French nationalists complained that "the Jews have no *patrie* in the sense we understand. . . . For them it is the place where they find the most advantage. . . . The Jews find their *patrie* wherever their best interests lie." Despite the very best effort on the part of the Jews to assimilate themselves to the lands of Europe, it was widely believed that no Jew could be truly loyal to the country in which he lived. That this representation was patently and demonstrably false did not hinder anyone from believing it to be true, or from acting on that belief. As for the feelings of the Jews in the matter, Theodor Herzl spoke for them all when he wrote:

> We are a people—one people. We have honestly endeavored everywhere to merge ourselves in the social life of surrounding communities and to preserve only the faith of our fathers. We are not permitted to do so. In vain are we loyal patriots, our loyalty in some places running to extremes; in vain do we make the same sacrifices of life and property as our fellow citizens; in vain do we strive to increase the fame of our native land in science and art, or her wealth by trade and commerce. In countries where we have lived for centuries we are still cried down as strangers, and often by those whose ancestors were not yet domiciled in the land where Jews had already had the experience of suffering. . . . In the world as it is now, and for an indefinite period will probably remain, might precedes right. It is useless, therefore, for us to be loyal patriots, as were the Huguenots, who were forced to emigrate. If we could only be left in peace. . . . But I think we shall not be left in peace.

(From *The Jewish State*)

Germany
Anti-Semitism
& Migrations

In 1871, Bismarck succeeded in unifying the masses of independent Prussian principalities through an appeal to "nationalism," his armies having decisively defeated the "common enemy" of all

Prussians—the French. Bismarck's "nationalism" was identical in form to that system of government which philosophers like Kant, Fichte, and Hegel had been advocating for the past sixty years: a Christian German nation in which the will of the state took precedence over the needs of the individual. Determined to preserve his new German Empire, Bismarck worked to suppress all separatist tendencies. In 1873 he launched a merciless campaign, the *Kultur Kampf,* against the Catholics, persecuting and imprisoning aged and respected priests for no greater offense than loyalty to their religion. In 1879, a nationwide campaign of extraordinary violence, directed against the National Liberal Party, swept through Germany. The Jews, who were largely identified with the National Liberals, and who therefore represented everything a good German should avoid, became the target of this campaign, which swiftly took on the character of an anti-Semitic attack. "I expressed my disapproval of it," Bismarck later rationalized, "but I did nothing more as it was a most useful means of attacking the progressives." The conservatives were, in addition, supported by the brilliant theoretical writings of men like Treitschke and Friedrich Nietzsche, who helped to pollute the air with contempt for the Jews.

Austria-Hungary   Anti-Semitism in the Austro-Hungarian lands, as in Germany, was cloaked as dislike for the urban, middle-class liberal party. Austrian Jews, to an even greater extent than their German coreligionists, had played a substantial role in the development of modern capitalism in their adopted land. The campaign against them became particularly virulent in the 1880s, when a highly contentious Catholic anti-Semite, August Rohling, received the Chair of Theology at Prague University. Despite his sketchy knowledge of Hebrew, Rohling unhesitantly denounced the religious pronouncements of the Talmud and proclaimed the veracity of all the old medieval libels concerning alleged Jewish use of Christian blood.

Ritual murder accusations soon proliferated. A case which attracted much attention involved the murder in 1882 of a young girl living in Tisza-Eszlar in Hungary. A number of Jews were arrested on grounds of ritual murder, but owing to insufficient evidence, they were acquitted. Anti-Semitic feeling had been strong throughout the trial. Even the socialists tried to create an anti-Semitic party by employing an agitator to stir up anti-Semitism among the working classes in certain industrial suburbs, by charging

that rich Jewish capitalists had managed to secure the acquittal of their "guilty" coreligionists. Owing to the courageous intervention of Dr. Joseph Bloch, the rabbi who served the suburbs chosen by the socialists for their propagandizing, the attempt failed. It was in fact this same Dr. Bloch who finally silenced Rohling. The rabbi published such scathing attacks on Rohling that the professor of theology was finally compelled to bring him to court for libel. The day before the trial, Rohling withdrew the charge, thereby publicly acknowledging the falsity of his own statements concerning the nature of Judaism.

By far the most solid conceptual support for modern anti-Semitism as it developed in Western Europe came from the theory of racism which was a doctrinal element in conservative German nationalism in the nineteenth century. This theory provided biological "proof" of the racial superiority of Germans, and, conversely, of the racial inferiority of all non-Germans, foremost among them the Jews. The new theory of racism, as expounded in pseudo-scientific form by European anthropologists and historians, was based on the assumption that human beings belong to different race groups, each group possessing a particular physiognomy and a common language source. German racism grew out of the "Aryan" myth, according to which Roman, Germanic, and Slavic tongues could be reduced to a common Aryan source; the next step was to attribute to the Aryan race a single physical type, that of the blond, blue-eyed Nordic. Finally, it was deduced by Count Joseph de Gobineau, a French diplomat, that all civilization began with the Aryan race, representatives of which were now to be found only in Central Europe. All this having been established, it followed that the Germans, the living embodiment of this pristine racial purity, were entitled to lay claim to an inherent superiority over the short, black-haired, dark-eyed Jew.

The idea of racial superiority had a terrific impact on the German people. Richard Wagner, the eminent composer, warned the Germans against racial degeneration: "We may explain the decay of the German folk by the fact that it is now exposed without defense to the penetration of the Jew." Out of this theory grew the concomitant fear that German blood was in danger of contamination by physical contact with the Jews, intermarriage with whom would result in the subversive decay of the German nation.

The masterpiece of German racism was written by a renegade Englishman, Houston Stewart Chamberlain, under the title *Die Grundlagen des Neunzehnten Jahrhunderts* ("The Foundations of the Nineteenth Century"). In this work Chamberlain traced the history of the German race with impressive documentation; even Jesus was transformed by him into an Aryan. The Jews he deemed a worthless race whose mission was to contaminate the German racial stream, and to "produce a band of pseudo-Hebraic *mestizos*, a people beyond all doubt degenerate physically, mentally, and morally." These sentiments, repeated cautiously at first, and held in check by the civilized restrictions of law and order, would in later years become the rallying cry of an entire social system, and in the twentieth century would set off the most fearful eruption of hatred in all human history.

France France, too, had at this time a strong conservative party which longed for the days of the *Ancien Régime* and disapproved of the Republicans. The conservatives believed that France, in order to become powerful, must rid herself of liberals, internationalists, aliens, and Jews. The "Action Française," founded on this principle, was the first movement in Western Europe to transform the ideology of modern anti-Semitism into organized physical violence, although the objects of its assault included non-Jewish liberals as well. One of the most outspoken of French Jew-haters was Edouard-Adolphe Drumont, an unscrupulous and able conservative, intent on attacking the Republicans but cynical enough to resort to anti-Semitism in order to attract followers. A bitter and frustrated man, who frequently sought escape from reality in spiritualism, Drumont was the author of a work entitled *La France Juive*, in which he maintained that the Jews were the cause of economic and social distress in France. Although the Jews constituted only one quarter of one per cent of the French population, Drumont credited them with ownership of over half the wealth of France. He advocated the expropriation of all Jewish property, which, he charged, had been unfairly acquired, and he encouraged the workers of France to help themselves to Jewish possessions. Drumont also "exposed" an international plot on the part of the Jews and Freemasons to destroy Christendom and gain world control, France being the first target of this alleged cabal. His book was dressed in the garb of religious inspiration and love of justice—God, he claimed, was on his side. The book was a great popular success, in its first year alone selling 100,000 copies; within ten years it went through more than 140 editions. Spurred on by this success, Drumont took every available occasion to lash out against the Jews, using as his mouthpiece the newspaper *La Libre Parole*. He became the chief spokesman of the anti-Dreyfusards, and was on record as approving any persecution of the Jews at any time. In the words of one of his own disciples, "What Drumont proclaimed, Hitler achieved."

England In England the danger of anti-Semitism was felt only briefly when Disraeli, as Conservative Prime Minister, was preparing for the negotiations about the future of the Balkans which led up to the Treaty of Berlin in 1878. The British Liberals, whom Jews usually supported, were on the side of Russia against Turkey. Russia, however, was known as the great oppressor of Eastern Jewry, while Turkey treated her Jews fairly well. Calumny fell on Disraeli and those Jews who, it was alleged, were putting their own interests before those of England. But when Disraeli returned from Berlin with a *fait accompli*, the treaty signed, the weed of anti-Semitism faded before it even had a chance to blossom.

Russia Russia's problem was different from that of the Western European countries. There the Jews were far more numerous than in any other single country, constituting in all about two-thirds of world Jewry. But they were not citizens. The Jews of Russia suffered from restrictive legislation with regard to rights of residence, economic opportunities, marriage, etc. Having been given little incentive to assimilate, they continued to live apart from the general populace. A small number of Jewish financiers and speculators, it is true, helped to pioneer in the railways and other commercial developments, and these few were granted permission to settle in towns outside the Pale of Settlement, but Jewish participation in early progressive activities was small. Nevertheless, Jews were blamed for the assassination of Alexander II in 1881, and for the next twenty years were called to account for the spread of liberal ideas in Russia. This was a blatant misrepresentation, since liberal and revolutionary ideas and activities were fermented in the intellectual atmosphere of the universities, to which only a minuscule percentage of Jews was admitted. There was, however, a small group of Jewish youths, with Leon Trotsky (Bronstein) at their head, who joined the revolutionary party and were to share in the Bolshevik rise to power in 1917.

In 1894 Nicholas II succeeded his father Alexander III as Tsar. A weak and mild ruler, Nicholas was persuaded by those about him that his greatest enemies were his Jewish subjects. The main instrument used in the official propagation of this notion was the "Protocols of the Elders of Zion," a forgery prepared for the enlightenment of the Tsar. The Protocols were fabricated at the Paris office of the Russian police between 1901 and 1905. In 1905 they were issued to the public and presented to the Tsar. As the latter did not believe them to be genuine, they seem to have been discarded temporarily. It was only after 1919 that copies were evidently circulated widely, particularly in Western Europe. The Protocols purported to show, from reports of an alleged International Jewish Congress, that there was a widespread international Jewish movement to destroy existing Christian organizations and to replace them by Jewish world domination. (This is essentially the same plot that was "exposed" by Drumont in France and by Hillaire Belloc in England.) The Bolshevist revolution of 1917 was claimed as evidence that this fantastic Jewish plot had begun to be realized. After all, were not Trotsky and Bela Kun (the Hungarian Communist) Jewish? The message of the Protocols was clear: "resistance to liberalism and socialism was vital if the world was to be rescued from malevolent Jewish conspiracy."

Such resistance was rapidly forthcoming. In Southern Russia, anti-Bolshevik forces slew in their fury thousands of defenseless Jews. Translations and adaptations of the Russian original of the Protocols appeared in most of the languages of Western Europe, and later even in Japanese and Arabic. They were even passed off as a record of the proceedings of the First Zionist Congress. In 1921, the London *Times* exposed the Protocols as an outright forgery, a fabrication based on blatant lies, but it was already too late; the Protocols had impressed themselves deeply on too many people who needed to believe them, and upon these people the disclosure of the truth had no effect. Anti-Semites to this day have persisted in believing the Protocols and have used them as an illustration of the perfidy and treachery of the Jews. Nazis, Arabs, and rabble-rousers in every land have taken them to heart and used them for the most outrageous kinds of incitement. In the United States, they were circulated by Henry Ford, who published them in his newspaper, *The Dearborn Independent,* and by Father Charles E. Coughlin in his *Social Justice.* Today they are the stuff of anti-Semitic vilification issuing from recognized sources in the Soviet Union and from various Arab governments—a potent example of the Big Lie and the twentieth century's substitute for the blood libels and religious superstition of the Middle Ages, they are medieval myths that die hard even in modern times.

Nineteenth-century anti-Semitism came as a bitter blow to the Jews of Europe who had hoped that as citizens they would be accepted wholeheartedly into the society in which they lived. The new doctrines of non-religious anti-Semitism shook their equilibrium and threw them into confusion. On the one hand they were attacked by men like Treitschke, supposedly for not having lived up to German expectations, that is, for not having become assimilated enough. On the other hand they were assaulted for having assimilated too well, to the point where they were "contaminating" German society. Everything seemed to conspire to lure the Jews deeper and deeper into confusion and self-hatred. The result was both a race for feverish assimilation and an awakening, at long last, of Jewish nationalism.

For no liberal program of effort could bridge the wide gap which centuries of hatred and discrimination had opened up between the Jew and his neighbors. Anti-Semitism had now assumed political colors, as longstanding popular prejudices against Jews were used now by one party, now by another, to win the support of the masses. Intensified by racism, exacerbated by economic crises and political insecurity, modern anti-Semitism on the eve of the twentieth century was well on the way to its final extreme measure: physical annihilation.

The Dreyfus Affair In December 1894, Alfred Dreyfus, a captain in the French army and a Jew, was convicted of treason and sentenced to life imprisonment on Devil's Island. The controversy surrounding this event was to rock the very foundations of the French Republic and to engage the minds and consciences of men everywhere for many years. At stake was not only the reputation and integrity of a single man, but the good name of an entire culture.

Alfred Dreyfus was accused of having passed secret army information to the Germans. The corpus delicti was the famous *bordereau,* an unsigned letter salvaged by a cleaning-woman from a wastepaper basket at the German Embassy and handed over to

French Military Intelligence. A comparison of the handwriting of several officers with that of the *bordereau,* and a slow process of elimination, led to the arraignment of Dreyfus, an artillery officer, as the most likely culprit. That his writing was by no means identical with that of the *bordereau* was unimportant to his accusers. Dreyfus was rich, cold, snobbish, boastful, ambitious, and, although highly assimilated, a Jew. He was arrested, held incommunicado, judged before a military court martial, and formally accused of treason. At the trial, the very fragile evidence of the *bordereau* was bolstered by a "secret dossier" submitted to the judges only; its contents were to remain secret so as not to jeopardize state security. Dreyfus was condemned to military degradation and perpetual imprisonment despite his persistent pleas of innocence and a clear lack of motive.

There was widespread indignation in France against the "traitor." Jean Jaurès, a socialist leader, regretted that he had not been shot. Anti-Semitic journalists, like those on the staff of *La Libre Parole,* who had helped to bring about the decision to prosecute, found in the condemnation of a Jewish officer a powerful argument in favor of their thesis of Jewish subversion. Nearly all were convinced of the guilt of Dreyfus.

In the minds of a few, however, there lingered a doubt. Dreyfus's brother Mathieu, determined to see a resumption of the trial, searched for evidence pointing to the real traitor. In the meantime, changes had been made in the Intelligence staff; Sandherr, the chief, had retired and was replaced by Picquart, an anti-Semite but a man of honor and intelligence. In March 1896, a further document passed into the hands of the French Intelligence, a special delivery letter for use within Paris and known as *le petit bleu.* It too was concerned with the passing on of information; its writing was identical with that of the *bordereau.* Dreyfus at this time was on Devil's Island; who, then, was the culprit? Picquart, who had discovered the *petit bleu,* had cause to suspect Major Esterhazy, an officer with a reputation as a "dissolute spender" and, at the time, overburdened with debts. Picquart revealed the information to his assistant Henry. Henry adopted the attitude that under no circumstances could the Army afford to admit that it had made an error, and he set about forging new evidence to strengthen the case against Dreyfus. He also informed his superiors that Picquart was about to make embarrassing investigations into the original conviction. Picquart was hastily transferred to Tunisia, but before leaving, he transmitted his discovery to his attorney, who in turn informed

Cinq Centimes

L'AURORE

Littéraire, Artistique, Sociale

ERNES…

LES ANNO…
142 — Ru…
AUX…

Les manuscri…

ADRESS…
à M. A.

J'Accuse…!

…RE AU PRÉSIDENT DE LA RÉPU…

Par ÉMILE ZOLA

…RE

FAURE

…République

…résident,

…s, dans ma grati-
…llant accueil que
… jour, d'avoir la
…gloire de et vous
…, si heureuse jus-
…e, la plus honteuse,
…ble des taches?

…sain et sauf des bas-
…us avez conquis les
…paraissez rayonnant
… de cette fête patrio-
…sse russe a été pour
…us vous préparez à pré-
…el triomphe de notre
…verselle, qui couronnera
…cle de travail, de vérité
…Mais quelle tache de boue
… —j'allais dire sur votre
… cette abominable affaire
…onseil de guerre vient,
…crime social a pu être commis,
…ils ont osé, j'oserai aussi.
…vérité, je la dirai, car j'ai pro-
…dire, si la justice, réguliè-
…isie, ne la faisait pas, pleine
… Mon devoir est de parler, je
…pas être complice. Mes nuits
…t hantées par le spectre de l'in-
… qui expie là-bas, dans la plus
…des tortures, un crime qu'il
…commis.

…s, monsieur le Prési-
…vérité, de

lieu, des papiers disparaissaient
…core; et l'auteur du bordereau était
recherché, lorsqu'un a priori se fit
peu à peu que l'on
être qu'un officier de l'état-major, et
un officier d'artillerie : double er-
reur manifeste, qui montre avec quel
esprit superficiel on avait étudié ce
bordereau, car un examen raisonné
démontre qu'il ne pouvait s'agir que
d'un officier de troupe. On cherchait
donc dans la maison, on examinait
les écritures, c'était comme une affaire
de famille, un traître à surprendre
dans les bureaux mêmes, pour l'en
expulser. Et, sans que je veuille re-
faire ici une histoire connue en partie,
le commandant du Paty de Clam entre
en scène, dès qu'un premier soupçon
tombe sur Dreyfus. A partir de ce moment, c'est lui qui a inventé Dreyfus, il se fait
l'affaire devient son affaire, il se fait
fort de confondre le traître, de l'ame-
ner à des aveux complets. Il y a bien
le ministre de la guerre, le général
Mercier, dont l'intelligence semble
médiocre; il y a bien le chef de l'état-
major, le général de Boisdeffre, qui
paraît avoir cédé à sa passion cléri-
cale, et le sous-chef de l'état-major, le
général Gonse, dont la conscience a pu
s'accommoder de beaucoup de choses.
Mais, au fond, il n'y a d'abord que le
commandant du Paty de Clam, qui les
mène tous, qui les hypnotise, car il
s'occupe aussi de spiritisme, d'occul-
tisme, il converse avec les esprits. On
ne croira jamais les expériences aux-
quelles il a soumis le malheureux
Dreyfus, les pièges dans lesquels il a
voulu le faire tomber, les enquêtes
folles, les imaginations monstrueuses,
toute une démence torturante.

Ah! cette première affaire, elle est
un cauchemar, pour qui la connaît
dans ses détails vrais! Le commandant
du Paty de Clam arrête Dreyfus, le met
au secret. Il court chez madame Dreyfus, … la terrorise, lui dit que, si elle
… t'est perdu. Pendant ce

Est-ce donc vrai, les choses indicibles,
les choses dangereuses, capables de
…mettre l'Europe … flammes, qu'on a
… enterrer … derrière ce
huis clos? Non! il n'y a eu, derrière,
que les imaginations romanesques et
démentes du commandant du Paty de
Clam. Tout cela n'a été fait que pour
cacher le plus saugrenu des romans-
feuilletons. Et il suffit, pour s'en assu-
rer, d'étudier attentivement l'acte d'accusation lu devant le conseil de guerre.

Ah! le néant de cet acte d'accusation! Qu'un homme ait pu être con-
damné sur cet acte, c'est un prodige
d'iniquité. Je défie les honnêtes gens
de le lire, sans que leur cœur bondisse
d'indignation et crie leur révolte, en
pensant à l'expiation démesurée, là-
bas, à l'île du Diable. Dreyfus sait
plusieurs langues, crime; on n'a trouvé
chez lui aucun papier compromettant,
crime; il va parfois dans son pays d'o-
rigine, crime; il est laborieux, il a le
souci de tout savoir, crime; il ne se
trouble pas, crime; il se trouble,
crime. Et les naïvetés de rédaction,
les formelles assertions dans le vide!
On nous avait parlé de quatorze chefs
d'accusation : nous n'en trouvons
qu'une seule en fin de compte, celle
du bordereau; et nous apprenons
même que les experts n'étaient pas
d'accord, qu'un d'eux, M. Gobert, a
été bousculé militairement, parce qu'il
se permettait de ne pas conclure dans
le sens désiré. On parlait aussi de
vingt-trois officiers qui étaient venus
accabler Dreyfus de leurs témoignages.
Nous ignorons encore leurs inter-
rogatoires, mais il est certain que
tous ne l'avaient pas chargé; et il
est à remarquer, en outre, que tous
appartenaient aux bureaux de la
guerre. C'est un procès de famille,
on est là entre soi, et il faut s'en sou-
venir : l'état-major a voulu le procès,
l'a jugé, et il vient de le juger une
seconde fois.

Donc, il ne restait que le bordereau,
sur lequel les experts ne s'étaient pas
entendus. On raconte que, dans la
…mbre du conseil, les juges allaient
… acquitter. Et, dès lors,
…l'obstination

profondément, s'inquiètent, cherchent,
finissent par se convaincre de l'innocence de Dreyfus.

Je ne ferai pas l'historique des dou-
tes, puis de la conviction de M. Scheurer-Kestner. Mais, pendant qu'il fouil-
lait de son côté, il se passait des faits
graves à l'état-major même. Le colonel Sandherr était mort, et le
lieutenant-colonel Picquart lui avait
succédé comme chef du bureau des
renseignements. Et c'est à ce titre,
dans l'exercice de ses fonctions, que ce
dernier eut un jour entre les mains
une lettre-télégramme, adressée au
commandant Esterhazy, par un agent
d'une puissance étrangère. Son devoir
strict était qu'il n'a jamais agi en
dehors de la volonté de ses supérieurs.
Il soumit donc ses soupçons à ses supérieurs hiérarchiques, le général
Gonse, puis le général de Boisdeffre,
puis le général Billot, qui avait succédé au général Mercier comme ministre de la guerre. Le fameux dossier
Picquart, dont il a été tant parlé, n'a
jamais été que le dossier Billot, j'en-
tends le dossier fait par un subordonné
pour son ministre, le dossier qui doit
exister encore au ministère de la
guerre. Les recherches durèrent de mai
à septembre 1896, et ce qu'il faut affir-
mer bien haut, c'est que le général
Gonse était convaincu de la culpabilité
d'Esterhazy, c'est que le général
Boisdeffre et le général Billot ne met-
taient pas en doute que le fameux
bordereau fût de l'écriture d'Esterhazy.
L'enquête du lieutenant-colonel Picquart avait abouti à cette constatation
certaine. Mais l'émoi était grand, car
la condamnation d'Esterhazy entraî-
nait inévitablement la révision du procès Dreyfus; et c'était ce que l'état-
major ne voulait à aucun prix.

Il dut y avoir là une minute psycho-
logique pleine d'angoisse. Remarquez
que le général Billot n'était compromis
dans rien, il arrivait tout frais, il pouvait faire la vérité. Il n'osa pas, dans
la terreur sans doute de l'opinion pu-
blique; certainement aussi dans la
crainte de livrer tout l'état-major, le
général de Boisdeffre, le général Gonse,
… compter les sous-ordres. Puis, ce
… qu'une minute de combat en-
… croyait

avec lui une correspondance amic…
Seulement, il est des secrets qu'i…
fait pas bon d'avoir surpris.

A Paris, la vérité marchait, ir…
tible, et l'on sait de quelle faço…
rage attendu éclata. M. Mathieu…
fus dénonça le commandant Est…
comme le véritable auteur du…
reau, au moment où M. Sc…
Kestner allait déposer, entre l…
du garde des sceaux, une dem…
révision du procès. Et c'est i…
commandant Esterhazy pa…
témoignages le montrent …
folé, prêt au suicide ou …
Puis, tout d'un coup, il pay…
il étonne Paris par la viole…
attitude. C'est que du seco…
venu, il avait reçu une let…
l'avertissant des menées …
mis, une dame mysté…
même dérangée de nuit…
mettre une pièce volée …
qui devait le sauver. …
m'empêcher de retrouv…
nant-colonel du Paty …
connaissant les expédi…
gination fertile. Son …
bilité de Dreyfus, et …
a voulu sûrement co…
vre. La révision…
c'était l'écrouleme…
leton si extravag…
dont le dénouem…
lieu à l'île du …
qu'il ne pouvait …
le duel à avoir…
lieutenant-colonel Pic…
colonel du Paty…
sage découvert…
les retrouvera…
deux devant la…
c'est toujours…
fend, qui ne la…
crime, dont…
d'heure en h…

On s'est d…
étaient les…
dant Ester…
l'ombre, le…
de Clam …
tout conn…
moyens la…
néral de …
Gonse, …
même, …
acquit…

Scheurer-Kestner, the liberal vice-president of the French Senate. Scheurer-Kestner determined to take up the fight for justice.

The persistence of the small circle of Dreyfusards proved successful, at least in part. Esterhazy was tried by court martial, but was found innocent. The news aroused a terrific response. The newspaper *L'Aurore* published an open letter to the President of the Republic written by the novelist Emile Zola. Zola denounced the acquittal of Esterhazy as a "crime against humanity" and accused members of the General Staff of having openly falsified and forged evidence, of deliberately trying to destroy an innocent man and whitewash a guilty one. Zola, as Anatole France remarked, became for a moment "the Conscience of Man." For his pains he was accused of libel, and had to flee the country to escape imprisonment. But his outrage had had an effect. In 1898 the new Army Chief of Staff, Cavaignac, felt obliged to study the "secret" Dreyfus dossier, due to certain incriminating information he had received about Esterhazy. Cavaignac could not fail to detect the clumsy forgery which had been compiled by Henry. The latter was arrested, thrown into jail, and there committed suicide. For the anti-Dreyfusards Henry died a hero, a great patriot who had tried to save the army from humiliation and possible ruin.

In June 1899, Dreyfus was returned to France for retrial. Only thirty-nine years old, he was bent, gaunt, and almost bald: a broken man. Despite the irrefutable evidence in his favor—the *bordereau,* Henry's forgeries, newly revealed data pointing to Esterhazy's complicity—Dreyfus was again pronounced guilty. His sentence was reduced to ten years because of "extenuating circumstances." Now the liberal reaction to this verdict, both in France and in the rest of Western Europe, was violent. The new President of the French Republic, Emile Loubet, himself a liberal, hastily pardoned Dreyfus. In 1906, twelve years after the inception of the case, Dreyfus was fully exonerated and reinstated in his rank; shortly afterward, he received the medal of the Legion of Honor.

For the French army, the question of the role of anti-Semitism in the Dreyfus Affair was secondary; of greater importance was the question of secrecy. But the motives of a Jew who wished to follow a military career were nevertheless made a matter of public doubt. Why should a Jew have renounced the life of commerce and finance pursued by so many of his coreligionists in order to enter the army? And because his motives appeared questionable, his potential disloyalty came to seem likely. If Dreyfus was not found guilty because he was a Jew, the idea of his guilt was more easily and readily accepted because of the fact of his Jewishness.

Front page of the Paris daily L'Aurore *on Thursday, January 13, 1898, features Emile Zola's* J'Accuse, *an open letter to Felix Faure, President of the French Republic, denouncing Dreyfus's rigged trial.*

Still, the anti-Semitic impetus in the case came less from the army than from the press, and principally at first from Edouard Drumont, whose newspaper, *La Libre Parole,* became the anti-Dreyfusard mouthpiece. The real popular reaction against the Jews occurred not until after Zola's protest, when huge crowds plundered Jewish stores, beat up Jews, publicly burned Zola's article, and hanged the author in effigy. In Paris, a mob paraded along the boulevards demanding "Death to Zola! Death to the Jews!" Petitions to expel the Jews were submitted to the government in large numbers. Legislation was proposed to deprive Jews of the vote. The nationalist press incited employers to dismiss Jewish workers. University professors who had identified themselves with the revisionist cause of the Dreyfusards were hooted down and their lectures disrupted by the mobs; some were suspended from their functions, some forced to resign. When the truth was discovered very soon after the nation had accepted the lie, it made little difference. The lie continued to find a necessary acceptance. To reject it would have been to reject the material force of the army as a shield against Germany, and to embrace instead an abstract ideal. Between the two alternatives, many Frenchmen unhesitatingly chose to believe in the lie. The anti-Dreyfusards, among whom must be numbered the Church, can be said to have favored order over justice and truth. For them, it was not legitimate to disturb social order and public peace and threaten national cohesion simply to prevent an innocent man from being submitted to an unjust punishment. Theirs was the logic of the *Ancien Régime.* The logic of the Dreyfusards, on the other hand, the logic that finally triumphed, was that of the French Revolution, and the victory was a victory of its ideals over self-interest and prejudice.

For the Jews, the Dreyfus case had a special significance, because Dreyfus had become a symbol of Jewish acceptance in European society. A Dreyfus guilty might have destroyed the civil rights they had so recently acquired. A Dreyfus innocent re-established the honor of the Jewish people, not only in France, but elsewhere in the world as well. But once again Jewish hopes were to be dashed. The Dreyfus case was not the turning point in world liberal attitudes that Jews had hoped it would be, and the gains the Jews had won in prestige and respect were to be short-lived indeed and counteracted by a public outpouring of anti-Semitic hatred.

One of the foreign correspondents witnessing the ceremony at which Dreyfus was stripped of his rank was Theodor Herzl, then serving as a reporter for the Vienna *Neue Freie Presse.* About this event he wrote later in his Diaries:

. . . What made me into a Zionist was the Dreyfus Case. Not the present one in Rennes, but the original one in Paris, which I witnessed in 1894. At that time I was living in Paris as a newspaper correspondent and attended the proceedings of the military court until they were declared secret. I can still see the defendant coming into the hall in his dark artillery uniform trimmed with braid. I still hear him give his credentials: "Alfred Dreyfus, Captain of artillery," in his affected nasal voice. And also the howls of the mob in the street in front of the Ecole Militaire, where he was degraded, still ring unforgettably in my ears: "Death! Death to the Jews!" Death to Jews all because this one was a traitor? But was he really a traitor? At that time I had a private conversation with one of the military attachés who has been much talked of recently. The Colonel did not know much more about the whole affair than had appeared in the paper; yet he believed in the guilt of Dreyfus, because to him it appeared impossible that seven officers should have been able to declare a comrade guilty without the most convincing proof. I, on the other hand, believed in his innocence, because I did not consider a Jewish officer capable of being a traitor to his country. Not that I regarded the Jews in general as better than other human beings. But under the particular circumstances in the case of Captain Dreyfus, who personally did not even make a favorable impression on me, the whole thing appeared unlikely to me. A Jew who, as an officer on the General Staff, has a career of honor lying open before him, is incapable of committing such a crime, I said to the Colonel. In a lower stratum of society, I would deny such a possibility among Jews as little as among Christians. In Alfred Dreyfus's case, however, it was psychologically impossible. A wealthy man, who had chosen this career only through ambition, simply could not have committed the most dishonorable of all crimes. The Jews, as a result of their long having to do without civic honor, often have a pathological urge for honors, and in this regard a Jewish army officer is a Jew raised to the highest degree. My line of reasoning at that time was probably that of all of our coreligionists since the beginning of the affair. Just because for all of us, the psychological impossibility was so clear from the very beginning, the Jews had foreshadowings on all sides as to the innocence of Dreyfus, even before the memorable campaign to establish the truth began. . . .

. . . But the Dreyfus case contains more than a miscarriage of justice: it contains the wish of the vast majority in France to damn one Jew and through him all Jews. "Death to the Jews!" the crowd yelled when they ripped the Captain's stripes from his uniform. And since that time, "Down with the Jews" has become a battle cry. Where? In France. In Republican, modern, civilized France, one hundred years after the Declaration of the Rights of Man. . . .

. . . And here we are at the matter that concerns us, here we are at the lesson in history that any unprejudiced observer must draw from the Dreyfus case. Up to that time, most of us had believed that the solution of the Jewish question was to be expected from the gradual progress of mankind toward tolerance. But if an otherwise progressive, surely highly civilized people could come to such a pass, what was there to be expected from other people, who even today are not at the height at which the French have already been for a hundred years? . . .

From the time of the expulsion of the Jews from Spain, which sent hundreds of thousands of Jewish refugees in quest of new homes, until the nineteenth century, the main element in Jewish migrations had been Sephardim, fleeing for the most part in the direction of the Levant, with small contingents arriving in Holland and England. Though the discovery of the New World coincided with the catastrophe of Spanish Jewry, America did not offer a haven of refuge until 150 years later, when the Dutch established themselves in Brazil and neighboring territories. Most of the settlers who went there were wealthy merchants or manufacturers, traveling on ships belonging to them and contributing enormously to the countries wherein they settled.

The nineteenth century witnessed a large-scale flight of Central European (mostly German) Jews to America. What had begun as a small trickle at the end of the eighteenth century grew into a mighty stream after the revolutionary movements of the nineteenth century failed to better the lot of the Jews. (Jewish emigration was paralleled by an immense German emigration at the same time.) Bitterly disillusioned with the false promises of emancipation, many Jews decided to break their ties with the Old World altogether and to escape the prevailing conditions of humiliation. America offered freedom; her Constitution made a special point of the individual's right to the "pursuit of happiness." Already in 1783 a German Jew had addressed a letter to the President of the Congress of the United States, in which he appealed to the young republic to grant asylum to two thousand of his coreligionists in return for a guarantee that they would pay "twofold taxes," were they but permitted to become subjects of the thirteen states. "Do we not believe in the same God as the Quakers do?" he wrote. "Can our admission become more dangerous and precarious than that of the Quakers?" There is no evidence that Congress considered his appeal.

The number of migrants rose considerably during the 1830s and 1840s, in the wake of anti-Jewish movements in Europe. Jewish leadership subscribed to the notion that refuge was to be found in the freedom of America, and organizations were formed to help the immigrants. Migration became a regulated process. Provisions were made for religious needs: kosher food was made available, Torah scrolls were wrapped in waterproof silk for the journey, and special prayer books, containing prayers for those at sea, were printed for the use of the emigrants.

The flow of Jewish migrants which began at that time has yet to stop; indeed, there is scarcely a Jew today whose family did not participate in the vast process of uprooting and resettlement that has been Jewish history in the past 150 years. When Jewish emigration from Central Europe declined, after full emancipation was achieved in Germany and Austria (1869), Russian Jewry began its great exodus. The years 1881–1882 mark the great population shift and the forming of large Jewish centers in the Western hemisphere. Those who went East, to their ancient homeland, laid the foundations for the future Jewish state. The majority, however, went West, to England and the British dominions (especially Canada and South Africa), to Argentina, and above all to the United States.

The Beginnings of American Jewry

The discovery of the New World and the expulsion of the Jews from Spain coincided. Unfortunately, since Spain and Portugal took possession of the new countries, these became immediately closed to Jews. The few Marranos who had succeeded in removing there, were persecuted with no less severity than at home, the new colonizers having brought the Inquisition with them to the New World. Not until the Dutch occupied Brazil, and later some of the neighboring territories, did the Jews gain a foothold in the Americas. But Dutch rule in South America was of short duration, as was the sojourn of the Jews, who found themselves fugitives again by the middle of the seventeenth century.

The first Jews to arrive in North America were twenty-three refugees from Recife (Brazil) who arrived in September 1654 at the little Dutch community of New Amsterdam, an outpost of the Dutch West India Company on the Hudson River. Wearily they disembarked, only to be told by the Governor, Peter Stuyvesant, that they must leave. Stuyvesant asked permission of the Dutch West India Company to expel them:

. . . The Jews who have arrived would nearly all like to remain here, but learning that they (with their customary usury and deceitful trading with the Christians) were very repugnant to the inferior magistrates, as also to the people having the most affection for you; the Deaconry also fearing that owing to their present indigence they might become a charge in the coming winter, we have, for the benefit of this weak and newly developing place and the land in general, deemed it useful to require them in a friendly way to depart: praying also most seriously in this connection, for ourselves as also for the general community of your worships, that the deceitful race—such hateful enemies and blasphemers of the name of Christ—be not allowed further to infect and trouble this new colony.

A bold petition from the Jews in Amsterdam and the intervention of Jewish stockholders in the West India Company resulted in the countermanding of Stuyvesant's orders. The Jews were to be allowed to remain, with the following proviso: "that the poor among them shall not become a burden to the company or to the community, but be supported by their own nation." Thus began the first Jewish community in North America and, in time, its greatest.

Years later, when the British pushed the Dutch from North America, Jewish history in the new land became interwoven with the story of British colonization. Jews were refused admittance into Massachusetts and Connecticut by the Puritans, whose idea of religious liberty was limited to their own brand of faith. However, in liberal Maryland, and in Rhode Island, where freedom of conscience was an unshakable principle, they found acceptance. Soon Newport became a hub of Jewish commercial activity. A Jewish cemetery was established in 1677. The leader of the community, Judah Touro, was responsible with his brother for the preservation of the Colonial Synagogue of Newport.

In the Southern states of South Carolina and Georgia, Jews were granted freedom to practice their religion and trades, and in South Carolina they were allowed to vote as early as the beginning of the eighteenth century. On the eve of the Revolution, in 1776, Jews in the thirteen provinces were relatively secure. They had religious and economic freedom and certain political rights. In New York, two Jews were chosen as constables in 1718, symbolic affirmation of their equality under the law. In 1740, an Act of Parliament was passed permitting Protestants, Quakers, and Jews to be naturalized in the English colonies after seven years of residence—a landmark in the history of Jewish emancipation.

At the outbreak of the Revolution, the Jews numbered about

White ark and altar of the famous Touro Synagogue at Newport, Rhode Island, named after the first prominent Jewish philanthropist in America, Judah Touro.

2000–3000 of a total population of two million, or one tenth of one per cent. Some of these Jewish settlers had developed extensive interests in the principal seaport towns of Newport, Philadelphia, New York, Charleston and Savannah. They were chiefly engaged in inter-colonial and English trade. Jewish traders were among the largest shipowners in America. Their business interests, therefore, lay on the side of England. To support the Revolution meant certain economic ruin. Nevertheless, the Jews almost to a man were supporters of the cause of separation. Jews were among the first volunteers when war with England broke out, and their record as soldiers was brilliant. Concerning Jewish participation in the War of Independence President Calvin Coolidge later said:

> The Jews themselves, of whom a considerable number were already scattered throughout the colonies, were true to the teachings of their prophets. The Jewish faith is predominantly the faith of liberty. From the beginning of the conflict between the colonists and the Mother country, they were overwhelmingly on the side of the rising Revolution.

The early history of Jews in America is one of individuals rather than of communities. In Texas alone one learns of pioneers like Adolphus Sterne, who fought in the war against Mexico and later became a member of the Texan Congress; David S. Kaufman, a graduate of Princeton College, who was also elected to the Texas legislature; Moses Albert Levy, who served as surgeon-general in Sam Houston's army; Henry Castro, a descendant of a Marrano family, who served as consul-general in France for the Republic of Texas. Other states soon followed suit. Within the first half of the nineteenth century traces of legal discrimination in the economic, political, and social life of the nation had disappeared for all religious groups in America.

The nineteenth century witnessed a tremendous emigration from Germany to America. Overpopulation, land hunger, unemployment, new methods of production which displaced the small farmers and artisans, revolutionary unrest—all these factors conspired to drive thousands and thousands of Germans from their homes. In 1827–28 more than 10,000 Germans landed in New York. In 1847, 50,000 Germans left for the United States. By 1910 there were six million Germans in America. Thousands of disappointed and disillusioned Jews of Germany who had pinned their hopes on the European Revolution now moved to America, the refuge of freedom and progress. In America, these immigrants received genuine, if condescending, encouragement; one influential newspaper wrote:

The wealth and enterprise of the Jews would be a great auxiliary to the commercial and manufacturing, if not agricultural interests of the U.S. A new generation, born in more enlightened times, and having the benefit of education, would be free from those errors generally imputed to the Jews, and participating in the blessings of liberty, would have every inducement to become valuable members of society. That toleration and mildness upon which the Christian religion is founded, will lend its influence to the neglected children of Israel, who in the U.S., can find a home undisturbed; land which they dare call their own; laws which they will assist in making; magistrates of which they may be of the number, protection, freedom, and, as they comport themselves, respect and consideration.

The German-Jewish immigrant, fleeing the reaction in Europe, found in America the realization of his dreams. Here he found, with the exception of the Negro slave or freedman, a land offering equality without distinction of creed or nationality; freedom of speech and press and a developed democracy which accepted him in its folds as an ardent patriot.

Most of the German Jews who emigrated to America were penniless. Many of them were dependent on Jewish charities. With little more than the clothing on their back, many turned to petty trading with which they were familiar and which required little capital, but large doses of perseverance. With a pack on his back, or a covered wagon laden with trinkets and household goods, the Jewish peddler set out for the wilds, close behind the agricultural pioneer. He became almost the sole contact between the isolated settlers and the large town, and served to bring not only goods but much longed-for news. The settler came to depend on this wandering Jewish peddler, welcoming his visits with warmth and friendship. As the settlements grew bigger, the peddler stopped roving, and established a little depot in the midst of the growing village. Soon the village became a town, and then a city, and the little depot became a flourishing department store on Main Street and an important focus of the city's mercantile life.

In truth, trade and settlement monopolized the energies of this generation of immigrants. They settled in almost every new town which sprang up between 1820 and 1860. The Gold Rush in California in the 1850s swept the Jews along in its wake, and congregations soon sprang up in the mining camps as well as in the cities. The largest community was in San Francisco, where a Jewish middle class expanded and consolidated its position within a matter of decades.

After 1870 Jewish immigration to America became predominantly Eastern European. Eastern European society was at this time disintegrating as a result of the break-up of old feudal orders. Squires, priests, and guildsmen could not hold their own against the powerful new social orders and against modern technology. Large-scale landownership squeezed out not only the peasants but the Jewish middlemen as well. Modern manufacture destroyed the artisan. The masses in the Jewish villages of the Pale struggled harder and harder each year to eke out a living. Pogroms, cholera, famine, persecutions, compulsory military service, confinement within the Pale of Settlement—all added to the determination of the Jews to search for a new and better home. They left in droves, for Western Europe, England, South America, South Africa, Palestine, and above all the United States. Whereas the Jews had been a minority among the emigrants from Germany, from Eastern Europe they poured out in hundreds of thousands.

The impact made by the arrival of Eastern Jewry in America was tremendous. With surprising dexterity, the Eastern Jews molded themselves to this new and different life, whose efficiency and tempo were alien to them. Unlike the German Jews, they clung to their traditional Orthodox way of life and so brought with them to America a strong measure of genuine Old World Judaism. It was their very steadfastness and tenacity which helped to save American Jewish Orthodoxy from extinction and to make the American community the most significant and powerful in the world, until the founding of the State of Israel. Sixty-five per cent of the Jewish immigrants settled in metropolitan areas. The rest dispersed inland, some moving into the small towns, others into the country to farm. Settlement in the cities was part of a natural process in America, industry being a magnet attracting all and sundry.

In the cities these immigrants lived in grossly overcrowded tenement buildings, reeking from bad sanitation. They became peddlers, small retailers, contractors working at home on a piecework basis for factories or shops. They went into tailoring and dressmaking and many kinds of manual labor. By 1890 over 13,000 Jews on the Lower East Side of New York alone were toiling to clothe a nation; after 1890 the manufacture of clothing in the United States was almost entirely a "Jewish" industry, operated, directed, managed and even owned by Eastern Jewry. The American author Jacob Riis wrote about them:

> Take a Second Avenue Elevated and ride up half a mile to the sweatshop district. Every open window of the big tenements, that stand like a continuous brick wall on both sides of the way, gives

A turn-of-the-century Russian-Jewish immigrant, typically accoutered, arrives in the United States.

*Street scene of the old Jewish section of New York,
just prior to World War I, gives the characteristic air, the
vigorous, jostling life of the sidewalks, the carts and peddlers
crowding the streets, the signs both in Yiddish and English.*

you a glimpse of one of those shops as the train speeds by. Men and women, bending over their machines or ironing boards at the windows, half-naked . . . The road is like a big gangway through an endless workroom where vast multitudes are forever laboring. Morning, noon and night, it makes no difference, the scene is always the same.

Not many of these Eastern immigrants engaged in heavy manufacture, mining or agriculture. But they were lured to the professions, which, unlike those in Europe, required only ability rather than personal contacts. By 1905 there were almost five hundred Russian Jewish doctors in New York City alone. Some professionals reached the very summit of their field, men like Louis Brandeis and Felix Frankfurter, who were appointed to the Supreme Court of the United States. Although famous cases like these were remote from the Jews who labored or traded, they nevertheless set the goals toward which the millions strove, goals which were not in America, as in Europe, completely unattainable.

The German Jewish immigrants had found in America freedom of movement, of contacts, of thought, of religion; freedom from hatred and discrimination, freedom to roam and vanquish a vast country abounding in innumerable opportunities. The Russian Jew, on the other hand, came to an America which had already entered a more advanced stage of development, where to earn a living in the city one had to sweat and grind day after day, night after night, where exploitation was part and parcel of the capitalist system. His task was harder, but even so his life was freer and more secure than it had been in Eastern Europe, and no restrictions were placed upon him. The immigrant's awareness of this fact, and of the boundless opportunities available to him, had an immensely liberating effect, as he was finally freed from the confinement which centuries of discrimination and prejudice had imposed upon him.

NATIONALIST movements played a large part in the history of Europe during the nineteenth century. As a result of such movements Germany was to be united into one empire, the Italian principalities became one country, programs for independence began stirring in the Balkans, Poland tried to break loose from Russia, and Ireland demanded home rule. The essential ideal of nineteenth-century nationalism was the right of every nation to complete sovereignty, a right which did not always suit the imperial and colonial policies of the great nations. Nationalist movements were greatly enhanced by the spiritual climate of the era, which, influenced by Romanticism, fostered a concern with the national heritage of every people.

Nationalism also deeply affected the Jewish world. Lacking their own national center, the Jews found themselves involved in this issue at the profoundest level. Their status as an ethnic-cultural entity had been upset by the French and American Revolutions, as the new egalitarian state superseded the corporate division of medieval society. In France, the National Assembly had granted the Jews full equality of rights as individuals, but not as a national group. The Jews were advised to give up their peculiar "state within a state," to discard their separate laws and self-governing institutions, and to accept French national culture. "Otherwise, if they refuse,

308

let them say so and be banished," declared Clermont-Tonnière, a delegate to the French National Assembly.

Country after country in Europe extended to the Jews equality of rights, so as to facilitate their incorporation into the national majority. (Some governments temporarily withheld equality until the Jews had completed their so-called reeducation and prepared themselves for this privilege.) An ideological nexus held forth the twin and inseparable goals of emancipation and assimilation. Reform Judaism was considered by many of its adherents as the most effective instrument for the adjustment of Judaism to this new national situation. The main exponents of Jewish emancipation during the great struggle in Europe before and after 1848 were at the same time children of the Enlightenment and of its opposing movement, Romanticism. As enlightened rationalists, they demanded recognition of Jews as men, endowed with the natural qualities and privileges of all humanity. As romantics, however, they felt the great power of historic heritages, and of those man-made and history-made divisions that were particularly evident in nationalist movements. It occurred to these champions of emancipation that the assimilation demanded from Jews could in practice not be accomplished by acculturation to some abstract ideal, but had to be carried out in conjunction with one or another historic nationality. In other words, Jews were not merely to become men, but specifically Frenchmen, Englishmen, Germans, etc. Many Jewish leaders were prepared to accept this. But there existed resistance to such whole-hearted surrender, especially in countries where the general cultural level was low. To become French or German was one thing, but the Lithuanian or Latvian nationalities seemed utterly unattractive. Western nationalism's appeal to the Jews was heightened, at least in its heroic stage, by its messianic fervor, by its vision of a nation devoted to the service of humanity; such a vision was held by Mickiewicz in Poland and Mazzini in Italy. Messianic credos elicited in Jewish hearts a responsive echo. Many Jews flocked to this standard; others, however, saw the realization of the messianic ideal through their own, genuinely messianic Jewish nationality.

German nationalism, which coincided with the liberation of the Jews from the ghetto, promised to bring salvation through an identification with the state. Many Jews, in an effort to outdo their gentile neighbors in patriotism, openly proclaimed that they did not wish to have a national existence of their own and that such as had previously existed had been imposed on them by their enemies. Now that religion had become the private concern of the individual, they could in all things think and feel as Germans.

Thus, the enlightened Jew of the nineteenth century felt fully prepared to become at one with the national majority. All national ingredients in the Jewish faith were to be given up, and Jews were to become individual members of the various Western nationalities. But this did not happen. Jews continued to be held together by a powerful tradition and emotional attachment; in addition, their inherent sense of solidarity was constantly being reinforced by the unceasing flow of migrations, and by the need for unity in the struggle for equality of rights, in interterritorial charities, and in the fight against anti-Jewish prejudice. Experience had taught them that the fate of one community, in one country, was deeply affected by developments in another. Besides, blind identification with the surrounding nationality was often fraught with danger. Often Jewish populations found themselves siding with German minorities against Polish, Czech, or Magyar majorities who claimed nationality rights for themselves.

Out of this international as well as inner Jewish situation, a new Jewish nationalism was born. It was formed not only by Jewish reaction to modern anti-Semitism, as has been asserted by its opponents, but by an internal need and readiness as well. Zionism derived its values from the general milieu in which it was born, and its aims can easily be identified with those of the age: national freedom and individual liberty, coupled with social and economic progress. The first Zionists were all men of the nineteenth century, deeply involved with the problems of their time.

The fact that a hundred years after the American and French Revolutions the Jews were still denounced as an alien group had led many to look for some more effective solution. Until the era of emancipation, no one doubted the existence of a Jewish nationality. Jews were generally considered a separate cultural entity. Only under secular modern nationalism did the fiction arise of the Jews as a religious group alone, a fiction that even the ultra-Orthodox agreed to, albeit with qualifications. The peculiar Jewish situation brought about new alignments and postures, and a division between Diaspora nationalists and Zionists or other territorialists. The protagonists of Diaspora nationalism wanted minority rights for Jews to be established in all countries throughout the world, wherever Jews lived in significant numbers. Simon Dubnow, the noted historian, was the most influential spokesman for such a program of emancipation without assimilation. Many nationalists

A handbill with a series of drawings to show the life of a newly founded Russian-Jewish 19th-century farming community in the Dakota territory. The handbill was used to attract new members for the community. The settlement was named for its leader, the Reverend Dr. Wechsler, whose portrait appears top center.

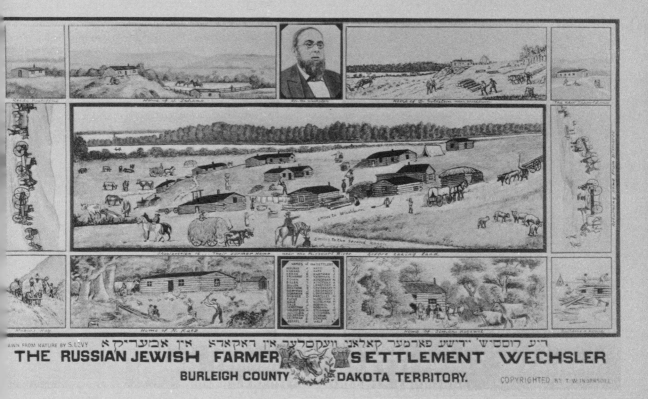

resented the apologetic attitude which this view entailed. They looked for absolute normality, for complete similarity between Jewish nationalism and that of other peoples. Out of such attitudes grew movements for the territorial concentration of Jews, as illustrated by the experiment of Mordecai Manuel Noah of New York, whose project was the settlement and concentration of all Jews on an island in the Niagara River which he called Ararat. Many European Jews of that time agreed with Noah insofar as they too regarded America as the ideal land for Jewish colonization, as a land which had given the Jews equal rights and which had no traditions of persecution.

Even in areas of dense Jewish population Jews formed a minority, and minority status involved more than numerical inferiority alone. Therefore, philanthropists as well as nationalists turned to the vast, unexploited areas of the old and the new worlds in hopes of finding a solution to the Jewish problem. Non-Jews too, frequently supported Jewish territorial claims or agreed on the desirability of removing European Jewry to a country of their own. The most ambitious project of Jewish settlement was initiated in 1891 by Baron Maurice de Hirsch, who founded the Jewish Colonization Association. His grandiose plan was the transfer of three million Jews to settle on Argentine land as farmers, but this program ended in failure. In 1903 the British offered Uganda for Jewish settlement, but by that time it was much too late for such *ersatz* homelands. The Palestine ideal alone reflected the age-old yearnings of the Jewish people and seemed therefore to offer the only realistic alternative. These deep-rooted Jewish loyalties alone can explain the immediate response of the Jewish masses to the calls of Moses Hess and Leon Pinsker for national action which preceded the political Zionism of Theodor Herzl.

East-European Diaspora 1897

At the time of the Spanish expulsion, the world's Jewish population stood at about one and a half million, and was evenly distributed between the Oriental and the European countries. This figure remained substantially unchanged until the seventeenth century, when it diminished considerably as a result of pogroms and Cossack massacres. By the middle of the nineteenth century, the Jewish population of the world had climbed to about 4,750,000, of which 72 per cent lived in Eastern Europe, 14.5 per cent in Western Europe, about 1.5 per cent in America, and only 12 per cent in the Oriental countries. At the beginning of the twentieth century, with the distribution figures radically changed, the number of Jews in the world had risen to about ten and a half million.

The nineteenth century witnessed a complete transformation in the Jewish situation, particularly in Western Europe. Jewish life became closely interwoven with that of the non-Jewish environment. Jews very often attained leading positions in the economy; they gained access to the many important posts in the economic, social, and political world. Their capacity for social and cultural progress was unmatched by any other group. In Eastern and Central Europe, more so than in the West, Jews played a predominant part in industrial and commercial development. This was truly an epoch of great achievements.

Before the partitions, Poland, for instance, relied almost totally on Jews for her commerce and trade. This trend was maintained even later; in the Galician provinces of Russia, most factories were founded by Jews. And in Russia at large, individual Jews had risen to great prominence by establishing banking firms and sugar industries, and by promoting railway and utility construction. Despite their significant contribution to Russian economic life and culture, however, Russian Jewry's emancipation was unsuccessful.

The progress of acculturation, to be sure, was rapid during the reign of Alexander II. The number of Jewish students in gymnasia increased substantially. In 1873, the proportion of Jewish students in all secondary schools for men rose to 13.2 per cent. In Poland, the rate of acculturation was even more rapid than in the Pale of Settlement until the Polish insurrection in 1863. Polish Jews were to be found at the top in banking, commission houses, export concerns, and liberal professions. They were patrons of some of the most important journals and newspapers. The book trade and theater were largely in their hands.

The emergence of the Russian Jews from isolation resulted in a profound change in the Jewish attitude toward non-Jews. Jews now became hypersensitive to gentile opinion, whereas, while living in the ghetto, they had remained totally indifferent to the outside world. They also felt the need to become citizens and to destroy the ambiguity of their situation: although highly educated, they were still denied civil rights. If anything, their secular education only accentuated their feelings of inferiority. No longer fitted for their old environment, they yet remained excluded from gentile society.

The later years of Alexander II saw a sharpening of Russian anti-Jewish policy. The anti-Jewish press became alarmed at the large

number of Jews to be found in Russian educational institutions. A *numerus clausus* was introduced in progressive stages. Russian public opinion, too, especially since the Polish rebellion, was decidedly anti-Jewish at this time, as was soon evidenced by the wave of pogroms that began in Odessa in 1871.

The general unfriendly spirit toward the Jew prevailing in government circles also found expression at the Berlin Congress of 1878. The *Alliance Israélite Universelle* had petitioned the delegates to this Congress to guarantee religious freedom and civic and political equality to the Jews of Serbia, Bulgaria, Rumania, and Turkey. The representatives of all the great powers, with the exception of Russia, agreed to equalize the Jews with the rest of the population of the Balkan countries. The Russian delegate, Prince Gorchakov, in explaining his objection, asked the Congress not to compare the Jews of Berlin, Paris, London or Vienna with those of Serbia and Rumania, or those who lived in some provinces of Russia. The former, he admitted, were deserving of civic and political equality, while the latter were the scourge of the native populations.

At the same time that it intensified its anti-Jewish program, the Russian government continued its policy of granting special privileges to selected groups of Jews. Government service was opened to Jews, Jewish physicians received army posts, and some Jews even became judges. There were even isolated voices calling for the removal of the Pale restrictions. It is therefore no wonder that the Jews did not give up the hopes which the era of initial reforms had kindled. Despite Alexander's failure to grant them emancipation, the Jews continued to regard him as their friend. But the sad fact remained that in Russia as in Germany, so long as the Jews remained Jews, they had no chance of acquiring civic equality. The error of the *maskilim* lay in their belief that Russification would earn them the prize of equal rights.

Tsar Alexander II was killed by a bomb in May, 1881. His son, Alexander III, inherited the throne and took as an adviser his former tutor, Constantin Pobiedonostsev, now Chief Procurator of the Holy Synod, a man who preached reactionary nationalism. With few exceptions, a period of political and social reaction set in, in which the nobility regained many of its old privileges and entrenched itself anew as the lord and master of Russia. The new government's Jewish policy was inaugurated with police cooperation in the pogroms of May 1881. The fact that Alexander II had been killed by a revolutionary's bomb, and that a Jewess was arrested for being involved in the assassination plot, provided enough

A characteristic scene from the Jewish "Pale" in Eastern Europe, this one in Ostrolenko, Poland.

proof to put the blame on the Jews. A wave of massacres and officially-condoned riots began which was to provide the final impetus for hundreds of thousands of Russian Jews to flee their homeland for America.

Life outside the Pale was made intolerable by expulsions; the greatest blow was reserved for Moscow's 20,000 Jews who were expelled in the most brutal fashion. Only about one third were allowed to stay, but their lives too were made almost unbearable. The new Minister of the Interior, Ignatiev, was responsible for the infamous "May Laws" which strictly forbade all new settlements either within or outside the Pale. Villagers were given the right to expel "vicious" Jews, a privilege which was frequently and vigorously exercised by the local *muzhiks*. A strict *numerus clausus* was introduced, preventing thousands of youngsters and students from attending schools and universities. The quota of Jews in the liberal professions was reduced. All this was enforced with an official chicanery designed to humiliate the Jews. In a report to his government Ignatiev stated that "the policy of toleration of Alexander II had failed," and that the new, stern policy was necessary to deal with "popular protest in Russia itself."

Russian policy had the additional effect of driving the Jews into a state of abject poverty, until a full 40 per cent were dependent on charity. Under Nicholas II, the situation continued very much the same. Police vigilance was intensified over the Jews both inside and outside the Pale. The closing years of the century witnessed violent pogroms against which the Jews were not allowed to defend themselves. When representations were made to Pobiedonostsev, he gave the following prognosis concerning the future of Russian Jewry: one third would die out, one third would leave the country, and one third would be completely dissolved in the surrounding population. During his tenure, he did his utmost to see this program of liquidation carried out. It was a fitting monument to the waning age of the Tsars.

The first reaction in Russia came in 1882 from an Odessa Jew, Leon Pinsker, in a pamphlet entitled "Auto-Emancipation." Pinsker sought a synthesis between the two current ideologies: traditionalism and emancipation. Emancipation had an obvious ethical and humanitarian appeal. But even when it had seemingly been won, it stood always in danger of being lost afresh. Europe had given the

In the spring of 1909 the group which was
to found and build Tel Aviv stands on the
barren sands from which the city was to rise.
Here the Tel Aviv Museum is now placed
and here too the State of Israel was
officially proclaimed in 1948.

Jews no guarantee that the new atmosphere of liberalism would be anything like permanent.

On the other hand, Pinsker saw, it was no longer possible to return to the ghetto, to throw emancipation aside as if it did not even exist. The generation which had tasted freedom was not about to relinquish it. The problem, then, was to find a form of emancipation which would not abandon the Jews perpetually to the mercy of others. The answer was found for the Jews, as for other oppressed nationalities, in the idea of national liberation.

The Jews alone of all the oppressed nationalities were not in actual occupation of the territory in which they envisaged their liberation to take place. To compensate for this deficiency, they invoked historical memories of political and religious independence. In 1862, Rabbi Zvi Hirsch Kalischer had written a book to prove that the messianic promise of the Bible meant the actual re-nationalization of the Jewish people on the ancestral soil of Israel. Moses Hess, in his book *Rome and Jerusalem,* demanded the establishment of a Jewish state based on ethical principles as the most radical and equitable solution of Jewish distress. Kalischer and Hess had been unable to organize a movement in support of their ideas. But in these two men the two streams which were to give birth to Zionism were already represented: messianism and social idealism.

A third appeal came from Leon Pinsker, whose pamphlet, subtitled "An Admonition to his Brethren from a Russian Jew," became one of the canonical writings of Zionism. A founder of the Society for the Spread of Culture among Russian Jews, Pinsker was led to a change of attitude regarding the destiny of the Jews as a result of the wave of pogroms and the anti-Jewish policy of the Russian government in the early 1880s. In "Auto-Emancipation," Pinsker set out to make a diagnosis of the Jewish problem and to prescribe a remedy in the form of a "territorial" base, which he later identified with Palestine.

Neither the intellectual constructions of Kalischer, nor of Hess, nor those of the leading Haskalah writers, had brought about a change in the basic attitude of those Jewish leaders who saw in assimilation the destiny of the Jewish people. Only when liberal nationalism had disappointed Jewish expectations, only when racist theories intensified social and economic anti-Semitism, only then did Jews begin seriously to doubt the ideology of Jewish assimilation on which they had pinned their hopes.

Two events at the end of the nineteenth century marked a turning point in modern Jewish history—and both of them signaled a change in Jewish political thinking. In the West, the Dreyfus Affair provided the impetus for the creation of a new movement, political Zionism. In the East, the same result—in the form of the *Hibbat Zion* (Love of Zion) movement—was produced by the outbreak of anti-Jewish massacres in Tsarist Russia in 1881. Together, these two events sufficed to engender in many a new attitude toward Jewish life in the Diaspora, and to suggest the need for a new solution to an age-old problem. Once again in Jewish history, men's minds and hearts were to turn eastward, toward the ancient homeland where once the Patriarchs had herded their flocks.

The Seed of Nationhood

It is not surprising that the idea of Jewish nationhood struck root so quickly among the Jews of the Russian Empire. Their lives, however miserable, went forward in an atmosphere of autonomy. Isaiah Berlin has vividly described their outlook and form of life.

> The bulk of them lived under their own dispensation. Herded by the Russian Government into the so-called Pale of Settlement, bound by their own traditional religious and social organization, they constituted a kind of survival of medieval society, in which the secular and the sacred were not divided as they had been (at any rate since the Renaissance) among the middle and upper classes in Western Europe. Speaking their own language, largely isolated from the surrounding peasant population, trading with them, but confined within their own world by a wall of reciprocal distrust and suspicion, this vast Jewish community formed a geographically continuous enclave that inevitably developed its own institutions, and thereby, as time went on, came to resemble more and more an authentic national minority settled upon its own ancestral soil.
>
> There are times when imagination is stronger than so-called objective reality. Subjective feeling plays a great part in communal development, and the Yiddish-speaking Jews of the Russian Empire came to feel themselves as a coherent ethnic group—anomalous indeed, subject to unheard-of persecution, remote from the alien world in which their lives were cast, but simply in virtue of the fact that they were densely congregated within the same relatively small territory, tending to resemble, say, the Armenians in Turkey: a recognizably separate, semi-national community.
>
> In their involuntary confinement they developed a certain independence of outlook, and the problems which affected and some-

*Yemenite Jews study the Talmud. Because books were scarce at
that time, several people shared one while studying and many
learned to read upside down so that they could read along
together and take part in the discussions.*

times tormented many of their co-religionists in the West—in particular the central question of their status—were not crucial for them. The Jews of Germany, Austria, Hungary, France, America, England, tended to ask themselves whether they were Jews, and if so, in what sense, and what this entailed; whether the view of them by the surrounding population was correct or false, just or unjust, and, if distorted, whether any steps could be taken to correct it without too much damage to their own self-esteem; whether they should "appease" and assimilate at the risk of losing their identity, and perhaps of the guilt that comes of the feeling of having "betrayed" their ancestral values; or, on the contrary, resist at the risk of incurring unpopularity and even persecution.

These problems affected the Russian Jews to a far smaller degree, relatively secure as they were—morally and psychologically—within their own vast, insulated ghetto. Their imprisonment, for all the economic, cultural and social injustice and poverty that it entailed, brought with it one immense advantage—namely that the spirit of the inmates remained unbroken, and that they were not as powerfully tempted to seek escape by adopting false positions as their socially more exposed and precariously established brethren without. The majority of the Jews in Russia and Poland lived in conditions of squalor and oppression, but they did not feel outcast or rootless; their relations with each other and with the outside world suffered from no systematic ambivalence. They were what they were; they might dislike their condition, they might seek to escape from it, or revolt against it, but they did not deceive themselves or others, nor did they make efforts to conceal from themselves their own most characteristic attributes that were patent to all—particularly their neighbours—to see. Their moral and spiritual integrity was greater than that of their more prosperous and civilized, and altogether grander, brothers in the West; their lives were bound up with religious observance, and their minds and hearts were filled with the images and symbolism of Jewish history and religion to a degree scarcely intelligible in Western Europe since the waning of the Middle Ages.

In 1897, Palestine was ruled by the Ottoman Empire, as it had been since 1517 and would continue to be until 1917. The country had long been languishing under Ottoman rule. After a short cultural rebirth in the sixteenth century, a long period of economic and political decay had set in, accentuated by a series of earthquakes, famines, and crop plagues. With the opening of trade routes to India around the Cape of Good Hope, Palestine had lost her vital position as a transit country, and had become a stagnant corner of the Mediterranean basin. The country was largely devastated, partly through neglect, partly as a result of invasions and local wars. A new movement of Jews during the hundred years from 1730 to 1830 had brought to its shores scholars and rabbis, businessmen and artisans, but the country remained largely backward and deserted, due to the inefficiency and indifference of its rulers and the apathy of its inhabitants.

Time and again, the idea of restoring Palestine to the Jews had arisen. During the eighteenth century Potemkin had begun training a cavalry unit for the recapture of the Holy Land; Napoleon Bonaparte, during his campaign in the Near East (1799), had issued a proclamation to the Jews of the world as the rightful heirs to Palestine. Many Christians saw the restoration of the Jews to their own land as a fulfillment of divine prophecy or as a simple ethical duty. In the nineteenth century, various Jewish groups in Central Europe, disillusioned by political reaction and economic depression, began to show interest in Palestine. Student organizations adopted as part of their platform the restoration of a Jewish state in Palestine.

The Damascus Affair of 1840, in which the medieval blood libel was evoked once more, awakened the Jews of Western Europe and the United States to the sufferings of their fellow Jews in other countries, and gave rise to the idea of colonizing Palestine. Both Adolphe Crémieux and Moses Montefiore had expressed an interest in Palestine as a center of Jewish settlement. Now this notion was taken up by the non-Jewish world, particularly in England. Lord Palmerston, Foreign Secretary and later Prime Minister of England, sent the following letter (August 1840) to Viscount Ponsonby, the British Ambassador to Turkey:

> There exists at present among the Jews dispersed over Europe, a strong notion that the time is approaching when their nation is to return to Palestine, and consequently the wish to go there has become more keen, and their thoughts have been bent more intently than before upon the means of realizing that wish.

Stressing the economic advantages that would derive from a large settlement of European Jews in Palestine, Palmerston continued:

> It would be of manifest importance to the Sultan to encourage the Jews to return to, and to settle in, Palestine.

A week later the London *Times* published an article on Palestine in which the following statement appeared:

> The proposition to plant the Jewish people in the land of their fathers, under the protection of the Great Powers, is no longer a matter of speculation, but of serious political consideration.

Nevertheless, few Jewish leaders at the time supported this idea, Montefiore being one of the handful who clung to the Palestine project even though others seemed more alluring.

Foremost among the protagonists of the project was Sir Laurence Oliphant, a writer and diplomat and, for some time, member of Parliament. He advocated the establishment of a Jewish center in Palestine under the protectorate of Great Britain, and he presented a plan for large-scale Jewish settlement in his book, *The Land of Gilead*. It appears that Prime Minister Disraeli approved of this plan and had it submitted to Lord Salisbury, then Foreign Minister. Oliphant's plan was to obtain a charter from the Turkish government for a company whose object it was "to develop the material resources and the administration of Palestine." He included in the rights of the company that of controlling immigration, feeling sure that Russian Jewry would stream to Palestine en masse. Both the French and the British Foreign Offices approached the Turkish Porte with this project, but the Charter was refused.

The same plan was to crop up again at the Berlin Congress of 1878. Disraeli had prepared a memorandum beforehand with a view toward submitting the entire problem to the Congress; his draft appeared anonymously in the Vienna press under the title "Die Jüdische Frage in der Orientalischen Frage" ("The Jewish Question in the Oriental Question"). Anticipating the certain decline of the Ottoman Empire as a result of the negotiations of the Congress, Disraeli suggested that the Jews should obtain Palestine and establish there a state of their own under the protectorate of Great Britain. (There is no doubt that Disraeli was motivated in this scheme first and foremost by concern for England's interests.) "Is it not probable," asked Lord Beaconsfield, "that within, say, half a century, there would be developed in that land a compact Jewish people, one million strong, speaking one language, and animated by one spirit—the desire to achieve autonomy and independence?"

In 1845, there were about 12,000 Jews in all of Palestine, most of them concentrated in the holy cities of Jerusalem, Safed, Tiberias, and Hebron. They were poor and, in large measure, supported by charity from outside. By 1882 their number had risen to 24,000, of whom only about 480 lived on the land. It was a country with a reputation of being impoverished, disease-ridden, arid or swamp-covered, disordered.

But the year 1882 also marked the turning point in the history of Palestine. The first group of *Biluim* (fifteen men and one woman) arrived from Russia in that year, and became the first modern settlers in the land, establishing farm colonies in Gedera, Rishon Le-Zion, Petach Tikvah, and other places. They belonged to a group known as *Bilu*—a Hebrew acronym standing for the phrase, "House of Jacob, come let us go" (Isaiah 2:5)—and their aim was to normalize Jewish experience by returning to the soil and becoming tillers of the land. In fifteen years they established eighteen colonies in the districts of Judah, Sharon, and Galilee, an enormous effort of will and devotion on the part of men and women determined to place before an incredulous world the achievements of a new Jewish prototype, and to revive in a Diaspora-bound Jewry the dream of independence and meaningful existence rooted in the soil.

By the time the First Zionist Congress met in Basle, modern Jewish Palestine was fifteen years old. Though the achievements of the First Immigration were slight, the *Biluim* and their disciples had paved the way for those to follow. By 1897 there were eighteen Jewish settlements in Palestine, and one agricultural school at Mikveh Israel. From Rishon Le-Zion to the south of Jaffa, to Rosh Pinah in the Galilee, islands of cultivation arose amid the swamps and dunes, islands created in a spirit of boundless enthusiasm and unending self-sacrifice. None of these settlements had a legal right to its existence: permission to reside in Palestine, to buy land and to build on it, could only be got through bribery or by cheating the law. Originally, it is true, the members of *Bilu* had sought to obtain from the Turkish government permission to settle legally in Palestine. From Constantinople, the first group of *Biluim* had sent out a manifesto: "We want a home in our country—it is given to us by our God. We beg it of the Sultan, and, if it be impossible to obtain this, to be allowed that we may possess it, at least as a state within a larger state. . . ." When permission was withheld, the group decided to proceed anyway. Sharp controversy arose over this point at the First Zionist Congress. Theodor Herzl demanded that immigration be suspended until a Charter could be obtained which would grant free immigration, self-defense, autonomy, and planned settlement. The "practical" Zionists, on the other hand, maintained that all this would entail a loss of valuable time, and that no effort should be discouraged that hastened the settling of

*The stark stony magnificence of the
Judean hills at Ein Kerem near Jerusalem
is softened by the clusters of
melancholy evergreens.*

the land. All, however, were by this time agreed that settlement in Palestine was a necessary solution to the vexed problem of Jewish survival. They differed only as to the means and to the timing of such settlement. Herzl had shown the way, and had come forward with the first systematic program of settlement the scope of which was commensurate with both the breadth of the Zionist aim and the extent of Jewish distress.

Theodor Herzl

Vienna, 1897: "At Basle I created the Jewish State. In five years, perhaps, and certainly in fifty, everyone will see it."
— HERZL

Fifty-one years after this incredible statement was made, the establishment of Israel was proposed by the United Nations.

Theodor Herzl was born in Budapest on May 2, 1860, an only son to adoring parents. His father, Jacob, was an energetic and capable merchant and at one time the director of the Hungarian Bank. Jeannette, his mother, was a highly intelligent, spirited and sensitive woman who generated in her home love, warmth, and comradeship.

Herzl's Jewish education terminated with his Bar Mitzvah, and his knowledge of Hebrew and of Judaism remained scant throughout his life. Herzl studied law at the University of Vienna, but was never completely absorbed by it. From an early age he had begun to write—essays, theater reviews, poems, feuilletons—and he burned with ambition to be successful in this field. At twenty-two he wrote in despair:

> I haven't even the tiniest success to show, not the slightest achievement of which to be proud . . . 22 years! And damn all done!

His literary activities diminished as his rejection slips accumulated. The young man became subject to fits of depression. During his student days, Herzl had also begun to delve into the Jewish question, and became convinced, for a time, that over the years assimilation would prove the best solution. He was rudely shaken from this conviction when he read Eugen Dühring's book, *The Jewish Problem as a Problem of Race, Morals, and Culture*, a work evincing a deep and unconquerable hatred and fear of Jews. The phenomenon of anti-Semitism began to trouble this young, assimilated Jew. In 1883 he resigned from one of the university societies which had begun to demonstrate anti-Jewish tendencies and had refused to accept any new Jewish members. In his letter of resignation, he wrote: "It must also be clear to every decent person that under these circumstances I cannot wish to retain my membership."

On July 30, 1884, Herzl was admitted to the bar in Vienna, but his briefs played a role subordinate to his literary writings. Within a year he withdrew from legal work and threw himself into writing, impatient and anxious for success. Overeager, he discouraged easily. It was in journalism that he made the greatest strides. In 1887 he was installed as the feuilleton editor of the *Wiener Allgemeine Zeitung* and within no time was recognized as a "superb feuilletonist." In 1891 he was appointed to the enviable position of Paris correspondent to the *Neue Freie Presse*, the leading daily newspaper in Vienna at the time. He applied himself to this task with the same enthusiasm and thoroughness which were to characterize his later Zionist activities.

As a leading journalist in Paris, invited to all important occasions and moving among all circles, Herzl again became conscious of the suffering of the Jews and of the marks of anti-Semitism evident in Paris, such as Drumont's *La France Juive* and the Panama scandal. The Jewish question began to haunt him. He almost convinced himself that the definitive solution lay in the complete disappearance of the Jews through baptism and intermarriage. But the futility of such daydreaming became clear to him when he considered the fate of the Marrano Jews. In 1894, plagued by thoughts like these, he wrote a play called *The New Ghetto*. It was by far the most daring of his literary creations and it heralded his complete spiritual return to his people. Until then, despite his emotional involvement in the question, he had stood outside it as an observer or even as a defensive alien. Now he was immersed in it, he identified with it, and he became its spokesman. The last words uttered by the hero of the play are: "Jews, my brothers, there will come a time when they will let you live again—when you know how to die. Why do you hold me so fast? I want to get out! Out! Out-of-the-ghetto!"

The Dreyfus case horrified Herzl: "Death to the Jews!" howled the mob, and Herzl could not forget it. Ideas began to crystallize in his mind. He had to convey them to someone. In June 1895, he called on Baron Maurice de Hirsch, the well-known Jewish philanthropist, and presented him with a 22-page memorandum which constituted the first written expression of his new ideas. He

An "atelier du couture" sponsored by the Alliance
Israélite Universelle for Jewish girls in Paris at the
end of the 19th century, gives some sense of
how far the Jewish community had become part
of French society since Napoleon.

placed before Hirsch two solutions, one including migration and one without that provision. Herzl stressed the need for political leadership, hoping that Hirsch would assume this leadership:

> Throughout the 2000 years of our dispersion, we have lacked unified political leadership. I consider this our greatest misfortune. If only we had unified political leadership . . . we could initiate the solution of the Jewish question. I propose to call a congress of Jewish notables to discuss migration to a sovereign Jewish State.

Hirsch thought he was dealing with a dreamer and barely let Herzl read him six pages of his notes.

Undaunted by his failure to win the approval of Hirsch, Herzl commenced to keep a diary which he called "The Jewish Question." The project enveloped him entirely, and of it he wrote:

> For some time now, I have been engaged upon a work of indescribable greatness. I do not know yet whether I shall carry it through. It has assumed the aspect of some mighty dream. But days and weeks have passed since it has filled me utterly, it has overflown into my unconscious self, it accompanies me wherever I go, it broods above all my commonplace conversation, it peeps over my shoulder at the comical little journalistic work which I must carry out, it disturbs and intoxicates me.

Having completed his thesis, now entitled "Address to the Rothschilds," Herzl presented it to several political leaders, including Bismarck. He was rebuffed by all. One person remarked to him: "You are making a ridiculous and tragic figure of yourself." Undaunted, as if driven by some inner force and conviction, Herzl strove on. His own newspaper refused to be associated with the idea. Then came the turning point in Herzl's career: he won Max Nordau over to his plan. Heartened by Nordau's enthusiasm, he rewrote his treatise and entitled it *Der Judenstaat*—"The Jewish State." Herzl wrote: "The idea which I have developed in this pamphlet is a very old one; it is the restoration of the Jewish State." This, then, was to be the answer to anti-Semitism, to the cries of *"Juden raus!"* Herzl outlined the practical physical functions to be performed by the State. He ignored the question of the national or cultural features which it was to assume, and did not necessarily associate it with Zion or fix its language as Hebrew. In detail he described the prerequisites to the establishment of the sovereign state: the need for a congress of Jewish representatives recognized as the official spokesmen of world Jewry, for money to be raised by a Jewish financial company, for engineers and technicians to make the state a model of modern industrial efficiency. He concluded thus:

> Therefore I believe that a wondrous generation of Jews will spring into existence. The Maccabeans will rise again.
>
> Let me repeat once more my opening words. The Jews who wish it will have their State.
>
> We shall live at last as free men on our own soil, and die peacefully in our own homes.
>
> The world will be freed by our liberty, enriched by our wealth, magnified by our greatness.
>
> And whatever we attempt there to accomplish for our own welfare, will react powerfully and beneficently for the good of humanity.

This fervid messianic document, published in 1896, broke upon the world like a bolt of thunder. Reactions were varied, but they were numerous, and loud. The German press, Jewish and non-Jewish, laughed about the "escaping Maccabees" and about Herzl, a Jewish Jules Verne, whose fantastic dream could only have been produced by a mind that had become unhinged by Jewish enthusiasms. Zionists suspected this unknown writer who rejected the Hebrew language and ignored his predecessors, particularly Hess and Pinsker. But the fact was that Herzl was completely unaware of the existence of these men. (He told Wolffsohn later that he might never have written his own book if he had known of Pinsker's "Auto-Emancipation.") Herzl had been driven to pour out his ideas in the belief that they were original, and it was this freshness of imagination that lent them their pristine force. Many were deeply stirred by *Der Judenstaat*. Wolffsohn wrote that after he had read it, he had become "another man." The Zionist youth were particularly impressed; in his autobiography, Chaim Weizmann recalls their reaction:

> It was an utterance which came like a bolt from the blue. We had never heard the name Herzl before; or perhaps it had come to our attention, only to be lost among those of other journalists and feuilletonists. Fundamentally, *The Jewish State* contained not a single new idea for us; that which so startled the Jewish bourgeoisie, and called down the resentment and derision of the Western rabbis, had long been the substance of our Zionist tradition. We observed, too, that this man Herzl made no allusion in his little book to his predecessors in the field, to Moses Hess and Leon

Pinsker and Nathan Birnbaum. . . . Apparently Herzl did not know of the existence of the Hibbat Zion; he did not mention Palestine; he ignored the Hebrew language. Yet the effect produced by *The Jewish State* was profound. Not the ideas, but the personality which stood behind them appealed to us. Here was daring, clarity, and energy. The very fact that this Westerner came to us unencumbered by our own preconceptions had its appeal. . . . We were right in our instinctive appreciation that what had emerged from the *Judenstaat* was less a concept, than a historic personality. . . . What has given greatness to his name is Herzl's role as a man of action, as the founder of the Zionist Congress, and as an example of daring and devotion.

From everywhere came calls to Herzl to take up the leadership of the Jews; was he not the man who had given clear and vigorous expression to the deepest feelings of the Jewish people, and who urged them to struggle for their ultimate freedom? Herzl then became absorbed in the task of realizing his plan. He appealed for assistance to the influential aristocracy, the Grand Duke of Baden, the Papal Nuncio of Italy, the Turkish government. He succeeded, in private interviews, in charming them all by his imposing appearance—thick beard and penetrating black eyes—but he failed to convince them or gain their support, just as he failed, in France, to convince Baron Edmond de Rothschild, the man who had until then been the support of the *yishuv*, and of the movement for Jewish self-help in the Land of Israel. It was indeed the Baron's refusal to grant moral or financial support which brought home to Herzl the realization that he would obtain nothing from above. His only hope lay in the masses, whom he would have to arouse by propaganda. "Let us organize our masses immediately," he resolved. And thus, political Zionism was born.

On one point Herzl was adamant—the convening of a Jewish Congress. "The Congress will take place!" The audacity of this idea caused great consternation within European Jewry. Did he want to sentence the Jews to death by exposing them as a nation within a nation—as the anti-Semites, who were just waiting for the right excuse to destroy them, had all along claimed? Herzl pressed on. Out of his own funds, he founded a weekly publication, *Die Welt*, for the defense and propagation of his idea. As one of the participants in the preliminary conference reported later: ". . . the Congress was made by Herzl alone, it was his money, his labor which brought it into being." On August 29, 1897, the Zionist Congress assembled in Basle. It was the first official and world-wide gathering of the Jews since their dispersion, and it was the work of one man. One hundred ninety-seven delegates attended this Assembly. They came from Eastern and Western Europe, from England, America, and Algeria—young and old, orthodox and reform, capitalist and socialist. As the delegates entered the great conference hall, they glanced up at the words "Zionisten Kongress" and at a flag, white with two blue stripes and the Star of David (designed by Wolffsohn). Herzl attached great importance to the need for a flag. "It is with a flag that people are led whithersoever one desires, even to the Promised Land. For a flag men live and die. . . ."

Then Herzl rose, "a marvelous and exalted figure." "It is a scion of the House of David, risen from among the dead, clothed in legend and fantasy and beauty. Everyone sat breathless in the presence of a miracle. And in truth was it not a miracle which we beheld?" Herzl expressed his plan as he had outlined it in the *Judenstaat*, but stressed now that the homeland would be Palestine, openly recognized and legally secured. During the Congress, a World Zionist Organization was established, with Herzl as its president; a Jewish flag and a national anthem, *Hatikvah* (The Hope), were adopted; an Actions Council was set up with headquarters in Vienna and resolutions for its program drawn up. On this note of practical activity, the historic occasion came to a close, amid cries of joy and pledges of devotion. The wheels had been set in motion. An extraordinary, powerful, and energetic individual had tapped the latent springs of Jewish unity, had brought to expression the hidden resources of the Jews as a people, one people, wherever they might live. On Herzl, the Congress made one vital impression; he was struck by the force of Russian Jewry:

> And then . . . there rose before our eyes a Russian Jewry the strength of which we had not even suspected. Seventy of our delegates came from Russia, and it was patent to all of us that they represented the views and sentiments of the five million Jews of that country. And what a humiliation for us, who had taken our superiority for granted! All these professors, doctors, lawyers, industrialists, engineers and merchants stand on an educational level which is certainly no lower than ours. Nearly all of them are masters of two or three languages, and that they are men of ability in their particular lines is proved by the simple fact that they have succeeded in a land where success is peculiarly difficult for the Jews. They possess that inner unity which has disappeared from among the Westerners. They are steeped in Jewish national sentiment, though without betraying any national narrowness and in-

Theodor Herzl, that "marvelous and exalted figure . . . scion of the House of David risen from among the dead, clothed in legend and fantasy and beauty."

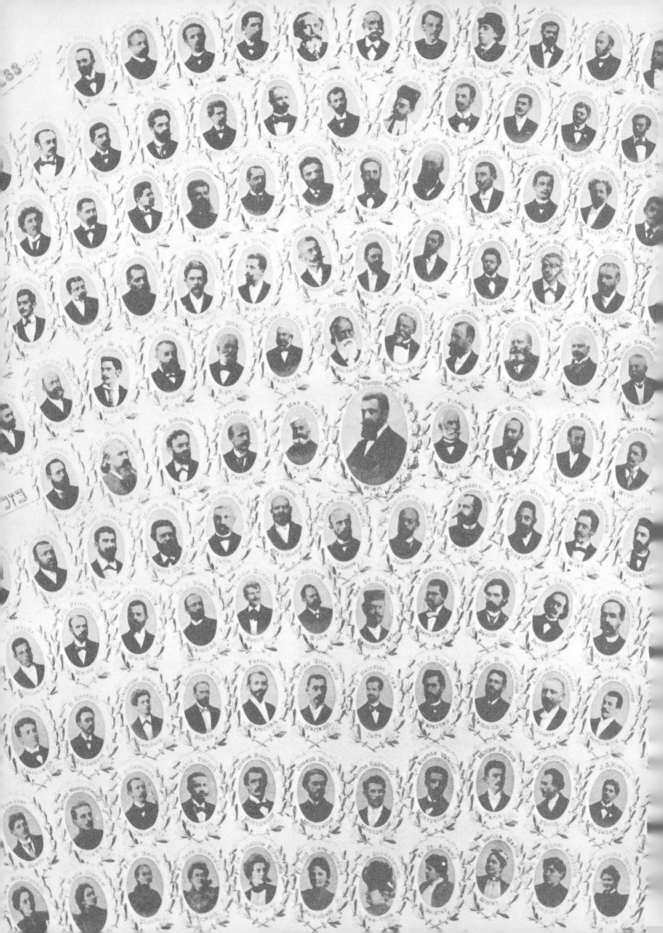

tolerance. They are not tortured by the idea of assimilation, their essential being is simple and unshattered. . . . And yet they are ghetto Jews! The only ghetto Jews of our time! Looking on them we understood where our forefathers got the strength to endure through the bitterest times.

After the Congress, Herzl threw himself into the execution of his program. He was the only one whose willpower and drive were proportional to the greatness of the cause. He was now determined to obtain a charter from the Turkish government which would legalize Jewish settlement in Palestine on a corporate basis. He believed that he could achieve this through diplomatic contacts and negotiations. But the vague promises he was given at his interviews were not kept. His first attempts were directed to Kaiser Wilhelm II of Germany, Turkey's only ally in Europe. Herzl obtained his interview with Wilhelm in October 1898. From the beginning the anti-Semitic bias of the Kaiser and his officials was evident. Yet politically the Kaiser favored Herzl's scheme, as it was most desirable to move "certain elements" to Palestine. The Kaiser promised to take up the matter of a "Chartered Company" with the Sultan at a suitable opportunity. Shortly afterward Herzl met again with the Kaiser on Palestinian soil and again the Kaiser expressed his approval of Herzl's scheme. For months Herzl waited feverishly for some further word. None was forthcoming. This had been Herzl's first visit to Palestine and he had been deeply moved. Trailed by Turkish detectives, he visited Mikveh Israel, Rishon Le-Zion, Ness Tsiona, and Rehovot, where the enthusiastic reception he received amid the singing of Hebrew songs and shouts of *Heydad!* and *Hoch Herzl!* brought tears to his eyes. Herzl saw the dire need for water in this desiccated land. The oriental filth of Jerusalem depressed him and he expressed an urgent desire to create "a glorious New Jerusalem."

Herzl now endeavored for two years (1899–1901) to make direct contact with the Sultan. This he achieved through bribing avaricious Turkish officials at terrific rates. In May 1901 he was granted a two-hour interview. Herzl suggested to the Turkish ruler that perhaps the wealthy Jewish bankers of Europe would help Turkey defray her many debts in return for a Charter of Jewish settlement in Palestine. The Sultan appeared interested. But on Herzl's side, the proposal had been made utterly without foundation. He had had no promises of financial support from Europe. Thither he now rushed, and furiously tried to raise the necessary financial assistance.

Nationalism, Assimilation, Zionism

335

He failed everywhere, and became disheartened to the point of disgust. Less than a year later, Herzl met again with the Sultan, from whom he tried to extract a definite offer. The Sultan now placed conditions on Jewish immigration: it was to be scattered rather than corporate. Herzl deposited three million francs in Turkish banks as a pledge of good faith, and to whet the Sultan's appetite. But as with Germany, nothing materialized. Indeed, it finally dawned on Herzl that the Sultan had merely taken advantage of him, and was using the threat of a Jewish loan to obtain better interest terms from French creditors. This time Herzl was bitterly disillusioned and seriously considered resigning from the presidency.

Herzl's novel, *Altneuland*, appeared in 1902. Its purpose was to illustrate the future of Palestine, to show "how much justice, goodness, and beauty can be created on earth if there is a decent will to it." He closes the book thus:

> But if you do not will it, then it remains a legend which I have recited. Dream and action are not as widely separated as many believe. All the acts of men were dreams at first and become dreams again.

Yet despite this note of failure, Herzl's achievements far outweighed his setbacks. From year to year, the number of people attending the Zionist Congresses increased, as did general interest in Zionist activity. By the time of the Second Zionist Congress, the number of groups which had joined the organization had risen to 913, triple the amount of the previous year. The total number of delegates was 400, and press representation was also greater. The movement was gaining world-wide recognition and status. Herzl was accepted as its guiding spirit and leader. In 1901, the Jewish Colonial Trust was established; whereas by 1904 it had sold only a million dollars' worth of shares, much to Herzl's chagrin and despite his never-ceasing endeavors in this regard, out of it arose the Anglo-Palestine Company, which in 1950 became the bank Leumi Le-Israel—an institution that played a leading role in the development of Palestine. At the Fifth Congress in 1901, the Jewish National Fund (Keren Kayemet Le-Israel) was created, which was to confine itself to purchasing, developing, and afforesting land in Palestine, to be the inalienable property of the Jews. It was this Fund which later made possible the experimental socialized cooperative farm settlements. At the Congresses, Herzl invariably received enthusiastic ovations despite the growing impatience and discontent of the delegates at Herzl's failure to produce rapid and spectacular results. Herzl himself was well aware of the discrepancy between his will and his actual achievements. He saw only too clearly how far he was from his goal—the Charter for Palestine. Weizmann wrote on this point:

> Herzl spoke in large terms, of international recognition, of a charter for Palestine, of a vast mass migration. But the effect wore off as the years passed and nothing remained but the phrases. Herzl had seen the Sultan. He had seen the Kaiser. He had seen the British Foreign Secretary. He was about to see this or that important man. And the practical effect was nothing. We could not help becoming skeptical about these nebulous negotiations.

It was this failure to achieve positive results that drove Herzl to the proposal of a homeland other than Palestine. His proposition of a settlement in El Arish, in the Sinai peninsula, which was adjacent to Palestine and had historic associations for the Jews, was presented by Herzl to Lord Nathan Rothschild, a member of the British Parliament. Rothschild was not unimpressed and secured Herzl a meeting with Joseph Chamberlain, then Britain's Secretary of State for Colonial Affairs. This marked the beginning of many long discussions with British leaders on the subject of a home for the Jews. The El Arish plan fell through because of disagreement between the Egyptian and Turkish governments. Herzl was now frantic to find a homeland, all the more so because of reports reaching the West concerning the misery of the Rumanian Jews and the anti-Jewish demonstrations in Kishinev, Russia. Thus, at the Sixth Congress, he laid before the delegates the idea of a homeland in Uganda, as offered by the British government. At first, the magnanimity of the British offer "eclipsed all other considerations." Herzl specified that this was not a replacement for Zion. "It is, and must remain, an emergency measure," he said, "which is intended to come to the rescue of ever helpless philanthropic enterprises and prevent the loss of those detached fragments of our people." What Herzl failed to perceive, in Weizmann's words, was that "with all their sufferings, the Jews of Russia were incapable of transferring their dreams and longings from the land of their forefathers to any other territory." A battle ensued. With the acceptance of a plan to send an exploratory commission to Uganda by a majority vote of 298 to 178, the Russian delegates staged a spontaneous walkout. The possible collapse and disintegration of the Zionist movement was imminent and threatening.

But on one point Herzl had always insisted—unity within the ranks at all costs; without unity, the Jews would achieve nothing. Astounded at the Russian demonstration, Herzl declared, "These people have a rope around their necks, and still they refuse!" During the next few days, the gap grew wider. The Russian delegates refused to accept any departure from the original Basle program and felt that the task of Zionism was to achieve its ultimate aim—a home in Palestine—and not to concern itself with the temporary suffering of the Jewish masses. Deep depression hung heavily over all. The epithet "traitor" was thrown at Herzl. He requested an opportunity to explain his position to the rebels: "This is my situation. Money you do not give me. There remains diplomacy, but in the last two days, I have seen how you help me, how you support me in my diplomatic moves. . . . And I am supposed to have violated the Basle Program? Never! I have always stood, I still stand, upon the Basle Program; but I need your faith in me, not your distrust. . . ." The Russian leaders, after a conference held at Charkhov, presented Herzl with the demand that he lay before the Congress no further territorial projects other than those connected with Palestine and Syria. The struggle ended only after Herzl convened a conference of the Greater Actions Committee (1904). He had determined to heal the breach and clear the air:

> We want the continuous growth of Zionism, we want Zionism as the representative of the people. Why do we want this? Because we believe that we cannot achieve our goal without great forces, and these great forces are not to be found in a federation of little societies. Such a federation you had twenty years ago, and you are always telling me that you were already Zionists twenty and twenty-five years ago. You are always throwing that up to me. But what do you prove thereby? What could you achieve so long as you did not have political Zionism? You lived in little groups and collected money. Undoubtedly, your intentions were magnificent, your idealism unchallengeable. Nevertheless, you could not achieve anything because you did not know the path to the objective. This path is the organization of the people, and its organ is the Congress.

Nationalism,
Assimilation, Zionism

This reconciliation conference was Herzl's last achievement, and in the sphere of human relationships, it stands as one of his greatest.

For him personally, the end was near. He had been very ill before the conference and only through sheer determination had he gathered enough strength to attend it. After it was over he was hurried to Franzensbad for a six-week rest cure. Herzl was fully aware that death was close at hand. "There is no time for joking," he said to a comrade, "it is in deadly earnest now . . . there is no time to lose. The last weeks or days. We must hurry. . . ." Not even during these weeks when he was in dire pain, and near to dying, did Herzl cease his work. He wrote letters, conducted interviews. Wrenched by fits of coughing, spitting blood, Herzl continued his fight. On July 3, overcome by pneumonia, he died at the age of 44. His funeral was a testament to the profound impact Herzl had had on the Jewish masses. Six thousand Jews accompanied him to his grave, in mourning for a national hero. Indeed, news of his death shattered the Jewish world. Even during his lifetime, the masses had seen their longings reflected in him. They saw in him their redeemer, a messiah who would lead them out of darkness and into light, into the Promised Land. Ahad Ha'am, one of his most vehement critics, wrote on the death of Herzl:

> The actual living Herzl said and did much that was open to question. . . . But the ideal figure of Herzl which is being created before our eyes in the popular mind—what a splendid vision it will be, and how potent its influence to cleanse that very mind of the taint of the *galut,* to awaken it to a sense of national self-respect, and to whet its desire for a real national life! The people will make him the embodiment of its own national ideal, in all its radiance and purity, and will derive from him strength and courage to struggle onward indefatigably along the hard road of its history.
>
> Herzl gave us the Congress, the Organization, the Bank, the National Fund. . . . But one thing Herzl gave us involuntarily which is perhaps greater than all that he did of set purpose. He gave us himself, to be the theme of our Hymn of Revival, a theme which imagination can take and adorn with all the attributes needed to make a Hebrew national hero, embodying our national aspirations in their true form.

Through Herzl the Jewish people overcame its passive role as the endurer. The Jews began to shape their own life and to take the future into their own hands. Herzl restored to them strength, courage, and purpose, giving himself body and soul to the realization of his utterances. "Why is it," he once asked, "why is it that the best must always fall? Is it because they give to the last ounce of their strength—and beyond—that they are the best?"

In 1949 Herzl's remains were brought to Israel and were reinterred on a hill overlooking Jerusalem, named Mount Herzl. The Jewish State had erupted from his imagination into the world of reality. His sombre dignified countenance became an emblem of the sovereignty which he had pursued with desperate but constant faith.

18 ❧ World War I and the Balfour Declaration

WORLD WAR I inaugurated a period of disintegration in the East-
European Jewish community, which had hitherto been an arena of
both spiritual and political renaissance. The political decline of this
Eastern center was accompanied by an intensive economic degeneration which forced two and a quarter million Jews to emigrate
between the years 1881 and 1914. Most of them turned to America.

On the eve of World War I, eight million out of the ten million
Jews in Europe still lived in the Russian and Austro-Hungarian
Empires. In Russia, where Jews were mobilized into the army, the
military authorities used the war to strike at the Jews, who were
considered anyway to be traitors. Arbitrary expulsions and deten-
tions were added to the normal miseries of life in wartime. One
and a half million Jews were affected by the evacuations, and hence
were visited with total economic ruin.

The situation was drastic, and drastic steps were taken to remedy
it. Jews all over the world began to realize that they must press for
protection of their coreligionists in Europe. In America, which had
not yet entered the war, a congress was founded specifically to agi-
tate for "the national rights of the Jews," rights that were to be
internationally guaranteed at the forthcoming Peace Conference in
Paris. Parallel centers were established in Denmark, Switzerland,
and Holland. These organizations worked in close cooperation with
the American Jewish Congress. They issued literature to keep Jews

abreast of events in Jewish communities all over the world, they appealed to various governments to listen to their claims sympathetically, they held conferences, organized meetings, and generally tried to influence public opinion in favor of Jewish rights. A conference of socialists of neutral lands, held at The Hague toward the end of 1916, declared itself in favor of autonomy for the Jews as well as for other national minorities.

In the countries affected by the war, Jewish nationalist activity was almost dormant. Jewish youths were fighting in the armies, and all dissenting activities had been smothered by the government. The Jews of Russia were branded by the Tsarist officials as disloyal.

When Poland and Lithuania fell to the German-Austrian armies in 1915, the Jews hoped that their condition would be improved. But Jewish aspirations were once again ignored, and no steps were taken to remove legal disabilities. In Russia, the situation changed, for a short time, after the Bolshevik Revolution, not, however, until after tens of thousands of Jews were slaughtered by the White armies of Denikin and Wrangel and the Ukrainian Cossacks of Ataman S. V. Petlura. Thousands of Jewish nationalists now burst upon the scene. Mass meetings, conferences, conventions abounded. Parties were reconstituted. A Jewish press appeared overnight. Jewish political rights were theoretically no longer in question, since the new government had promised to remove all restrictions which Russian subjects had suffered on account of their religion or nationality. Instead of political rights, then, Russian Jews began to press for national-cultural autonomy. In 1917 a congress was held of all Jewish nationalist groups. The proposed program sought the furtherance of Jewish self-government in Russia, and the acquisition of legal guarantees for the Jewish national minority. The Copenhagen office of the World Jewish Congress, anticipating a shaky future, issued a proclamation hailing the removal of the Tsarist restrictive laws, but adding that although the emancipation of the Russian Jews was welcomed, it must not be made conditional upon the renunciation of Jewish national individuality.

At the end of World War I, the great Jewish concentration in Eastern Europe was broken up and its fragments now became part of one or another of the newly established states. The greatest blow fell when the Jews of Soviet Russia were cut off by their government from contact with the Jewish people as a whole. Three million people, about one third of European Jewry, were sealed off behind an impenetrable barrier which to this day has not been pierced. The remaining five million lived now in the newly created countries

Some of the founders of the Joint Distribution Committee, relief organization of all American Jewry. In the left foreground is seated Felix M. Warburg, philanthropist and first Joint chairman.

between the Soviet Union and Western Europe. All of these countries had been major battlefields during the war, and all of them had endured much suffering. With the end of the fighting, all of them eagerly looked forward to the possibilities of a new national existence and a cultural flowering.

The Paris Peace Conference

The Peace Conference of Paris in 1919 began its work in an atmosphere of exhilaration, anticipating nothing less than a new start for mankind and eternal peace. The chief peacemakers among the twenty-seven allied powers were Clemenceau of France, Lloyd George of Great Britain and Woodrow Wilson of the United States. President Wilson had outlined his ideas for the future world order in Four Principles which embodied the doctrine of the "self-determination of peoples." In his famous Fourteen Points, issued a year before (January 1918), he foresaw the creation of an "association of nations to be formed under specific covenants for the purpose of affording mutual guarantees of political independence and territorial integrity to great and small states alike." This association was to be the League of Nations.

The outlines of the new Europe were largely drawn by the delegates to the Paris Peace Conference. Altogether nine new independent states came into being in Europe (Finland, Latvia, Estonia, Lithuania, Poland, Czechoslovakia, Yugoslavia, Austria, and Hungary). Despite every conceivable attention to nationality rights, the drawing up of new national borders to coincide with ethnic and linguistic frontiers resulted inevitably in the transfer of large numbers of Germans, Austrians, and other nationals to the newly created countries. The consequent discontent and ferment were to break out in the crisis of 1938–1939.

President Wilson had made it absolutely clear that "national aspirations must be respected" and that "peoples may now be dominated and governed only by their own consent." Other Allied leaders proclaimed similar concern for minority rights; the victors stood committed to guard the liberties of the weaker peoples. But the problem was a difficult one. Empires were being dissolved, new states were being created, small principalities were demanding more territorial acquisitions. National autonomy alone seemed to offer an adequate solution. That minority groups needed international guarantees for their protection was obvious, but what should those guarantees consist of?

The most persistent advocates of minority rights were the Jews. The delegates sent to Paris by Jewish national organizations insisted that more than civil, political, and religious equality was necessary for the welfare and safety of the Jews. On the other hand, Jewish nationalists and anti-nationalists alike felt that specific assurance made to the Jews alone would tend to segregate them and might arouse hostility. They urged, therefore, the enactment of general provisions to safeguard other minorities as well.

This marked a new milestone in the history of the Jewish struggle for social justice. No longer were Jews attaching themselves to larger groups in search of some abstract ideal which, if attained, would benefit them as well. Nor were they engaging solely in special pleading to improve their own lot, dire though that lot in fact was. Rather, they had taken the forefront in a battle for the principle of liberty. Only if liberty could be secured for all would the Jews benefit from its blessings; by turning outward, by taking upon themselves the responsibility and the burden of securing the larger liberty for all, the Jews announced to the world their new-found confidence in the moral rectitude of their cause.

The Jewish delegates had come prepared. The American Jewish Congress had adopted resolutions to serve as guideposts at the Conference in Paris. Their delegation consisted of nine men, headed by Judge Julian Mack, Rabbi Stephen S. Wise, and Louis Marshall. French Jewry was represented by the *Alliance Israélite Universelle,* a body that was completely anti-nationalist and considered the national claims of the Easterners to be positively dangerous to the cause. Britain's delegation, while not nationalist, was in principle in favor of "minority rights" in the political—as opposed to the narrowly religious—sense.

Eastern Jews were also well represented. Bukovina, Poland, the Ukraine, and even Hungary (in a surprising gesture, since Hungarian Jews had long considered themselves Magyars of the Mosaic persuasion), all sent claims to the Peace Conference for recognition of Jewish national rights. Some, like the Ukrainian Jews, asked the Conference to recognize a United Jewish nation and to admit it to the League of Nations, and to restore Palestine as a Jewish center.

In April of 1919 all sides aired their differences openly and clearly. Nahum Sokolow wanted educational and linguistic autonomy for the Eastern Jews, as well as proportional representation on a national basis and an untrammeled communal life. Claude Montefiore, of the British delegation, conceded on all these points, but opposed a world Jewish Parliament or Jewish membership in the

League of Nations—points that were being demanded by the more extreme Jewish nationalists. No basis for unity could be found so long as the Easterners adamantly refused to dispense with the word "national" and the Westerners refused to accept it. Because of this failure to find unity, the Committee of Jewish Delegations on the one hand, and the anti-national French and British delegations on the other hand, each presented its own memorandum at the Peace Conference. Nevertheless, although attempts at unity had failed, a verbal understanding was reached to cooperate on matters on which all were in accord, and to avoid conflict on disputed questions. The Committee of Jewish Delegations was therefore free to present its claims for national rights, secure in the knowledge that other groups would "abstain from acting in hostility" to these proposals.

The Committee of Jewish Delegations consisted of Mack as chairman and six vice-chairmen including Marshall and Sokolow. Leo Motzkin, who represented the World Zionist Organization, was general secretary. Commissions were set up to deal individually with various matters. Delegates were elected democratically in their respective countries. Their official memoranda demanded guarantees of citizenship for all Jews resident in any state, and national minority rights for Jews and all other minorities. The term "national" denoted an ethnic and cultural community which sought loyally to serve the state of which it would form an integral part. The work done by the leaders of this Committee, particularly by Marshall, Mack, and Sokolow, was conducted in secrecy for fear of prejudicing the claims before they reached the Supreme Council. Unfortunately, this very secrecy tended to deprive their work of the wholehearted confidence and approval of the Jewish delegates.

At the beginning of 1919, President Wilson's draft, which demanded not only recognition of minorities, but guarantees of fair and equal treatment for "national and religious groups," failed to win the support of leading delegates to the Conference. The article was temporarily dropped. The Jewish delegations now acted to try to save the situation. The French and English representatives placed memoranda before the Peace Conference and enlisted the aid of important personages. In March 1919, Mack, Marshall, and Wise submitted memoranda to President Wilson in America. The President in his reply stated his approval of the Jewish claims with regard to Palestine, but the reply was vague on the subject of national rights in Eastern Europe, stating only that the President was "sympathetic to the incontestable principle of the right of the Jewish people to equality of status everywhere."

In Paris, the Committee of Jewish Delegations sought to arouse public opinion in favor of its programs through the medium of the press and through mass meetings. It negotiated with representatives of the small states which would be affected by the Jewish demands. Proposals were formulated, presented, and, when rejected, reformulated. The results were meager. Finally, the Committee on New States and for the Protection of Minorities met to examine the obligations of Poland and the other new states with regard to the protection of racial and religious minorities.

The most important work done by this committee was the drawing up of the Polish Minorities Treaty which was approved by the Supreme Council. The American heads of the Jewish delegations were shown the draft of this treaty. They complained that the provisions were inadequate, and they requested that the minorities themselves be granted the right of appeal to the League. These leaders pressed too for recognition of the Polish Jews as a "legal entity." But their efforts were of no avail and the Supreme Council approved a treaty without the modifications proposed by the Jewish delegates. The activity of the Jews nevertheless continued unabated, their case strengthened by reports of recent excesses against Jews in Eastern Europe and the brutal massacres in southern Russia. In the meantime, the proposed treaty was submitted to Poland, which reacted strongly against it. The small powers now banded together to launch a common offensive attack against the proposed guarantee of minority rights. The provision of these rights, they maintained, would invade the sovereignty of their states and jeopardize their national unity. President Wilson stood firm, refusing to grant any additional territory to these states until they accepted the terms of the treaty. Then, suddenly, at the end of June, Poland signed the treaty. With tremendous relief the Jewish delegates held a long interview with the Polish head of state, and both parties expressed their desire for cooperation and understanding.

The Polish treaty confirming minority rights granted the Jews the right to use their own language in primary schools; furthermore they were to be exempted from performing any duties which would violate their Sabbath, but were of course obligated to perform certain duties to the state such as military service, national defense, and the preservation of order. The League of Nations would guarantee that these acts were carried out; any complaints were to be voiced before the Permanent Court of International Justice. The provisions of the Polish Minorities Treaty bore a close resemblance to the guarantees sought in the formula of the Committee of Jewish

"And they posed for the picture." On August 10, 1919, on the route from Bohuslav to Tarastcha, Ataman Zeliony's Cossacks unashamedly display the corpses of Jews they have murdered.

Delegations and in the proposals presented by the Joint Foreign Committee and the *Alliance* in February 1919.

The other new states were now placed on the agenda. Rumania and Serbia refused to be bound by any provisions for the protection of minorities and would not have the "Jewish Articles" included in their treaties. Again the Jews acted, leaving nothing to chance. Their efforts were not wholly successful. The Jewish clauses were deleted from the treaty with Czechoslovakia, from the Serbo-Croat-Slovene Minorities Treaty, and from the Rumanian Treaty, although in the last a new article was introduced which guaranteed Jews full rights as Rumanian citizens. The treaties with the defeated states of Austria, Hungary, Bulgaria, and Turkey were largely based on the Polish one with the omission of the "Jewish Articles."

Russia was not dealt with at this stage. Louis Marshall, however, appealed to President Wilson that in the final treaty with Russia, which was to be settled by the League of Nations, provisions be made for the protection of minority rights.

In May 1922, the Lithuanian Declaration on the protection of minorities was signed: it was almost identical to the Polish Treaty. Latvia and Estonia refused to accept the minorities treaties but made a declaration to the League which included the basic conditions of the Polish Treaty. Albania signed a similar declaration.

Thus, due primarily to the efforts of the Jewish representatives, the Peace Conference was induced to guarantee racial, religious, and linguistic minority rights which exceeded the accepted levels of civil, political, and religious equality. Minority groups of new and enlarged states were assured group rights in religion, language, education, and culture. Thus the ideal of complete national uniformity, which had prevailed before the war, was superseded by the new ideal of pluralism and variety.

Even so, the more radical demands of the East-European Jewish nationalists had not been met. These nationalists had thought in terms of separate states or federated nationalities within a larger body. Their demands, due to the opposition of the Western Jews, had never been voiced publicly at the Peace Conference. Indeed, even some of the more modest desires of the Committee of Jewish Delegations were not fully realized. Nevertheless, Jews everywhere acclaimed the Minorities Treaties as a great victory. The general attitude of the Jews was expressed in a letter which Marshall, Cyrus Adler, and Nahum Sokolow sent to Boris Bogen, the administrator of Jewish relief in Poland:

> Its [Polish Treaty's] clauses are far-reaching. It confers civil and political rights upon all, regardless of race, language, nationality

or religion. It carefully defines citizenship. It prevents discrimination. It affords ample security for the free exercise of religion, assures equality before the law, and free use of languages of the several minorities and the right of management by them of their schools and other communal institutions with that of sharing in the public funds appropriated for educational and other like purposes.

These rights of minorities are declared by the Treaty to be matters of international concern. This is an act of the first magnitude. In truth it constitutes a genuine charter of liberty for all minorities because its effectiveness is guaranteed by the sanction of the League of Nations.

The Jews of Europe now looked forward expectantly to a happier and safer future. It was a future which—through patient and determined effort—they had secured for themselves and for all other minority groups. It was, however, to be a future whose blessings would be of brief duration and of tragic end.

Collapse of Minority Rights The new order in Europe held forth the promise of international protection of minorities under the League of Nations. The provisions of the "minority clauses" guaranteed national privileges with regard to schools, choice of language, state-supported institutions, and the like. In this way, Jewish national rights were safeguarded by law in Latvia and Lithuania, in Poland and in Czechoslovakia. In Latvia, for instance, Jews were granted full educational autonomy. In Lithuania, a special Jewish Ministry was established. In Rumania, the classical locale of the pogrom, the new constitution guaranteed the Jewish population broad national and civil rights.

On the whole, the Jewish masses were stirred to new heights of activity by the proclamations of equal rights on the part of the new governments. Their belief in the high ideals of national liberation triggered an intense social and cultural revolution, which led to country-wide organizations of community life and to the establishment of numerous Yiddish and Hebrew schools.

But from the very beginning, political democracy in Europe was highly fragile, and in a fairly brief time the formal equality and constitutional guarantees agreed upon by these governments were disclosed as nothing but gestures of conciliation toward the Western liberators. A process of disenfranchisement, economic expulsion, and forced emigration now began in earnest, and once

A small synagogue, shabby and dilapidated,
outside of Moscow.

again the environment became one in which Jews found themselves physically insecure and psychologically desperate.

Such was the situation in most countries of Eastern and Central Europe. Scarcely had the Polish Republic been established when the Jews of that land became subject to physical assault, high taxation, and the introduction of a *numerus clausus.* Almost all of Poland's political parties were agreed that there was no room in their country for her three million Jews, despite the fact that Jews had lived there for almost a thousand years and had pioneered in every phase of the country's development. Economically, their situation deteriorated to the point where Polish Jews became frantic about finding a new homeland—this, long before the era of Hitler.

The situation was no better in Rumania, especially in the provinces of Bessarabia and Transylvania, where unrestrained, government-inspired terror resulted in the persecution and imprisonment of numerous Jews accused of lingering attachment to Hungary or Russia, from which countries these territories had been acquired. In Hungary itself, the policy of repression resulted in a steep drop in the percentage of Jews attending universities—from 34.6 per cent before the war to 7.8 per cent after it. In every country between the Soviet Union and Western Europe, an area inhabited by five million Jews, institutions of higher learning were transformed into centers of savage anti-Semitism.

Thus, in nearly every country in Eastern Europe, Jews became the victims of the new sovereign majorities, which pursued a policy of rabid nationalism despite all their promises to the contrary. In Poland, which was struggling to survive economically, it was erroneously believed that the destruction of one economic group, namely the Jews, was inevitable if others were to survive. The economic assault upon Jews did not, however, take the form of open anti-Jewish legislation. During the 1920s, the government resorted instead to Estatism, a kind of state capitalism which nationalized the tobacco, liquor, salt, and match industries, as well as all branches of public transportation. It was no coincidence that these were the industries in which Jews had been most prominently represented. The new government owners now dismissed all Jewish employees. In addition, Jews were completely frozen out of all civil service positions and from all government contracts. Tens of thousands of Jews joined the unemployed. Nearly every stratum of Jewish life was affected. In the mid 1920s, of 2800 Jewish shoemaking concerns in Poland, 2060 were closed. The same held true in many other branches of industry.

In Rumania, national and local authorities tried to evade the simplest and most reasonable of the obligations which they had undertaken. In the university city of Cernauti, for example, in the northern province just acquired from Austria, a Jewish businessman, desiring to show his good faith to all the inhabitants of the city, built, equipped, and presented to the university a fine social center for all its students. The first step taken by the authorities was to exclude any Jewish student from the use of the new center.

In Hungary, the situation was also unhappy, but it was of a different tenor. In the old Imperial days, the sons of the middle and upper classes found ample employment in the army or the civil service. They willingly left to the Jews the fields of finance, journalism, commerce, manufacturing, and entertainment. After the war, these fields were virtually all that remained. In the civil service, Jews who had university degrees were stiff competitors. An unsavory economic anti-Semitism thus developed, centering in the universities. The Hungarian Jews bitterly resented this turn of events, being more emancipated than most other Eastern Jews and hence accustomed to a more open society.

Then, too, the small states in Eastern and in Southeastern Europe had become covetous of their neighbors' territory. Disregarding the territorial arrangements of the Peace Treaty, they took what they wanted by force. Local squabbles were fiercer than ever before, and Jews frequently found themselves in the middle, accused by the petty politicians on each side of disloyal scheming.

That the treaties failed was perhaps inevitable. The League of Nations had no power to see them enforced, and neglected to exercise the impartiality and justice which were essential to their proper execution. The Great Powers, moreover, played their own political game with the League, hindering any attempts of real progress. Then, too, the peacemakers had paid little attention to the economic problems of the newly established states. No aid was extended to the defeated nations to enable them to return to a normal economic existence. In consequence, poverty and hunger, bitterness and hatred, grew from day to day. As ever in such situations, the Jews provided the most likely scapegoat for all the ills of society.

The Balfour
Declaration

Zionist hopes for the establishment of Palestine as a home for the Jews became a living political reality in 1914, when Turkey entered the Great War on the side of Germany. With the envisaged liquidation of the Ottoman Empire, which had long been leading a precarious existence as the "Sick Man of Europe," various parties put forward their claims to the inheritance of Palestine. The leading contender at this stage was France, which based its claim to the territory on the fact that most of the Crusaders in the Holy Land during the Middle Ages had hailed from France. For centuries France had played the role of protector to Christians living in the Turkish dominions, a role which had been acknowledged by the Turkish Porte as early as 1553, although in actual effect, the religious interests of most Christians in the Empire were vested mainly in the Russian Orthodox Church, to which the majority belonged.

In 1882 France had been forced to accept the consolidation of British interests in Egypt. At this time she insisted even more strenuously on retaining her influence in Syria, whose territory also included Palestine. Since Great Britain was concerned principally with the fate of the Suez Canal, at the outbreak of the Great War it agreed, at least by implication, that France pursue the leading role in the economic and cultural development of Syria. England expressly disavowed any political or territorial aspirations. This attitude, however, was to change very soon, when the fear arose in Britain that a major power, so close to the Suez Canal, might jeopardize the British lifeline to India. England thereupon made it clear to France that her hopes for incorporating Palestine in the larger scheme for Syria would not be tolerated.

At this stage, British intentions ran concurrent with Zionist aims. Offering her protection to a Jewish Palestine was a means of justifying Britain's role in the Middle East. Zionist leaders began to receive hints of Britain's preparedness to assist in a realization of the Zionist program for the establishment of a legally secured home in Palestine, in accordance with the Basle Program.

On the eve of World War I, the visible strength of the Zionist movement was not impressive. The world membership in 1913 had reached a total of 130,000, but advances were slow. Despite the fact that the underlying strength of the movement was vastly greater than this figure would suggest, the Zionists were still being looked upon by most of their fellow Jews as unworldly dreamers, out of touch with reality. Politically, no headway had been made since the Sixth Congress. The period of close friendship with Great Britain during the years 1902–1905 (at the time of the Uganda proposal) had ended. The French were convinced that the Zionists worked for the Germans (Herzl had striven to interest the Kaiser in a Charter) and the Turks in general were hostile to Zionist endeavors. In the words of Chaim Weizmann, "we were standing before a blank wall." Therefore the main efforts had been concentrated on practical work in Palestine, on settlement, agriculture, and the development of a new culture.

Renewed contact with the British government was made by Weizmann late in 1914 through his friend C. P. Scott, the editor of the *Manchester Guardian*. In January 1915, he met Lloyd George, who had become chairman of the Munitions Committee and had encountered difficulties with the production of acetone. Lloyd George approached Weizmann, the brilliant scientist, for a solution to the problem; Weizmann's success in evolving a new process for producing acetone was of great importance to the war effort, and it gained him a friend in the man who was to become Prime Minister.

The real turning point in the British-Zionist relationship, however, went back beyond this episode to an encounter between Arthur James Balfour and Chaim Weizmann in 1906. Balfour had wanted to meet Weizmann in order to convince him that it had been wrong to refuse the British offer of Uganda. In a curious reversal, Weizmann succeeded in convincing Balfour that it was he who was wrong; that Zion, and only Zion, was a suitable homeland for the Jews. Thereafter, Balfour became a dedicated Zionist; without his help, there would have been no Declaration. When Weizmann met Balfour again, as Foreign Secretary in Lloyd George's cabinet, Balfour said: "You know, I was thinking of that conversation of ours (in 1906), and believe that when the guns stop firing, you may get your Jerusalem."

From now on, Weizmann worked feverishly toward this goal. He won the support of many leading British personalities as well as that of certain prominent British Jews, such as Herbert Samuel, the first professing Jew to be a member of the British cabinet, Walter Rothschild (son of Nathaniel), Harry Sacher, Israel Sieff, and Simon Marks. Weizmann outlined his plan in a letter to Scott: ". . . that the Jews take over the country; the whole burden of the organization falls on them, but for the next ten or fifteen years, they work under a temporary British protectorate. A strong Jewish community in the Egyptian flank is an efficient barrier against any danger likely to come from the North."

In many countries, Zionist aspirations had been denounced by the Jewish leadership, which regarded the possibility of a Charter as a calamity which would endanger Jewish rights in the Diaspora. Sometimes, the most vehement protests came from the very organizations which encouraged Jewish philanthropic efforts in Palestine.

These circles were careful not to disclaim the historic ties between the Jews and Palestine, but were anxious to preserve the equality which had been gained so recently, and at such cost, in Western Europe. They saw in the conception of a Jewish State an invitation to their enemies to raise the vexed question of divided loyalty.

Toward the end of January 1917, despite this opposition, Weizmann and his committee submitted to the Foreign Office an official memorandum of proposed policy in Palestine, called the "Outline of Program for the Jewish Resettlement of Palestine in Accordance with the Aspirations of the Zionist Movement." The main points were that the Jews in Palestine were to be recognized as a nation and given every freedom, civic, national, political, and religious, as well as the right to purchase land and to immigrate.

The anti-Zionists, alarmed at the headway the Zionists were making in 1917, determined to foil the effort. Weizmann writes:

> It was an extraordinary struggle that developed within English Jewry in the half-year which preceded the issuance of the Balfour Declaration—a struggle which probably had no historic parallel anywhere. Here was a people which had been divorced from its original homeland for some eighteen centuries, putting in a claim for restitution. The world was willing to listen, the case was being sympathetically received, and one of the great Powers was prepared to lead in the act of restitution, while the others had indicated their benevolent interest. And a well-to-do, contented and self-satisfied minority, a tiny minority of the people in question, rose in rebellion against the proposal, and exerted itself with the utmost fury to prevent the act of restitution from being consummated. Itself in no need—or believing itself to be in no need—of the righting of the ancient historic wrong, this small minority struggled bitterly to deprive the vast majority of the benefits of a unique act of the world conscience; and it succeeded, if not in balking the act of justice, at least in vitiating some of its application.

In an address to a special conference of delegates from all Zionist societies of Great Britain, Weizmann said that he considered it a matter of deep humiliation that the Jews could not stand united in this great hour. "We do not want to offer the world a spectacle of a war of brothers. But we warn those who will force an open breach that . . . we shall not allow anybody to interfere with the hard work which we are doing, and we say to all our opponents: 'Hands Off the Zionist Movement!' "

The anti-Zionists heeded no threats. A long statement was published in *The Times*, repudiating the Zionist position and urging the government not to favor the Zionist demands. *The Times* itself rebutted this statement, answering cryptically: "Only an imaginative nervousness suggests that the realization of territorial Zionism in some form would cause Christendom to turn around on the Jews and say 'Now you have a land of your own, go to it.'"

Nevertheless, anti-Zionist agitation resulted in a delay in the issuing of the Balfour Declaration, and its final wording was not as precise or as unconditional to the Jews as it had been before this interference. When the Palestine item was laid before the War Cabinet, Edwin Montagu (then Secretary for India), a Jewish anti-Zionist, made a passionate speech against the proposed move. Finally, on October 16, President Wilson cabled to the British government America's support of the substance of the Declaration; the deadlock created by the anti-Zionists was broken. On November 2, 1917, the British Foreign Office issued the following declaration in the form of a letter addressed to Lord Rothschild, the head of the British branch of this family and himself not a banker but a scientist and a member of the House of Lords.

> Dear Lord Rothschild,
>
> I have much pleasure in conveying to you, on behalf of His Majesty's Government, the following Declaration of sympathy with Jewish Zionist aspirations which has been submitted to, and approved by, the Cabinet:
>
> "His Majesty's Government view with favour the establishment in Palestine of a national home for the Jewish people, and will use their best endeavours to facilitate the achievement of this object, it being clearly understood that nothing shall be done which may prejudice the civil and religious rights of existing non-Jewish communities in Palestine, or the rights and political status enjoyed by Jews in any other country."
>
> I should be grateful if you would bring this declaration to the knowledge of the Zionist Federation.
>
> Yours sincerely,
Arthur James Balfour

The Balfour Declaration signalled the start of a British military campaign in Palestine which a month later led to the liberation of Judea from the Turks. On the first day of Hanukkah, 1917, Lord Allenby entered Jerusalem. Among his troops were three Jewish battalions of the Jewish Legion, formed by volunteers from England, the United States, Canada, and the indigenous Jewish population of Palestine, and led by Vladimir Jabotinsky and Josef Trumpeldor. At the San Remo Conference of the Allies in 1920,

the Palestine question was finally settled. Lloyd George parted from Weizmann with the following words: "Now you have your State. It is up to you to win the race." The Mandate was formally conferred on Britain by the League of Nations in 1922.

Importance of the Balfour Declaration

The Balfour Declaration is the decisive diplomatic victory of the Jewish people in modern history. The subsequent political victories of 1947 and 1948 seem to overshadow the Balfour Declaration, which was Weizmann's salient contribution to the Israeli revolution. But 1917, not 1948, was the initial turning point. It is true that the 1948 partition seemed to have more revolutionary consequences. But it did not depend on an exclusively visionary impulse. It reflected a manifest balance of existing forces. The Jewish settlement in Palestine had grown too large to be dominated by Arabs, too self-reliant to be confined by tutelage, and too ferociously resistant to be thwarted in its main ambition. Thus to urge partition in 1948 was not to disappear from solid reality into an outer space of mystical faith.

On the other hand, to propose in 1914, as Weizmann did, that international recognition should be given to the right of the Jewish people "to reconstitute a National Home in Palestine" was to rebel against the inertia of established facts. Nobody knew what a "National Home" was or was not. The "Jewish people" was not a recognized juridical entity. There was not even such a country as "Palestine"; there was only the southern district of Syria. It was also an awkward fact that the country whose fate Britain was invited to decide happened to be under the effective domination of the Ottoman Turks, against whom Britain was then waging a remarkably unsuccessful war.

Weizmann's power lay in his capacity to grasp and to convince others that the needs of Jewish history must ultimately prevail against those mountainous obstacles of rationality. He was only a lecturer in Manchester University, with no authority to speak even for the small Zionist movement of those struggling days. But there was a promise in the air—of new and wonderful opportunities to be snatched from the changing interests and fortunes of the powers. And Chaim Weizmann was young and free, unburdened by history, failure, disillusion, or public office. It was the springtime of his people's hope and it was good to be alive. He swiftly gathered a few men around him, watched and nursed his chances, and then

Officers and men of the Jewish Legion pray near the Western Wall. The Legion, organized during World War I and commanded by British General Allenby, made a brilliant record in the Middle Eastern fighting.

intervened in the central political arenas with such massive authority and sureness of timing as to change the whole direction of his people's history. It was an age in which victorious nationalism was setting many leaders of liberated peoples on their pedestals. Weizmann towers above them all in the poignant disparity between the ends which he sought and the means that he commanded.

A leading diplomatic historian has written:

> No one will dispute that Dr. Weizmann was the main creator of the national home, and without the national home there could have been no State of Israel today. But even now I doubt whether this part of his great achievements has ever received in contemporary history all the recognition that it deserves. It was, in my opinion, the greatest act of diplomatic statesmanship of the First World War. That period produced several great leaders of small nationalities who obtained much for their people when the world was transformed by the conflict between the great powers. But none of them in my view, not even the two most renowned amongst them, Masaryk and Venizelos, can compare in stature with Dr. Weizmann. The obstacles which they had to overcome to achieve their aims were far smaller than those which confronted Dr. Weizmann. Their peoples were already in physical possession of their territories. But Dr. Weizmann had no such advantage. The people for whom he strove to create were dispersed over all the five continents. The home which he sought to create was in a country whose inhabitants, except for a small and all-important body of pioneers, belonged to another people. He had to go back nearly 2,000 years to establish a claim upon it. There was no precedent for what he asked.
>
> (From Sir Charles Webster: *The Art and Practice of Diplomacy*)

The Weizmann Era

The wave of this victory brought Weizmann high on its crest to a position of unrivaled leadership in Jewish life. His triumph had been in the arena of diplomacy. But he knew that the final verdict would be decided in more strenuous fields. He implored the powerful Jewries, with only partial success, to turn their minds away from diplomacy toward the concrete forces which alone gave diplomacy its content. The Balfour Declaration and the Mandate for Palestine were no more than opportunities. They carried with them no inherent certainty of fulfillment. Everything depended on whether they could be replaced by a geopolitical reality more substantial than themselves.

Between the two world wars he was to pursue his task in the clear understanding that he was conducting a race against time. Arab nationalism would soon awaken to a stronger virulence; and British statesmen would not for long ignore the calculations of space, population, and strategy in which the Arab world seemed so vastly to outweigh the imponderable values which Zionism expressed. Weizmann's task was to convert a generous vision into solid fact.

His own position in international life conveyed a premonition of Jewish sovereignty. Heads of state received him with courtesy, ministers and high officials with apprehensive respect. They stood a good chance of being charmed into an unwanted commitment or exhausted by the tempest of his emotion. But they behaved toward him as though he were already president of a sovereign nation, equal in stature to their own. He and they knew that this was not strictly true; but something in his presence and in their own historic imagination forbade them to break the spell. The Jewish people had produced a president before it had achieved a state; and somehow this made the claim of statehood seem less farfetched in many eyes than it would otherwise have seemed.

From the masses of his own people he was separated by the range and distinction of his contacts, by his taste for elegance, order, and sophistication in daily life, and by the broad scope of his cultural experience, extending from Jewish folk tradition across European humanism into the atmosphere and discipline of scientific method. But in style and spirit he was not remote from them. They admired his balanced attitude toward his own personal eminence. They knew that he was gripped by their central interests. He refused to dissipate his versatile attainments in varied and scattered fields. The strands of his multiple interests were woven together in a single texture.

For this total consecration to their purposes his followers rewarded him with an awed respect. He was deeply rooted in their memories and origins. To foreign chancelleries he might come as a skilled diplomat. To the Jewish masses he was the gifted son of a timber merchant in Pinsk. His language, voice, and mannerisms never ceased to convey the rich and solid culture of the Jewish Pale of Settlement. Sometimes in the heat of political combat, his people would reject him formally, only to fall into a passion of repentance and move heaven and earth for his restoration to their head. Even when he was removed from office, Jewish communities refused to recognize anyone else as the paramount envoy of Zionism.

Israel's national rebirth had already begun with the *Biluim*. They were followed by ever-growing numbers of pioneers who, as distinct *aliyot* (waves of immigration), laid the foundations for the structure of modern Israel. At a time when immigration to England and America was still free, these men and women had turned to Zion. Their ambition was to create a radical transformation in the basis of Jewish existence. They consciously took up agricultural settlement and manual labor, out of a determination to cleanse Jewry of the odium of the ghetto by a return to the soil. If not all of them withstood the test they had imposed on themselves, the best formed an elite under whose leadership a new type of Jewish society gradually began to take shape. Redemption of the soil, personal labor as a kind of salvation—these were the ideals which inspired the "normalization" of Jewish life undertaken with partic ular ferocity by the pioneers of the second *Aliyah*, which began in 1904 and lasted until the outbreak of the war. These ideals became a living reality in the cooperative settlement, or *kevutzah,* a unique experiment in social organization which began at Deganiah in 1909. Here a society was created which functioned according to the utopian norms conceived by the great reformers of nineteenth-century Russia; here a mode of life was evolved in which everybody in truth gave according to his abilities and received according to his needs. These embryonic units would later develop into the *kibbutz* movement—a successful embodiment of the egalitarian ideal and an inspiration to democratic societies all over the globe.

At first, the idea of a return to Zion was the exclusive preoccupation of the intellectual Jewish youth of Eastern Europe. Among the men and women who came in those days were young people of great promise, all eager in their devotion to the rebuilding of Palestine. Their philosopher was Aaron David Gordon, who wrote of physical labor as the basis of renewed Jewish existence. It was a time of experiment, of danger and of difficulty, but also a period of close comradeship and ardent spirit. By 1914 only a small beginning had been made, but enough had been achieved not only to inspire the Zionists with confidence in the future, but to enlist the sympathies of many Jews who did not call themselves Zionists. The settlements had begun to be self-sustaining. There existed a nucleus of Jewish labor in the cities, and a new culture was in the making. It was all on a small scale but it was enough to give weight to the claims of the Zionists, and it was proof that their schemes were not idle daydreams. Now, when Jewish statesmen like Weizmann and Sokolow appeared on the international scene to claim the rights of

Tel Aviv in 1921. Today this is one of the city's busiest shopping and commercial centers, Mograbi Square. In the background the promontory of Jaffa juts into the Mediterranean.

the Jewish nation, the civilized world listened. Achievements in Palestine spoke more eloquently than centuries of supplications and tears.

The return to Zion, and the creation of a new national life there, demanded the quick evolution of a national culture attuned to the spiritual values of Zionism. The instrument of this cultural renaissance was the Hebrew language, revived by the Zionists as a medium of communication in the life and literature of the nation. In Europe Hebrew had already experienced a revival of sorts a few decades before it began to be used in Palestine, where it became an issue only with the Zionist immigration. That it was desirable to have a single unifying language for the new "ingathering" was obvious to everyone, but it was initially not so obvious that this language should be Hebrew. At that time most Jews spoke Yiddish and enjoyed Yiddish literature. Hebrew was a language known in the synagogue and school, a language of prayer and study, but it was spoken by few and had not kept pace with the modern world. Nevertheless, a decision was made that Hebrew should be the national language. One man, Eliezer ben Yehudah, dedicated his life to the remolding of Hebrew as the vehicle of a new Jewish life; the enormous dictionary which he compiled contained hundreds of new idioms. Yiddish for the new pioneers came to symbolize the exile, humiliation. The return to freedom meant a concomitant return to the language of the ancient Hebrews, the forging of a link between the people and the land, in proud affirmation of past glories.

The first to propagate Hebrew had been the workers in the agricultural colonies, those early settlers who had been inspired to come by the *Hibbat Zion* movement. These settlers insisted on using Hebrew in conversation, in reading and in writing. Had they not displayed such obstinacy, Hebrew might not have established itself as the unifying language of the homeland. The struggle for Hebrew was long, bitter and involved. The ancient pietist community of Palestine regarded Hebrew as the holy tongue, reserved for prayer and study. Many refused to use Hebrew for everyday purposes, and were appalled at this profanation of the sacred language. All these factors had to be overcome before Hebrew could become a natural, rather than an artificially imposed, element in the national life and culture.

By 1913 there existed several schools in Palestine in which Hebrew was the language of instruction. The measure of the Zionist victory in this regard may be taken from an incident which occurred in 1913 when the Haifa Technion was opened, with German as its official language. Both students and teachers went on strike; their slogan: "No Hebrew—No Technion." No amount of pressure on the part of the supporting philanthropic organization, the German *Hilfsverein,* could convince the striking scholars to give up their new language.

To all intents and purposes, Jewish life in Palestine was from the beginning a national life. It was so by virtue of the basic emotions of the settlers; their efforts to rehabilitate the country were under taken not only to improve their own economic and political situation, but to further the cause of the nation as a whole. To achieve that goal they were prepared to undergo a complete change in the traditional structure of Jewish society; the result of their devotion was the conversion of a desolate land into a flourishing and productive country. The adoption of Hebrew as a spoken language and the creation of many new cultural institutions inaugurated an era of profound spiritual revival, an expression of a new national consciousness whose reverberating effects on the Jewish and non-Jewish world at large were entirely disproportionate to the numerical strength of these early pioneers. Their wealth was puny and their physical strength negligible. But they enlarged their small reality by a utopian vision. Thy were resolutely convinced that it was their destiny to make a new communication of freedom to Jewry and to all mankind.

*T*HE BALFOUR Declaration was greeted by world Jewry as a kind of Magna Carta. The caution and ambivalence of its formulation could not dim its inner glow. The idea of Jewish national independence had passed from fantasy into the real world of politics. In some parts of the Jewish Diaspora, the messianic fervor was so intense that Weizmann found it necessary to sound a cautious note.

> A State cannot be created by decree but only by the forces of the people and in the course of generations. Even if all the governments of the world gave us a country, it would be a gift of words. But if the Jewish people will go and build Palestine, the Jewish State will become a reality and a fact.

The conditions under which the reality was to be built were unusual. There were scarcely any funds, there was little experience and not much training in the pursuits most closely relevant to the task at hand. People who for centuries had been divorced from the land now threw themselves into intensive agricultural development. Intellectuals, shopkeepers, merchants, students, turned by an act of conscious will toward the soil. By every rational test, the experiment seemed doomed to fail. Yet the Jewish population of Palestine grew from 55,000 at the end of World War I to 450,000 in 1939. Each new immigrant made way for the next. The central aim was to create opportunities for those to come.

The era of the National Home began with the third *Aliyah*. Among the tens of thousands who came after World War I, a nucleus of dedicated pioneers gave the new society its motive force. The word *pioneer* does not fully exhaust the meaning of *halutziut* which became the central ethic of Palestinian Jewish life. The concept is one of self-abnegation, austerity, practical mysticism, and a creative refusal to face uncomfortable facts. The pioneer was totally consecrated to the social and national vision. His satisfactions came not from personal advantage but from the spectacle of growth and expansion of which he was the architect and sometimes the victim. The first task was to make the land itself a fitting environment for civilized pursuits. The draining of swamps, the planting of trees, the building of roads, gradually deprived part of the land of its incredible harshness. Deadly malaria carried by clouds of mosquitoes hovering over neglected bogs and swamps took a heavy toll. A Jewish idealism, suppressed for many centuries, now found heroic outlet. The emerging society was nothing like anything heretofore associated with the Jewish image. The new national prototype was not the businessman or ascetic scholar, but the farmer and laborer.

Suffering was the badge of this new Jewish tribe. They lacked money and medical facilities, and sometimes were short of food. In their outlying settlements, they were subject to sharp cultural isolation and very often to physical danger. There were times when men went hungry in order that their cattle might eat. The explanation was engaging, "We are Zionists, but our cows are not." The new society was marked by a deep sense of moral preoccupation. The settlers tormented themselves with endless debates about the meaning of their lives, the purpose of their actions and the shape of the nation that they were struggling to build. Rigorous ideals of justice and equality were pursued in the socialized communities which they founded. They were driven by a fierce and constant sense of mission. They learned from experiment and failure. Above all, they sought an inner spiritual rebuilding of their souls, a total reconstruction of the national will.

With each wave of immigration, the community became more complex. Various social and religious outlooks clashed about the ultimate aim of the National Home. But nearly all managed to combine for immediate goals. In 1925, the fourth *Aliyah,* consisting of over 30,000 immigrants, poured in suddenly. Half of them came from Poland in flight from new persecution. They were nearly all of middle class. They had had no contact with primary

sources of production. They found vast economic difficulties and many turned away disheartened. The crisis ended in 1928. New factories had been established and these, together with the expanding farms, were absorbing a growing labor force. The Jordan waters were now harnessed for an electric power station at the Rutenberg Works. The Dead Sea's mineral potential was being exploited by volunteer workers. The Jewish sector of Palestine was by Middle Eastern standards becoming a progressive society.

Progress was rapid in social organizations. From the beginning, the *yishuv*, or settlement, resolved to govern its internal life and develop its own institutions. In Eastern Europe the Jews had been familiar with this pattern. They had created their own social environment in almost complete oblivion of the central governments which ruled over them. Now, too, the British Mandatory Administration was strangely external to the close-knit autonomous structures which the Jews established and sustained.

The democratic habit was fostered at every level. In general balloting the *yishuv* elected its own representatives, the *Asefat Ha-nivharim*, a body which in turn appointed an executive organ, the *Vaad Leumi* (National Council). The *Vaad Leumi* organized an educational system which covered almost the entire Jewish population. This indeed was one of its decisive achievements accomplished with little encouragement by the Mandatory Power. The educational level was just as high among the alert and vigorous farm population as among city dwellers. A new nation was being fashioned from an ancient mold.

The national leadership placed strong emphasis on intellectual progress. In his early romantic years, Weizmann had dreamed of a Hebrew University as the supreme expression of the renascent culture. He felt that the Jewish spirit would thrive best on its own soil where masters and disciples, inspired by the same traditions, would in their own language create an authentic national culture. The Hebrew University was conceived as a kind of power station generating spiritual and intellectual energy throughout the Jewish people as a whole.

In July 1918, while guns could still be heard, the foundation stones of the Hebrew University were laid on Mount Scopus in the presence of the British General Allenby and his staff, representatives of the Allied armies, Moslem, Christian, and Jewish dignitaries from Jerusalem, and representatives of the *yishuv*. It was one of the formative assemblies of the new Israel. Of that day, Weizmann wrote:

The toil of hands in the fields under the hot sun once again makes the barren valleys of the Promised Land fruitful. Driven by the urge to rebuild the land, pioneers labor in sight of the ancient hills of Zion.

The physical setting of the ceremony was of unforgettable and sublime beauty. The declining sun flooded the hills of Judea and Moab with golden light, and it seemed to me, too, that the transfigured heights were watching, wondering, dimly aware perhaps that this was the beginning of the return of their own people after many days. Below us lay Jerusalem, gleaming like a jewel.

We were practically within sound of the guns on the northern front, and I spoke briefly, contrasting the desolation which the war was bringing with the creative significance of the act on which we were engaged; recalling, too, that only a week before we had observed the Fast of the Ninth of Ab, the day on which the Temple was destroyed and Jewish national political existence extinguished—apparently forever. We were there to plant the germ of a new Jewish life.

. . . The ceremony did not last longer than an hour. When it was over, we sang *Hatikvah* and *God Save the King.* But no one seemed anxious to leave, and we stood silent with bowed heads, round the little row of stones, while the twilight deepened into night.

In 1925, the University was officially opened. The ceremony brought guests from all corners of the world. They assembled in a natural amphitheater, commanding a sublime view all around: the tumbling hills of Judea, the steep descent into the Jordan Valley with a glimpse of the blue waters of the Dead Sea across to the mountains of Gilead and Moab beyond.

Lord Balfour, who had faithfully accompanied Zionism in its early struggle, delivered the inauguration speech. In scarlet Cambridge robes and white-haired majesty, he seemed to symbolize a gentile world coming to terms for the first time with Jewish national equality.

It is not the magnificence of the view which is stretched before you. It is the consciousness that this occasion marks a great epoch in the history of a people who have made this little land of Palestine a seed-ground of great religion, and whose intellectual and moral destiny is again, from a national point of view, reviving, and who will look back to this day which we are celebrating as one of the great milestones in its future career.

Jerusalem and Mount Scopus were one expression of the national rebirth. Several hundred feet below and forty miles away emerged another. There on the shores of the Mediterranean, Tel Aviv, founded in 1909 as a suburb of Jaffa for a population of ten thousand, was growing rapidly as an active Jewish city. Tel Aviv

Planned at the First Zionist Congress in 1897, the Hebrew University begins on Mt. Scopus in 1925 with completion of its first building, the Institute for Jewish Studies.

became the nerve center of the nation. Commerce and industry grew. Hebrew newspapers were published every morning; poets and writers flocked to weekly meetings on Friday night; the city's intellectual atmosphere was illuminated by the masters of modern Hebrew, Hayyim Nahman Bialik, Saul Tchernikovsky, and for a few declining years, the philosopher Ahad Ha'am. Theaters performed Hebrew and foreign drama. Here, the first concert of the Palestine Symphony Orchestra, formed by Bronislaw Hubermann, was conducted under the baton of Arturo Toscanini to the music of Beethoven and Mendelssohn. It appeared that the years of hardship and sacrifice had begun to flower. Men and women who had come to Palestine in grave defiance of obstacles were now claiming their cultural heritage and embarking on their people's revolution.

The fifth *Aliyah,* beginning in 1932, saw the absorption of tens of thousands of German Jews into the homeland. The terror from which they fled had not reached its final paroxysm, but the dangers and humiliations were intolerable enough. There was something poignant in the contrast between their previous confidence and their present ruin. German Jews were often more remote from Zionism than even the most assimilated among Polish and Russian Jewry. They had given their German "fatherland" every loyalty and service. They were intensely European in manners, taste, dress, refinements. Their adaption to the hot and arid Middle Eastern land was proportionately more difficult. They presented the National Home with a sharp challenge concerning its central vocation as the receptacle of Jewish communities and Jewish hopes. Could these sophisticated Jews develop any affinity with Palestine? Their road was hard, but they were to traverse it with grace and assume a creative place in the national society.

The British Mandatory Power gave a conservative interpretation to its task of facilitating the establishment of a Jewish National Home. The British policy had become an international charge with the embodiment of the Balfour Declaration in the Palestine Mandate, which had been worked out at the Peace Conference in Paris and ratified at San Remo in 1922. Supervision by the League of Nations was formal and somewhat lax. There were no real inhibitions on British sovereignty. The main burden of facilitating the establishment of the National Home fell to the Zionist organization, which created instruments for administration, financing, and political representation. The *Keren Kayemet* (Jewish National Fund) had been established in 1900 at the Fourth Zionist Congress for the purpose of purchasing land in Palestine as the inviolate possession of the Jewish people. Now the *Keren Ha-Yesod* (Jewish

Foundation Fund) was created. Its funds were to be used for all purposes: facilitation of immigration, education, health services, settlement. It was to be launched as a mass undertaking; Jews everywhere were called to give one-tenth of their income in the manner of the ancient Biblical tithe. Finally, an over-all organization was set up, called the Jewish Agency, for the administration of Jewish Palestine and the supervision of its relations with world Jewry and the Mandatory Power.

It was not until 1929, when non-Zionists joined the Jewish Agency, that all organized Jewry began to take an active interest in the Palestine enterprise. Before that time the response of wealthy Jews to the Zionist appeal had been grudging. The movement had a distinctly populist aspect. Much more would have been achieved had the full weight of world Jewish support been applied to the Zionist project at this stage. Many opportunities for land purchase and for rescue activities among harassed Diaspora communities were lost through lack of funds. The *yishuv* depended on voluntary contributions and collections. Weizmann himself and eminent Jewish luminaries such as Albert Einstein, Justice Louis Brandeis, Henrietta Szold, combined their roles as statesmen and administrators of Zionism with that of the zealous and urgent fund raiser.

In the twenty years from the end of World War I to the White Paper of 1939, the *yishuv* developed its independent community. It maintained a network of schools, health services, and labor organizations. It had even developed its own defense system. The Mandatory Power had no choice but to recognize this "state within a state," but in order to transform this nucleus into an articulate political society, one thing more was needed: national independence. There was no hurry in Zionist minds about this. A constitutional situation was tolerable so long as it enabled the practical task of social expansion to go forward and the stream of immigration to flow. The vital purpose was to prevent the country from coming under a regime even more hostile to Jewish national hopes than the Mandatory regime. In the second and third decades after the Balfour Declaration, the Zionist leaders looked with anxious eyes on the growing strength and ardor of Arab nationalism.

The Beginnings of
Arab Nationalism
Palestine
Between the Wars

Israel came to birth in a region where political nationalism has recorded signal advances in this century. Five decades ago, every Arab, and indeed almost every Moslem on the face of the globe, lived in subjection either to the rule of the Ottoman Empire or of the colonial powers. The great Moslem and Arab cultural traditions were nowhere the center of independent political and economic life. Within fifty years, a vast and astonishing transformation was to come over this scene. Today, fourteen sovereign Arab states extend over a huge continental expanse of four million square miles, embracing all the centers which owe their historic fame to their connection with the Arab and Moslem traditions. Cairo, Baghdad, and Damascus, the scenes and centers of the Caliphate; Mecca and Medina, the holy cities of Arabia, the sources and origins of the Moslem faith—are today centers of independent Arab nationhood. This vast good fortune in their political evolution came to the Arab peoples less as a result of their own sacrifice and effort than as a consequence of international influence in two world wars, and more recently, of the revival throughout the world of sympathy for national liberation.

In comparison with the Jewish people, the Arab nations achieved very much, very quickly, and with very much less toil and tears. But for four preceding centuries, the Western colonial powers had done great injury to Arab interests and to Arab pride. The Arabic-speaking world, once the cradle of culture and the arts, had fallen behind the best levels of political and technological progress. As far as the Arab world was concerned, the French Revolution might never have occurred. The doctrine of political equality and social justice which spread through Europe and later across the Atlantic had no impression on the dark hinterland of Arabia, which continued to organize itself on medieval feudal patterns. Similarly, as far as the Middle East was concerned, the Industrial Revolution might never have come to pass. The developments in human technology which had revolutionized material progress left no mark on the squalor of teeming millions who dwelt in the subcontinent between the central Mediterranean and the Persian Gulf. If we were to strike the balance at the end of the nineteenth century, an attitude of grievance and injury by the Arab world toward the West had deep justification.

In the decade before World War I, when the Ottoman Empire was in full decadence, Arab nationalist groups began to demand their nation's birthright. The movement lacked a mass following, but its torch was carried high with moving intensity and often at the expense of sacrifice by the intellectual elite in all countries where Arabic was the spoken tongue. The Arab nationalists, like the Zionists, saw the approach of the British epoch in the Middle East. Their representatives sought and elicited promises of national freedom to be fulfilled when the fighting ceased. By 1921, an Arab king, Feisal, was installed in Iraq. His brother, the Emir Abdullah, had been awarded Transjordan, and the Hejaz territories with their holy cities were the seat of the kingdom of Saudi Arabia.

Contact between Britain and the Arabs had existed before the outbreak of World War I, but only on a limited scale. Britain had hesitated to undertake definite commitments toward Hussein, the Sherif of Mecca, when he asked for modest assistance for an impending revolt of the Arabs against the Turks. After the outbreak of World War I, it was Britain who tried to influence the Arabs to begin their revolt against the Turks. By then, Hussein was reluctant to take action. Negotiations were held between the British High Commissioner in Egypt, Sir Henry McMahon, and the Sherif Hussein, who demanded Arab sovereignty over a very large area. Eventually, an agreement was reached. Contrary to later Arab claims, Palestine was explicitly excluded in the Hussein-McMahon negotiations. McMahon himself was later to deny any contrary allegation, but it was one which Arab politicians of the postwar era repeated indefatigably in their condemnation of "the broken pledge of Britain with regard to Palestine."

Arab demands for an independent state in Palestine had no roots in any memory of prior Arab independence on that soil. Until 70 C.E., Palestine was recognized universally as "the land of the Jews." It had been so in the universal consciousness for over a thousand years. Only with the fall of Bar Kochba did the Jews give up their attempts to retain sovereignty in the land. Palestine fell to the Arabs in 634, and remained under the rule of the Caliphs for approximately four centuries before it was conquered by the Crusaders and in the sixteenth century by the Ottoman Turks. Thus, from the sixteenth century onward, the land had been under non-Arab rule.

That Palestine was not like other Middle Eastern territories in its relationship to Arab history was implicit in the cautious attitude of Arab leaders after World War I. They hesitated to advance claims on Palestine. The Arabs of Syria and Iraq demanded fully independent control. In regard to Palestine, their leaders were willing to compromise. At the Paris Peace Conference, the Palestine issue was for the Arabs still of secondary importance. Their main task was to secure the promise of independence in those territories whose Arab character was unreserved. The Arab cause at the Peace Conference was represented by Emir Feisal on behalf of his father, the Sherif of Mecca. His demands for independence in the Arab countries were uncompromising, but on Palestine he showed an intuition for the historic forces which had shaped that land.

In 1918, Chaim Weizmann approached Emir Feisal for the purpose of reaching an understanding with the Arab leader. The meeting between Feisal and Weizmann, which took place at Aqaba, led to the first, and to this day, the only understanding ever recorded between leaders of the two national movements.

In November 1918, the World Zionist Organization congratulated Feisal on his coronation as King of Syria. After a meeting with Jewish leaders in London, Feisal issued a statement, which was published in *The Times* of December 12, 1918:

> The two main branches of the Semitic family, Arabs and Jews, understand one another, and I hope that as a result of the interchange of ideas at the Peace Conference, which will be guided by the ideals of self-determination and nationality, each nation will make definite progress towards the realization of its aspiration. Arabs are not jealous of Zionist Jews, and intend to give them fair play; and the Zionist Jews have assured the Nationalist Arabs of their intention to see that they, too, have fair play in their respective areas. Turkish intrigue in Palestine has raised jealousy between the Jewish colonists and local peasants, but the mutual understanding of the aims of Arabs and Jews will, at once, clear away the last trace of this former bitterness, which indeed had already practically disappeared even before the war, by the work of the Arab Secret Revolutionary Committee. . . .

The concept of Arabia for the Arabs, Judea for the Jews, emerges with even greater clarity from letters signed by Feisal, at the time of the Peace Conference, concerning his understanding with Weizmann. In 1936, a British Royal Commission was to express this historic record succinctly. "If King Hussein and Emir Feisal secured their big Arab State, they would concede little Palestine to the Jews."

The hour of grace was short. The Arabs did not "secure their big Arab State." They therefore declined to "concede little Palestine to the Jews." Britain dominated Iraq, and France expelled Feisal from Damascus. Savage disappointment gripped the Arab national movement. The moderate position of Feisal was weakened. Arab nationalism made its claim for the complete liberation of Syria, its union with Palestine, and total resistance to the Jewish National Home.

In Palestine itself Arab nationalism was organized in an oligarchic pattern. Its leaders were the large landowners, Moslem holy men, and the prosperous members of the free professions. Those who had played a dominating role in the Arab community under Turkish rule retained and strengthened their influence. The unbalanced class structure of the Arab nationalist organizations expressed itself in sympathies and orientations which were later to align the movement with the policies and aims of Mussolini and Hitler.

The central position was won by Haj Amin el-Husseini, Grand Mufti of Jerusalem and the President of the Supreme Moslem Council, which was supposed to deal exclusively with religious affairs of the Moslems. But all the leading Arab families were agreed on one point: they demanded the abolition of the Jewish National Home and the Balfour Declaration, and the establishment of an Arab independent state. Their case was that sovereignty belonged to Arabs wherever they were and to Jews nowhere at all. In their propaganda they ranted against the sale of land to Jews which, they claimed inaccurately, would render the rural population landless. Arab national leaders themselves, however, sold large tracts of land to Jews.

Arab resistance to Jewish national claims was intense during this period but by no means insuperable. No attempt was made by the Mandatory government to express the ideological foundations on which its charge rested: namely that Arab nationalism was to express itself fully and freely over vast areas of the Middle East while the Jewish people was to be accorded national self-determination in "little Palestine," the source and cradle of its identity and tradition. A clear support of this idea by the international community could in the 1920s and 1930s have prevented the approaching conflict. But Feisal's vision was allowed to perish. Arab nationalism and Zionism were henceforward locked in mortal combat.

Arab opposition was not the only challenge which harassed the Zionists in the postwar period. Relations between them and the British Mandatory Power deteriorated sharply. The British authorities in Palestine pushed the Balfour Declaration and Mandate into the background of their concern. The British attitude to Jewish development became obstructive and later repressive.

The policy of the Jewish leadership in Palestine and of the world Zionist movement was marked by unrequited good will toward the Mandatory Power. It was still hoped that Britain, nudged and prodded by world opinion, could be persuaded to fulfill its obligations. Zionist leaders were convinced that ties with Britain were for the time being the best guarantee for the development of the Jewish National Home. This conviction became steadily undermined. Relations between Britain and the Zionists became increasingly tense until they reached a virtual breaking point with the publication of the White Paper in 1939. By drastic limitation of immigration and land settlement this policy statement proposed to stunt the growth of the Jewish National Home and to hand it over after ten years to the all too predictable "mercies" of an Arab government.

All this was still far away when the British Civil Administration was established in July 1920 with the arrival of Sir Herbert Samuel as the first High Commissioner for Palestine. The appointment of a Jewish governor in Jerusalem was enthusiastically hailed in Palestine and by world Jewry. There were messianic undertones in Samuel's arrival. He was soon to disappoint the most extreme of these expectations. One of his first actions was to declare a general amnesty for all Arab participants in the Jerusalem riots of 1920. Soon after he made a gesture of good will toward the Arabs by pardoning the leaders of the riots, among them Amin el-Husseini, whom he later installed as the Grand Mufti of Jerusalem and who became the guiding spirit of subsequent disturbances, and during World War II, a staunch ally of the Nazi cause.

The greatest of all the shocks was caused by Herbert Samuel's announcement after the May riots of 1921 at the gathering of Arab dignitaries in Ramleh that Jewish immigration would be suspended. Henrietta Szold remarked, "Both the decision and the form of its announcement came as a severe shock to Jews everywhere. Immigrants already within the sight of Palestine's shores were not allowed to land." The suspension of immigration brought about the first open conflict between the British administration and the Palestine Jews. The Zionist Commission, composed of Zionist leaders who had come to Palestine in 1918 in an advisory capacity and who were later replaced by the Jewish Agency Executive, resigned in protest, as did the Executive of the *Vaad Leumi*. They resumed their functions only after reassurances from the Colonial Secretary, Winston Churchill, that immigration would be renewed.

It is certain that Herbert Samuel acted in sincere conviction that a policy of cautious good will toward the Arabs would be to the best interests of the Mandatory Power. Before his appointment as High Commissioner, Sir Herbert held the view of most British statesmen of that period that the ultimate aim of the Balfour Declaration was the establishment of the Jewish State. Indeed, his courageous advocacy of the Zionist policy within the Cabinet had been a crucial factor in the adoption of the Balfour Declaration. He was never to lose his dedication to the central interests of the Jewish people. But he was also and above all the first representative of the British government to displace the center of gravity in British policy. Henceforward the main purpose was not to facilitate the establishment of the Jewish National Home but to subject that aim to the task of securing tranquillity within the Arab community.

In addition to applying stricter regulations against immigration and Jewish land purchase, the British government turned to the appeasement of Arab demands in the constitutional sphere. It sponsored proposals for independence which gave full weight to the existing Arab majority and little or none to Jewish immigrants who were the potential citizens of the National Home. The paring down of the Mandate's positions began with the Churchill White Paper, issued in June 1922. In this document the British government enacted the exclusion of Transjordan from those provisions of the Mandate which referred to the establishment of the Jewish National Home. It set up an Arab government as the Hashemite Kingdom of Transjordan. Settlement of Jews in Transjordan was henceforth prohibited. Limitations on Jewish immigration in western Palestine were also set forth in the White Paper.

By this unilateral act the British government committed itself to a serious restriction of the Mandate. Nevertheless the Zionist Organization accepted the White Paper. It acknowledged some of the objective reasons behind the new policy. Britain had encountered difficulties in Mesopotamia and in other parts of the Middle East. It had been forced to take account of Arab demands which became progressively more extreme. On the other hand, the idealistic expectations that had found expression at the end of World War I had been slowly corroding. Disenchantment with the possibilities of international collaboration had set in. The prestige of the League of Nations was steadily diminishing. The Zionists hoped that if their energy and zeal were excluded from the eastern part of the mandated territory it would be given freer reign in the western area.

The White Paper was accepted in the Zionist Organization even by Vladimir Jabotinsky, then a member of the Executive, who later regretted his decision and organized a political party, the Revisionists, dedicated to the establishment of a Jewish State on both sides of the Jordan. Weizmann and his colleagues believed that to accept the White Paper was "the lesser evil." As long as immigration and the investment of capital and the purchase of land remained possible, the Jews could develop the country, enable it to grow, and enhance its opportunities for the consolidation of a national society. The Zionist strategy was to create stronger realities on the ground and to postpone the constitutional confrontation until later. When legislative councils with Arab majorities were proposed, it was incongruously the Arab leadership which prevented their establishment. Thus the British administration continued in unchallenged control. The opportunities available to the Zionists were too small for satisfaction but too large for despair.

When Herbert Samuel ended his administration in 1925, relations between the British administration and the Zionist movement were still correct. The year 1925 was one of record immigration: nearly 34,000 Jews had reached the shores of Palestine. The Hebrew University had opened its doors. The *yishuv* was flourishing. The Jews gave Herbert Samuel a friendly farewell. And the Zionist Executive issued a statement expressing gratitude for the way in which he had accomplished his historic task.

Herbert Samuel was followed by Lord Plumer, an experienced general, whose administration was marked, to the relief of Jewish leaders, by unflinching severity toward civil riots and intimidation. Arab revolts in Egypt and Syria had been successfully suppressed by the British and French authorities. Jewish immigration during years of economic crisis was spontaneously diminished. In these circumstances the Arab-Jewish confrontation became less acute. But the basic problem of reconciling the national claims of two peoples remained unsolved, as it did during the undistinguished administration of the third High Commissioner, Sir John Chancellor.

In 1929, tranquillity was shattered by Arab riots in which 133 Jews were killed, several hundred wounded and Jewish property destroyed on a large scale. The shock was all the greater for the realization that the British administration, in Dr. Weizmann's words, had shown "indifference, inefficiency, and hostility, which had helped give the Arab leaders their opportunity." The disturbances brought about the appointment of an investigative body, the Shaw Commission, to inquire into the causes of the Arab riots. In its report the commission acknowledged that the Arabs were the first assailants. It passed in discreet silence over the behavior of the Palestine administration. It did, however, express the grotesque opinion that the land was now too thickly settled, and that the non-Jewish authorities should be consulted as to limits on further immigration, ostensibly on economic grounds. Later developments were to pour derision on this narrow concept of the country's absorptive capacity.

This political setback for the Jews was followed by another. In October 1930, The Simpson Report on the problem of land settlement was published, together with the White Paper, bearing the name of the Colonial Secretary, Lord Passfield. This document was a clear repudiation of the Mandate and the Balfour Declaration. The first Labour government virtually proposed that the Jewish National Home be handed over to the decisive control of an Arab majority. Weizmann summarized the main thrust of the White Paper in the following terms:

> Immigration would no longer be determined by the test of the country's economic absorptive capacity, but by other considerations of entirely non-economic nature, such as the widespread suspicion existing among the population. While paying lip service to the need for the development of Jewish settlement, the government intended to limit itself to the settlement of Arabs.

In protest against the Passfield White Paper, Weizmann resigned as President of the Jewish Agency. Lord Melchett and Felix Warburg also tendered their resignations. The outcry by Jews all over the world, as well as by British statesmen and parliamentarians, was intense and passionate. The British government was taken aback by the scope of this resistance. Negotiations were held by the government with Dr. Weizmann and the Jewish Agency, which resulted in a reversal of policy expressed in the White Paper. The new position was announced in a letter addressed to Dr. Weizmann by Ramsay MacDonald, the Prime Minister, in which the main provisions of the White Paper against Jewish immigration and land settlement were canceled. The conflict left its scars, but enough room was left for a further spate of Zionist energy.

The MacDonald letter gave a respite in which British policy and Zionist aims could coexist in circumstances which fell short both of harmony and of collision. During this period the economic development of the country progressed quickly. In 1935, with the intensification of anti-Jewish measures in Hitler's Germany, Jewish immigration reached an unprecedented figure of 62,000. Relations between the Jewish Agency and the new High Commissioner, Sir Arthur Wauchope, were cordial. Sir Arthur showed a tactful sensitivity for Jewish emotions and a practical interest in the promotion of the Jewish National Home. In 1935, however, he urged the

establishment of a Legislative Council with an Arab majority. According to his proposals, the council would be composed of Arabs, Jews, and British officials. All decisions on immigration would be reserved to the High Commissioner. The Jews feared that once the Arabs gained their majority they would in the course of time demand that the vote apply to the immigration problem as well. This, together with the cold attitude of British officialdom in Palestine, would lead to a stoppage of immigration and to stagnation in the development of the Jewish National Home. The British proposals were rejected by the Jews because they offered them too little, and by the Arabs because they offered the Jews too much. Under the leadership of the Grand Mufti, Arab nationalism had developed an all-or-nothing philosophy which was to prove its undoing in subsequent years.

The disorders which began in April 1936 had the dimensions of a full-scale Arab revolt. At first they were sporadic but under the instigation of the Arab leadership they soon spread throughout the country. An Arab Higher Committee, established to organize the disturbances, proclaimed a general strike which was to last until Arab demands for the immediate cessation of Jewish immigration were granted by the British administration. The committee also demanded a prohibition of the sale of Arab lands to Jews and the establishment of a national government. The British authorities attempted a policy of conciliation. They offered to re-examine their proposals on the Legislative Council in order to make them still further congenial to Arab demands. The disorders continued with a tax on Jewish settlements and then on British army personnel. Ultimately the Mandatory government called in reinforcements and even issued arms to Jews for their self-defense. A British officer, Colonel Orde Wingate, cooperated with Jewish rural settlements in the organization of night squads to resist and attack Arab terrorist bands. The situation became so grave that the government issued a strong ultimatum to the Arab Higher Committee, warning that drastic military action would be taken if the disorders were not halted. The Arab Higher Committee called off the strike in October 1936.

The Palestine problem now entered a new and decisive stage. A Royal Commission, headed by Lord Peel, went to Palestine to investigate the riots and propose measures to insure peace. The commission's report was published on July 7, 1937, together with a government White Paper. The report recommended a partition plan for Palestine, according to which the Arab part of the country

The byways of Jerusalem during the 1936 riots. Soldiers stop and search passersby for arms on a dark and narrow street.

would become an Arab state, and a smaller area would be constituted as a Jewish state, within an area of less than 2000 square miles which was less than one-fifth of western Palestine. At the Zionist Congress in Zurich in August 1937, Dr. Weizmann criticized the commission's report for the parsimony of its proposal but drew attention to the historic importance of the recommendation for the establishment of a Jewish State. The Jewish Agency was empowered to negotiate with the British government in an effort to improve the partition proposal, to which the Arabs were uncompromisingly opposed. Once the partition idea had been proposed, its inherent logic was to dominate the Palestine problem for the next decisive years. The Peel Commission had understood the central fact: Jews and Arabs in Palestine did not pursue common aims or strive for common aims. The choice was either to subordinate one to the other or to create a framework of separate sovereignty for each.

Britain recoiled again before Arab opposition. The Woodhead Commission was sent to Palestine ostensibly to establish the practical implications of the partition plan; actually to find means of retreating from its implications. The commission declared the Peel partition plan to be unworkable, suggested some even more unworkable plans on its own account, and allowed the project to recede. Its central idea was to come to life a decade later.

Violent disorders continued through 1937 and 1938. With clouds of war gathering on the horizon, the British government made a drastic attempt to appease Arab intransigence. All inhibitions in favor of Jewish interests were swept away. A White Paper issued in May 1939 contained a virtual sentence of death on the National Home. A maximum of 75,000 Jewish immigrants would be admitted during the next five years; and five years thereafter the British Mandatory Administration would be replaced by an independent Palestine government with an Arab majority. The Jewish Agency denounced the White Paper as a "breach of faith and surrender to Arab terrorism"; addressed a reasoned protest to the Permanent Mandates Commission of the League of Nations; and obtained the verdict that "the policy set out in the White Paper was not in accordance with the interpretation which, in agreement with the Mandatory Power and the Council [of the League of Nations], had been placed upon the Palestine Mandate." The Zionist victory was hollow and ineffective. Palestine Jewry was to enter the Second World War with all its ambitions, and indeed its very survival, in dangerous suspense.

In the period between the two wars the National Home had developed a shield on which its life and fortune were to depend. An unprovoked Arab attack on Tel Hai in March 1920; the assault on Jewish Jerusalem in April of that year; the rioting in Jaffa in 1921, all pointed to the need for an organization of Jewish self-defense. Ever since the days of the second *Aliyah*, there had existed a small defense organization, founded in 1907 as *Bar Giora* and later to be called *Ha-Shomer*. The early militia men were fighters and farmers. They pioneered in agricultural settlements and stood watch over remote outposts lying isolated amidst hostile Arab populations. The *shomrim* saw their work as a personal mission undertaken for the benefit of an entire nation. Their example was to inspire the *yishuv* with courage and self-reliance which were to prove vital in later years in the face of massive Arab assaults.

In the 1920s the *Ha-Shomer* movement, exhausted and decimated by the great war, pressed for a realignment of forces in the *yishuv*. The British Military Occupation Force under generals Bols and Storrs had shown excessive indulgence to the instigators of Arab riots. It was plain that no foreign trustee would be willing to spill the blood of its soldiers for the life of the Jews. Therefore provision had to be made for the acquisition of arms and the training of a defense force to meet any eventuality. A new approach to the problem of security was incumbent in the face of threatening Arab opposition and well-organized political attacks. It was not enough to provide guardsmen for the agricultural colonies as *Ha-Shomer* had done. The cities, too, had to be defended. The entire *yishuv* had to look to its security.

The *Haganah* (defense) was formed in 1920 at a conference of the *Ahdut Avodah* party, which also undertook a reorganization of the labor movement in conformity with new needs. The problem of defense now became a responsibility of the *yishuv* together with its other tasks in economic, political, and cultural development. The Haganah was rigidly subservient to the civil authority provided by the Jewish Agency.

From a handful of guardsmen who went out at night to watch over the fields, the new organization would grow into an important instrument in the shaping of Palestine's political destiny. Three great undertakings—settlement, immigration, and defense—would have been impossible without it. The Israel army, which was to spring from its loins, would in later years make national and regional history.

From the beginning, Haganah was an active element in every

new settlement. Its task was especially difficult in the years 1936–1939, when the answer of the *yishuv* to Arab rioting was self-restraint (*havlagah*). The new settlements, often isolated in undeveloped regions, were vulnerable points, frequently lacking a single stone building to serve as protection. A system was now developed to erect defensible settlements with great rapidity, preferably in the span of a single day. By nightfall the defenses of the new settlement had to be established, at least with a wall, barbed wire and watchtower. Necessary components were therefore prepared in advance and assembled at the nearest village during the night before possession was taken of the land. At daybreak, members of the new settlement, with the help of volunteers, would move up in trucks to the chosen site. By sunrise the tower would stand; by midday the outer wall was erected; in the early afternoon a whole camp would be functioning, complete with chickens and cows. The government sometimes allowed two official rifles for its defense. The first of these settlements, which bequeathed to Israel's history the legendary name "Stockade and Tower" (*Homah u-Migdal*) was Tel Amal at the foot of Mount Gilboa. Many others were to follow, from Hanita to Dan, from Tirat Zvi to Sha'ar Ha-Golan.

Thus, through the troubled years of 1937 to 1939, more new communities were established than in any previous period. Settlement, cultivation of the land, and self-defense, were the practical answer of Palestine Jewry to Arab hostility and British vacillation. The response was colored by an awareness of the inherent right of peoples to self-protection and by a belief in the inalienable dignity of human life as a principle from which Jewish life should not be excluded. The years 1939 to 1945 would see that principle shattered across the bloodstained continent of Europe.

The Eve of War 1939

In the two decades between the wars the Jewish people had neither squandered its opportunities nor fully used them. By 1939 the National Home had a population of 450,000. Its economic and technological levels were spectacular by Middle Eastern standards, but well below the best European average. Nevertheless, it was a source of pride for the Jewish people and for the world a fascinating and original spectacle. Here, and only here, the Jews faced history in their own authentic image. They were not a marginal gloss on other societies. The national attributes were all reflected

The B'nai B'rith settlement in the Valley of Jezreel symbolizes the hopes and hardships of Israel's resettlement. The characteristic watchtower rises squat and peering over the halutzim's *living quarters and the animals' sheds to stand guard against Arab marauders. The similarity to early American pioneer settlements in the West is striking.*

on a miniature scale but in growing completeness. The salient feature of this society was its Hebrew character. The ancient language, expanded and renewed, was not only the vernacular and mother tongue of a newborn Jewish generation, it was also the vehicle of an impressive literary movement. More than anything else it gave individual form and color to the nascent community. It was also a link with a cherished and universally revered past. In order to be itself, a Jewish national society had to be different from everything else. The driving force was the quest for identity. An intense solidarity inspired its Jewishness. Its ideals and priorities were collective, not individual. What mattered was a man's service to the growing nation, not his prowess in self-advancement. Palestine Jewry had a utopian outlook and was gripped by a profoundly moral preoccupation. Life was earnest, austere, responsible, resolute, effervescent, somewhat irrational and, to strangers, a little ponderous and self-conscious. Every first tree, road, street, settlement, school, library, orchestra, university, was ecstatically celebrated. The Jewish people lived at last with the unique taste of creativity.

In its social structure Palestine Jewry pursued original goals. The *kibbutz* (collective village) and *moshav* (cooperative village) set the national tone. Socialist ethics predominated. The *Histadrut* (General Federation of Labor) had trade unionism at its core; but it carried the cooperative principle into an endless list of enterprises: industrial, agricultural, social, and every other. Apart from links with world Jewry, the *yishuv* found its strongest affinities among social democratic governments and international institutions. In an intensely libertarian climate politics flourished with strong emphasis on ideological loyalties. Hegemony belonged to the labor movement. But Orthodox Judaism was firmly established in the communal hierarchy with the Mizrachi movement standing political guard over its interests. Different shades of leftness and rightness divided the *kibbutz* movement and the Histadrut.

General Zionism was the domain in which national purposes were empirically pursued without dogmatic commitment. At the extremity of the political gamut was Jabotinsky's Revisionist movement, combative, strident, and more concerned with the symbolism and manners of nationalism than with the ostensibly prosaic and yet inherently poetic tasks of land settlement and pioneering. A man who came to Jewish Palestine in the 1930s found a cultural climate that was not completely European and yet more charged with European energies than with the customary Middle Eastern tranquillity or fatalism.

Far above its other achievements was the *yishuv's* genius for autonomy. It was a microcosmic but fully articulated body. It was theoretically a community within a colonial dependency. But this was little more than a fiction. The ties with the British Mandatory Administration remained formal and tenuous. With Arabs there was a more intimate commingling in commerce and conflict; but there was no intention or prospect that Palestine Jewry could be assimilated to an Arab environment. It had built a wall around itself for protection against external hostility and internal corrosion. It was very nearly a national State in miniature. It largely administered its own agriculture, industry, education, and social welfare. It commanded its own labor organizations. It spoke its own tongue. Defense and foreign policy are usually the last prerogatives which a community attains in the pursuit of its sovereignty. Even here the *yishuv* was becoming increasingly independent. A citizen army was at its control; and its leading representatives, Weizmann, Ben Gurion and Moshe Sharett, were accepted and admired in the international diplomatic community as representatives of an entity that was a state in all but name. The Peel Commission, despite its disappointing territorial recommendations, had given the concept of Jewish statehood a new stature in political thought.

In a normal epoch these achievements would have held the assurance of ultimate and even early success. But the clouds were gathering thick on the horizon. Arab nationalism was in rampant and confident mood. Britain had deserted the vision which had originally inspired its Mandate and there was soon to break around the head of the Jewish people the most violent and destructive torrent of hate that had ever afflicted any family of the human race.

*T*HE EUROPE on which the Nazi plague descended was a land of rich and diverse cultures. Outside the Soviet Union the Jewish thread in the European tapestry was represented by eight million Jews some of whom were closely assimilated to their countries of abode while others lived strange and aloof on the outer margin of European society, bearing witness to ancient faith and rituals. European tolerance seemed broad enough both to welcome the assimilated and to grant freedom to the separatists. Had there not been sporadic but visible progress for over a century toward enlightenment, liberalism, scientific rationalism, and expanding religious toleration? Did not Jewish names glow brilliantly in the constellation of European science, literature, and art? Here and there the residue of nineteenth-century anti-Semitism could be perceived, but there was no premonition of a violent storm.

Into this scene there erupted the German Nazi, shrill and strident with hatred, endowed with an uncanny capacity to find and conquer all the dark places of the German mind. On January 30, 1933, Adolf Hitler was appointed Chancellor of the German Reich. The Nazi plot was born out of a monstrous wedlock between lust for power and a perverted ideology which mocked the insights of religion and the conclusions of science.

It is difficult even now to remember how short was the time

within which this tyranny was to ravage the life of a generation. A contemporary historian has written:

> It lasted twelve years and four months, but in that flicker of time it caused an eruption on this earth more violent and shattering than any previously experienced, raising the German people to heights of power they had not known in more than a millennium, making them at one time the master of Europe, from the Atlantic to the Volga, from the North Cape to the Mediterranean and then plunging them to the depths of destruction and desolation. At the end of the world war which their nation had cold-bloodedly provoked, during which it instituted a reign of terror over the conquered peoples which, in its calculated butchery of human life and the human spirit, they outdid all the savage oppressions of the previous ages.

There are three distinct periods in the procession of Nazi violence. The first extends from the attainment of power in 1933 to the outbreak of war in 1939. The second from 1939 to 1941 when the "final solution" was resolved; the third from 1941 to 1945 when physical extermination was the ordained lot of the Jews in every land over which German power was established.

The spectacular events of the third period have come to overshadow the significance of the first. Physical violence was intermittent during those early years. Newspaper readers became familiar with the cruel and vacuous grins of Nazi youths leading bearded Jews with self-condemnatory placards on their chest to clear the refuse and wash the pavements of German streets. But the emphasis was "only" on disposition, arbitrary arrest, social ostracism and endless humiliation. The rubber truncheon and other tortures were still reserved for the relatively few who were dragged to the concentration camps from which they sometimes emerged beaten, crushed in spirit, but still alive.

The impunity with which Nazism survived the first period made the next two inevitable. It was in the relatively bloodless years before the war that the German people was spiritually prepared for acts which, without deep indoctrination, no human being could bring himself to perform.

The central theme of the new ideology was the absence of a common basis for all humanity. "All human culture, all the results of art and science that we see today," declared Hitler, "are almost exclusively the product of the Aryan stock." The Aryan in this outlook is a definite biological species with its characteristic shape of skull, tint of complexion, and strain of blood. Non-Nordic man is closer to animals than to the human race. To suppress and destroy non-Nordic man is an elevated destiny to be pursued with discipline and sacrifice to the utter end.

This blasphemous doctrine, soon to become the formal religion of the German nation, can still be read in the files of fading newspapers and books of the 1930s. It was expounded in a literature of morbid sexuality with strong sadistic and masochistic overtones. The unexpected and horrifying fact is that professors and trained scientists were found willing to give their endorsement to these aberrations. An eminent physicist was solemnly enlisted to purge science of the "Jewish Einstein corruption." "In reality," said Professor Lenard of Heidelberg, "science like every other human product is racial and conditioned by blood." Thus, encouraged and sheltered by academic applause, Goebbels presided over a public bonfire in which the works of Heine, Thomas Mann, Einstein, Zola, and Freud went up in smoke. "The soul of the German people" he shrieked, "can again express itself. These flames not only illuminate the final end of our era, they also light up the new age."

As the Third Reich approached its decision to plunge the world into war, the persecution of German and Austrian Jewry became increasingly violent. The war on the Jews was not limited to modern considerations of politics, economy, and culture. It extended to religion as well. A Christian Nazi institute was established which set about proving that Jesus was not of Jewish origin. A team of jurists, psychologists, and theologians was put to work to expunge all traces of Jewish influences from religious tradition. All these endeavors were dwarfed by Alfred Rosenberg's Institute for the Exploration of the Jewish Question, which became the central disseminating organ of Nazi instruction and training. From this institute a crusade against the degenerate democracies was conducted to the greater glory of the "Aryan race."

In March 1933, in the first act of physical violence against Jews in Germany, bands of Nazis attacked Jewish lawyers and judges in the courthouse of Breslau. In the following weeks thirty-five Jews, mostly assimilated doctors and lawyers, were murdered. In April of the same year a boycott was declared. Guards of the SS and SA were posted before every Jewish business or office and Aryan clients were prevented from entering. As soon as the boycott ended a series of laws was passed which, before the year was out, had practically excluded the Jews from all possibility of earning a livelihood in Germany.

Goebbel's bonfire was dedicated to the extinction of Jewish influence on literature. This was not the only target of primitive

Nazi zeal. In the following months the new era of German civilization extended its control over every sphere of culture—music, theater, the press, radio and films were purged. German museums were cleansed of such "decadent" masters of art as Picasso, Matisse, Cézanne and Kokoshka. Universities and scientific institutions were made *judenrein*. Einstein, and later Sigmund Freud, the two men whose luminous intelligence were the acme of a once glorious German Jewish culture, joined the stream of illustrious émigrés.

In September 1935, the passage of the Nuremberg laws placed the Jews beyond the pale of citizenship, depriving them in one sure stroke of their status as Germans. The new laws neatly cut the Jew off from any physical contact with the master race. Hitler had invented a new definition of Jewishness: a Jew was any person three of whose great-grandparents had been Jews. He also introduced the category of fractional Jews (of first or second degree), defined according to the number of Jewish grandparents.

By the end of 1935, 8000 German Jews had committed suicide; 75,000 had emigrated; countless others were besieging foreign consulates for exit visas to any place under the sun which would grant them asylum. The immigration laws of the world, however, had made no provision for emergencies such as this. And the gates to Palestine were open or shut according to the "schedule." Soon the names of exotic and little-known cities, countries, and islands joined the Jewish travelogue of flight over the centuries.

As always under adverse conditions, the Jews began to organize for their own spiritual survival. Enforced segregation stimulated a sudden interest in Jewish history and in the Hebrew language; the thirst for self-understanding found expression in the publication and sale of numerous copies of Jewish encyclopedias, history books, and Hebrew grammars. But as the life of the spirit became more intense, physical existence became more precarious. In all quarters of the civilized world, the suffering of German Jewry met with an uncanny silence. The Jews were utterly bewildered at the failure of the Nazi onslaught to evoke universal disapproval. But the fact is that many democratic leaders felt, with the best of intentions, that loud protests would only make matters worse for German Jewry—a position taken with equal self-assurance, and equal fallaciousness, with regard to the plight of Soviet Jewry even today. These leaders decried anti-Nazi propaganda and denounced a boycott against Germany which had been launched in a disorganized manner. Warnings from Zionist leaders that the Jewish persecutions in Germany were but a preliminary to a general Nazi assault on all human liberty were dismissed as "warmongering."

Weizmann had prophetically declared to Lord Halifax, the British Foreign Secretary: "They are burning the synagogues now, tomorrow they will burn British cathedrals."

Thus, throughout the first phase of the Nazi assault, the Jews were faced with the spectacle of the world's great democracies retreating from one position to another. An international conference on the refugee problem, convened at Evian in the summer of 1938, failed to recognize the urgency of the hour and adopted half-hearted resolutions which did next to no good at all. The savage attacks which began in Germany on November 9, 1938 (after the murder of Vom Rath in Paris), generated a far greater need than could be met by the meager provisions made at the conference to deal with the problem. Only the Dominican Republic was prepared to make more than a token gesture toward the fleeing refugees. As boatloads of Jews were shunted from port to port, brushed off by humanity like bothersome insects, the humanitarian conscience expressed concern by allowing emergency quotas of a few hundred or a few thousand to enter Western lands.

In the philosophy of *Mein Kampf* neither love nor mercy nor justice was counted among the cardinal virtues of the Nazi spirit. That these virtues should suddenly disappear from humanity at large was less expected. News of the horrors being perpetrated in Nazi Germany met with incredulity and indifference. The human imagination was not yet prepared to recognize that the twentieth century was capable of a wholesale descent into barbarity. It was not until the outside world finally came to the realization that the liberty of all was at stake that it took up arms; by that time, it was too late to save the victims.

German troops crossed the frontier of Austria on March 12, 1938. Unified now with the Reich, Austria in turn adopted the entire body of anti-Jewish legislation. With unabated fury the 400,000 Jews of Austria were subjected to the same restrictions, humiliations, and persecutions as their brethren in Germany, only at an accelerated pace.

By the outbreak of the war, half a million Jews still remained in the territories under direct German control. In time, all occupied Europe was to become a field of carnage and agony.

Nazism in Eastern Europe

The Holocaust

In Eastern Europe—an area permeated by long-standing traditions of anti-Jewish feeling—Hitler's rise to power was greeted with joy. Poland, Lithuania, Latvia, and Rumania adopted anti-Jewish measures in 1934; Hungary followed suit in 1935. Anti-Semitic parties

Last Chance: The summer of 1939. Four hundred Jews, men, women and children, try to escape Hitler and the Holocaust. Huddled together with animals on the upper deck of the Greek ship Atratto, *they were intercepted by the British Navy and brought captive into Haifa.*

were formed and gradually their platforms became the official policy of the various governments. As in the preceding century, anti-Semitism served as a common ground, uniting otherwise antagonistic factions.

The threatening atmosphere of a pogrom pervaded Poland in the years before the war. Attacks against Jewish merchants, which had begun immediately after World War I, now became intensified. Jewish stores were picketed, and Christian customers prevented from entering. In 1934 the Polish Premier, Skladhowski, legally sanctioned this picketing provided that it was not accompanied by violence. The drive against Jewish professionals was carried on with equal energy. The number of Jewish university students rapidly diminished. Colonel Beck, the Polish Foreign Minister, announced that there were one million Jews too many in Poland.

In Rumania, Goga-Cuza, who came to power at the end of 1937, enforced harsh legislation against the Jews. Economic barriers were erected; Jewish employees were dismissed from factories; ritual slaughter was forbidden; Jews were forced to work on their Sabbath. In Hungary, a massive expulsion of Jews from economic life began officially in 1939.

With the exception of the Jews in Poland, virtually no active resistance was offered by the various Jewish communities to the physical and economic persecutions. In Germany, resistance was out of the question; Jews were no longer represented in the political institutions. In other countries, Fascist regimes controlled the parliaments or had deprived these bodies of the right to take action. In Poland, self-defense organizations, formed largely by the *Bund* and the *Poalei Zion,* succeeded in mounting some resistance; in Warsaw these groups frequently met anti-Semitic attacks with force. But the total impression was, nevertheless, one of tragic weakness: a defenseless minority in the midst of a murderous, overwhelming majority. Equally ineffective was the small number of socialist or liberal gentiles who protested against the treatment of the Jews. The world outside was indifferent.

As the crisis mounted, the opportunities for emigration decreased. Visas were impossible to obtain. Many Jews fled anyway, in a desperate attempt to save their lives. Often they were turned away from one port to the next because they were "illegal" immigrants. Ships sank, Jews drowned. Many were forcibly returned to Europe.* In a statement before the Palestine Royal Commission

* Toward the end of October 1934, a ship bearing 318 Jews from Poland and Czechoslovakia was found wandering in the Black Sea. It could not land because its passengers had no visas. In March 1939, 68 Jewish refugees from Germany were

on November 25, 1936, Chaim Weizmann, who had gone up to Jerusalem to deliver his evidence, declared:

> . . . There are six million people doomed to be pent up where they are not wanted and for whom the world is divided into places where they cannot live, and places which they may not enter. Six million!

In eight years' time, the problem presented by these six million Jews was to be solved. In 1945, these six million were dead.

Nazi Conquests and Deportations

When World War II broke out on September 1, 1939, Nazi rule already extended over much of Europe; the persecution of Jews now entered a new phase, a phase more hideous than anybody could have imagined. Almost the entire European continent, except for the Soviet Union, was dominated by German might for most of the Second World War. The Germans swallowed Poland, Denmark, and Norway, Holland, Belgium, Luxemburg, and France. Then followed all the Balkan countries. At the conclusion of the military campaigns, the German occupying forces set about imposing Nazi ideology and Nazi rule upon the conquered peoples. In thrall to a diabolic logic, and with no diminution of energy, they undertook the relentless persecution of the Jews who had fallen under their power.

The entire machinery of the Wehrmacht, the Nazi Party, and the State, participated in the work. Every German mission had a special consultant on Jewish questions, and every propaganda medium was used to foster anti-Semitism among the local populations. This work was carried out even by missions in countries not involved in the war, such as those in Ankara, Madrid, Lisbon, and Stockholm.

Reichsminister Alfred Rosenberg was placed in charge of a special bureau—the *Einsatzstub*—which undertook the organized plunder of art museums, libraries, and other institutions in all occupied territories. The Gestapo, meanwhile, set up the machinery for the "final solution," under the supervision of Adolf Eichmann, whose direct superiors were Heydrich and Himmler.

Jewish freedom ceased to exist: it had been replaced by curfews, yellow badges, economic and intellectual isolation, social exclusion.

---

repatriated from Buenos Aires because their temporary visas had expired. In the same month the "Capo," with 750 Jewish refugees aboard sank. In June 1939, 900 Jewish refugees sailed along the coast of the U. S. for three weeks. No American country would admit them, and the ship finally returned to Europe.

At first, Jews in the East were concentrated in specified urban centers, to be used for slave labor. Jews from the occupied Western countries—France, Belgium, and the Netherlands—were deported to the East for this purpose.

In France, the assistance given by the Vichy government to the Germans was essential to the success of the German plan. It assured the isolation of the Jews from the rest of the population and relieved the occupiers of the necessity to assume police operations, which were carried on in both the Free and the Occupied zones by the French police. As in the East, stringent anti-Jewish legislation was passed, but no ghetto was created in Paris. In fact extensive assistance was given to the Jews by the rest of the French population—a factor which saved the lives of many French Jews who managed to escape the mass roundups.

In Belgium, the smallness of the country and the consequent ease of surveillance made the lives of Belgian Jews more precarious. The situation was even worse in the Netherlands where the Nuremberg laws were introduced in May 1941. In addition, Dutch Jews were ghettoized in three districts in Amsterdam.

Hungary's 800,000 oppressed and harried Jews remained comparatively safe until the spring of 1944. Then, when the Germans occupied the country, Eichmann took bitter revenge on the Hungarian Jews for having escaped him so long. When transport for deportation procedures became unavailable, 30,000 Jews were walked on foot from Budapest to Vienna.

The deportations of Greek Jews were particularly gruesome. The trip lasted ten days, during which time the Jews were reduced to such a debilitated state that upon arrival in the camps they were exterminated en masse without the customary selection. Several hundreds of Jews from the isle of Rhodes were crowded into antiquated boats and sunk in the Aegean.

The Italians gave refuge to Jews in their occupied regions. Although in other areas they adopted Nazi legislation and cooperated with the Germans, they could not bring themselves to collaborate in genocide. Such was also the case in Nice and in the French Alps. Jews from other regions soon began pouring in by the thousands to place themselves under Italian protection. As long as the Germans did not take over the country, non-cooperation remained possible, despite the violent protests lodged by Ribbentrop against Mussolini. But in the end, the Nazis swallowed the "unoccupied" zone as well.

Loopholes in the deportation system, together with the assistance rendered by the French, Dutch, and Belgians, made possible many

The Holocaust

399

attempts at escape. Some Jews were able to hide, or "Aryanize" themselves with the help of false papers, or flee to unoccupied France. The number of *camouflés* in France and *onderduikers* in the Netherlands ran into the tens of thousands. Slowly, bit by bit, numerous clandestine organizations sprang up in these countries to help the camouflaged Jews. Jews and non-Jews cooperated in this effort. Whole factories for falsifying papers operated in the large cities. Aiding the Jews became a subsidiary activity of resistance movements. Across the Alps and the Pyrenees, along hazardous routes, Dutch, Belgian, and French Jews were convoyed by the thousands to Switzerland or Spain. But almost as often, refugees were tragically sent back to enemy territory.

The Scandinavian countries alone took a firm and positive stand with regard to their Jews. Danish solidarity was particularly effective; King Christian even threatened that he would be the first to wear the Jewish star if it were introduced in Denmark. Informed in time of the Germans' intentions, most of the 7500 Danish Jews scattered and hid; the majority slipped over to Sweden. Finland too, despite its alliance with Germany, refused to let its Jewish citizens be deported.

In July 1939, Goering had given orders to devise an over-all plan for the "final solution" of the Jewish question. The plan was accepted by the Wannsee Conference in January 1942:

> Under suitable control, the Jews should be brought to the East in the course of the Final Solution, for use as labor. In big labor gangs, the sexes separated, the Jews capable of work will be transported to those areas and set to road building, in the course of which many, without doubt, will succumb through natural losses. The surviving remnant, surely those with the greatest powers of resistance, will be given special treatment [*sonderbehandlung*], since they will constitute the natural reserve for the re-creation of Jewry, as history has proved.

> In execution of the Final Solution, Europe will be combed from West to East. The Jews will first be driven into Ghettos, and from there to the East. . . . In the Occupied Territories and in those under our influence in Europe, the officer designated by the Security Police will operate in coordination with the appropriate representative of the Ministry for Foreign Affairs.

Annihilation in the East

The Holocaust

The Blitzkrieg in Poland was over in less than one month. The entry of the German forces signaled the commencement of pogroms, plunder, collective fines, the destruction of synagogues. All this was only the beginning. A year later, all the Jews of Poland

They wait—for their different fates. Polish Jews about to be trucked to extermination camps—and their Nazi exterminators.

were placed in ghettos, cut off completely from the outside world, deprived of their sources of livelihood, condemned to a living death. In Warsaw alone, in an area where 35,000 people had lived previously, 500,000 persons were herded together under conditions of unimaginable terror. Starvation was imminent; bread, potatoes, and ersatz fat made up the paltry daily diet of 800 calories. Epidemics ran wild. The entrances to the ghetto were guarded by German and Polish sentries who shot on sight any Jew who ventured to come too close. Communications with the outside world were completely severed.

The ghetto had become the pattern of Jewish life in Poland before the inception of the "final solution." Ghettoization was a most effective means of ensuring submission, but it could be used by the Germans only in the East, where the Jews were a well-defined national unity and where they were densely populated. Once ghettoized, the Jews were exploited as slave labor in workshops and factories. Those unable to work were deported. The tragic irony of this economic "collaboration" is that Jews were forced to sell their souls in order to survive; there was simply no other alternative, except death. Emmanuel Ringelblum, whose Warsaw ghetto diary was found after the war, epitomized the situation thus:

> The history of man knows no similar tragedy. A nation that hates the Germans with all its soul can ransom itself from death only at the price of its contributions to the enemy's victory—a victory which means its complete extermination in Europe and perhaps in the whole world.

Under such conditions, the struggle for mere survival became an obsession. Small committees were organized in each building to aid the poorest tenants. Youth organizations attempted to reduce the spreading famine by cultivating tiny patches of ground on the sites of bombed houses, on balconies, on roofs. A few youths even courageously volunteered to cultivate fields outside the ghetto. But all this activity helped little. Beggars became an increasingly frequent sight in the ghetto streets.

Whatever its ordeals of survival, the ghetto nevertheless supported a flourishing culture; artistic and intellectual activities seemed to burgeon as physical strength flagged. Theaters functioned to the end. Even teaching, which was forbidden, was secretly carried out on a large scale at all levels. A group of doctors even undertook a series of studies on the pathological aspects of starvation. The results were found and published after the war. People read works of history and literature with boundless voracity.

But the chief source of comfort lay within, in the inner resources of the Jews themselves, in their vitality and optimism. It was this same faith that had helped the Jews face every threat and survive centuries of misery and persecution. Almost the only suicides in the ghettos were those of highly assimilated German Jews who had lost the traditional resources of their Polish brethren. For them the Nazi terror had come as a sudden, smashing blow. For the Polish Jews, on the other hand, present circumstances still made a certain amount of sense when placed in the context of past experience. It was thus easier for these Jews to take up the cause of resistance. After all, an apparatus of communal and political solidarity had existed for some time in the Polish community, and it could be adapted to present needs with relative ease.

In June 1941, Hitler broke his pact with Stalin and marched into Russia. At once, the Jewish population in the invaded territories was systematically exterminated by special SS detachments, known as *Einsatzgruppen*. Jews were rounded up, shot on the spot, and dumped into common graves. Extermination squads spread over the country, inciting the native masses to initiate pogroms and "spontaneous massacres." Jews were forced to assemble their brethren. They were then herded into trucks and freight cars, taken outside the town to some ravine or ditch, stripped of valuables and even clothing, and then—men, women, and children—shot. The countryside became one immense graveyard, the ground drenched with the blood of innumerable anonymous corpses. Sometimes, as in the case of Babi Yar, near Kiev, the site of these mass executions was not discovered until years later. Other methods of execution were also employed, such as mass drownings, burnings, and gassings in mobile gas chambers which were usually disguised as convoy trucks.

As the war proceeded, extermination ceased to be instantaneous. In many cases, before being killed, the Jews were exploited by the Germans for their labor potential. An SS economic empire of slave labor was created to overcome the lack of manpower in wartime Germany. The Jews were either hired out to public or private industry or employed in factories owned by the SS. Jewish labor was also used to clean streets, clear the ground, dig ditches, etc. Hundreds of work camps sprang up all over Soviet territory. Work and death, from blows, torture, hunger, or murder, became almost synonymous in these camps.

But the final pillage took place in the concentration camps

where, before and after death, the Jews were systematically stripped of everything they possessed, not only removable valuables, but hair, gold teeth, false limbs. Even their bones were turned into phosphate and their fat into soap. Men gave free rein to their most demonic instincts; all barriers were swept away in the mad pursuit of self-aggrandizement. Hundreds of thousands of German nationals became rich from the pillage. In the words of Himmler: "We have written a glorious page in our history. A story which should never be told. We have taken everything they owned."

By the middle of 1942 deportation had begun to the death camps of Auschwitz, Maidanek, Treblinka, and many others. The sheer number of those exterminated at these camps staggers the imagination. Hoess, the camp commander of Auschwitz, stated at his postwar trial:

> I commanded Auschwitz until December 1, 1943, and estimate that at least 2,500,000 victims were executed and exterminated there by gassing and burning, and at least another half a million succumbed to starvation and disease, making a total dead of about 3,000,000. Apart from 20,000 Russian prisoners of war delivered there by the Wehrmacht, the victims were Jews from Holland, Belgium, France, Poland, Hungary, Czechoslovakia, Greece, and other countries. We executed about 400,000 Hungarian Jews alone at Auschwitz in the summer of 1944.

Nothing affected the tempo of genocide except technical factors, such as the number of men Eichmann could spare for his operations, or the availability of transport.

The Death Camp at Auschwitz   Auschwitz was situated in a sparsely populated, unhealthy, swampy region. The abundance of manpower made available by the camp attracted industries to the site, whose periodic selections provided the only link between the Auschwitz of the crematories, the Jewish Auschwitz proper, and the international Auschwitz of slave laborers. Thousands of prisoners, Jews and non-Jews alike, worked in the I. G. Farben factories making artificial rubber and synthetic gasoline. Others worked elsewhere. Selections were made on the basis of those fit for labor, and usually took place upon the arrival of each new convoy. The "unselected" went straight to their death. The survivors joined the ranks of the slaves and were assigned civil status and tatooed with a number. Their life span was approximately three months. Selections were rapid and superficial.

The Holocaust   Along with the principal selections upon arrival, partial selections

Bergen-Belsen ranked with the worst of the German death camps. When the British army took it at the end of the war they forced one of the chief Nazi executioners, Dr. S. S. Klein, to stand before a truckload of his Jewish victims so that they could show the world his handiwork.

took place constantly in order to eliminate those whose work output was no longer adequate. The manpower needs of the moment determined the frequency and severity of the selections.

The unfit were led to the gas chambers on the pretext that they were going to have a shower. They undressed and were handed a cake of soap. The gas chambers had simulated shower heads in the ceiling. Canned Zyklon "B" gas, which was used to disinfect the camp from vermin and bugs, was dropped through little windows in the ceiling. The asphyxiation process lasted three to ten minutes. One half hour later, the bodies were removed by the *Sonderkommando*, Jews who had been selected to clean out the installations, to pull the bodies out of the gas chambers, to search, bury, or burn them. Stripped of all that might remain, they were transferred to the crematoria. After cremation the ashes were dumped into ditches or loaded onto trucks. The *Sonderkommando* was kept strictly isolated. The members of this squad were better fed and consequently less debilitated than other work details. Indeed, the only recorded uprising in Auschwitz, as in Chelmo, was attempted by the *Sonderkommando*. These Jews, too, were exterminated at regular intervals.

The units assigned to guard the camps, known as the "Death's-Head" details (SS *Totenkopf*), had been trained since 1933 in the systematic degradation and torture of "sub-humans" and enemies of the Reich. It was they who crushed the slightest attempt at resistance on the part of the prisoners, and who surrounded their bleeding expiations with horror and mystery.

Nazi crimes were not undertaken haphazardly. The enslavement of millions, the deportations to Germany, the murder and ill-treatment of prisoners of war, the mass executions of civilians, the shooting of hostages, and the fulfillment of the "final solution" of the Jewish question—all were the result of long-term planning. The Germans themselves have provided unchallengeable evidence of this in the records, returns, inventories, orders, and other documents, all carefully preserved, collected, and tabulated, that are part of the legacy of the Nazi era. To see these documents is to behold a monument to the bureaucratic temperament. To read them is to enter into a vertiginous world of horror.

Rescue

The extermination plans of the Nazis had been laid on a grand scale; by contrast, rescue activities undertaken by Jewish organizations, notably the Jewish Agency and the Joint Distribution Committee, seemed infinitesimal in scope. Yet untold effort, anguish, and frustration went into the work of these organizations, centered in the few neutral countries left in Europe and engaged in an unending battle with the homelessness, hunger, and fear that were the lot of the few who had managed to gain their freedom.

In the East, the attitude of the mass of people toward the Jews was one of hostility and indifference; only the small democracies in the Western countries reacted with firmness and unanimity to the plight of the Jews. The response of the Church to the persecutions was equivocal, ranging from strong protests, to silent humanitarian efforts, to silence. In France and in the Netherlands a number of prelates held public prayers for the Jews, and pamphlets were distributed to apprise the people of what was happening. The Pope himself aided and protected a number of Jews, even contributing fifteen kilograms of gold when the Jewish inhabitants of Rome had to supply an exorbitant amount to the Nazis in October 1943. But in general he carried on his humanitarian activities in a cautious way. The Papacy was careful not to strain its relations with Germany and thus refrained from using its full moral authority. On the other hand, the lower clergy, especially in France, and the monastic orders rivaled one another in their energy and daring to protect and hide Jews.

The Allies were inactive toward the fate of the Jews. Not until 1943 did the United States government set up a committee for the victims of war. This action came too late. Only a few individuals could be saved. The Roosevelt administration on this question showed none of the humanity associated with it in other spheres.

When a spokesman for Hungarian Jewry appeared in Cairo to negotiate with the British on a deal for the release of Jews, he was imprisoned by British authorities. Even before that time, in February 1941, the new Colonial Secretary, Lord Moyne, had written to Weizmann refusing an impassioned appeal for a "substantial allocation of immigration certificates to be issued immediately to Rumanian Jews." "Rumania," wrote Lord Moyne, "is regarded as enemy occupied territory. The machinery for verification of the bona fides of applicants . . . has disappeared."

Weizmann and his Zionist colleagues were tireless in their efforts to break the public silence on the subject of the Holocaust in Europe. On March 1, 1943, he took the floor at Madison Square Garden in New York to deliver a resounding cry of anguish:

> When the historian of the future assembles the black record of our days, he will find two things unbelievable: first, the crime itself; second, the reaction of the world to that crime. He will sift

the evidence again and again before he will be able to give credence to the fact that, in the twentieth century of the Christian Era, a great and cultivated nation put power into a band of assassins who transformed murder from a secret transgression into a publicly avowed government policy to be carried out with all the paraphernalia of State. He will find the monstrous story of the human slaughterhouses, the lethal chambers, the sealed trains, taxing the powers of belief.

But when that historian, overwhelmed by the tragic evidence, sets down the verdict of the future upon this savage phenomenon, unique in the annals of mankind, he will be troubled by still another circumstance. He will be puzzled by the apathy of the civilized world in the face of this immense, systematic carnage of human beings whose sole guilt was membership in the people which gave the commandments of the moral law to mankind. He will not be able to understand why the conscience of the world had to be prodded, why sympathies had to be stirred. Above all, he will not be able to understand why the free nations, in arms against a resurgent, organized barbarism, required appeals to give sanctuary to the first and chief victim of that barbarism.

Two million Jews have already been exterminated. The world can no longer plead that the ghastly facts are unknown or unconfirmed. . . . At this moment, expressions of sympathy, without accompanying attempts to launch acts of rescue, become a hollow mockery in the ears of the dying.

The democracies have a clear duty before them. Let them negotiate with Germany through the neutral countries. Let havens be designated in the vast territories of the United Nations which will give sanctuary to those fleeing from imminent murder. Let the gates of Palestine be opened to all who can reach the shores of the Jewish homeland. The Jewish community of Palestine will welcome with joy and thanksgiving all delivered from Nazi hands.

Jewish rescue and relief efforts were undertaken on several fronts. During 1939 and 1940, Russia consigned 350,000 Polish Jews, whom she had acquired by the partition of 1939, to the bleak Asian border of Persia. Most of them died of cold and hunger. The remaining survivors gathered into small towns along the frontier of Persia, where they struggled to set up their own communities. To their rescue came a member of the Joint Distribution Committee in 1942, who established a relief service for these starving Jews. After the war, most of them escaped, either through Persia or by way of Poland and the DP camps, and made their way to Palestine.

In Lisbon, which was one of the chief transit ports for Jews escaping from Europe, the Joint's work consisted largely of chartering ships to sail for Cuba and the U. S., or buying up all berths on regular passages. Trains ran regularly to Lisbon from Berlin, Vienna, and Prague. The Joint, working through the Jewish Immigrant Aid Committees of several countries, even through German tourist agencies, arranged the schedules of these trains and met them upon arrival at Lisbon. There the Joint cared for the passengers until they boarded the chartered ships.

In France, the Joint financially assisted any group which tried to save the lives of Jews. From Marseilles a courier route was continued across the demarcation line so that cash could be delivered to Paris. It was a dangerous route, but Jews and non-Jews volunteered for service on it. Children were smuggled into Switzerland, the Joint being the chief financial assistant in this traffic. The Joint also supported, by means of its courier routes, canteens in Occupied France, for those who did not even possess a forged food card.

In Vichy France, the Joint's task was threefold: to get Jews out, to care for those who had been caught and put in concentration camps, and to hide the many who had not been arrested and who could still escape. In Unoccupied France, during two and a half years of operations there, 10,000 French Jews were rescued through Lisbon and another 1200 through Casablanca.

In the Vichy concentration camps, the Joint supplied food, clothing, and medicines. The Jews in these camps managed to stay alive until the dreaded moment when the Germans collected them for deportation. When the Germans finally crossed the demarcation lines, the Joint went underground. Its work was kept up all during the occupation.

Jewish Resistance Many questions may be raised about Jewish resistance to the Nazi onslaught, but the fact of such resistance is beyond dispute. It took various forms: service in every army fighting Hitler, actual revolt in the ghettos, partisan activity in the forests, even the clandestine writing of diaries kept in secret hiding places in cellars and attics. All these were manifestations of an obstinate refusal to submit to the Nazi ordeal.

The Jewish resistance movement differed from the general resistance movement in several crucial ways. The Jewish movement, for one thing, was forced to fight under more difficult conditions: it had no backing and in some countries did not receive any assistance from the local population. In Soviet Russia, to be sure, Jewish resistance fighters were part of the Soviet partisan movement, and the same is true for such Western countries as France, Belgium, and Holland, where the Jewish resistance worked hand in hand with the rest of the population. In the Ukraine, however, Jewish resistance fighters often faced two enemies: the nationals and the Germans. In Poland, too, the Jewish partisan movement was a separate undertaking. These countries were also the scene of the most brutal exterminations of Jews by the Nazis.

From the first, the Jewish resistance movement was not simply an undertaking of courageous individuals or groups, but a mass movement, an integral part of the battle waged by the Jewish people against the Nazis. Even though this struggle was doomed to failure, it embodied a vision of popular liberation and national rebirth. Many of the fighters were drawn from the ranks of the Zionists, people who believed in the idea of a Jewish State or in a free socialist world, or in a synthesis of both. And just as other freedom fighters named their partisan units after their own revolutionary heroes (Garibaldi in Italy, Kosciuszko in Poland, Alexander Nevski in Russia), Jewish partisan units were named after Bar Kochba and Judah Maccabee.

Jewish resistance movements were active in the ghettos, in the camps and in the forests. Individual groups carried out acts of sabotage right in the centers of Nazi rule. A group of German Jews was in Berlin in 1944; others struggled within the French underground in Paris. Jews participated in the general underground movements in all countries where they were allowed to join in them.

The drive for spiritual and economic self-preservation was ever present in the Jewish resistance movement. The splendid records of mutual aid in the ghettos, of newspapers appearing in the camps and ghettos, written under the shadow of death, the rescue of Torah scrolls from the ruins of destroyed synagogues, all these were expressions of resistance to the enemy. The spirit of revolt in the ghettos must be seen in relation to the general orientation of Jewish leadership at the time. Zionist youngsters in Nazi Europe lived together, sharing every drop of water and every crumb of food. They assumed responsibility for other Jews in the crowded ghetto, became teachers, kindergarten nurses and smugglers. They brought in weapons and trained themselves in their use. All this, while living under the same harsh conditions as their fellow Jews.

The most spectacular of all the resistance efforts took place in the Warsaw ghetto. From the beginning, the young members of the Warsaw *"kibbutz"* had struggled to remain together and to retain their group identity. In this they were not alone. The Jewish Bund members, too, published clandestine newspapers and plotted armed resistance, as did other political groups. When the deportations began, the various groups coordinated and established contact with the Polish resistance in order to obtain arms and ammunition. The Polish underground, however, was reluctant to help them, and endless obstacles had to be overcome to smuggle even a single weapon into a ghetto that was swarming with spies. Several hundred Jewish fighters trained secretly in shelters. (A network of camouflaged hiding places with false entrances had been dug deep under the earth.) Within a short while the Jewish combat group became a powerful and respected society.

The Nazi liquidation of the Warsaw ghetto began in July 1942. In one month, almost 100,000 Jews were taken away on the pretext that they would be transported to work camps. In fact, they were taken to the extermination camp at Treblinka and put to death. By the Day of Atonement, 1942, 60,000 Jews were all that remained of the half-million inhabitants of the ghetto.

The Germans' last entry into the ghetto met with violent resistance from the small combat group. Twice the Germans were forced to retreat; artillery and flame throwers were called in to overcome the Jewish fighters. Finally, the defenders took to the sewers. Despite the unbearably overcrowded conditions and the lack of air, they continued to offer savage resistance. Little by little, the organized Jewish resistance was extinguished, and the action was temporarily stopped. But this was only a breathing spell. Every minute was now used to procure and manufacture arms. None of the Jewish leaders had illusions about the outcome. None of that hope which encouraged other resistance fighters was permitted them, neither dreams of victory nor the expectation of saving their own lives. They were animated solely by a lucid resolve to preserve dignity, to die fighting, to redeem Jewish honor.

The Nazis were staggered by these first acts of resistance. Himmler had given orders to destroy the ghetto. Now the eve of Passover, April 19, 1943, was chosen for the final assault. The ghetto was placed under siege and a fierce bombardment began. The advancing troops were supported by tanks, many of which were driven off with home-made bombs. The desperate battle had been joined. Fighting was street-to-street and house-to-house. Buildings were set on fire to drive out those hiding within; gas was

*Nazi squadrons round up the Jewish survivors of the Warsaw ghetto
for the concentration camps as the ghetto goes up in smoke behind them.*

tossed into the bunkers. Finally even the sewers and dugouts were blown up. The commander of the German force reported to his headquarters:

> The resistance put up by the Jews and bandits could be broken only by relentlessly using all our force and energy, day and night. . . .

Twenty-eight days later, the fighting ended with the blowing up of the ghetto synagogue. The German commander reported on the termination of the action: "We did succeed in catching a total of 56,065 Jews whose extermination can be proven. To this should be added the number of Jews who lost their lives in explosions and fires. . . ." What General Stroop did not know was that close to a hundred resistance fighters succeeded in escaping through the sewers, finding their way to freedom in order to tell the world of this heroic chapter in Jewish history.

As in Warsaw, so in other ghettos resistance groups were born when news of the extermination camps spread. Some of these groups were quashed before they had a chance to defend themselves, as in the Vilna ghetto, where the group's existence was betrayed and its leader executed. In Cracow, a group of young Zionists created havoc through bombings and individual attacks. In Byalistok, a concerted resistance took place within the ghetto itself. The Jews defended the ghetto as long as possible. A few of them escaped into the neighboring woods, where they joined partisan groups. In the forests, several Jewish partisan groups undertook successful action against the Nazis, like the Vilna Avengers or the Tobias Belski division which operated farther south in the Lida region. A veritable free Jewish city had sprung up near the end of the war in the forests of White Russia, a refuge for escaped Jews which the local peasants called "Jerusalem." It held out until the Red army arrived.

On the day of the final "action," the Jews of the city of Tukzin set their ghetto afire and perished in the flames rather than fall into the hands of the Germans. The same happened at Dvinsk in Latvia. There are also astonishing accounts of isolated feats, or veiled references to "camouflaged" Jews who slipped into the German administration or even into the army to spy and sabotage until they were finally denounced. In Latvia, Jews engaged in sabotage and set fires after the entry of the German forces. And in Russia itself, the Jews played a major role in partisan battles. In Holland, Belgium, and Italy, Jews took an essential and sometimes preponderant part in the resistance movements.

In France, the proportion of Jews in the resistance organizations ran between 15 and 30 per cent. Among the many individual Jewish heroes, one in particular deserves mention: José Aboulker, a young Algerian medical student, who at the age of 22, organized the resistance in Algiers which made the American landing possible. In Paris, Jewish guerrillas and partisans carried out several attacks, some of them among the most important of the resistance.

All these organizations were also engaged in setting up escape routes, in undercover work, in fabricating false papers to help Jews escape—this, too, was part of their resistance to the Nazis. And finally, in Jewish Palestine, a national Jewish resistance movement was formed. Perhaps the most unforgettable exploit of this group was the parachuting of a handful of young Palestinians into Hungary and Rumania in 1944 in order to establish contact with the Jewish underground there and to comfort European Jewry in its last death throes. Many of these youths were captured and executed by the Germans, among them the young poetess Hannah Senesch and Enzo Sereni.

The efforts of these youngsters, as of so many more like them, may be said to have been doomed to failure from the start. And so, in one sense, they were. But the example of their devotion was not lost. Jewish resistance to the Nazis was all the more glorious for its apparent futility. For even in the darkest hour, in a world gone mad and brutish, the dignity of life was fiercely vindicated and upheld.

Examples of the Holocaust

It is important, though frightening, to realize that the murder of Jews had become a normal pursuit for thousands of Germans throughout all the occupied territories. The normality was horrifyingly evident in the business world. Captured German documents include laconic minutes from industrial firms such as this one from I. A. Topf, manufacturer of heating equipment:

12 February 1943

> To the Central Construction Office of the SS and
>   Police, Auschwitz.
>
> Subject: Crematoria 2 and 3 of the camp.
>
> We acknowledge receipt of your order for five triple furnaces including two electric elevators for raising the corpses and one emergency elevator. A practical installation for stocking coal was ordered, and one for transporting ashes.

William Shirer, in his *Rise and Fall of the Third Reich,* quotes the obsequious efforts of a firm called C. H. Kori, soliciting the Belgrade business upon the grounds of successful achievements in Dachau and Lublin where it claimed to have given "full satisfaction" in practice.

> Following our verbal discussion regarding the delivery of equipment of simple construction for the burning of bodies, we are submitting plans for our perfected cremation ovens which operate with coal and which have hitherto given full satisfaction.
>
> We suggest two crematorial furnaces for the building plant but we advise you to make further inquiries to make sure that two ovens will be sufficient for your requirements.
>
> We guarantee the effectiveness of the cremation ovens as well as their durability, the use of the best material and our faultless workmanship. Heil Hitler.
>
> —C. H. Kori

Until the Nazi Holocaust there was an innocent assumption that no man, however depraved, can stand unmoved before the innocence and fragility of childhood. The human race can no longer allow itself even this consolation. Here are the words of the Attorney General at the Eichmann trial in Jerusalem in 1961:

> We shall present you with the instructions about the transport of children. The children were to be divided among transports intended for Auschwitz. Children of fourteen were considered independent for purposes of transport to the extermination camps. Nor shall we say who suffered the more terrible fate—those who died or those who concealed themselves in every conceivable hiding place, who lived in perpetual terror of expulsion, who survived by the grace of Christian neighbors who agreed to hide them. Children would come home from the schools and centers organized by the community to find their parents' home empty for they had been sent by some special operation to their deaths and the apartment was in the meantime occupied by others. You will hear evidence of tender infants, pressed by their mothers to their bodies in the gas chambers so that they were not immediately poisoned until the executioners came and threw them alive into the furnaces.

The Jerusalem courtroom was hypnotized into electric silence as it heard a description of the children's convoy from Drancy in France dispatched to Auschwitz on Eichmann's orders that "children's transports can get under way."

The children would arrive at the Drancy camp packed in buses, guarded by policemen. They would be put down into courtyards surrounded by barbed wire, guarded by a platoon of French gendarmes. The police and the gendarmes, hard people, not easily moved, could not hide their feelings and abhorrence for the task they were compelled to carry out. On the arrival of the buses they would begin to remove the children and lead them in groups to the halls, the older ones holding the hands of the smaller children, or carrying them in their arms. They did not weep, the children. They walked terrified, disciplined, miserable, and complied with the orders like a flock of sheep, one helping the other.

On the day of deportation they would be awakened at 5 o'clock in the morning. Irritable, half asleep, most of the children would refuse to get up and go down to the courtyard. The volunteer women would have to urge them gently, patiently, and so tragically, so as to convince the older children that they must obey orders and vacate the halls. On a number of occasions the entreaties did not help. The children cried and refused to leave their mattresses. The gendarmes would then enter the halls, pick up the children in their arms as they screamed with fear, struggling and grasping at each other. The halls were like a madhouse. The scene was too terrible for even the hardest of men to bear.

In the courtyard they would call out the names of the children one by one, mark them off in the register, and direct them to the buses. When a bus filled up it would leave the camp with its cargo. Since many of the children remained unidentified and others would not answer to their correct or assumed names, they would include them in the convoy to make up the number.

Each convoy consisted of about five hundred children and five hundred adults chosen from the camp prisoners. Within a period of about three weeks during the second half of August and the first part of September 1943, 4000 children thus made into orphans were transported in this fashion, exterminated with adult strangers.

The dimensions of these actions are vitally important if we are to understand the scope of the mental disease which had gripped the German nation. Thousands of officials were necessary to carry out these tasks. They could not have been fulfilled except against the background of overwhelming social acquiescence. The anti-Jewish prejudice, burning fitfully throughout history, sometimes as a tiny spark, sometimes as a vast flame, had now left its scorched path across the territory of the human spirit.

Jewish history and consciousness will be dominated for many generations by the traumatic memories of the Holocaust. No people in history has undergone an experience of such violence and depth. Israel's obsession with physical security; the sharp Jewish reaction to movements of discrimination and prejudice; an intoxicated awareness of life, not as something to be taken for granted but as a treasure to be fostered and nourished with eager vitality, a residual distrust of what lies beyond the Jewish wall, a mystic belief in the undying forces of Jewish history, which ensure survival when all appears lost, all these together with the intimacy of more personal pains and agonies, are the legacy which the Holocaust transmits to the generation of Jews grown up under its shadow.

The Effect of the War in Palestine   The Allies were conscious of the great strategical importance of the Middle East and Palestine during World War II. C. L. Sulzberger summed up the position in *Foreign Affairs*, July 1942.

> The geographical triangle stretching between the Mediterranean, the Black Sea and the Indian Ocean, and vaguely known as the Middle East, is the most important link between the key members of the United Nations: the United States, Britain and her central Asian empire, China and the U.S.S.R. The Suez Canal and the shipping lanes westward through the Mediterranean, eastward to India and southward around the Cape are the heart of an area including the richest petroleum deposits in the Old World, the greatest road and air network between East and West, and regions valuable not only from a purely strategical point of view but for cotton, grain, fruit, gold and chromium. Finally, the Middle East is not only the barrier between the two expanding ends of the Axis—in Europe and Asia—but contains the gateway to Europe through the Balkans, the back-door to the Soviet Union through the Dardanelles and over the Caucasus, the road to India through Iran and Baluchistan. . . .

The attitude of the Arabs toward the Allies during the war, at least until it became entirely clear that the Allied cause would win, was an unfriendly one, ranging from open hostility to grudging neutrality. In contrast, the Jews of the *yishuv* were eager from the first to join the battle against Nazi Germany. Jewish enlistments in the British army were so numerous as to prove embarrassing to the British authorities, who tried to keep them down to the level of the Arabs. The Palestinian Jewish units made *The Holocaust* an honorable contribution to the victory in the Middle East. Of

very great importance, too, was the contribution of Jewish Palestinian industry and skilled labor to the war effort. This fact was recognized by the British, but did not change their political attitude toward the Jewish National Home.

On September 3, 1939, when Britain officially declared war on Germany, the Executive of the Jewish Agency at Jerusalem issued a statement:

> His Majesty's Government has today declared war against the Germany of Hitler.
>
> At this fateful moment, the Jewish community has a threefold concern: the protection of the Jewish homeland, the welfare of the Jewish people, the victory of the British Empire.
>
> The White Paper of May 1939 was a grave blow to us. As heretofore we shall defend to the utmost of our ability the right of the Jewish people in its National Home. Our opposition to the White Paper was, however, never directed against Great Britain or the British Empire.
>
> The war which has now been forced upon Great Britain by Nazi Germany is our war, and all the assistance that we shall be able and permitted to give to the British Army and to the British People, we shall render wholeheartedly.

Yet despite its wholehearted willingness to join the Allied ranks, the *yishuv* had to plead incessantly with the Mandatory Power to be allowed to take an effective part in the war against Nazi Germany. Britain was apparently afraid that such efforts might cause the Arabs to think of the war as one being waged for the Jews, or for the Middle East, which was still far removed from the scene of battle. The result, the British feared, might even be to throw the Arabs to the side of the enemy. Every effort was made to discourage the *yishuv* from expressing its desire to help.

Obstacles to Jewish recruiting were put forward in different ways: low rates of pay, absence of family allowances, barriers to the obtaining of commissioned ranks for "aliens." The British authorities even began trials against Jews who had been found in possession of arms. Forty-three members of the *Palmach*, who belonged to Orde Wingate's "Night Squads," and had been trained by the British army for special duties against Arab marauders, were among those brought to trial. Yet despite these affronts, the Jews continued to clamor for the right to serve in the army. The Jewish Agency demanded the formation of special Jewish military units for the defense of Palestine which was threatened by the Axis forces. The Civil Administration regarded this suggestion

The Jewish Brigade passes in review, the desert dust on their shoes, the desert tan on their faces. The Brigade contained Jews from more than twenty-five different countries and made a distinguished combat record with the British army in World War II.

with open disfavor, fearing that it would strengthen the Jewish position and antagonize the Arabs. Finally, in December 1939, Dr. Weizmann made an official proposal for the training of Jewish junior officers in preparation for a Jewish military unit at a later stage; this proposal was received favorably by the military authorities in England, but was killed by bureaucratic delay.

When Italy entered the war in June 1940, Weizmann again pleaded for a Jewish military unit and urged speedy action. No reaction was forthcoming. Weizmann then addressed a letter to Winston Churchill in August 1940. After urging the British interest and the ardent desire of the *yishuv* to fight against the common enemy, Weizmann stated:

> Palestinian Jewry can furnish a force of 50,000 fighting men, all of them in the prime of their strength—no negligible force if properly trained, armed, and led. If Palestine be invaded and the Jewish community be destroyed for lack of the means of self-defence, a grave responsibility will attach to the British Government which refused them.

This letter from Dr. Weizmann soon had consequences. In October 1940, the British government approved a limited scheme for the enlistment of Jews in separate units in the British army. A sense of national and moral obligation made the Jews accept these conditions, ambiguous though they were. While the formation of a special Jewish division was postponed until the autumn of 1944, Jewish units under Jewish officers were formed in Palestine and took part in the war. The advance of Rommel's armies in North Africa and Egypt, and the need for manpower, had meanwhile made the recruitment of the Palestinian volunteers an urgent necessity. Men and women now served in many capacities and took part in the decisive battles of the Eighth Army under Montgomery which drove back Rommel from El-Alamein.

In August 1943 there were 22,000 Jews in the British forces organized in special units, excluding the Supplementary Police force and civil defense workers. When, at last, after lengthy discussions, tenaciously pursued by Moshe Sharett, the Jewish Brigade was formed in September 1944, the number of Jewish soldiers grew to 35,000. The formation of the Brigade was announced by the British War Office: "His Majesty's Government have decided to accede to the request of the Executive of the Jewish Agency for Palestine that a Jewish Brigade Group be formed to take part in active operations."

On October 31, the Jewish Agency could announce that the

flag and the insignia of the Jewish Brigade had been approved—low horizontal blue stripes on a white background with a blue Shield of David in the center. A blue and white shoulder flash with a golden Shield of David was also authorized. The Brigade fought gallantly in Italy and moved up to Austria and Germany, and finally to Belgium and Holland. Every Palestinian Jewish officer and soldier was also a member of the Jewish self-defense organization, the Haganah.

Jewish-British Relations When Britain declared war against Germany, only three and a half months after the publication of the White Paper, it was hoped that the Paper, together with the entire policy of appeasement pursued by Chamberlain's government, would be abolished. The White Paper had been strongly criticized in British parliamentary circles. The Permanent Mandates Commission had declared that it was not consistent with the terms of the Mandate.

These hopes proved to be in vain. British policy in Palestine, as formulated in the White Paper of 1939, was rigorously applied during the war. It is, perhaps, possible to understand the attitude of Britain in this regard during the first stages of the war, when the danger existed that the Middle East would fall to the armies of the Axis, and there were plans for the evacuation of British forces from Palestine. But the cruel implementation of the White Paper with regard to Jewish immigration into Palestine, especially "with the turning of the tide" of war, is less understandable. In this hour, as disaster befell European Jewry and the policy of non-cooperation drove the smallest of Jewish communities into a death struggle with the occupying power, the *yishuv* was powerless. It was not for the safety or economic progress of the six hundred thousand who lived in Palestine, but for the millions trapped in war-stricken Europe, and for the right to come to their rescue, that the *yishuv* undertook its protracted struggle against the Mandatory Power.

The White Paper of 1939 had stopped immigration almost completely and had sealed off the gates of the country at the precise moment when the Holocaust engulfed European Jewry. Britain refused to open the gates of Palestine even to those refugees who managed to save themselves from the Nazi inferno. At no point were immigration restrictions relaxed. Sometimes there was a stoppage of immigration altogether, when according to the government the quota had already been exhausted by the so-called "illegal" immigration. Only at the end of 1943, when it became clear that the quota of 75,000 immigrants allowed in the White Paper would not be reached, did the British administration announce as a gesture of "generosity" that the full number of 75,000 would be permitted to enter Palestine after the stipulated cut-off date of April 1, 1944.

The infinitesimal number of entrants permitted according to the "schedule" (1500 souls per month) made illegal immigration an immediate necessity. Something had to be done to save Jews from certain doom. For some years past, the Haganah had counteracted the limits on immigration by smuggling immigrants into the country. In the first years they were brought over the border from Lebanon or from Syria. Many an Arab smuggler helped in these operations, being paid per capita for his human cargo. Kfar Giladi, a *kibbutz* on the Lebanese border, was the crossing point into Palestine. From 1934 on, illegal immigrants were also brought by ship, an enterprise much more dangerous because far greater numbers were involved at one time; more costly too, owing to the necessity of acquiring and preparing boats which, if intercepted, were confiscated by the British. The first boat to arrive at the shores of Palestine with illegal immigrants was the "Velos," carrying *halutzim* from Poland (1934).

After the British capitulation at Munich, when war became imminent, Jewish refugee boats were to be seen everywhere, sailing the waters of the earth like ghostly galleons of despair. They were to be found as far away as Cuba and Ecuador, Shanghai and Mauritius. A stern watch was kept over the few-hundred-mile-long coastline of Palestine to prevent any human cargo from disembarking. In March 1939, the boat "Sando," which had set out from a Rumanian port with 239 Jewish refugees on board, was received at Palestine's shores by the shots of coastal guards. The "Sando" was forced back to sea without water or fuel. Such incidents occurred repeatedly, enraging public opinion everywhere but encountering a deaf ear in the chambers of Whitehall.

As the Nazis conquered one country after another, Jews tried to get into Palestine by every means possible. Most of them came by sea, frequently on unseaworthy vessels; some attempted the land routes, often traveling by foot and taking many months for their journey. Illegal immigrant ships sailed along the coast of Palestine for weeks, looking for an opportunity to land. Fearing deportation, many immigrants destroyed their identification papers. The British government established the cruel practice of sending these immigrants to some island under British control. Thus, the deportees of the "Atlantic" were sent to the island of Mauritius in the Indian Ocean. These 1600 souls lived under the most primitive conditions for the duration of the entire war.

The worst of the tragedies was that of the "Struma." A converted yacht of about two hundred tons, the "Struma" carried on board 769 Jews, among them children between the ages of ten to sixteen. Badly overcrowded, the small boat reached Istanbul in the middle of December 1941. There the tragedy began. The Turkish authorities declared that they would not permit the immigrants to remain in Turkey, while the British insisted that they would not be allowed to enter Palestine. After lengthy negotiations, Britain agreed to admit the children to Palestine. But the Turks decided to send the ship on to the Black Sea. On February 24, news was received that the "Struma" had sunk, probably torpedoed by a Nazi U-boat. All but one of its passengers perished.

Fierce protests were lodged in Palestine, and all over the free world. Britain offered excuses, and expressed regret on the fate of the refugees. But no measures were taken to alleviate the immigration restrictions. The British Colonial Secretary offered the condolences of his government: "His Majesty's Government earnestly hope that such a tragedy will not occur again. It does not, however, lie in their power, amid the dangers and uncertainties of the war, to give any guarantee, nor can they be party to any measures which could undermine the existing policy regarding illegal immigration into Palestine in view of the wider issues involved."

A further element in the continued strain between the Jews and Britain was the application of the Land Transfer Regulations of 1940. The White Paper of 1939 had declared that "there is now in certain areas no room for further transfers of Arab land, whilst in some other areas such transfers of land must be restricted if Arab cultivators are to retain their existing standard of life and a considerable landless Arab population is not to be created." The prohibited zone included some 6615 square miles, or approximately 63 per cent of the land of Palestine. According to the Land Transfer Regulations, only 2.6 per cent of the land area could freely be purchased by the Jews from the Arabs. The publication of these regulations led to turbulent Jewish demonstrations against the Mandatory government. Demonstrations were organized daily during the first week of March in Jerusalem, Haifa, Tel Aviv, and Petach Tikvah. British police and troops were stoned. The government had to resort to the use of force and a curfew was imposed. The government action was sharply criticized in Parliament, where the position was taken that the Land Transfer Regulations were inconsistent with the Mandate, but the regulations were not withdrawn.

In general, the struggle against the White Paper was carried out by the *yishuv* at the same time that it participated to the utmost of its ability in the larger struggle against Hitler, side by side with the Allied powers. The attitude of the *yishuv* during those years was accurately reflected in the statement of David Ben Gurion, "We shall fight the war as if there were no White Paper, and we shall fight the White Paper as if there were no war." But to the injury caused by the rigid application of the White Paper, a deeper, more lasting insult had been added: this was British perfidy toward the Jews—their allies—in the darkest period of Jewish history. The *yishuv* felt betrayed.

The Jewish Problem and World Politics

During the first part of 1943 the prospect of Allied victory brightened. Palestine was now safe from invasion and the urgent business was to create a favorable climate for the postwar settlement. It was clear that the United States would play a decisive role, but the vehement support which the Jewish cause enjoyed in the public and on Capitol Hill was not reflected in the corridors of the State Department. Weizmann now engaged leading American diplomats, including Sumner Welles and the heads of the Near East Division, in a concentrated and patient seminar on the Jewish problem and its solution. Moshe Sharett and Nahum Goldmann joined him as powerful reinforcements.

On May 7, 1943, Weizmann saw Lord Halifax, then the British Ambassador in Washington, and reminded him that a deadline was approaching. The White Paper required that there be no further Jewish immigration into Palestine at all after March 1944. "Now, Lord Halifax, do you think you can really maintain that position? Somehow or other you have allowed everybody to get away with the idea that if one additional Jew enters Palestine there will be a revolution. For all I know there will be. But the Jews have nothing to lose. If you allow the position to drift it will lead to disaster." He carried the same warning to President Roosevelt on June 12. The President was full of smiling but noncommittal charm. He proposed a Jewish-Arab conference with the possible participation of Mr. Churchill and himself. "Did you see Churchill here in Washington?" he asked. Dr. Weizmann replied: "No, Mr. Churchill doesn't like to see me because he has very little to tell me."

In October, Weizmann returned to London and resumed his assault on Downing Street. On October 25, he lunched with Churchill together with the Deputy Prime Minister, Clement Attlee, and Air Marshall Lord Portal. Churchill presented Weizmann affectionately to the other guests and plunged into words of firm commitment about the Jewish future. "When we have crushed Hitler," he said with sonorous emphasis, "we shall have to establish the Jews in the position where they belong. I have had an inheritance left me by Balfour and I am not going to change. But there are dark forces working against us. Dr. Weizmann, you have some very good friends; for instance, Mr. Attlee and the Labour Party are committed on this matter." Mr. Attlee said, "I certainly am." "I know the terrible situation of the Jews," said Churchill. "They will get compensation and will also be able to judge the criminals. God deals with the nations as they deal with the Jews. . ."

In May 1944, a Hungarian Jew, Joel Brand, reached Istanbul and contacted the Jewish Agency emissaries. He told a fantastic story. Adolf Eichmann, the Nazi officer in charge of the extermination of the Jews, was now engaged in the liquidation of Hungarian Jewry. Much of the grisly work had already been accomplished, but hundreds of thousands of Jews still remained alive. Allied armies were converging on Germany and the doom of Nazism and its leaders was certain. Brand explained that Eichmann had told him, in the presence of Dr. Kastner, the representative of the Jewish Rescue Committee, that if 10,000 trucks were made available to Himmler, the expulsion of Jews to the Auschwitz death camp would be stopped. Brand insisted that if he could return to Budapest with the reply that the offer was being seriously considered, the "mills of death would stop grinding." Jewish representatives urged that despite all natural skepticism the macabre offer should be treated as genuine. There was an objective possibility that Himmler was seeking to curry favor with the advancing Allies by belatedly saving Jewish lives.

On July 6, Weizmann and Sharett carried their plea to the Foreign Secretary, Anthony Eden, whom they found maddeningly hesitant. His main argument was that "there must be no negotiations with the enemy." Weizmann admitted that "the Gestapo offer must have ulterior motives. It is not impossible, however, that in

In the home city of
Kafka only names and
dates appear on the
mourning scroll of
Czechoslovak Jews
murdered in Nazi
concentration camps.

the false hope of achieving their ends they would be prepared to
let out a certain number of Jews, large or small. The whole thing
may boil down to a question of money and the ransom should
be paid."

On the following day Weizmann urged the Foreign Office to
approach the Royal Air Force with the proposal to bomb the
death camps at Auschwitz. He admitted that this measure might
do no more than delay the extermination. But the bombing "would
have a far-reaching moral effect. It would mean that the Allies
waged direct war on the extermination of the victims of Nazi
oppression." "Secondly," he added in a parenthesis of terrible
import, "it would give the lie to the oft-repeated assertions of
Nazi spokesmen that the Allies are not really so displeased with
the action of the Nazis in ridding Europe of Jews."

The Foreign Office was living in a moral vacuum, of which the
White Paper was both a cause and an effect. Brand's mission was
allowed to fail despite Eden's assurance to Weizmann that there
would be no objection to his returning to Europe. And on September 1, the Foreign Office informed Weizmann that his proposal
for the bombing of the death camps had been rejected by the
Royal Air Force "for technical reasons." Once again, British policy,
in the test of administrative action, had proved to be incongruous
with its stated aims.

The Jewish World in 1945

Jewry came out of the war orphaned. Six million of its people—
over a third of the prewar total—had perished. Utterly extinguished were the hundreds of Jewish communities which had represented the centers of national consciousness and creativity, its
cultural and spiritual resources. East-European Jewry had been the
people's heart, the source of its vitality. For centuries, the great
majority of Jewry's spiritual leaders had either lived there or
originated there. From Eastern Europe had come the giants of
Biblical learning. In Eastern Europe were the great academies of
Talmudic studies. Many of the originators of the Zionist idea, and
the architects of the Zionist movement, the *halutzim*, the writers
and thinkers, had hailed from Eastern Europe.

Poland had become a Jewish graveyard. Before the war large
and virile Jewish communities had existed in some two thousand
cities and villages in Poland alone. In August 1945, a census carried out in that country showed that Jews were to be found in

only 224 places. Almost 90 per cent of the communities had been completely obliterated from the map. And those that remained were pale, weak, debilitated shadows of former glory.

The total Jewish population before the war, in the countries of Europe which were later occupied by Nazi Germany, was 9,800,000. Of these, at least six million were killed. In Poland, whose former Jewish population had been 3,300,000, fewer than 74,000 remained in 1945. Of 356,000 in Czechoslovakia, only 14,000; of 156,000 in Holland, fewer than 20,000.

The Germans had not only killed millions of individuals; they had destroyed innumerable communities, the sources of new Jewish life, of values, of learning. Those who survived had run the gamut of existence at the brink of death: beatings, starvation, thirst, inhuman labor, degradation, loss of family, and the constant reminder that their turn was next. At the end of the war, in May 1945, Europe was chaos—politically, economically, morally, and spiritually. The Jewish situation everywhere was still insecure, not only physically, but psychologically. The Jews had never been made so fully aware of their exposure to the whims of human depravity. The shock was even more intense after the bloodbath had ended, when there was time to digest and reflect upon what had come to pass.

Equally confounding was a resurgent anti-Semitism. This phenomenon, far from dying out after the war, had now become intensified. New pogroms broke out against those who had presumptuously survived. Now a desperate urge seized these survivors to flee from Europe, that cursed and bloody continent. But opportunities for large-scale immigration remained few; no country, not even America, was prepared to jeopardize its peace for these people. Who might or might not enter became a matter of careful selection. And Palestine, the one pre-eminent goal for most survivors, was closed to the Jews. So they were forced to linger on in internment camps and provisional homes, dreading to be cut off again from the rest of Jewry. The approximately three hundred thousand Jewish survivors became a "huddled, homeless humanity," most of them grouped together after the war in DP camps. They had not yet recovered from the scarring experience of human degradation. They were hounded by memories of waking nightmare, memories which they could not begin to forget so long as they still remained in the very countries which had perpetrated such atrocities upon them.

They were afraid. Afraid of the Germans, from whom they

asked to be separated by a barbed wire around the camp. Neurotically afraid of having to remain where they were, in the country of the people who had murdered their families. Afraid of the growing manifestations of anti-Semitism all about—an anti-Semitism that was too deep-rooted, too ingrained by Nazism, to be overcome within a few years. They were afraid to put their faith in the Americans or British, or in any other European nation which offered them assistance or permission to enter their countries. They could not trust the people about them. Indeed, they distrusted the world; they distrusted humanity and its promises.

There was no initiative or will to improve conditions within the camps. There was no future there. To tidy a room, install curtains in the window, to work—this was an act of submission to the miseries of the present. This the refugees refused to do. A pathetic but obstinate determination to survive made them assert that each day in Germany must be lived as though it were the last, when food is eaten hurriedly, when bags are packed ready for the journey out of the Land of Bondage and into the Promised Land.

An ardent urge overtook these homeless survivors to emigrate to Palestine. Hitler had made them nationalists. It was, they reasoned, because they had no land of their own that six million of them had been inhumanly slaughtered. Although they were aware that Jews lived happily in some lands, they had suffered too much to take another chance. They were too tired to attempt a new life in a place where, someday, someone might cry, "Jew, get out!" It was unimportant to them that life in Palestine was hazardous and uncertain. Whatever was involved, they would rather die in Palestine than live in Poland or Germany. For had not Hitler taught them that they were not Poles or Germans, but merely members of the Jewish nation, despised and rejected by "civilized Europe"? Far away in Palestine, a National Home was eager to receive them and offer them a chance to rebuild their own lives as Hebrews in their own land. To judge by the sober realities of Europe, they had no other hope but in a Jewish Palestine.

*A*T THE END of the Second World War the curtain went up on the burned and mangled bodies of six million Jews, including a million children. The Jewish people had fallen victim to the most fearful agony which had ever beset any nation or group of people. A whole continent was saturated with its blood and haunted by its unexpiated sacrifice. But as the world rose from the ravages of the Second World War, it came perilously near to creating an injustice more heinous than any which had been eliminated by the triumph of the Allied cause. It became horribly but seriously possible that every nation would be granted its freedom, among those which had suffered under the heel of tyranny, except the people which had suffered the most. All the victims of tyranny would be established in sovereignty, except the first and the most sorely ravaged among the targets of persecution. If the world order had been established upon this discrimination, it would have been conceived with an intolerable measure of guilt.

From this spiritual peril the community of nations cleansed itself belatedly, perhaps a little too grudgingly, but nevertheless decisively, when it ordained and later recognized the establishment of the State of Israel. The process was long and arduous by which the acknowledgment and satisfaction of the Jewish claim to equality pressed itself upon the conscience of the human family; it was attended on the one side by heartbreak and occasional despair, on the other by hesitation, postponement, and even outright deception. That finally it issued, in an act of universal equity, is a tribute to the deepest ethical motivations of the international society, and to the indomitable will of a people newly risen from the most horrible blood-letting the world has ever witnessed.

Betrayal by
the Labour
Government
When the war ended, the Jewish situation, both in and out of Palestine, indeed appeared hopeless to Chaim Weizmann, who in 1945 wrote to Churchill, shortly before Churchill's defeat at the polls:

> The position of the Jews in liberated countries is desperate. The political position in Palestine is becoming untenable. And so is my personal position as President of the Jewish Agency. This is the hour to eliminate the White Paper, to open the doors of Palestine and to proclaim the Jewish State.

Churchill's short unhelpful reply of June 9, 1945, made the situation even more desperate:

> My dear Dr. Weizmann,
>
> I have received your letter of 22 May, enclosing a memorandum on behalf of the Jewish Agency for Palestine. There can, I fancy, be no possibility of the question being effectively considered until the victorious Allies are definitely seated at the Peace Table.

Weizmann had invested endless hope and toil in Churchill and Roosevelt. By the summer of 1945, Roosevelt was dead and Churchill swept from power. The two had been endowed with unchallengeable powers to set the Jewish cause on the road to consolation and recovery. They had not used these powers. When they left the scene which they had dominated for six years, the Jewish people stood at the lowest point of its historic fortune—stunned with anguish, ignored, rebuffed, with no glimpse of light ahead.

The new Labour government was committed to a pro-Zionist program. Its policy, as formulated by Hugh Dalton only a few months before, had bravely declared, "There is surely neither hope nor meaning in a Jewish National Home unless we are prepared to let Jews, if they wish, enter this tiny land in such numbers as to become a majority. There was a strong case before the war. There is an irresistible case now after the unspeakable atrocities of the cold and calculated German Nazi plan to kill all Jews in Europe. . . ." The statement went on to propose a voluntary population exchange: "Let the Arabs be encouraged to move out as the Jews move in." However, Ernest Bevin was appointed Foreign Secretary, and he proved hostile to Jewish national survival.

At his first meeting with the new Foreign Secretary, on October 10, 1945, Weizmann found him in irritable resentment at President Truman's proposal for the admission of 100,000 Jewish "displaced persons" from Europe. The President's suggestion to the Prime Minister, Mr. Attlee, had been made in August on the basis of a report by his special emissary, Earl G. Harrison, who had visited the concentration camps where the Jewish survivors lingered on in dull despair. "They want to be evacuated now," said Harrison. "Palestine is definitely and pre-eminently the first choice. . . . Only in Palestine will they be welcome and find peace and quiet and be given an opportunity to live and work."

Not only did Bevin negate Truman's proposal, but he issued a statement of policy wherein he refused to cancel the White Paper, repudiated the Labour Party's Conference Statement of December 1944, observed that "we cannot accept the view that the Jews should be driven out of Europe," and announced the appointment of an Anglo-American Committee of Inquiry to consider the position of the Jews in Europe and to propose a solution to the two governments. Bevin's callous statement burst the dikes of Jewish restraint. British troops and Jewish resistance groups were now in almost daily conflict in one place or another on Palestine soil. The Zionists focused more hope on American intervention.

The Anglo-American Committee issued a report which advocated that the White Paper be abolished; 100,000 immigrants should be admitted into Palestine at once, land restrictions be removed, and Palestine be prepared for trusteeship with no statehood either for the Jews or the Arabs. Admittedly, the report rejected Jewish long-term proposals for a sovereign state, but with a great infusion of Jewish immigrants and a broadening of the territorial structure, the prospect of establishing a Jewish State seemed to many observers to have been enhanced. Yet, far from accepting this unanimous report, Bevin rejected it, saying that its implementation would require American military aid; he also insisted on the disarming of the Jewish population. Thus the Labour government, in cold cynicism, succeeded in dispelling the hopes of rescue which the Anglo-American report had raised in the hearts of tens of thousands of Jewish refugees.

The Zionist movement was entering a short but crucial phase of intense conflict with Britain. At Basle, in December 1946, the delegates to the Zionist Congress, the last which Weizmann attended, were torn between a deep affection for his person and a conviction that he symbolized a policy which both they and he no longer upheld, but with which a stubborn mythology had identified him beyond repair. The fact is that their resentment against Britain was as nothing compared with his. They felt politically frustrated. He felt personally as well as nationally betrayed. But a statesman remains a symbol of an attitude long after the attitude itself has passed away.

Yet Weizmann's presence dominated the Congress. In his opening address, he cast a glance inquiringly over the assembly, as if to wonder where German, Polish, Hungarian, Dutch, and Belgian Jewry had gone. His voice was choked, his eyes tense and painful behind the dark glasses. "The greatest malice in the annals of inhumanity was turned against us and found our people with no hope of defence. . . . European Jewry has been engulfed in a tidal wave. Its centers of life and culture have been ravaged, its habitations laid waste." He spoke of the White Paper: "Few documents in history have worse consequences for which to answer." He told of British ministerial promises which he had frankly believed: "It seemed incredible that anybody could be playing fast and loose with us when we were so battered and exhausted." He did not deny the existence of a strong anti-British current in the sentiment of the Jewish people: "If there is antagonism directed against the British government, its sole origin is indignation at Britain's desertion of her trust." He spoke lucidly of Arab hostility: "How can it be moderate for them to claim seven states and extreme for us to claim one? Sympathy belongs to those who have suffered. Restitution is the desert of those in need. The Arab people cannot compare with us in suffering and need."

Early in the next year, after Weizmann's despairing resignation, talks were held again with Britain in a last attempt to reach an agreement—this time, on the basis of partition. Not for a moment did Bevin allow a conciliatory mood. Discussion ranged from the proposal of partition, which Bevin professed himself unentitled to impose, to various federal schemes based on the Morrison Plan which Bevin had amended ferociously to the detriment of the Jews. While constantly asserting that it would be wrong under partition to place 300,000 Arabs under Jewish "domination," Bevin declined to explain why it would be right, under his proposal, to subject 700,000 Jews to the domination of the Arabs. On February 18, 1947, the following public announcement was made:

His Majesty's Government have of themselves no power under the terms of the Mandate to award the country either to the Arabs or to the Jews, or even to partition it between them. . . . We have therefore reached the conclusion that the only course open to us is to submit the problem to the judgment of the United Nations.

The Yishuv: 1946 and 1947

By 1946, the atmosphere in Palestine was volcanic. The small nation of Jews in Palestine had sweated and toiled to reclaim its promised homeland. They had given all their mental and physical energy to the rebuilding of their land. They could not conceive the surrender of this home. It was their last historic station.

The *yishuv* was dominated by a sense of unity in a common cause. In the Histadrut, the Haganah, the Jewish Agency, in the humblest settlements, all dreamed the same dream of the homeland. There was a common bond within the *yishuv* and an inextricable knot which bound it to the Jews of the Diaspora and particularly to the survivors of the Second World War. The British authorities had been sending intelligence units all over Europe to ascertain when refugee boats were scheduled to depart, so as to intercept their arrival in Palestine. They used diplomatic pressure to interfere with the purchase, fueling and departure of ships. A hunt began in Europe for the organizers of *Mossad*, the illegal immigration organization. Activities had to be shifted frequently from one port area to another, from Greece to Albania, and thence to Italy and France. Nevertheless, in less than three years the *B'riḥah* (flight) movement had emptied the DP camps, rescued from countries in the east all the Jews still able to leave and sent them to Palestine.

Meanwhile, in Palestine, the British government was perfecting plans to crush Jewish resistance. By a concentrated "purge" of the settlements, mass arrests, disarming of the Haganah, the detention of Jewish Agency executive members and widespread military operations, Britain hoped to shake the *yishuv* to its very core and to place the entire structure in danger of collapse. They underestimated the strength, purpose, and determination of the *yishuv*. At one extreme were the "dissidents" whose strategy ranged from personal violence to guerrilla tactics; at the other was the pacifist wing, which opposed physical violence and urged political effort coupled with unauthorized immigration. The majority, despondent and hesitant, stood between the two extremes, grappling with the issues posed by the "activists" and "anti-activists," the extremists and the moderates, those who supported violence and those who were ready to enter the fray solely in defense of immigration and land settlement.

Collisions with authority became increasingly more drastic. On June 18, 1946, the Haganah blew up eight bridges on the Palestine frontier and paralyzed communications with neighboring territories. This operation was the crowning act of an organized struggle against the White Paper administration in Palestine. Ten days later, the British authorities launched their own action against the *yishuv*. A strict curfew was imposed, and widespread military operations were launched against the *yishuv*, the Jewish Agency, and the Haganah, which were accused of organizing and conducting acts of violence against the government. Armored cars cruised along the deserted thoroughfares. British infantry patrolled the sidewalks, while now and again warning shots were fired into the air to keep people well indoors. Jewish Agency executive members were arrested—Moshe Sharett, David Remez, Itzchak Gruenbaum, Dov Joseph, Rabbi Fishman. All those arrested were moved to the detention camp at Latrun.

The *yishuv* was tense and helpless, confined indoors with only telephone and radio to connect it to the outside world. In an act of political identification with the detainees, it was decided not to set up any new official leadership lest such action be misinterpreted as surrender. Communication by a secret code was inaugurated with the detained leaders at Latrun, and daily reports were relayed to them. Their replies—sent along the same grapevine—contained instructions, ideas, impressions, and news of the camp. Contact was maintained in this way until the day of their release. All relations with the Mandate government were suspended. Overseas communications were also established with David Ben Gurion and Eliezer Kaplan. Moshe Sneh went underground with other Haganah leaders. Arrests, searches, and extensive military operations were the order of the day throughout the country. Settlements were surrounded by cordons, and painstaking searches for concealed weapons were made in every corner. Hundreds of young men were arrested and taken to concentration camps in Rafa, Atlit, Latrun, and Eritrea. Quantities of arms and ammunition were discovered and impounded, especially at Yagur, where, after a pro-

longed search, British troops unearthed a large arsenal of mortars, machine guns, and other weapons. The *yishuv* knew that its only hope lay in whatever arms it possessed, and that its defensive power would be destroyed if it were disarmed.

The *yishuv* regarded British policy as arbitrary and cruel, imposed by force, without moral or legal basis, on a tormented people at the gravest juncture of its history. The situation was now untenable. Continued British hints that the Jews in Palestine should become a minority under Arab rule were viewed by the *yishuv* as a sentence of extinction. There had been too many disastrous examples of Jewish minority existence in other countries.

The resistance groups continued their activities; on July 22, 1946, a section of the King David Hotel in Jerusalem, where the civil and military administrations of the Mandatory government had their headquarters, was blown up. Most Jews in Palestine were angered by this and other acts by the "dissidents," who had also wrought fiendish murders on many Jews, Arabs, and Britons. A nagging helplessness, sorrow, bewilderment, and oppressive anxiety set in during the days after this action. The crisis reached its height in August, when British authorities began the expulsion of refugees from Palestine to Cyprus. At first, it had been the practice to intern the unauthorized newcomers in special camps in Palestine until their turn for release came under the monthly immigration quotas. But this arrangement was apparently unsatisfactory to the authorities, and reports began trickling through of the establishment of detention camps on the island of Cyprus. Large forces of the navy, army, and air force had been mustered for this purpose. The first expulsion of Jewish refugees to Cyprus was carried out under a curfew, behind barbed wire and under army guard. Additional expulsions later provoked a series of clashes between the army and police and the *yishuv*'s forces, the Haganah, and the refugees themselves. Several attempts were made by Haganah frogmen to blow up the ships engaged in refugee expatriation.

Four months after their initial arrest by the British, the detained Jewish Agency leaders were freed. Armed resistance and British reprisals were mounting. The situation appeared menacing. The downhearted *yishuv* then suffered a further blow. An immigrant ship sank at sea and the rescue of its passengers was attended by great difficulties. As the sinking ship went down, the people on board scrambled ashore on a barren, lonely island in Greek waters, without food or clothing and exposed to severe winter cold.

Aliyah: A part of the remnant that was saved from the Holocaust sights the Promised Land in 1949.

This incident provoked still greater feeling in the country, and profound anxiety as to what might next develop. Relations with the government were strained. Even though Britain had given humanitarian assistance in this case, the whole affair was seen as the agonizing result of British policy.

At the
United Nations

As long as the League of Nations had existed, Jewish diplomatic activities with regard to Palestine had revolved about its Permanent Mandates Commission. But within the League the Mandates Commission was weak, and therefore had no practical influence on mandatory policy. The outbreak of World War II ended the effective life of the League of Nations.

On April 2, 1947, the British government asked that the question of Palestine be put on the agenda of the United Nations, declaring its inability to propose any concrete policy and thus leaving the whole question in the hands of the General Assembly. Under the circumstances, this decision was welcomed by some Zionists and feared by others.

For some time prior to the calling of the United Nations' special session, democratic public opinion had been uneasy at the prospect of a discussion of the Palestine problem in a forum in which the Jewish people were not represented. This discomfort also extended to leading officials of the United Nations. When the special session met on April 28, it was immediately faced with a request by the Jewish Agency for Palestine, as the representative Jewish body recognized under the Mandate, for participation in the deliberations. In its note, the Jewish Agency made it clear that the deliberations of that session were of great importance to it and that it was only just that the Jewish Agency be allowed to participate. Following the request of the Jewish Agency, other organizations, Jewish and non-Jewish, made similar demands.

Independently of the Jewish Agency, a plea for the admission of a representative of the Jewish people for consultation with the United Nations was made by several delegates. Mr. Wineiewicz, the Polish delegate, viewed the question as follows:

> The difficulty arises out of the fact that the Egyptian proposal and others suggest in a most decisive form the termination of the Palestine Mandate, even before we have heard the opinion of the most interested party, the Jewish people, for which the Mandate in Palestine provided special rights. We cannot, therefore, vote

for the inclusion of this additional item at this special session of the General Assembly of the United Nations. We shall abstain from voting, urging at the same time that this committee should take up as soon as possible the admission of a Jewish representative body for consultation with this Assembly.

Another clear expression of the problem was put forward by Mr. Asaf Ali of India:

> ... today, and yesterday also, we are playing Hamlet without the Prince of Denmark. Where is Palestine here? Where are the people whose actual rights we have got to consider? Where are the great representatives of the Jewish people who are also interested in this problem?

The problem was not easily solved. The General Assembly had never admitted non-governmental organizations at political discussions, the petitions and communications of such bodies having been heard by a special subcommittee. Now the Assembly found itself charged with unfairness toward the Jewish Agency, which had had no opportunity to be heard, whereas the Arabs, through their member states, had taken an active part in the preliminary proceedings. Their sense of fair play offended by these proceedings, the leading powers now underwent a change in attitude with regard to the question of organized non-governmental access to the General Assembly. After much deliberation, a resolution was passed by an overwhelming majority for the granting of a hearing to the Jewish Agency. The representatives of the Jewish Agency for the special hearing were immediately appointed: David Ben Gurion, Dr. Abba Hillel Silver, Moshe Sharett, Hayim Greenberg, Mrs. Rose Halprin, Nahum Goldmann, Dr. Emanuel Neumann. It was made clear to these representatives that they were to state their views only on the subject that the General Assembly was then debating, namely, the constituting and instructing of a special committee to deal with the Palestine issue.

As a result of these hearings, the General Assembly established the special committee on Palestine, the UNSCOP. Over strenuous Arab objections, the UNSCOP decided to link its investigation with a careful study of the situation of the displaced persons. At a meeting held before its tour, the question of Arab-Jewish cooperation was fully discussed by the special committee. Ben Gurion expressed the Jewish standpoint:

> A Jewish-Arab partnership, based on equality and mutual assistance, will help to bring about the regeneration of the entire

Middle East. We Jews understand and deeply sympathize with the urge of the Arab people for unity, independence and progress, and our Arab neighbors, I hope, will realize that the Jews in their historic homeland can, under no conditions, be made to remain a subordinate, dependent minority as they are in all other countries in the Diaspora. The Jewish nation in its own country must become a free and independent state with a membership in the United Nations. It is eager to cooperate with its free Arab neighbors to promote economic development, social progress and real independence of all the Semitic countries in the Middle East.

Mr. Chairman, I most earnestly suggest to your committee that the real, just and lasting solution of the problem before you is a Jewish State and a Jewish-Arab alliance.

The Jewish Agency representatives further urged the special committee, while in Palestine, to look into the real and fundamental causes of the unrest there: the unfair and tragic restriction on immigration, the unjust and severe restrictions on Jewish settlement as imposed by the Mandatory government, as well as discriminatory racial laws.

The Arab speakers, in their turn, constantly stressed the great danger which the Palestine situation posed to the cause of peace and security in the Near East and in other parts of the world. They stated that the desire of the Jews for a National Home, should, in view of this, not be granted. If the Jews should receive Palestine, they said, war would result.

The Jewish case was presented to the special committee by only three spokesmen (Dr. Silver, Ben Gurion, and Moshe Sharett). In view of the restrictive rules on the granting of a hearing, the presentation of its case by the Jewish Agency was concise and rather limited. No real opportunity was granted for entering into any detailed discussion and rebuttal of the numerous anti-Jewish arguments. The Jewish case was a legal one, based on the Balfour Declaration and the Mandate for Palestine. Dr. Silver urged that these international commitments, which had flowed from the recognition of historic rights and of present needs, and upon which so much had already been built in Palestine by the Jewish people, could not now be erased. Both Dr. Silver and Mr. Sharett were emphatic in their contention that the purpose of the Balfour Declaration and the Mandate was the establishment of a Jewish State. Dr. Silver cited Lloyd George's own words given before the Palestine Royal Commission in 1937:

There could be no doubt as to what the Cabinet then had in their minds. It was not their idea that a Jewish State should be set up immediately by the Peace Treaty. . . . On the other hand, it was contemplated that when the time arrived for according representative institutions to Palestine, if the Jews had meanwhile responded to the opportunity afforded them . . . and had become a definite majority of the inhabitants, then Palestine would thus become a Jewish Commonwealth.

The Arab spokesmen sought strenuously to destroy the legal foundations of the Jewish case. They defied the legality, as well as the moral, human, and political validity of the Mandate, which they had never recognized. The Jewish Agency tried to outline the justice of Jewish claims to Palestine. The Arabs sought to disprove and disqualify these claims, rather than present an independent justification of their own case.

The majority of the governments did not express their sympathies on behalf of either of the directly interested parties in the Palestine issue. While there was a group which solidly supported every move in the interests of the Arab Higher Committee, no such group existed to support the Jewish position. So far as the Jewish aspect of the problem was concerned, several states, particularly among the Slavic and the South American groups, expressed their sympathy with the Jews and stressed their sufferings, especially during the Nazi occupation. Some, such as Norway and South Africa, went further and emphasized the link between the fate of the insecure Jews and Palestine. Poland, Czechoslovakia, and, in a more qualified manner, the Soviet Union and China, expressed their sympathy and understanding for Jewish national aspirations. The Soviet Union abandoned a long anti-Zionist tradition to hint at the possibility of support for an independent Jewish state.

Upon its arrival in Palestine, the UNSCOP was greeted enthusiastically by the *yishuv*. During its sojourn, a dramatic event occurred which cast a shadow over the deliberations and shed new light on the tragedy accompanying the debacle of the Mandate. "Exodus 1947," largest of the refugee vessels, was forcibly returned to Europe by the British authorities after a bitter fight at Haifa. As the wretched immigrants languished in agony at a small French port, refusing to leave the ships which later took them back to the DP camps of Hamburg, the members of UNSCOP sailed off to Geneva, amid mountains of files, testimony, and theories.

Some members of the committee had been present at Haifa and witnessed the squalid spectacle of the Jewish refugees being violently returned by British troops to the "Exodus." It was not surprising that the first recommendation of the entire committee upon its return to Geneva was that the Mandate come to an end. The death of the Mandate had in fact been advocated by those who had given it birth—Churchill, Smuts, Weizmann. It only remained to prescribe an alternative arrangement. The majority suggested a partition scheme which included the Negev in the Jewish State. At midnight on September 1, 1947, the report proposing partition was handed to the Jewish Agency representatives, Abba Eban and David Horowitz, in the *Palais des Nations* at Geneva. Although this was an authentic turning point, it was only potentially decisive. If the committee had rejected the Jewish case, the United Nations would never have adopted a favorable recommendation. Now that it advocated Jewish statehood, there was at least a chance for General Assembly endorsement. A splendid gleam of friendship had lit up the darkened corner of Jewish solitude.

The arena now shifted to United Nations headquarters where the most crucial political struggle in modern Jewish history was joined. Everything depended on the possibility of gaining American and Russian support of the committee's proposal. By mid-October it was plain that American and Soviet support could be counted on. But even then, a two-thirds majority was not automatically assured. Vast efforts were made to persuade the uncommitted and wavering delegates who were being shaken by the strong blasts of Arab pressure. The aging Weizmann was responsible for two great achievements: the retention of the Negev area in the United Nations' plan for a Jewish State, and the spectacular recognition of Israel by the United States. He rose from his sickbed for a talk with President Truman to convince him that the southern Negev must not be excluded from the Jewish State, as was the announced intention at the time. Weizmann buttressed his case with the following memorandum:

> Akaba, which is found on the southern end of the Negev and the Red Sea, represents the only outlet for the Jewish State to the Indian Ocean, India, the Far East, Australia and New Zealand. For the Jewish State this outlet will be one of the most important routes for commercial relations with that part of the world. The Jewish State, in order to absorb the refugees coming from Europe, will have to do its utmost to develop its industrial and commercial capacities and in this connection the importance of Akaba is much greater than just a piece of land on the Red Sea. . . . Akaba in the hands of the Arabs, may be a permanent threat in the rear of the Jewish State. The Arab States have an outlet to the Red Sea and the Gulf of Akaba through Transjordan, Egypt and Saudi Arabia.

Truman was convinced. The struggle for the Negev ended in victory. The way was now clear for the final decision. In the desperate, unforgettable weekend of 27–29 November, the Jewish delegation threw itself into the frenzied pursuit of wavering votes. When the prospect of French abstention threatened to disrupt the West European front, Weizmann cabled Léon Blum, summoning the Socialist statesman to a supreme effort: "Does France really wish to be absent from a moment unfading in the memory of man?" On the 29th of November, France added its vote to the others in favor of partition. There were many other capitals in which governments wrestled with conscience and interest in a spirit of sharp responsibility.

Prelude to War On November 29, 1947, the United Nations General Assembly in a session at Flushing Meadows passed its resolution on the partition of Palestine. The vote was thirty-three to thirteen with ten abstentions; the required two-thirds majority had been exceeded. The majority included the United States, the Soviet Union, many European states, most of the Latin American countries and members of the British Commonwealth. Britain, on whose initiative the UN had taken up the Palestine issue, abstained.

The majority had rallied around the basic ideas which had inspired the Peel Commission a decade before. The alternatives were to subject Palestine Jewry to Arab domination or to establish a defined framework for its independent development. The first choice would involve the affirmation that Arabs must be sovereign wherever they are—the Jews nowhere at all. If an Arab minority lived under Jewish rule this would not destroy the very concept of Arab national freedom, which had expression in seven sovereign states, soon to become thirteen. On the other hand, if Palestine Jewry became a minority, Jewish nationhood would be repudiated forever. The international community took the line of lesser injustice. Its verdict was enhanced by a sense of guilt toward the people whom the United Nations had been unable to save from horrifying disaster. Many communities were to enter the United Nations whose attributes of nationality were no more salient than those developed by Palestine Jewry. The *yishuv* was already a state in all but name. Some delegates had spoken in a mood of historic emotion about the nobility of Israel's return to the family of nations. Others looked forward to the fascination of a distinctive Jewish contribution to the emerging world society. Some argued, on prag-

Israel Is Born

443

matic grounds, that the *yishuv* was too big to be swallowed by the Arabs, and too vigorously dissident for subjection to international rule. Many were impressed by a cause capable of bringing the United States and the Soviet Union together in a common vote.

The discussion enacted on a broad international stage before the gaze of world opinion was pitched on a distinguished note. It was a high moment for the Jewish people, as well as for the United Nations which had not known an occasion of similar elevation. Palestine Jewry passed overnight from the status of an unconsidered rebel to that of a nation on the verge of recognized statehood. The partition plan was complex and tortuous. Its frontiers were of serpentine intricacy. Jerusalem was to be an international enclave, and the new Jewish and Arab states were to be linked in economic union. But the central theme of the 1947 resolution was the innovation of Jewish sovereignty. All else might change, but this concept was now an integral element of the international experience.

A wave of joy swept the *yishuv* when the news came. There was dancing through the streets of Tel Aviv, Jerusalem, and Haifa. But there was little time for celebration. Dawn brought the first shots and the first victims. The Arab Higher Committee announced a general strike; an Arab mob burned and looted in Jerusalem. The road to the Jewish State was to be long and full of blood and tears.

The population of Palestine in 1947, according to the figures of the Mandatory government, consisted of 1,200,000 Arabs, 650,000 Jews, and 150,000 "others." The number of Arabs may have been exaggerated, while the number of the Jews was almost certainly higher, as some "illegal" immigrants who had managed to reach Palestine did not appear in the records of the Palestine government. It is difficult to assess the military strength of the Palestinian Arabs at the outbreak of the hostilities. They had no professional military force, nor a unified command of their various military and para-military organizations. One the other hand, they had a substantial manpower potential and considerable quantities of arms.

The Palestinian Arabs believed that terrorism would undo the UN resolution. They also placed great hopes in the help to be received, in the form of arms, money, and men, from the surrounding Arab lands.

The Arab states, divided politically, economically, and socially, held widely divergent opinions on the Palestine question. Syria had never forgotten that Palestine had been part of its territory under Ottoman rule. As a minimum, Syria wanted to annex the "finger of Eastern Galilee," thus getting the Jordan sources under her control. For Egypt, the Palestine question was of secondary importance. Her primary political aims were the evacuation of the British from their bases in the Suez Canal zone and the annexation of Sudan. Lebanon did not take her participation in the Arab war seriously; because of her economic weakness, she was interested, above all, in self-defense. Saudi Arabia had no common frontier with Palestine and was not interested in military intervention. Most directly concerned with Palestine was Transjordan, where King Abdullah considered the Jordanian throne a springboard for a great Hashemite Kingdom, including Palestine. Abdullah's hopes were pinned on the Arab Legion, a strong force of well-trained men supplied and officered by Britain, and under the command of Glubb Pasha. Iraq, too, though lacking a common border with Palestine, was interested in gaining access to the Mediterranean through Haifa, where the Mosul pipeline ended.

But despite the diversity of their motives, the Arab states were united in one respect: they were all opposed to partition. In October 1947, the Arab League held a meeting at which resolutions were adopted requesting members to take military measures along the borders of Palestine and to support the Palestine Arabs in their struggle. The most significant resolution in connection with the various military preparations by the Arab League obliged all Arab states to absorb the Arab population which might be evacuated from Palestine, in case of military operations undertaken by the Arab armies in that country.

As for the *yishuv*, the bulk of the military forces at its disposal were organized in the Haganah. In addition, there were the two dissident underground groups, the *Irgun Zvai Leumi*—National Military Organization—and the Stern group—*Lohamei Herut Israel*, Fighters for the Freedom of Israel. Both these groups had a limited membership and their impact on the all-out war which now confronted the *yishuv* was relatively small. The primary objective of the Haganah was defense. The special unit of *Palmach* (striking force) consisting of 2100 men and women, with 1000 on active reserve, had to undertake the more dangerous operations, such as raids on enemy bases, headquarters, and lines of communications.

In weapons and equipment the Haganah fell grimly short of the Arab forces. The weapons which had been purchased abroad and smuggled into the country were a motley collection. A few underground workshops manufactured a small number of grenades,

Sten guns, and mortars. But the size of the Israeli arsenal was of secondary importance. What mattered was the will to survive. This spirit found expression in the military instrument of the *yishuv*— the Haganah and *Palmach*—an instrument which proved superior to the military might of the enemy. It inspired the improvisations, the sudden adjustments, and the sense of unity which gave the Israelis an advantage not only on the battlefield, but also in every community, settlement, and home.

In 1947, as in 1921 and 1936, the Arabs openly initiated hostilitics, hoping to achieve their political ends by violence. The unofficial war lasted from November 29, 1947, to May 15, 1948, and was characterized by Arab attacks on Jewish settlements and harassment of the lines of communications. Riots were a part of daily life in Palestine at that time. It was Haganah policy to hold onto even the most isolated settlements, which had to be supplied with food and arms in order to withhold attack. Arab assaults were concentrated on the convoys bringing food and manpower to the outlying villages. The Arabs were able to score successes against these Jewish transports, and they thereby threatened the network of communications in the Jewish-held areas. Within a single week, a convoy on its way to the isolated settlement of Yechiam in the western Galilee was ambushed and forty of its defenders killed; another convoy, returning from Kfar Etzion, was attacked on its approach to Jerusalem; two other convoys trying to reach Jerusalem were ambushed and badly battered. Thus, many of the armored cars at the disposal of the Haganah were destroyed in one week. Their skeletons on the roadside leading to Jerusalem are reminders to this day of the battle for Hulda and Etzion, for Jerusalem and Yechiam.

All this happened during a period when Britain was still responsible for the maintenance of law and order and had pledged responsibility for defending the lines of communication. In reality, the British attitude was one of weighted impartiality, mostly favoring the Arabs. Despite the ambushes on the roads, Jewish convoys were searched for weapons; Haganah men were frequently arrested, and the hunt for illegal immigrants continued while hundreds of armed Arabs were daily crossing the land frontiers of Palestine. The economic structure of the Arab population was such that Arabs were less dependent on road communications. And the "sympathetic neutrality" adopted by Britain enabled the Arabs to operate with ease, while it hindered the Jews.

The youthful courage and spirit of the defenders of Israel. A soldier stands guard on the desert near the Dead Sea.

The first round of the fighting ended with considerable Arab success. Though unable to capture any Jewish settlements, the Arabs had caused widespread disruptions of Jewish communications. Some parts of the *yishuv* were almost cut off from the center. Moreover, there were indications that the Arabs were about to achieve their political goal, the abolition of the partition resolution of the United Nations, by demonstrating that it could only be implemented by force. In March 1948, when the United States suddenly withdrew its support for the partition scheme, it looked as if the Arabs were approaching their objective.

They intensified the fighting. Under British eyes, Arab volunteers from across the border moved into Palestine in January 1948. The first battalion of Arabs from Transjordan was soon followed by others. The "Arab Liberation Army," under the command of Fawzi-el Kawakji, began attacking Jewish settlements in the North.

Despite its defeats, the Haganah prepared for the day when it could seize the initiative and transform the military situation to its advantage. Purchase of arms in Europe, especially in Czechoslovakia, was speeded up. Almost 1200 Jews, half of them civilians, had died since the beginning of the war. In March, the Haganah High Command prepared a comprehensive operation, "Plan Dalet," the purpose of which was both simple and revolutionary: "to gain control of the area allotted to the Jewish State and defend its borders and those of the blocs of the Jewish settlements and such Jewish populations as were outside those borders or inside the area of the Jewish State."

April 1948 was largely devoted to the *Nachshon* operation, the opening of the road to Jerusalem. The success of this difficult and bloody operation, coinciding with the successful defense of the *kibbutzim* Mishmar Ha'emek and Ramat Johanan, was a turning point in the war. In the same month, military operations on a large scale were undertaken by the Haganah. Tiberias, Haifa, and Upper Galilee were liberated. On the other hand, after a gallant battle against the Arab Legion, the Etzion bloc fell to the tanks of the Arab Legion on May 13. Communications with the isolated settlements in the Negev was maintained by precarious improvisation.

During the weeks before May 15, the Haganah was able to increase the quantities of small arms in its possession. A first ship carrying Czech arms arrived and was unloaded. Negotiations for purchases of further arms were hastily undertaken.

But whoever surveyed the military position on May 14, 1948, was bound to look to the future with very grave concern. The question was whether the Jewish forces could withstand the four regular Arab armies—the Egyptian, Jordanian, Syrian, and Lebanese —now joining the battle. These were fresh, well-organized according to the pattern of regular armies, and were also well-equipped. Two of them possessed tank units. All of them had field artillery regiments. Three had air forces with fighter squadrons, and Egypt had a squadron of bombers. The Haganah was unable to match this impressive superiority of Arab arms. It had exactly four field guns, a single tank, and a single fighter plane in addition to a few private planes. The first battle with an Arab regular army at the Etzion bloc had ended disastrously.

Meanwhile British evacuation was going on apace. The organs of the Mandatory government had ceased operations on May 1. Officials whose services would still be required for the liquidation of administrative and financial problems were transferred to Cyprus; others returned to Great Britain. Administrative authority had not been transferred. And a vacuum was created. This was the chaos which certain British officials had predicted ever since the partition resolution. Trains had stopped running, Palestine was no longer a member of the International Postal Union. The police had been disbanded. Judicial process had been suspended. On May 21, 1948, Yigael Yadin, Chief Operations Officer of the Haganah, surveyed the military situation:

> We will not discuss the problem whether or not there will be an invasion. We have been planning all this time on the assumption that an invasion will take place. Our information indicates that it is a certainty. Our plans for such an invasion are simple: all our forces and all our arms—all of them—will have to be concentrated in those places which are likely to be battlefields in the first phase of the battle.
>
> The regular forces of the neighboring countries—with their equipment and their armaments—enjoy superiority at this time. However, evaluation of the possibilities cannot be merely a military consideration of arms against arms and units versus units, since we do not have those arms or that armored force. The problem is to what extent our men will be able to overcome enemy forces by virtue of their fighting spirit, of our planning and our tactics. It has been found in certain cases that it is not the numbers and the formations which determine the outcome of battle, but something else. However, objectively speaking, there is no doubt that the enemy enjoys a great superiority at this time.
>
> Our Air Force cannot even compare with theirs. We have no Air Force. The planes have not arrived yet. It is possible that they

may yet come on the decisive day, but I cannot rely on that. Even then, if the neighboring Arab countries activate their Air Forces, a comparison will be invidious. Their Air Force is a hundred and fifty times the size of ours. At this moment, our planes operate contrary to all the rules of aerial tactics.

No other pilots would dare to take off in planes like ours. The planes are antiquated and obsolete, some of them are patrol planes or trainers; even with these planes we have had grievous losses, and we are now in a poor state, so it would be best not to take them into account as a military factor.

To sum up, I would say that the outlook at this time seems delicately balanced. Or—to be more honest—I would say that their superiority is considerable, if indeed their entire forces enter battle against us.

Israel Is Born

The skeleton of an ambushed armored car on the road to Jerusalem. During the 1948 war these armored cars tried to pierce the Arab lines to bring supplies to the besieged defenders of the Holy City. Each Independence Day, Jerusalem schoolchildren commemorate their efforts by placing wreaths of flowers against their burned-out metal flanks.

The successes of the Haganah in the first weeks of May had the effect of sowing confusion among the Arabs. In spite of Jewish victories, however, the political situation remained favorable to the Arabs. Arab "liberation troops" poured in from all sides to reinforce the revolt of Palestinian Arabs against the United Nations resolution. The British administration, formally responsible for law and order, held the door open to the Arab incursions with one hand, while with the other it proceeded to harry the desperate defense of the Jews. As it became apparent that the Arabs would not peacefully acquiesce in partition, second thoughts began to grip many members of the UN who had supported the plan. In Washington, the State Department repented of its partition policy on the very morrow of its adoption. It is difficult to describe the choking suspense in which Jewish life was lived during the winter of 1947–1948. The community in Palestine was under violent attack by Arab invaders. The British authorities neither protected the Jews, as they were legally bound to do, nor allowed them freedom of self-protection as moral duty commanded. The commission, established to carry out the partition plan, languished impotently in New York. Both political collapse and military defeat appeared to be imminent. The 19th of March was to become known in Jewish diplomacy as "Black Friday." Warren Austin, the American Ambassador to the UN, addressed the Security Council with a sensational request. All efforts to implement partition should be suspended. The General Assembly was to be convened in special

session to work out a plan for temporary trusteeship. The dream of Jewish statehood, which had illuminated the preceding winter, was now to be shattered.

The American withdrawal from the partition plan convinced the Arabs that they did not have to take quick military decisions. The Arabs also had second thoughts about the Jewish war potential, which they had come to respect. Arab military commanders suggested a postponement of the invasion, while the politicians of the Arab League insisted on immediate invasion after the expiration of the Mandate, on May 15. A military plan was drawn up on the assumption of a "blitz" attack. The Arabs had not enough ammunition and reinforcements for a prolonged war. The Jewish settlements in the interior were to be isolated from the coast, their only source of reinforcements and supplies.

But internal conflicts among the Arab states prevented the military "master plan" from being put into operation. King Abdullah withheld his consent from the plan, fearing that the conquests of his Arab Legion would be worthless if afterward he found that he had to defend the existence of his kingdom against his Arab enemies, above all the Mufti. In secret negotiations held with the Jewish Agency in October 1947, Abdullah had agreed to the annexation of Arab Palestine by his forces without making war. The Jewish Agency Executive decided early in May 1948, to reach an agreement with the King on that basis. Golda Myerson (now Golda Meir), disguised as an Arab woman, met King Abdullah in the house of a friend in Amman. Abdullah did not deny his former promise, but claimed that the situation had changed. "Then I was alone. Now, I am one of five." However, if the Jews agreed to refrain from proclaiming the establishment of a State, stopped immigration, and agreed to his annexation of the whole territory of Palestine, he might influence the "moderates" among the Arab leaders to abstain from war. His proposal was rejected.

In Palestine, the last High Commissioner prepared for the end of the Mandate. He was adamant in refusal to permit the orderly handing over of authority. British policy was to avoid doing anything which might be construed as cooperating with the UN resolution. There was to be non-cooperation to the last moment in the setting up of the Jewish State. Railways ceased to run. The post ceased to function. Official files were burnt. The assets of the State were transferred to England, offered for auction, or turned over to the Arabs. Though there had been a substantial surplus, not a penny was left in the Treasury for the use of a successor government.

The Jewish leaders carefully planned their independent administration. Committees were formed to deal with various administrative departments. Provisional stamps and currency were printed, and a complete proto-administration was established. At the beginning of April, a National Council numbering thirty-seven members was set up, composed of the elected members of the World Zionist movement resident in Palestine, and executives of the *Vaad Leumi* and of other public bodies. The council appointed a National Administration, answerable to itself. They authorized an internal loan; set up a manpower and supply organization; and brought about an agreement between the Haganah and the dissident organizations for full cooperation in military operations.

On May 14, 1948, Sir Alan Cunningham, the High Commissioner, with the last of his staff, left the soil of Palestine. From a cruiser outside territorial waters he signaled the end of the Mandatory era. It had been born in high exaltation. It had now expired in chaos and discredit. In a short ceremony at the Museum of Tel Aviv at 4 P.M. that day the State of Israel was born. Two hundred forty men witnessed a new page in Jewish history, as David Ben Gurion read the Proclamation of Independence:

ERETZ-ISRAEL [the Land of Israel], was the birthplace of the Jewish people. Here their spiritual, religious and political identity was shaped. Here they first attained to statehood, created cultural values of national and universal significance and gave to the world the eternal Book of Books.

After being forcibly exiled from their land, the people kept faith with it throughout their Dispersion and never ceased to pray and hope for their return to it and for the restoration in it of their political freedom.

Impelled by this historic and traditional attachment, Jews strove in every successive generation to re-establish themselves in their ancient homeland. In recent decades they returned in their masses. Pioneers, *ma'apilim* [immigrants coming to Israel in defiance of restrictive regulations], and defenders, they made deserts bloom, revived the Hebrew language, built villages and towns, and created a thriving community, controlling its own economy and culture, loving peace but knowing how to defend itself, bringing the blessings of progress to all the country's inhabitants, and aspiring toward independent nationhood.

In the year 5657 (1897), at the summons of the spiritual father of the Jewish State, Theodor Herzl, the First Zionist Congress convened and proclaimed the right of the Jewish people to national rebirth in its own country.

This right was recognized in the Balfour Declaration of the 2nd November, 1917, and reaffirmed in the Mandate of the League of Nations which, in particular, gave international sanctions to the historic connection between the Jewish people and Eretz-Israel and to the right of the Jewish people to rebuild its National Home.

The catastrophe which recently befell the Jewish people—the massacre of millions of Jews in Europe—was another clear demonstration of the urgency of solving the problem of its homelessness by re-establishing in Eretz-Israel the Jewish State, which would open the gates of the homeland wide to every Jew and confer upon the Jewish people the status of a fully-privileged member of the comity of nations.

Survivors of the Nazi Holocaust in Europe, as well as Jews from other parts of the world, continued to migrate to Eretz-Israel, undaunted by difficulties, restrictions and dangers, and never ceased to assert their right to a life of dignity, freedom and honest toil in their national homeland.

In the Second World War, the Jewish community of this country contributed its full share to the struggle of the freedom- and peace-loving nations against the forces of Nazi wickedness and, by the blood of its soldiers and its war effort, gained the right to be reckoned among the peoples who founded the United Nations.

On the 29th November, 1947, the United Nations General Assembly passed a resolution calling for the establishment of a Jewish State in Eretz-Israel; the General Assembly required the inhabitants of Eretz-Israel to take such steps as were necessary on their part for the implementation of that resolution. This recognition by the United Nations of the right of the Jewish people to establish their State is irrevocable.

This right is the natural right of the Jewish people to be masters of their own fate, like all other nations, in their own sovereign State.

ACCORDINGLY WE, MEMBERS OF THE PEOPLE'S COUNCIL, REPRESENTATIVES OF THE JEWISH COMMUNITY OF ERETZ-ISRAEL AND OF THE ZIONIST MOVEMENT, ARE HERE ASSEMBLED ON THE DAY OF THE TERMINATION OF THE BRITISH MANDATE OVER ERETZ-ISRAEL AND, BY VIRTUE OF OUR NATURAL AND HISTORIC RIGHT AND ON THE STRENGTH OF THE RESOLUTION OF THE UNITED NATIONS GENERAL ASSEMBLY, HEREBY DECLARE THE ESTABLISHMENT OF A JEWISH STATE IN ERETZ-ISRAEL, TO BE KNOWN AS THE STATE OF ISRAEL.

WE DECLARE that, with effect from the moment of the termination of the Mandate, being tonight, the eve of Sabbath, the 6th

Iyar, 5708 (15th May, 1948), until the establishment of the elected, regular authorities of the State in accordance with the Constitution which shall be adopted by the Elected Constituent Assembly not later than the 1st October, 1948, the People's Council shall act as a Provisional Council of State, and its executive organ, the People's Administration, shall be the Provisional Government of the Jewish State, to be called "Israel."

THE STATE OF ISRAEL will be open for Jewish immigration and for the Ingathering of the Exiles; it will foster the development of the country for the benefit of all its inhabitants; it will be based on freedom, justice and peace as envisaged by the prophets of Israel; it will ensure complete equality of social and political rights to all its inhabitants irrespective of religion, race, or sex; it will guarantee freedom of religion, conscience, language, education and culture; it will safeguard the Holy Places of all religions; and it will be faithful to the principles of the Charter of the United Nations.

THE STATE OF ISRAEL is prepared to cooperate with the agencies and representatives of the United Nations in implementing the resolution of the General Assembly of the 29th November, 1947, and will take steps to bring about the economic union of the whole of Eretz-Israel.

WE APPEAL to the United Nations to assist the Jewish people in the building-up of its State and to receive the State of Israel into the comity of nations.

WE APPEAL—in the very midst of the onslaught launched against us now for months—to the Arab inhabitants of the State of Israel to preserve peace and participate in the upbuilding of the State on the basis of full and equal citizenship and due representation in all its provisional and permanent institutions.

WE EXTEND our hand to all neighboring States and their peoples in an offer of peace and good neighborliness, and appeal to them to establish bonds of cooperation and mutual help with the sovereign Jewish people settled in its own land. The State of Israel is prepared to do its share in common effort for the advancement of the entire Middle East.

WE APPEAL to the Jewish people throughout the Diaspora to rally round the Jews of Eretz-Israel in the tasks of immigration and upbuilding and to stand by them in the great struggle for the realization of the age-old dream—the redemption of Israel.

PLACING OUR TRUST IN THE ALMIGHTY, WE AFFIX OUR SIGNATURES TO THIS PROCLAMATION AT THIS SESSION OF THE PROVISIONAL COUNCIL OF STATE, ON THE SOIL OF THE HOMELAND, IN THE CITY OF TEL-AVIV, ON THIS SABBATH EVE, THE 5TH DAY OF IYAR, 5708 (14TH MAY, 1948).

No man was more instrumental in establishing a Jewish state in Palestine than Chaim Weizmann. Now, he had lived to see his efforts crowned with success; "a people which had been divorced from its original homeland for some eighteen centuries" had come home once more.

David Ben Gurion

Daniel Auster	Golda Myerson
Mordekhai Bentov	Nachum Nir
Yitzchak Ben Zvi	Zvi Segal
Eliyahu Berligne	Rabbi Yehuda Leib
Fritz Bernstein	Hacohen Fishman
Rabbi Wolf Gold	David Zvi Pinkas
Meir Grabovsky	Aharon Zisling
Yitzchak Gruenbaum	Moshe Kolodny
Dr. Abraham Granovsky	Eliezer Kaplan
Eliyahu Dobkin	Abraham Katznelson
Meir Wilner-Kovner	Felix Rosenblueth
Zerach Wahrhaftig	David Remez
Herzl Vardi	Berl Repetur
Rachel Cohen	Mordekhai Shattner
Rabbi Kalman Kahana	Ben Zion Sternberg
Saadia Kobashi	Bekhor Shitreet
Rabbi Yitzchak Meir Levin	Moshe Shapira
Meir David Loewenstein	Moshe Shertok
Zvi Luria	

When the proclamation had been read, its signatories advanced to the table to give it their sanction. The Hebrew benediction was recited. "Blessed art Thou, O Lord our God, King of the Universe, who hast kept us alive and preserved us and enabled us to see this day." The two hundred and forty filed out into the sun-drenched street. The air-raid sirens were sounding. A new and revolutionary date had been added to the calendar of Jewish history.

At the General Assembly in New York, Dr. Silver broke in on the committee's debate to announce that the State of Israel had been established. In the White House, President Truman sat with his secretaries of State and Defense, Marshall and Lovett, deliberating on a letter from Dr. Weizmann asking for recognition of the Jewish State. At 5:16 P.M. President Truman authorized the recognition of Israel by the United States. American diplomacy had taken an audacious and visionary course.

The news of President Truman's recognition broke like a thunderbolt on the representatives of the UN in the General Assembly. It astounded the American representatives themselves. The Soviet Union was next to grant recognition. The next morning, the young State of Israel was plunged into war. As Egyptian planes bombed the Tel Aviv area, the first immigrant ship brought detained "illegals" to the shores of a free country. In twenty-four hours a

Mandate had ended, a State had been proclaimed and recognized, and an armed invasion launched. It was the most crowded day in modern Jewish history.

By the end of March 1948, Jerusalem was besieged, cut off from contact with the coast except by a single-engine training plane that landed on an improvised air strip.

What the city lacked in equipment, food, and water, it had to replace by morale. There is a very thin line between panic and the capacity of a civilian population to endure the hardships of daily bombardment, hunger, and lack of water. Jerusalem's population found the median line. The darkest moments of the war were turned into the city's deliverance.

The ordeals which Jewish Jerusalem had to endure were beyond pessimistic forebodings. In April, when the city was still under the vigilance of the Mandatory Power, a convoy of medical staff, professors, and students, making its way to the Hadassah Hospital and the Hebrew University on Mount Scopus, was attacked and almost all were killed. On May 28, the Jewish quarter of the Old City fell to the Arab Legion troops.

In the New City, all the duties of the municipal and governmental bodies had been taken over by the Jerusalem Emergency Committee. During the winter of 1947–1948, the committee improvised services, from schools to radio broadcasting, from mail to water distribution. The English-language newspaper, *The Palestine Post*, never failed to appear, though it sometimes had to resort to mimeographed editions. In addition, the Jerusalem staff of the major Hebrew newspapers put out a Hebrew paper, *Yediot Yerushalayim* (News of Jerusalem). A radio station was improvised which functioned throughout the war, though its broadcasts could be received only on battery-run radios. The supply of electricity was erratic. Jerusalemites resorted to boy scout methods of cooking. Electricity could be supplied only to the most vital institutions. Transformers and connecting lines were maintained at great risk. One line, cut twelve times during a single night, was restored to service just as often. The shortage of food, water, and fuel overshadowed other concerns. The scarcity of supplies was ominous. Famine was a serious prospect.

Water had ceased to flow through Jerusalem's pipes. It was brought to the householders in water tanks mounted on trucks.

At first, the water ration was two gallons per day, of which scarcely four pints were drinking water; eventually it was cut down to six quarts per day.

When the last convoy in Operation *Nachshon*, which opened the road to Jerusalem, reached the city with its supplies on April 20, it was estimated that Jerusalem could survive for four more weeks. But the rations were stretched to last eight full weeks. With the road to Jerusalem blocked by the Arab Legion at Latrun, it became desperately imperative to find an alternate route to the coastal plain.

This road was planned and carved out of the rocks of the Judean mountains in secrecy while Jerusalem was still under siege. Engineers, bulldozers, and stonecutters worked diligently for many nights clearing a path through the mountains. Finally, the entire track was passable save for a stretch about one and a half miles long which was precipitously steep and covered with boulders. But there was no time to be lost. A new method of operation was devised: empty trucks were sent from Jerusalem to the edge of the ravine. There hundreds of men walked to the terminal of the supply trucks coming up from the south, and each of these men carried a forty-five-pound sack of flour over the hillside in the dark, each man holding the shirttail of the one ahead. A pipeline was laid down the hill for bringing fuel from the vehicles at the top to those waiting on the Jerusalem road.

The road was gradually improved. By the time of the first truce, Israel's Marcus Road—named for the American Colonel, David Marcus, who had commanded the Jerusalem sector—had broken the siege of Jerusalem by providing new access to the beleaguered capital.

The War of Liberation

Within eight hours of Israel's declaration of independence, the Arab armies had begun their invasion. From the north came the Lebanese; from the northeast, the Syrian armies; the Arab Legion and the Iraqi forces attacked at the center; and from the south, the Egyptian army moved up, supported by bomber planes. In a swift move, the Egyptians reached a town only twenty-two miles south of Tel Aviv, bypassing the few isolated settlements in the Negev. Impressive chapters in the story of Israeli resistance were written by the settlers of these Negev outposts. Negba, Nirim, Bet

Through the intricate swirls of barbed wire that separate Jewish and Arab sectors in Jerusalem, the Tower of David rises white and glittering in the bright hot sunlight.

Eshel, Revivim, Sa'ad, Be'erot Yitzchak, held out against attacks by infantry, artillery, armor, and aircraft. They defended themselves with rifles and mortars, refusing to surrender even when the enemy came within yards of their communities.

A decisive moment in the northern campaign came with a heavy armored assault on the Jordan Valley settlements, south of the Sea of Galilee. The Syrians had captured a police station on the outskirts of Deganiah and were within inches of conquering the Jordan Valley. The settlers of Deganiah pleaded with Premier David Ben Gurion for artillery. Two 65 mm. guns and a few shells arrived at the *kibbutz* just as the Syrian attack began. Five tanks had already broken through the settlement perimeter. The first was destroyed when one of the settlers ran out from the defense ditch and flung a Molotov cocktail through the turret, killing the crew. Another was knocked out by a flamethrower. Three other tanks were disabled. As the defense at Deganiah stiffened, the Syrians faltered and suddenly withdrew. This was on May 20. It marked a turning point in the War of Liberation. It seemed that the Arab forces had been convinced that they could move across Palestine without serious opposition. The resistance which they encountered surprised and confused them.

The next chapter of the war was written in the political arena. While Arab armies invaded Palestine, the Security Council met to debate whether a breach of peace had taken place, as the Americans charged. The Americans demanded sanctions and a cease-fire; Britain opposed. Arab delegates promised peace only if Israel's independence were rescinded. The Israeli answer was brief. "If the Arab states want peace they can have it. If they want war they can have that too. But whether they want peace or war, they can have it only with the State of Israel." On May 24, the provisional government of Israel announced its readiness to accept a cease-fire. The Arabs did not consent until thirteen days later, when their armies were near exhaustion. The cease-fire finally went into effect on June 11, 1948; Count Bernadotte, the United Nations mediator, established his headquarters on the Island of Rhodes.

The Arab armies had failed to gain any of their objectives. But the picture on the Israeli side was far from heartening. The invading armies still held more than one third of the territory allotted to the Jewish State by the United Nations. In the north, the Syrians were entrenched on the western banks of the Jordan; in the center, the Iraqis, at one point, were only ten miles from the Mediterranean; Jerusalem was without ammunition. The Israel Defense

Army *Z'va Haganah LeIsrael*—which had been formally established, was in urgent need of reorganization.

The publication of the mediator's tentative proposals for a permanent settlement caused great anger both in Israel and in the Arab states, with the exception of Transjordan to which Bernadotte proposed to give the Negev and Jerusalem. (Abdullah's Arab Legion had failed to take the New City of Jerusalem in a month of bitter onslaught and the Negev was in the hands of the Egyptians.) Bernadotte also proposed that Israel and Transjordan become a dual state, holding fiscal, foreign, and military policies in common. He secured British and, briefly, American support for his plan. But it was rejected by Israel and the Arab states on contrary grounds. The plan was based on the fallacy that a solution could be imposed on the parties from outside. Count Bernadotte's mission failed. His proposals for the prolongation of a truce were rejected by the Arabs, and on July 8, twenty-eight hours before the expiration of the truce, the Egyptians decided to reopen the war.

But the truce had transformed the military situation. Israel had been able to enlarge the number of its combatants—who now included almost 2500 volunteers and recruits from abroad. But the Arab armies, too, had increased considerably. Even more striking was the change in equipment. The Egyptians had managed to replenish their stocks of ammunition from British dumps in the Canal Zone. Israeli equipment had changed out of all resemblance to the resources of a month previously. The Israelis now had some tanks, some artillery, and a sufficient number of small arms. During the ten days of fighting before the second truce took effect, the Israelis scored important victories in the north and on the central front. This time, the British representatives at the United Nations pleaded for haste in fixing a cease-fire. There was urgent need to rescue the Arabs from their reverses.

When the second truce went into effect on July 18, there had been thirty-eight days of fighting. The Israelis had captured fourteen Arab towns and 201 out of 219 Arab villages within the area of the Jewish State. The Arabs had captured fourteen Jewish sites, including the Jewish quarter of the Old City of Jerusalem. Only one settlement captured by the Arabs, Mishmar Ha-Yarden, was within the area allotted to the Jewish State.

The second cease-fire, like the first, failed to bring peace. The Egyptians occupying the south, contrary to the truce conditions, refused to let supply convoys reach the settlements in the Negev. Repeated appeals to the UN mediator failed to bring results. The

Egyptian aim was to cut the Negev off from the main body of the State of Israel. On October 15, a convoy going south was attacked by Egyptian fire at the formal cross point. This was the signal for an Israeli decision to break through and to bring relief to the outlying *kibbutzim*. In the ensuing battles, the Israeli army made great advances. In the north, Kawakji's Liberation Army used the opportunity to attack. But in an operation which lasted sixty hours, he was driven out into Lebanon. The whole of western Galilee was now in Israel's hands.

The last operation in the Negev took place in December. This time, Israeli troops crossed the international border into Egypt; the Egyptians surrendered on all sides, and the Israelis were within grasp of the largest Egyptian army base, at El Arish. At this moment, the Egyptians received help from unexpected quarters. Britain saw in this threat to Egypt cause for invoking the Anglo-Egyptian friendship treaty of 1936. Shortly after Israeli forces crossed the frontier, Britain sent an ultimatum to Israel, calling for her immediate withdrawal from Egyptian territory. The Israelis called an enforced retreat, but on the way back threatened to take El Arish, in an action which would have cut a wedge between Egypt and the Gaza Strip. Now the Egyptians hastily announced their willingness to enter into armistice negotiations. On January 7, 1949, the fighting between Israel and Egypt was halted.

On January 13, armistice negotiations between Egypt and Israel began on the Island of Rhodes. The delegates of the two governments met face to face across the table on the morrow of their arrival with the mediator, Dr. Bunche, as their elected chairman. He had succeeded Count Bernadotte, who had been assassinated by terrorists in Jerusalem. The Israeli government had responded to this brutal act by summarily dissolving the dissident Jewish organizations. Dr. Bunche inherited his mission with equal courage and greater skill. When the Egyptian-Israeli talks ended, he invited representatives of the other Arab countries to join Egypt in armistice negotiations. Twenty months after the first Arab attack following the UN resolution, with the invading armies severely beaten, the war had come to an end.

Israel's victory stunned the world, and astounded even the Israelis themselves. It had cost the lives of 4000 soldiers and 2000 civilians—virtually an entire generation of the youngest and most vital members of the new state. But there had been no choice, and Israel's citizens had responded to the threat with the full

In a military cemetery outside of Tel Aviv a mother mourns her twenty-year-old son killed in the War of Liberation.

measure of their devotion. "If we are to condense all the various factors, and they were many, which brought about victory," said General Yigael Yadin, "I would not hesitate to credit the extraordinary qualities of Israel's youth, during the War of Independence, with that victory. It appears as if that youth had absorbed into itself the full measure of Israel's yearning, during thousands of years of exile, to return to its soil and to live in liberty and independence, and like a giant spring which had been compressed and held down for a long time, when suddenly released—it liberated."

22 ❧ *American Jewry in the Twentieth Century*

*B*Y THE END of the nineteenth century, Jews from Germany were
established in the American economy as contractors, retailers,
wholesalers, private bankers, manufacturers, and professionals.
They enjoyed the prestige of their status. The arrival of masses
of immigrants from Eastern Europe troubled their serenity. Though
willing to aid them through the establishment of charitable institutions, they made vain efforts to stem the tide of immigration, or
at least to divert the newcomers to the interior of the continent and
into agriculture.

The East-European immigrant was in a more difficult position
than his German coreligionists who had preceded him in mid-
century. Adaptation was difficult. Few could take up the ancient
occupations of peddler or pawnbroker in the ghettos of New York,
Philadelphia, Chicago, or Boston. The majority had to become
workers in "sweatshops." The immigrants suffered the inhuman
conditions of labor which characterized American industry in the
1880s. Only with the arrival of Jewish workers and intellectuals
who had been active in organized workers' movements abroad did
the situation improve.

The sweatshop system was difficult to accept in a land which
symbolized opportunity. The Jews, as foreigners, could be exploited
without arousing the traditional American spirit of social justice.
From their own midst there arose leaders who began to work for

467

better conditions. Their efforts did not go unopposed. The prominence of Jews in the trade-union movement and in socialist thought identified Jews with radicalism and anarchism. However popular Jews in the labor movement were to become in the 1930s, by the end of the nineteenth century they were viewed with animosity.

Despite the hardships that surrounded him, the Jewish immigrant's standard of living was never lower than in his home country. The pressure of the sweatshop and the squalor of the tenement were oppressive. So was the feeling of insecurity and tension in a strange land. But there was always the hope of saving enough money to give children an education and to secure the benefits of freedom. Most immigrants operated in the determined conviction that their present status was temporary. And, indeed, it was. The sons and grandsons of workers became entrepreneurs and entered the middle class. Every effort was made to save capital with which to open a small retail store or to buy sufficient stock to become a jobber or a contractor. By encouraging their children to take full advantage of free education in high schools and colleges, Jewish immigrants ensured their progeny a brighter career.

The Jews of the garment industry strove to improve sweatshop conditions through the establishment of trade unions. Still strangers to the language, they carried out the business of their unions in Yiddish. Their goals were simple: eight-hour workdays, decent pay, and abolition of the sweatshop and child labor. From the needlecrafts the labor movement branched out into other occupations. The United Hebrew Trades, founded in 1888, had among its affiliates, bakers, butchers, waiters, printers, teamsters, musicians, and actors. But the two large organizations which the movement created were in the clothing industry: The International Ladies' Garment Workers' Union and the Amalgamated Clothing Workers of America. Their struggle to end the sweatshop system benefited not only Jewish workers, but American workers of other faiths. In their fight for better conditions the unions organized strikes, some of which brought cruel suffering. The most famous uprising was the "great revolt" which began in July 1910 and lasted for two months. It ended with the "Protocol of Peace" concluded by the arbitrator Louis Dembitz Brandeis, later to become the first Jewish Justice of the Supreme Court. This arbitration made a lasting impression on Brandeis, who, through this experience, was drawn into Jewish affairs and activities.

By branching out into auxiliary services for their members, the Jewish unions became pioneers for the whole labor movement. They launched educational programs, instituted employment insurance,

American Jews in the garment industry led the fight
against sweatshop conditions early in this century.
Here, in 1915, a clothing workers' strike shows the
English, Yiddish and Italian signs of the picketing
Amalgamated Clothing Workers of America.

maintained health centers, and built low rental housing. Yet though the workers of that period were proletarians economically, it is difficult to associate them with a proletarian mentality. The conviction of each was that his present status was transitory. Psychologically the Jewish worker failed to adjust to his proletarian status. He was not class-conscious, nor did he wish his children to go into the sweatshops. At the first opportunity, he sought an outlet for individual enterprise.

As more Jews extricated themselves from the proletariat, radical and socialistic ideas receded in importance. By 1914 the Jewish immigrants were well on their way toward firm middle-class status. The Eastern European Jewish immigrant was neither the son nor the father of a proletarian. It was nevertheless through the efforts of this immigrant that the American proletariat in general found the means, and the will, to assert its strength and claim for itself the dignity of life in a free society.

Social and Cultural Patterns of Jewish Life

From the beginning of its life as a nation, America both advocated and legislated complete equality for its citizens. If there was social discrimination against Jews, this did not interfere with opportunities for work and study and the full exercise of citizenship. The only periods when anti-Semitism was felt strongly in America were periods of economic depression. But responsible American leadership and Jewish defense organizations have always been able to avert this threat effectively. Anti-Semitism, although a danger, has been a peripheral issue for American Jewry.

Rapid Americanization became the ardent wish of most new citizens. The immigrant generation up to World War I found it difficult to break the chains of tradition. It was torn between the desire for Americanization and the wish to preserve the human and Jewish values which it had brought from the Old World.

For the three million Jews who arrived in the United States between 1881 and 1924, the mother tongue was Yiddish. For more than five centuries, the thoughts, emotions, and dreams of millions of Jews in Poland and Russia had been expressed in that language. In the closing decades of the nineteenth century, Yiddish went through a literary and cultural renaissance through the works of such masters as Mendele Mocher Seforim, Sholom Aleichem, and I. L. Peretz. To the East Side of New York, the immigrant Jew transferred the cultural world of the old country. Together with the stream of immigrants there arrived thousands of teachers and writers, journalists and rabbis. These men could resume their professions in America without interruption. Their audience, their congregation, their public, had migrated with them. Yiddish theater and journalism, poetry and literature, now entered a new and American phase.

Like the Germans, Poles, Italians, Swedes, and Irish, Jewish immigrants tended to flock together. The newcomers moved gregariously into the "ghetto" areas of the city. As in the enforced ghettos of Europe, they found all needs provided: a *heder* for children; a kosher butcher; a synagogue around the corner. Thus, though living in a metropolitan area, the Jewish immigrant resumed the life of his small town in the Russian Pale or in the Polish village. His social life centered around the synagogue or the *landsmanschaften*—organizations, originally formed for mutual aid, which provided the framework for his social life. These *landsmanschaften,* which perpetuated the social structure of the native town in Europe, set up charitable organizations, built hospitals, took care of the old and the orphaned. All this took place within a tradition of Jewish philanthropy whose long history in the United States began with the demand of Peter Stuyvesant that the twenty-three refugees from Recife be admitted "on condition that they take care of their own poor."

America would not have fulfilled its promise had the children of these immigrants been forced to share the fate of their parents. What parents everywhere hoped for their children was offered to them in a land of seemingly unlimited opportunities. There was free education for all; and education opened the way into the professions. The children of the immigrants were eager to Americanize themselves as quickly as possible. They rejected the values associated with the Old World. Often, the same schools in which children studied during the daytime would serve as night schools for the older generation seeking an escape from the sweatshops.

The Yiddish press and stage offered rich cultural stimulation. Many writers who had achieved stature in the Old World joined their people in the New World and contributed to a literary, dramatic, and journalistic efflorescence which, among similar efforts by other immigrant groups in America, stands unsurpassed in scope and quality.

But interest could be maintained only as long as the first generation of Yiddish-speaking newcomers remained numerically significant. The strong attachment to Yiddish culture ceased with the second generation. Today it is nostalgically celebrated by the third and fourth.

There were two separate Jewish groups in the United States. The East-European immigrant parted company from the "German" Jew, the product of an earlier migration who had already become Americanized by the time the victims of the May Laws and the Kishinev pogroms arrived. The two groups inhabited two distinct worlds. But there arose a leadership in both segments of the community, ready to face common problems in collaboration. Though they were still not one, they learned to work together.

Community Organization

With the influx of East-European immigrants, America's German Jews soon became outnumbered. But their influence on the American Jewish community was hardly diminished. On the contrary, this group, which had become economically secure, took it upon itself to care for the "greenhorns." Through the initiative of the older community, philanthropic agencies were set up which extended their influence over the Jewish cultural agencies and fraternal orders that were to follow.

The immigrants from Europe were linked by a strong religious tie. Their faith branched out into three major groupings: Reform—for a long time the precinct of the "German" Jews; Conservative; and Orthodox. Until the end of the nineteenth century, scholarship had been "imported" to the new country from abroad. In the course of time, however, each stream added higher learning and scholarship to its program. Seminaries and rabbinical colleges were founded. The first permanent Jewish seminary in America was established by Isaac Mayer Wise in Cincinnati in 1875. A second liberal seminary was founded by Stephen S. Wise in 1922. The two schools were combined in 1950. At the same time, a number of American universities began to open departments of Jewish studies. In the Conservative movement, the central figure was Solomon Schechter, who joined the Jewish Theological Seminary in 1901. Mordecai M. Kaplan, head of the Teachers' Institute of the Seminary and later founder of the Reconstructionist movement, was the teacher of generations of rabbis, and a forceful influence in American synagogal life. In Orthodoxy, Yeshiva University, conceived in 1886, has grown from a rabbinic seminary and college to embrace a major university, including schools of medicine, social work, and education, as well as a faculty of higher Jewish studies.

The traditional and classical heder where Jewish children learn their Aleph-Bet under the alert eyes and pointing finger of the Orthodox melamed.

By the end of the First World War, the most important undertakings in the English language produced by Jewish scholarship were the monumental *Jewish Encyclopedia,* and a new translation of the Hebrew Bible prepared by the Jewish Publication Society. Most Biblical translations hitherto available in English had been made by Christian scholars. It was felt that their rendering differed greatly from the inherent spirit of the Scriptures.

For a long time the Yiddish press remained an important instrument of education. It introduced the immigrant masses into the history and institutions of their adopted country through the only language they understood. It taught them the meaning of American democracy and helped them to become naturalized. It promoted and did not retard their Americanization.

One factor which drew the diverse elements of American Jewry together was a common concern with the fate of Jews abroad. The defense of Jewish rights throughout the world had long preoccupied Americans. At various times the Jews had actively protested the infringement of those rights. Time and again the government of the United States had acted on behalf of the persecuted. In the 1840s there had been vigorous denunciations of the blood libel in Damascus; in 1858, of the Mortara case in Italy; later, of Swiss regulations discriminatory toward Jews; and of reactionary decrees in Rumania. The Dreyfus case in France had stirred American Jews to action. A long series of pogroms and discriminatory measures in Russia, Rumania, Morocco, and Austria elicited from them political, moral, and financial support for the victims. All these actions had been taken at the behest of *ad hoc* groups; the absence of a central body capable of speaking for all Jews had been deplored for some time. In the aftermath of the Kishinev massacres of 1905 the need for such a body became more acute. At this point it was decided that one voice should speak on behalf of American Jewry: this voice was initially to be that of the American Jewish Committee, founded in 1906.

But attempts to unite the Jewish citizens on a more encompassing basis remained unsuccessful. In 1909 an effort was made to unite New York Jews, who then numbered one and a half million, or one half of all of American Jewry, into one community, on the pattern of the Old-World *kahal.* Other communities were to follow suit, and thus put an end to the anarchy of Jewish life. Two hundred separate organizations in New York joined this new entity, which named itself the *Kehillah.* It embarked on a large and ambitious program. But the active life of the *Kehillah* lasted only about one decade. The unifying experiment soon came to an end. There was more to divide American Jewry than to unite it.

On one issue, however, the Jews of America were united: the need to give aid to their coreligionists in other parts of the world in times of need. In World War I, the plight of Jews in Eastern Europe confronted world Jewry with relief necessities of unprecedented scale. The Jews of America rose to the challenge. As early as November 1914, the American Jewish Joint Distribution Committee was created. The Joint became a beacon of hope for Jewish communities in many parts of the world, where distress and the havoc wrought by war called for relief and rehabilitation. The mission of the Joint did not end with the termination of hostilities. Indeed, it faced its hardest and most important tasks when the war was over. Its work was beset with problems which not only required the creation of specialized agencies and a far-flung network of activities in Europe but also an apparatus for the raising of funds. The Jews of America learned to give of their substance on a scale equaled by no other group in voluntary effort.

American Jews
and Zionism
(1897–1919)

In the two decades after the First Zionist Congress at Basle, Zionism did not play a spectacular role in American-Jewish life. American Jewry's share in the movement fell below its relative size and influence. Nevertheless, the issue of Zionism precipitated major tensions in the community. Some German Jews who had risen to wealth and influence rejected the idea of national restoration for the Jewish people. They believed that a Jewish State would undermine the position of Jews who were citizens of the lands in which they lived. The "Left" was even more adamant and vocal in its condemnation of Zionism. Labor leaders who embraced socialism saw in Zionism a deviation from the path of world progress. They labeled Zionism a bourgeois, parochial, and obscurantist movement; in this, they aligned themselves with the "Right" segment in its hostility to the "reactionary menace."

There were exceptions both on the Left and on the Right. Nor did the "center" form a solid bloc of support for the aspirations of the Zionist movement. A spiritual bulwark of Zionism was the Jewish Theological Seminary in New York, but it was so mainly by dint of the enthusiasm of its president, Solomon Schechter, who saw in Zionism a revitalized Judaism. Schechter inspired his students with his own convictions, and they in turn carried these convictions to the fast-growing Conservative congregations now ranged across the continent.

Zionism aroused greatest sympathy among the poor immigrants from Eastern Europe, for whom the restoration of a national home was a childhood dream, sustained by religious fervor. Their attachment was emotional; and the success of the movement filled them with growing excitement and a strong commitment to its aims.

At the beginning of this century, political Zionism began to make itself felt in American Jewish life. Parties were formed from Left to Right, from *Poalei Zion* to *Mizrachi* and the Zionist Organization of America (ZOA), which represented all shades of opinion and conviction. Until the outbreak of World War I in 1914 the Zionist Federation, the forerunner of the ZOA, was an "East Side" affair. But its outstanding leaders were not East-siders. Its first president was the professor of Oriental studies at Columbia, Richard Gottheil, and its first secretary was Rabbi Stephen S. Wise, who had turned down the office of Rabbi at Temple Emanu-El in New York City because the worshipers there had refused to listen to Zionist sermons. Another outstanding figure in the early period of Zionism was Louis Lipsky of Rochester, New York. Emissaries from abroad arrived in America as reinforcements to local leadership. The most persuasive were Nahum Sokolow and Shmarya Levin, who succeeded in drawing some of the foremost Jewish philanthropists into the orbit of Zionist activity.

The "parent" organizations gave birth to auxiliary bodies. *Hadassah,* the Women's Zionist Organization of America, founded in 1912, was to become the largest single Jewish movement in the United States, and indeed, in the Zionist structure.

At the First Zionist Congress in Basle in 1897, there was only one delegate from the United States. When the Eleventh Zionist Congress convened in Vienna in 1913, forty of the five hundred delegates were Americans. It was not a negligible contingent; and together with the twelve from Canada, it attested to the strides made by the movement in the New World.

American Zionists, together with the Joint Distribution Committee, were among the first to answer the urgent call for help which came from the *yishuv* in Palestine at the outbreak of World War I. The population of the *yishuv* at this time had grown to 85,000 most of whom still depended on the dole system of small donations from communities abroad. The number of pioneers who had settled on the land in farm colonies now approached 12,000. The fate of all these men and women was gravely menaced. The funds had ceased to flow with the outbreak of hostilities and the erstwhile recipients were faced with starvation. Nor were the economic afflictions caused by the war the sole cause for worry. The

Turkish government, suspicious of the loyalties of the Jews, arrested many and had the leaders of the *yishuv* exiled. Thousands of Jews, who were Russian subjects and hence Turkey's "enemies" in the war, were expelled. The war had also disrupted the activities of the *yishuv's* most important economical and political asset, the world Zionist movement.

The organized Zionist forces in America stepped in to redress the balance. An emergency fund was established which succeeded in transmitting urgently needed funds to Palestine. Louis Brandeis emerged as the leader of Zionism in America. Brandeis said: "To be good Americans, we must be better Jews, and to be better Jews, we must become Zionists." Brandeis gathered around him a group of influential leaders who became active in the cause of Zionism: among them Felix Frankfurter, who, in 1939, was to succeed Brandeis on the Supreme Court; the philanthropist Nathan Straus; Mary Fels of Philadelphia; Julian W. Mack, a judge of the United States Circuit Court; and many other prominent citizens and civic leaders. The Provisional Executive Committee not only kept Zionist institutions alive, but made it possible to send relief to Palestine and other parts of the Middle East.

Hadassah, established prior to the war, sent medical units of physicians, nurses, and social workers. Its work there is associated primarily with the name of Henrietta Szold, who was held by all in such deep affection that she was widely known as the "mother" of the *yishuv*.

The leaders of the Zionist movement in America played an important part in the negotiations which preceded the Balfour Declaration of November 2, 1917. President Wilson's approval, conveyed to the British Prime Minister, helped to tip the scales in favor of the Declaration against powerful forces in London arrayed in opposition to it. The Declaration was received in America with jubilant celebration. Even the American Jewish Committee, which had never identified itself with Zionism, issued a careful statement welcoming the Balfour Declaration.

The Zionist issue gave rise to demands that crucial Jewish questions be not the sole concern of the American Jewish Committee but be placed before a democratically elected Jewish Congress. Negotiations to bring opposing factions together lasted for years. The Congress did not convene until December 15, 1918, in Philadelphia, when the war was over. The Congress made three important decisions. The first was to send a delegation to Europe to cooperate with the representatives of Jews of other lands for the recognition of Jewish rights by the Paris Peace Conference. The

second was to instruct the delegation to cooperate with the World Zionist Organization "to the end that the Peace Conference might recognize the aspirations and historic claims of the Jewish people in regard to Palestine" as set forth in the Balfour Declaration, and might declare that such conditions should be established in Palestine as would assure its development "into a Jewish commonwealth." The third decision bore on the question of Jewish rights "in the new or enlarged states," which the Peace Conference might call into being.

In the early 1920s the American economy entered a phase of consolidation. The labor market reached an apparent saturation point. The United States acted to halt free immigration to its shores (Johnson Act, 1924). This development adversely affected the millions of Jews living in Poland and Russia. The fate of large Jewish communities in Russia, and later in Nazi countries, was thereby sealed.

The new immigration policy affected those who had been shut out. Those already living in America, however, continued to find ample economic opportunities. Swelling productivity and prosperity spawned myriads of new businesses. The vast growth of the white-collar occupations absorbed those with a higher education. The entertainment media, movies and radio, blossomed. The continued growth of higher education slowly opened jobs for teachers and scholars. The postwar decade saw the rise of a new Jewish middle class, composed chiefly of professional workers.

Jews were not prominent in all parts of the economy. Oil, steel, mining, the utilities, insurance, and the automobile industry attracted or allowed few Jews. Unofficial agencies imposed difficulties on the securing of jobs by Jews, in these pursuits. In some fields, professional societies even imposed a quota system. Such a system existed at almost every major university. A pattern of exclusion extended to the field of housing as well, closing whole urban areas to residents of "Hebrew descent."

Among the rows of crosses at an American World War II cemetery near Beja in Tunisia appears a white wooden Star of David over the grave of an American Jewish soldier.

Along with the rest of the population, Jews were hard hit by the Great Depression which began in 1929. But they could contribute to combating the ills of America's economy. Among the planners and administrators of the New Deal were many Jewish officials, economists, and lawyers.

In the time of the Depression and the New Deal, American Jewry was exposed to the most serious eruption of anti-Semitism in American history. Jews were accused of being the architects of America's disintegration. This anti-Semitism originated in the rural districts of the American South, whose inhabitants felt themselves in economic bondage to the cities, and above all to New York. The Jews were particularly connected with the city, and hence with finance. It was an easy step, when the need for a scapegoat was acute, to blame Jews for the economic disaster which the city had ostensibly wrought upon the rural areas.

Another precipitant factor in the rise of anti-Semitism was the development of racial prejudice. The argument that white Southerners had long used against Negroes could easily be applied to other groups as well. Unwilling to recognize the true sources of change in the old rural economy, Southerners began to blame the newcomers of "inferior" races for every ill. They demanded a restriction of immigration and a careful selection of those who knocked at the gates of the New World. The Jews were generally, although by no means exclusively, numbered among the unwanted immigrants. At the same time, the higher strata of society were suspicious of the Jews as competition. Retaliation often took the form of barriers against Jewish entry to vacation places, clubs, and societies. In some instances these social barriers were extended to other spheres, and Jews found themselves excluded from consideration for certain positions.

Many Americans accepted this pattern of discrimination, albeit with unease. World War I had thrown America back into chauvinistic isolation. "Patriotic" societies proliferated. The most ruthless of these was the Ku Klux Klan, whose membership by 1925 had reached four million. Its venomous hatred was directed against Negroes, Catholics, and Jews.

Anti-Jewish agitation became more virulent in times of economic depression, when currency was given to the myth of Jewish control of American finance. Investigations exposed the falsity of such accusations, but they did not always succeed in killing the myth. The rise of Nazism in Europe added fuel to anti-Jewish sentiment among Fascists in America. Jewish defense organizations were hard-pressed to cope with the problem of increased anti-Semitism. They were aided in their battle by inter-faith movements. But the main obstacle to the spread of anti-Semitic tendencies lay in the liberal traditions of the American people. With few exceptions, leaders in politics turned their backs on anti-Jewish demagogues, and joined in efforts to combat them.

The anti-Semitic movement of the 1930s is largely linked with the name of Father Coughlin. He argued that the Depression, which had caused havoc in the economy and wiped out savings, threatened now to unleash Bolshevism and anarchy. Bolshevism, he contended, was a system created by Jews. Father Coughlin's propaganda became more effective when Hitler's Germany began its persecution of Jews.

The virulent anti-Semitism of these years was especially ominous. It indicated that Jews were potentially more vulnerable than any other group in America. Jews found themselves bearing the brunt of responsibility for all visible ills. Then the measures passed by the New Deal proved effective, and the country was saved from collapse. An incipient American anti-Semitism was squelched. But the lesson had been learned: the position of the Jews in any society is only as secure as that society itself.

Escape and Return   Two or three generations ago, American Jewry was an enclave with transplanted institutions and ideologies which had little relevance to American life. Today the Jews are politically secure, economically prosperous, and culturally integrated. Their influence in the general society is greater than their numerical proportion would indicate. Constituting less than 3 per cent of the total population, they have made enduring contributions to America's economic, cultural, and intellectual life. In all fields of American culture during the past fifty years, they have originated decisive movements. Jewish playwrights, composers, actors, producers, and directors have made Broadway and Hollywood major institutions of American life. Among the country's most eminent philosophers, novelists, and artists are Jews who have won fame and distinction.

Thus, in less than a century, a mass of poor immigrants had become integrated into the American economy, attained a high level in its occupational and income structure, and became a significant factor in its spiritual life. This process has not been unattended by self-doubt; nor has it been completely free of confusion about Jewish identity. For the immigrant generation, which dominated the American-Jewish scene until the First World War, Jewishness was ingrained. This generation, however, was followed, between the two world wars, by a generation more vocal in its negation of Jewish values and more precipitate in its flight from Jewishness. Embracing every opportunity to assert its Americanism, this second generation fled the visible ghetto of its parents, only to erect about itself an invisible ghetto of mores and values. Many were obsessed by a feeling of insecurity and inferiority. "My dominant childhood memory," Meyer Levin has written, "is of fear and shame at being a Jew."

But flight from Jewishness was largely a second-generation phenomenon. Social forces were at work to change this pattern, and the upheavals of the 1930s and 1940s caused a resurgence of Jewish loyalties. The rise of Hitlerism, the plight of European Jewry, and Israel's fight for independence prompted American Jewry to a radical change of heart.

With the rise of Nazism in Germany, American Jewish organizations strove to alert public opinion to the approaching disaster. There were mass demonstrations and a boycott of German goods. The Zionist center had moved to America during the war. American Jewry became deeply involved in the aspirations of the *yishuv*. When Britain passed the Palestine question to the United Nations, the political battlefield was transferred to the country where the largest Jewish community lived and where the United Nations, providentially, had its headquarters. The Zionists no longer stood alone in their battle. Almost the entire Jewish community now worked to obtain the moral and political support of the American people and its government for Jewish aspirations in Palestine.

The Zionist movement had a persuasive and forceful spokesman in Rabbi Abba Hillel Silver, of Cleveland. He was a worthy successor to Louis Brandeis, who fought for the Balfour Declaration, and to Stephen S. Wise, who had kept the flame alive in the intervening years. Rabbi Silver, as chairman of the American section of the Jewish Agency, joined forces with Moshe Sharett, the Palestine Jewish spokesman, in leading the battle during the crucial debates at the United Nations. In November 1947, the General Assembly adopted the majority report of UNSCOP for the partition of Palestine. To be approved, the plan had to obtain a two-thirds majority. The Russian vote had been assured, but the United States, giving in to Arab pressures and to its own oil interests, was vacillating. All the influence and skill that the Jewish groups could muster was employed to win over the American delegation in favor of the plan.

During and after World War II, the American government was drawn more and more into the politics of the Middle East. Despite Middle Eastern considerations and its own formidable oil interests, it was moved to support Zionism and Israel. The Jewish vote was not always the prime inducement. Politics were often overruled by humanitarian impulses. At the time of the Balfour Declaration, President Wilson had disregarded the protests of State Department officials to give his approval to the Declaration. A Calvinist by heritage and temperament, Wilson found it agreeable to picture himself as the agent of Providence. As Stephen S. Wise remarked, "From time to time, it fell to Wilson to reach decisions on Jewish matters of gravest import. In reaching these decisions he never took counsel of expediency or self-seeking. He neither yielded to pressure nor consulted the hope of advantage. In all the discussions of Jewish problems covering nearly a decade, Wilson never in the faintest way indicated that he wished merely to please his Jewish fellow citizens, though I believe he rejoiced to be able to serve them and to have a part in the working out of Jewish destiny. A Christian in the Lincolnian sense, he respected self-respecting Jews, and I noted with unconcealed delight his scant patience with such Jews as imagined that they were 'forced to frame excuses for their birth.' "

The same impulse may have operated in 1948, in President Truman's decision to extend immediate recognition to the infant State of Israel. American public opinion had been deeply affected by the plight of the DPs, as well as by the struggle of the *yishuv* against overwhelming odds. A strong inclination for justice took precedence over other considerations. Deep chords of sympathy had been struck with a people battling for independence in its homeland. The formal recognition of the Jewish State was the inevitable result. Israel was rarely to find itself without United States support for its central interests.

Thus, the latent Jewish loyalties of the American Jewish community had come to the fore during the crisis. They would emerge again in later trials. The urgent need for action had crushed all dissension. American Jewry organized its power to help the resettlement of the survivors of the Holocaust and to give moral and political support to Israel. The benefit was mutual. A sense of dignity, security, and pride in collective achievement was American Jewry's reward for its intimate cooperation with Israel.

The Future of American Jewry

The growing strength of American Jewry ranks with Israel's statehood among the two most formative events in twentieth-century Jewish history. Never in that history had any Jewish community achieved a similar numerical size or a corresponding power and freedom to intervene in the events which shaped Jewish destiny. Despite the growth of liberation and tolerance, American Jews

were staunchly identified with the preservation of Jewish life and culture in its separate arenas of creativity. American society, as a whole, respected the particular solidarities of United States Jewry and its preoccupation with Jewish causes at home and through the world. The pluralistic structure of American life made the duality of American Jewish experience less exceptional than it might otherwise have been.

After the Second World War we find American Jewry elevated by a special exuberance. It was a full participant in America's advance toward world predominance; and it was also a recognized partner in the Israeli pioneering adventure. It is unlikely that any Jewish community, since the Diaspora began, had ever had such large scope for its vitality and enterprise. The satisfactions in American Jewish life far outweighed the frustrations; and the spiritual climate was robust and confident.

But over this hopeful scene several question marks hovered. Would Jewish individuality survive the assimilating influences of American tolerance? And would a new generation which knew neither the trauma of the Holocaust nor the elation of Israel's rebirth have emotional reason to give its thought and work to the task of Jewish conservation? The answer to those questions will have as large an effect on the Jewish destiny as will Israel's own national fortunes. There is no evidence that American Jewry will be effaced by the assimilative inducements of its environment or by a decline in the anxious tensions surrounding Jewish survival. True, there is erosion at the margin of the community through intermarriage and alienation. But the main body seems disposed to attempt the reconciliation between American national identity and the particular intimacies out of which Jewish loyalty grows and lives. Insecurity and frustration were once the incentives which drove Jews to conserve their special dreams and solidarities. Today, affirmative impulses of confidence and pride seem able to evoke the same unifying spirit. The existence of a large Jewish influence in the country whose strategic and economic power surpasses that of all the empires of history is a reality which enrages Arab nationalists and some others. But it is an organic part of the modern human situation. It may gratify some and irritate others—but it cannot fail to be taken into account.

23 ❧ *The Jewish World Today: Israel 1968*

*T*HERE ARE other free countries in which the Jewish situation differs from that in the United States only in scale. In Great Britain 500,000 Jews form a more cohesive and centralized group than American Jewry. Their organization reflects a British instinct for social coherence, just as American Jewry emulates the dispersion and organizational recalcitrance of a looser federal environment. Everything in British Jewry falls more neatly into place. Religious, communal and Zionist authority all have a recognized hierarchical framework. British sympathy for the Jews is enhanced by the memories of the anti-Hitler struggle and by a chivalrous remorse for the excessive anti-Zionism of the Bevin era. British leaders of all parties now prefer to evoke the generous audacity of the Balfour Declaration. The Biblical roots of British culture also promote a respect for Jewish individuality. These impulses seem strong enough to ensure security against occasional prejudices. Jews in Britain are more prominent in Parliament and the Establishment than in the United States; and many of them help to shape the innovating trends in British culture. The proximity to Israel is strongly expressed by British Jews in collective and personal contacts.

Across the channel, French Jewry, swollen to 600,000 by the arrival of Algerian and Moroccan Jewish immigrants, is losing its self-conscious and conservative traditions, in order to emerge more openly into the universal Jewish experience. President De Gaulle's reflections on Jewish history in his November 1967 address elicited a sharp debate about the Jewish place within the French community. The charge of "anti-Semitism" leveled against him was manifestly farfetched; but the notion that Jewish suffering had, in some ways, been "provoked" by the Jews, had a disturbing impact on Jewish serenity. The disquiet was eloquently formulated by Raymond Aron, in his book *The General and the Jews*, which showed how strongly Jewish pride was awakening among French Jews not previously aware of strong Jewish loyalties.

Beyond the oceans, free Jewish communities, attached both to their national environments and to their global Jewish responsibilities thrive in Canada, South Africa, and Latin America. Elsewhere, there are small dwindling remains, or exotically remote islands of Jewish survival.

Israel is everywhere the focus of Jewish solidarities. Economic and cultural Jewish conferences in Jerusalem during 1968 revealed world Jewry as a dynamic force for Israel's consolidation. There are other states which enjoy the emotional support of kindred communities overseas. But there is no parallel for the constancy and depth of active responsibility which Jewish communities assume for Israel's security and progress.

In the Soviet Union nearly three million Jews remain cut off from the mainstream of Jewish life and denied expression of their Jewish solidarities. In recent years the grief and pathos of their situation have aroused the interest of the progressive world. They are, at least, on the international agenda after years of submergence. There is evidence that their Jewish ardor has not been quenched. The prospect of their reunion with Jewish history is rationally remote; but the dream is still alive and fervently cherished. The enforced separation of this large community from the other parts of the Jewish people has historically been associated with the closed character of Soviet society. The reduction of tension between the Great Powers and the increased liberty of movement between Western and Eastern Europe may result in a liberalization of Soviet attitudes toward the Jews. It is unlikely that the Soviet Union will radically improve its image in Western liberal opinion without changing its policies toward the Jews.

The background of all Jewish Diaspora groups, whether in the democracies of the West or in the Soviet bloc, is the non-Jewish pattern of existence of the society in which they live. This poses a constant problem of harmonization between the gentile environment and the Jewish fidelity. But although Jews outside Israel form minorities in their respective countries, there is no evidence of a deep corrosion of Jewish identity. As European and American Jews advance to higher forms of social organization and technical power, they become increasingly responsive to voices from their past. It is unlikely that Jewish individualism will be surrendered by those who have freedom and opportunity to conserve it.

At the end of 1967 the number of Jews in the world was estimated at 13,600,000, distributed as follows: in North America, 6,100,000, of which 5,800,000 were living in the United States, 270,000 in Canada, and the balance of 30,000 in Mexico; in Europe (including Asian regions of the U.S.S.R. and Turkey), 4,054,000, of which the largest number, 2,568,000 were living in the U.S.S.R., and the next largest, 535,000 in France, with 450,000 in Great Britain and the balance of 501,000 in other countries; in Central and South America and the West Indies, 712,700, of which the greatest number, 450,000, were living in Argentina, 140,000 in Brazil, and the balance of 122,700 in other countries. By far the greatest part of Asia's Jews are, of course, the 2,365,000 living in Israel. The Jewish population of Africa numbered about 200,200, of which 114,800 lived in the Union of South Africa, and 50,000 in Morocco. Some 74,500 Jews lived in Australia and New Zealand.

Israel's First Two Decades

For twenty years Israel has advanced in sharp spurts of energy between recurrent wars. The special theme of her existence has been the implacable hostility of her neighbors. Being unable to mitigate the Arab assault, Israel has, at least, contrived to resist it.

Israel's first two decades are the story of this resistance: not only of its strains and hazards but also of its victory. The daily peril has sharpened every impulse of union. Historians will not find it easy to determine whether the surrounding enmity has, in the final account, been more of an obstacle than a stimulus.

The salient Israeli quality is the speed of growth. On Israel's twentieth anniversary in 1968, her population had grown from 650,000 citizens to 2,700,000. No other state in history has more than trebled its population in twenty years. The "ingathering" has held priority of interest and concern. Israel's Jewish vocation has been the context within which her other problems have been considered and approached.

The immediate task was to rescue the remnants of the European Holocaust. Refugee camps in Germany, Cyprus, and Mauritius were emptied in the first tempestuous months. Israel's Declaration of Independence on May 14, 1948, was followed, within an hour, by legislation abolishing the Mandatory's restrictions on immigration and proclaiming the right of every immigrant Jew to immediate citizenship. To be a Jew was now a title for entry into a sovereign country instead of being a total or partial disqualification. On May 18 an Israeli representative in the United Nations was telling other governments that the rate of immigration to Israel was not their concern; it had entered the domestic jurisdiction of a sovereign state. Immigration was the purpose of Israel's existence; sovereignty was the means which served the end.

That Israel would absorb the relics of European Jewry was expected. Far more astonishing was the torrential convergence of Jews from Moslem lands. Here the motive was not only the pressure of misery and discrimination. This after all had existed and been patiently sustained for centuries. Now, for the first time, there was an alternative to docile resignation. The most isolated of Jewish communities, which had lived in Yemen since the time of the Hebrew kingdoms, arose in all its mass and flew "on eagles' wings" to the land of promise. Iraqi Jews, descendants of the Babylonian dispersion, came in their wake, fleeing the vengeance of the Baghdad government, which showed greater valor in the persecution of its Jews than in confrontation with Israel on the battlefields. Bulgaria, Czechoslovakia, Yugoslavia, Poland, Rumania, and Hungary opened their gates for the exodus of Jews who sought to escape from the ghosts and memories of torment under Nazi occupation. The stream was swollen by tributaries from Iran, Turkey, Morocco, Tunis, and Libya. In 1949, 240,000 immigrants entered a country whose population of 650,000 had just emerged from a war of survival; 350,000 more came in the next two years. Within forty months Israel had doubled its population by immigration.

The absorption of this copious flood engaged the effort and responsibility of the entire Jewish people. In Israel the years of mass immigration were the epoch of nobility and self-sacrifice. Houses, schools, immigrant camps (*ma'abarot*), villages, social institutions, were improvised at great speed. The only historic parallel is the avalanche of immigration which carried the United States toward its massive growth in the late nineteenth and early twentieth centuries. But the immigration movement to Israel was relatively of greater dimensions, and far more diverse in the cultural experiences and outlooks of those who composed it.

The achievement does not belong to Israeli Jewry alone. The

Another "ingathering of
exiles" begins as
Yemenite Jews from one
of the oldest and most
isolated of Jewish
communities await their
turn to be flown to the
Promised Land in
Operation Magic Carpet.

Diaspora communities were partners in the enterprise. The United Jewish Appeal and Israel Bond Organization in the United States, and parallel institutions elsewhere, gave impetus to the reception and absorption of the newcomers. The novelty of the process touched deep chords in Jewish memory. There had been many banishments and exiles in Jewish history. Now the current was reversed.

An immigrant society cannot be conservative in its temperament. Significance belongs not to the achievement of today but to the perspectives which today's experience opens up for tomorrow's expansion. It is in the construction of new communities that men achieve their highest sense of creativity. The challenges, improvisations, necessities, and collisions which agitated Israel's society at the climax of the immigrant flood, became the formative influences in the nation's character. The autonomous institutions and pioneering impulses developed by Palestine Jews during the Mandatory era now had broad and free expression. The driving force in Israel's life is still generated by immigration movements—both those already received and those longingly anticipated. Everything is nascent, primordial, focused on new vistas of social expansion.

Thus, Israel abounds with people whose character and intellectual structure were fashioned outside itself. Yet the total impression after twenty years is one of coherence, not of anarchy. The unifying energies which weld a society into a single devotion have prevailed with great swiftness. For this there are several factors of explanation. First, there is the very fact of convergence. It is easy for a theorist to assert that a Yemenite coppersmith, a Johannesburg doctor, a Polish professor, a Moroccan shopkeeper, an Argentinian student, a Kurdish porter, a New York industrialist, have little or nothing in common. The truth is that they have in common a specific Jewish memory which, whatever their motive or predicament, pulled them to Israel and nowhere else. Then there is the cement of common danger. Beyond these there are the harmonizing influences which the Israeli army and school have applied to immigrant youth now grown to manhood. By the end of its second decade Israel began to lose the character of a predominantly immigrant society. More than 40 per cent of its population were of Israeli birth. More than half had received their education in Israeli schools and universities. Of the rest, a large proportion were those whose date of immigration lay far enough behind for them to have developed a more intimate relationship with Israel's landscape and culture than with their previous environment, which grew steadily

more dim. In 1948 a state had been born. By 1968 a nation of sharply defined identity had been created. Israel was something distinct from the aggregate of influences which had inspired its creation.

With the transformation of a people went a revolution of the land. There is probably no country whose physical countenance has changed more radically in so brief a time. Sandy wastes have given way to cultivation. The desert has retreated before the advancing plow and water-pipe. Urban aggregations of imposing modernity have given the country a new solidity of aspect.

The original resources of Israel are its land, sun, and occasional water. The agricultural progress of the first two decades was not dictated by economic needs alone. Zionism has always had a rural and agricultural mystique. The fertilization of land was only one part of the story. The other part, no less crucial, was the reconstruction of the national personality. The sense of basic creativity, of physical attachment to soil, of remoteness from urban degradations, all came together in the effort to transform the national prototype. Early Hebrew poetry of the Zionist period is obsessed with pictures of nature with which Jews are now in intimate reunion. The *kibbutz* and *moshav* added collective idealism to the normal virtues of farming communities.

Near the ancient city of Ashkelon students at the Kfar Silver Agricultural School sort the pipes used in modern irrigation.

There is no doubt that it is in farm and field that the Israeli enterprise has celebrated its greatest successes. In human terms the result is a generation of Israelis sprung from the soil, robust in body and spirit, who form the advance guard of the national progress. The *kibbutz* population is a small fraction of the community, but it has provided a disproportionate percentage of Israel's military officers, air pilots, and emissaries for development projects in Africa and Asia. It is now being reduced to a marginal role in the economy. But in the scale of values, in the determination of what is to be admired, emulated, cherished and pursued, it still holds first place. The national elite is country bred.

In economic development, too, the agricultural and rural sectors were at first the directing force. The years after 1948 were tense with the struggle for subsistence. Mass immigration made impossible demands on scanty agricultural resources. There were periods of severe rations and scarcity in food. The balance of payments was ominously dislocated. By the mid-fifties production had not only caught up with population increase but had so far overtaken it as to generate a surplus. Self-sufficiency was reached in all but cereals, fats, and part of the meat consumption. The farm glut had to be rigorously controlled to prevent falling prices. By 1968 the proportion of workers in agriculture had declined, but output had gone up in leaps and bounds. By 1968 the memories of austerity were far away. On a million acres Israel was producing enough food to sustain over 80 per cent of its population at a high level of nutrition, and was also exporting $130 million worth of agricultural products to the world markets. Israel's agricultural profusion had consoled and encouraged other developing nations. Hundreds of Israeli soil and water experts were at work in distant lands; and thousands of farmers from other continents had studied problems of rural development in Israel. In a world whose destiny would be largely controlled by the relation between steep population growth and slower increase of resources, Israel's achievement became a portent for study and emulation. The achievement was largely made possible by a new distribution and management of water resources. The waters of Lake Tiberias and the Yarkon had to be taken down to the northern Negev. The National Water Carrier, completed in 1964 with massive international aid, brought Israel's agriculture to the height of its potentiality.

But it was evident that an agricultural economy, however sophisticated, could not sustain a growing population in a small area at a tolerable level of material and scientific culture. The development of industry, technology, and communications is predominantly the achievement of sovereign Israel. There was much less to start with than in agriculture, of which the foundations had been firmly laid in the prestate period.

The rise of Israeli industry has been accompanied by endless criticism, experiment, doubt, and theoretical controversy. But the results speak impressively. In Israel's first year of independence, her exports were less than $30 million. They were 11 per cent of her imports. In the twentieth year, exports exceeded $500 million; they now covered 70 per cent of imports. Private capital, the bond issues and the German Compensation Agreement had provided massive funds for investment. After twelve years Israel was proudly repaying international loans granted with indulgent scepticism in the years of austerity. The trade gap, though still disquietingly large, in absolute terms had dwindled relatively from $214 per capita to

$80 National airlines and shipping were carrying the Israeli flag to all five continents. By 1968 tourists were reaching Israel at the annual rate of 450,000. New development towns from Upper Galilee to the Red Sea coast had risen on the crest of industrial growth. Beersheba had grown from a squalid village of 4000 souls to a hot, boisterous, dusty, but strangely exciting city with 70,000 inhabitants. A new deep-sea harbor had been carved out of nothing at Ashdod. An oil pipeline brought fuel from Eilat on the Red Sea to the Mediterranean coast. Electricity output had vastly multiplied, and in two research reactors, at Dimona and Nahal Sorek, Israeli engineers and technicians were preparing for the age of nuclear power. A man who had not seen Israel since the first year would have had difficulty in recognizing it in the twentieth.

Above all, the swift thrust of industry and technology had abolished the equation between land, space, and population. The question of "how many people Israel can support" was now a function not of her area but of her commercial and economic energies. The relevant examples are small countries such as Belgium, Holland, Denmark, and Switzerland, which have maintained denser populations than Israel's in restricted land areas at high levels of culture and prosperity. Israel's capacity to absorb population would henceforward have little or no relevance to her size.

The Israeli Culture The need to make the most of small possibilities inspired Israel from her earliest years with a strong reliance on science and technology. By the end of her second decade, Israel's research workers, technologists, and engineers had placed her high in the international scientific community. It was startling to find a small state on the western fringe of Asia endowed with research reactors, accelerators, computers, laboratories, hospitals and clinics, aircraft repair facilities, electronic factories, and other indications of scientific progress. The result is not to be measured in economic welfare or security alone. The intellectual climate of scientific enquiry, its rational spirit, its objective standards of judgment, its pursuit of reason and order, its constructive scepticism and its universal solidarities have all gone into the texture of Israeli life. A society in which a family of research workers takes part in the penetration of nature is intrinsically different from a society in which no such family exists. When Chaim Weizmann founded the Institute of Science in his name at Rehovot, he was as much concerned with Israel's intellec-

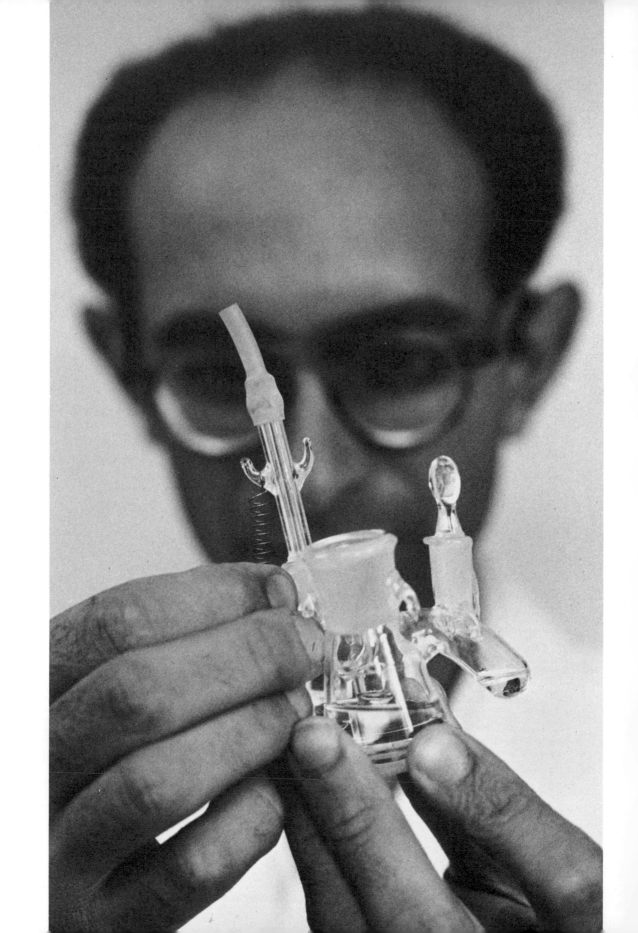

tual level as with the more pragmatic consequences of scientific progress. Israel's place in the scientific enterprise enlarged her position in the world. By the end of the sixties she had become regarded by the developing nations as the most congenial arena of contact between the world of national freedom and the world of scientific progress. For Israel stands at a crossroads not only in geography but also in the realm of ideas. She is one of the new states in the international community; and she is also a full partner in the universal scientific adventure. No other state stands in such simultaneous kinship with the movements of national liberation and technological advance which have thus far dominated the second half of the twentieth century.

But the scientific spirit is only one aspect of Israel's cultural personality. To many writers and thinkers Israel represents the modernist element in Middle Eastern life, striving for progress through scientific rationalism. But no less potent an influence in the life of the nation is its sense of association with Israel's past. The revival of the Hebrew language in daily speech, its astonishing growth in conceptual precision, the spectacular results in archaeological discovery, the central position of the Bible in secular as well as in religious education, the tendency to refer moral problems to traditional Hebrew ethics, are all symptoms of a profound yearning for continuity. The archaeological obsession is particularly instructive. Israel is not a new "esperanto" nation writing its history on a clean slate. It is the only state in the world which speaks the same tongue, upholds the same faith, and inhabits the same land as it did three thousand years before. The authenticity of the relationship between this people and its land is the most controversial issue in Israel's dialogue with the Arab region and the outside world. There is therefore a note of contemporary triumph in every new evidence of historic continuity. The fortresses of Judean kings are revealed south of Jerusalem. An Israelite temple is unearthed in the central Negev. Hebrew scrolls confirm the traditional story of the Jewish zealots' last revolt. Letters by Bar Kochba to his troops are found in the Judean wilderness, together with other indications of Hebrew life at the time of the revolt against Rome in 135. The skeletons of those who perished and killed their families to forestall humiliating surrender bear eloquent witness to the ancient heroisms. All of this exalts the historic imagination of the country's youth. A competition in Biblical knowledge is followed with the partisan tension which most nations devote to major sporting events.

All movements in Jewish nationalism take ancient Hebrew thought as their major premise. But Israel also garners the riches of medieval and modern Jewish literature, of European humanism, and of twentieth-century science. Its modern culture, apart from literature, belongs to the European and Mediterranean pattern with occasional Oriental overtones. In music and the plastic arts there is an experimental vitality. What is unique in Israel's culture is the egalitarian principle which governs its diffusion. There are no barriers in access or appreciation between town and village. Whatever is thought, written, composed, painted, acted, carved, or postulated is communicated across the whole national scene.

The prestate population was in many respects an elite community. It was born out of an idealistic impulse and it formed part of the cultural history of Europe. Mass immigration from countries of less advanced culture seemed to threaten the dilution of the nation's intellectual standards. In the longer term the variety and vigor of immigrant strains would have an effervescent effect. But the immediate effects could be disruptive. Meanwhile, the maintenance of equality in cultural opportunity became, in the sixties, a central preoccupation of the educational movement. A school network embracing more than 700,000 students in primary and post-primary schools was one of Israel's crowning achievements. The population had trebled; but the educational system had expanded sixfold. The question was whether an educationally retarded proletariat would be formed around the third of the population whose origins lay in Moslem lands. These immigrants had been sundered from the Jewish tradition of intellectualism, although their ingrained piety had given them a firm grounding in Hebrew lore. Would post-primary and higher education in Israel become the special domain of European immigrants and their children, while the "Oriental" part of the community languished at the wrong end of the cultural gap? If so, Israel had little chance of spiritual and social cohesion. The educational movement addressed itself vigorously to the social dilemma which ranked above the academic ambition in the hierarchy of its concern. Intensive efforts were made to broaden the flow of students from poor homes, mostly of Asian and African origin, into the secondary schools and universities. The progress was not as swift as many hoped—nor as slow as many feared. But it was perceptible enough to augur the day when Israelis of all backgrounds would be equal in their educational attainments, and therefore in their social opportunities. The transitory gap was sometimes exploited for infamous and exaggerated demagogy. But time and responsible labor were closing the gulf. The university network branched out from Jerusalem, Haifa, and Rehovot to the Tel Aviv University and to Bar-Ilan University at Ramat Gan. The broader foundation accommodated all the immigrant communities. By the second generation the inequalities would have been largely effaced.

There was no doubt that the equalizing trend would flow upward, not downward. Some writers who despaired of any Arab reconciliation with a "Western" and intensely Jewish Israel drew false comfort from two prospects. Israel would become increasingly "Orientalized" until it lost the qualities which separated it from the rest of the Middle East; and it would cease to be a "Zionist" state based on a particular sense of kinship with Jews outside. In other words, Israel would not be Israel much longer. It would be absorbed unobtrusively in the surrounding Levantine ocean.

Whether or not this is a desirable solution for the Arab-Israel predicament is beside the point. There is no chance at all of its coming to pass. Israel will continue to be conspicuously non-Arab in its speech, thought, and shape of mind. Its Jewish connections will be stronger than its links with the Arab environment. It learned in 1967 that its physical survival depended on its organic relationship to the science, technology, social cohesion, and democratic ethic which marked it off from its neighbors. The very qualities which it did not share with them were those which enabled it to withstand their assault. Israel would be part of the Mediterranean world and of the Jewish spirit rather than of the Arabian hinterland. It is more likely that the Arab world will become "Westernized" and adaptable to modern technology and democracy than that Israel will become what some Europeans condescendingly call "another Middle Eastern State." Israel's roots and geographical environment are older and just as authentically Middle Eastern as are those of the Arabs; but Israel will not be "another" anything. It will be itself and utterly specific. It responds to the natural diversity and not to the spurious homogeneity of the Middle Eastern world. The question is whether the region can recapture its higher moments, when Judaism, Christianity, Islam, Hellenism, and Roman civilization were all considered as part of its accumulated legacy. For to be Middle Eastern does not involve being Arab or Moslem. It is not an offense against the Middle Eastern tradition for a non-Arab and non-Moslem sovereignty to live and flourish in the original home of Hebrew memory and thought. The question is not whether Israel will change its special nature, but whether the Arabs will come to terms with Israel as it is.

There was no evidence of a positive answer in Israel's first two decades. Arab governments continued to regard Israel's emergence as a temporary disaster which would sooner or later be liquidated. The General Armistice Agreements concluded in 1949 with Egypt, Jordan, Syria, and Lebanon pledged all their signatories to the final renunciation of war and to respect for the armistice lines until they could be replaced, in a peace settlement, by permanent boundaries. These agreements were intended to be *de facto* settlements which would first become crystallized and later flower into a formal peace. But after the shock of their defeat in 1948 the Arab governments renewed their attempt to harry Israel out of existence. There is no precedent in modern international history for such a comprehensive and diversified hostility. The Arab governments organized a world-wide economic boycott in an effort to deny Israel access to world markets and sources of supply. In international diplomacy they challenged Israel's status as a sovereign state. They denied her the right to drain the Huleh marshes or to use any part of the Jordan River which flows through her territory for sixty-five miles. They sought to persuade other governments not to establish relations with her. They opposed her membership in international agencies. They asserted the right of Arab refugees to "return" to Israel ir-respective of Israel's will or security. They attempted to prevent Israel from acquiring arms. They maintained a constant campaign of vituperation and verbal assault. In writing and caricature Israel was portrayed as a hook-nosed verminous monster worthy only of physical extermination. There is not a single image, phrase, or adjective in the Nazi vocabulary which Arab propaganda, directed from Cairo, has not adopted and diffused in the political warfare against Israel. The vicious Protocols of the Elders of Zion were formally endorsed by Nasser. The murder of six million Jews by the Nazis was alternately denied and applauded. Political opposi-tion to Israel merged into a comprehensive anti-Jewish ideology. Jewish communities in Arab lands were either persecuted or ex-pelled. The blood libels are more copiously represented in Arab nationalist literature than they ever were in European anti-Semitism. Israel's very existence was portrayed in Arab writings and politics as a crime for which the only expiation lay in Israel's disappearance.

There were times when it appeared possible for this vehement hatred to be contained without erupting into general war. Israel would have preferred to flourish in peace with her neighbors. But she was also capable of flourishing without it. Behind the shield of strong military defenses, with an eye vigilantly fixed on hostile frontiers, Israel went on with its work. The Arab threats of Israel's destruction appeared at times to have become rhetorical and ritualistic rather than operative. But on two occasions belligerency was to explode into generalized conflict.

In each case the motive cause and the inflammatory occasion were provided by President Nasser of Egypt. He had come into power in 1953. He made hostility to Israel the rallying point for the union of the Arab world around his banner. His approach was blatantly hegemonistic. All Middle Eastern states and much of Africa were, in his conception, the vassals of Cairo. Hatred of Israel was the unifying slogan. His belief in his own propaganda was not always immaculate. The tap of anti-Israel incitement was sometimes allowed to flow gently, at other times to burst into profusion. Nasser's anti-Israel doctrine was a means, not an end. But it was advanced and articulated with such constancy that there was seldom a chance of prolonged regional stability.

In 1953–1956 a new technique was devised for expressing Arab hostility toward Israel. Terrorists (*fedayeen*) were trained and organized for infiltration into Israel where they carried out murders and acts of sabotage. In 1956 the raids became particularly intensive. Their gravity was underlined by a massive Egyptian armament program, and by the seizure of the Suez Canal from the international interests which had always controlled it. Alliances with Syria and Jordan under Egyptian command gave Israel a sensation of encirclement. The adversary was growing stronger. He was applying pressure from all sides. He was successfully expelling or subjugating the international and regional influences which stood in his way. And he was denying Israel the elementary safety of life and limb. At the end of October 1956 Israel burst out of the closing ring. She was not alone. France had been alienated by Cairo's disruption of her position in Algeria. Britain, under Anthony Eden's leadership, was moved to resistance by the seizure of the Suez Canal, which seemed to place her economy and crucial communications in hostile hands. The need to prevent Nasser's domination of the Middle East had been a constant theme in discussions between Jerusalem and Paris, and later between Paris and London. The convergence was not accidental. As Israeli troops under General Moshe Dayan moved across Sinai to break the blockade in the Gulf of Aqaba and expel the Egyptian army from Gaza, French and British forces occupied the Suez Canal area. The two governments justified their action by the eccentric explanation that they were bent on preventing hostilities in the Canal area.

Nasser's power was now threatened with extinction. A purposeful international policy might have translated the tension into a serious attempt to establish a permanent peace. The opportunity was frittered away. The United States, irritated by the independence of British, French, and Israeli action, joined with the Soviet Union in applying pressure against its friends and allies. Britain and France withdrew from the Suez Canal, which reverted to unilateral Egyptian control. Their failure marked the end of their independent influence in the Middle East and had a strong impact on their domestic politics. Israel was more obdurate. She declined to complete the withdrawal of her forces until she had secured the presence of a United Nations Emergency Force which was to ensure free passage in the Gulf of Aqaba and an international restraint on Gaza, which had been the springboard for terrorist assault. Israel was assured, especially by the United States and France, that these arrangements would remain in force until such time as their termination would not lead to renewed belligerency against her by land and sea. The association of Israel's resistance with a British and French enterprise had, in the first shock, prejudiced her political position. But when the justifications of her action were disentangled from the motives of her partners, they came into a clearer light. Of the three countries fighting against Nasserism, Israel alone was fighting for life and peace.

Israel's resistance had done more than secure her a new tranquillity in Sinai and Gaza and a maritime bridge to the Eastern world. It had deflated Nasser's hegemonistic pretensions, enlarged Israel's international prestige, and above all, imbued her with a sense of creative self-confidence. The decade between 1957 and 1967 was the most fruitful in modern Jewish history. Israel grew in population, economic strength, technical power, and international standing. She had established a network of political and economic relationships with the new nations of Africa and Asia. Over 10,000 future leaders of developing states received training in Israel and 3000 Israeli experts, scientists, engineers, doctors, agronomists, and economic planners played a valued role in the accelerated development of African, Asian, and Latin American states. The Arab threat to prevent the National Water Carrier from coming into operation was successfully defied in 1964. When 1967 dawned, Israel seemed to have defeated the attempt to isolate her. The Arab threat to destroy her lost credibility.

The extraordinary assault mounted by Egypt and Syria in 1967 may well have been inspired by a sense of "now or never." The

solidarity and permanence of Israel's statehood were becoming
deeply rooted and universally recognized. If final stabilization were
to be prevented, a swift and drastic challenge would have to be
mounted. The initiative came this time from the revolutionary
Ba'ath regime in Syria. It counted on uncritical Soviet support.
While the frontiers with Egypt and Lebanon were quiet and
Jordan evinced some interest in an ultimate settlement, Syria harbored and trained terrorist bands for penetration into Israel. Her
forces on the Golan Heights kept the settlements in Upper Galilee
under constant assault. Israeli resistance brought Damascus a heavy
toll of loss, especially in Syrian aircraft, which tended to fall into
the Sea of Galilee or elsewhere whenever challenged by Israeli
fighting planes. Syria turned to Moscow for help. The Soviet Union,
reluctant to provoke American intervention, turned the responsibility over to Cairo. In May 1967 Soviet spokesmen gave Egypt
false information on alleged Israeli troop concentrations on the
Syrian frontiers, and summoned Cairo to Syria's aid.

The Six Day War

At the beginning of May 1967 all Israeli and Western appraisals
predicted the indefinite continuation of the "unstable stability"
which had prevailed for ten years. There would be relative peace
on three armistice borders. Terrorist raids from Syria would be
contained by defensive vigilance or, in severe cases, by reprisals of
limited scale. Nasser would not invite a war which he was unlikely
to win. Syrian verbal militance was never matched by excessive
military prowess. And none of the major powers had any objective
interest in a major conflagration which would put their commitments and predilections to the test. The two things which seemed
least likely to happen were peace—and war.

Within three extraordinary weeks the prospect was transformed.
Nasser strode toward the precipice in a crescendo of reckless steps.
He gathered an army of 80,000 men with 900 tanks in Sinai. He
falsely announced that Israel had concentrated troops for a massive
assault on Syria. He dismissed the findings of the United Nations
Observers that no such concentrations existed. He expelled the
United Nations Emergency Force from Sinai, Gaza, and the entrance to the Gulf of Aqaba. On May 22 he announced the imposition of a blockade in the Gulf. In explaining this act of war he
made an ominous speech which settled for all time the question of
responsibility for the 1967 war:

We awaited the proper day when we would be fully prepared and confident that we would take strong measures if we were to enter the battle with Israel. I say nothing aimlessly. . . . Recently we have felt strong enough that if we were to enter a battle with Israel with God's help we could triumph. I said once that we could tell the United Nations Emergency Force to leave within half an hour. Once we were fully prepared we could ask UNEF to leave. That is what has actually happened.

Taking over Sharm-el-Sheikh means confrontation with Israel. *Taking such action means that we are ready to enter war with Israel. It is not a separate operation.*

The battle will be a general one and our basic objective will be to destroy Israel. I probably could not have said such things five or even three years ago. Today, some eleven years after 1956 I say such things because I am confident. I know what we have here in Egypt and what Syria has. I also know that other states—Iraq for instance—have sent their troops to Syria. Algeria will send troops. Kuwait will also send troops. They will send armored infantry units. This is Arab power.

While Israel steadied itself for the assault, the Western powers developed a purposeful attitude of irresolution and nonintervention. The United Nations Security Council, in ignominious silence, heard the Egyptian representative announce "an overt state of war" with Israel. It did and said nothing. It thus kindled the greenest of green lights before the exultant aggressor. Israel would not soon forget the abdication of the United Nations from its duty to defend her Charter rights. On May 30 Egypt and Jordan concluded an alliance against Israel. The encirclement was almost complete. On June 4 Iraq joined the hunt by signing a similar agreement. Troops from Algeria, Morocco, Kuwait, Saudi Arabia, converged toward Israel like greyhounds advancing to tear the quarry to pieces. An American plan to mount an international naval force to break the Egyptian blockade dwindled for lack of international support and domestic authority. Egyptian aircraft began to go into and out of Israel at will, carefully marking targets for the impending attack. The sudden departure of the United Nations force from Sinai found Israel's southern border thinly manned. Vast crowds in Cairo and other Arab capitals were hanging Israel in effigy and giving vent to an intense lust for Israel's blood.

These days were among the most dramatic in Jewish history. Their volcanic atmosphere was described a few weeks later by the

Israel Foreign Minister, appearing before the United Nations General Assembly:

> Nobody who lived those days in Israel will ever forget the air of doom that hovered over our country. Hemmed in by hostile armies ready to strike, affronted and beset by a flagrant act of war, bombarded day and night by predictions of her approaching extinction, forced into a total mobilization of her manpower, her economy and commerce beating with feeble pulse, her main supplies of vital fuel choked by a belligerent act, Israel faced the greatest peril to her existence that she had known since the hour of her birth. There was danger wherever she looked. And she faced it in deepening solitude. A crushing siege bore down upon us. Multitudes throughout the world trembled for Israel's fate. On the fateful morning of June 5 our country's choice was plain. The choice was to live or perish; to defend the national existence or to forfeit it for all time.

The sensation of peril in a dark hour was inscribed in the early summer of 1967 on the tablets of Israel's history. A new dimension was added to the national memory; and the exploration of it would take many years. So also would the six days of resistance be narrated as long as any memory of the past endured. Within a week an angry Israel had torn the strangling fingers from its throat. In a brilliant campaign, nourished by desperate valor, Israel's forces, under General Rabin's command, smashed their way to the Suez Canal, to the entire length of the Jordan River and to the Golan Heights. Jerusalem was reunited. The Western Wall, relic of Israel's ancient glory, was restored to its people after two decades of sacrilegious separation inflicted by Jordan's armies, which had invaded Jerusalem in 1948. The national history had celebrated one of its sharpest transitions. At one moment everything had seemed desperately vulnerable, fragile, and tenuous. A week later the air resounded with the note of salvation.

The Political Aftermath Victory in war did not end Israel's danger. The Soviet Union and the Arab states mounted an intensive and virulent political campaign in an effort to cancel Israel's gains. Their purpose was to force Israel back to the armistice lines without the conclusion of peace. This would have reproduced the juridical ambiguity and territorial vulnerability which had nearly spelled Israel's doom. In

resisting this proposal, Israel based her policy on the traditional foundations of international law. She announced her intention of maintaining the cease-fire lines until they were replaced by peace treaties establishing agreed territorial frontiers by negotiation. The Arab governments had never recognized the armistice lines as final boundaries. They had specifically reserved their right to propose changes in the peace settlement. Israel now claimed identical rights. The armistice regime had been shattered by years of hatred and violence. Above all, it had been repudiated by the Arab states in their declarations and acts of war in May and June 1967. Israel now sought a new order of relationships in which an armistice regime and provisional demarcation lines would be replaced by a contractual peace with secure and permanent boundaries. Her central resolve was never, under any circumstances, to return to the edge of the precipice.

This position won impressive international support. At meetings of the Security Council and the General Assembly in the summer and fall of 1967 Soviet and Arab proposals for restoration of the prewar situation were crushingly defeated. World opinion, which had looked on in helpless anguish when Israel seemed about to perish, now rallied fervently in her support. On June 19, President Lyndon B. Johnson of the United States, whose sympathy and responsibility had been engaged by Israel in the weeks preceding the war, declared that it would be wrong to restore the previous position. It would be "a prescription for the renewal of hostilities." A new structure of peace should be built in the Middle East by agreement between its sovereign states. On November 15, 1967, Ambassador Arthur J. Goldberg developed the United States doctrine on the territorial question. He said that neither the old armistice lines nor the new cease-fire lines established by Israel's victory could be regarded as the final boundary. This had to be fixed by agreement within the peacemaking process. A group of states from all five continents supported this approach. The authoritative international policy now favored an exercise in innovation. The past with its legacy of war and conflict should be left behind. Israel should not withdraw except to secure and recognized boundaries. The watchword was not backward to belligerency, but forward to peace.

On November 22, 1967, the Security Council, on British initiative and with American support, embodied these ideas in a resolution which was unanimously adopted. This represented a substantive defeat for traditional Arab policy. Withdrawal from occupied territories was made conditional on the establishment of peace, the total

After the liberation, in June 1967, Israeli soldiers stand at the Wailing Wall, or the Western Wall, of the Temple in Jerusalem.

abolition of belligerency, and the establishment of secure and recognized boundaries. A United Nations representative, Dr. Gunnar Jarring, the Swedish Ambassador in Moscow, was charged with the task of "promoting agreement" on a peaceful settlement.

The political struggle in 1967 had ended satisfactorily for Israel. All proposals seeking to condemn her resistance, to describe it as an act of aggression, and to urge withdrawal without peace, had been defeated.

Israel's military and political success placed Arab policy, for the first time, in a sharp dilemma. The situation created by war could only be changed by peace. But peace would involve a total renunciation of the ideas, slogans, and dreams which Arab leaders had embraced and cherished since Israel's establishment. The old ideology based on Israel's nonexistence had been repudiated in Middle Eastern fact and in world opinion. In a negotiated peace settlement Israel would probably have boundaries more compact than those of the cease-fire and more spacious and secure than the demarcation lines of June 1967. But if the Arab governments did not withdraw from belligerency and nonrecognition Israel would not withdraw from the cease-fire positions. If the Arab states behaved toward Israel as though there were war, Israel would not behave toward them as though there were peace. In a genuine peace settlement Israel would not insist on maintaining the entire cease-fire position. She would work with Arab states to achieve an agreed territorial settlement.

Thus an entirely new tactical situation had been born. There was now an inherent immobility which could only be unfrozen by a sharp change in Arab policy. Dr. Jarring's explorations during 1968 were designed to clarify whether such a change could be expected. Would Egypt agree to a final peace settlement? Would Jordan cut her losses which she sustained in the incredibly rash assault on Israel on June 5, 1967? Above all, would Arab governments grasp the existential truth about the Middle East as a region which can never be comprehended in Arab terms alone? Would they perceive that the destination of the Middle East lay in variety and pluralism, not in Arab monopoly, and that to accommodate Israel's sovereign and secure existence was the first condition of regional peace?

As 1968 came to an end there was no evidence that Arab governments were prepared to escape from the inertia of their previous policies. At a conference in Khartoum they had announced that they would seek a political settlement only if it accorded with three principles: no negotiation with Israel; no recognition of Israel; no peace with Israel. These were not promising ingredients for peace. In March 1968 the U.A.R. refused Dr. Jarring's proposal for joint meetings with Israel under his chairmanship for negotiations on all the matters covered by the Security Council resolution. On July 23, President Nasser reaffirmed his opposition in principle to peace with Israel or to recognition of her statehood. He was prepared for a "political settlement" only if it were consistent with the negatives formulated at Khartoum. He invitingly added that this political settlement was necessary as an intermediate measure until such time as the Arabs, rearmed with Soviet weapons, could resume the war. Meanwhile the terrorist organizations were busy killing and blowing up Israeli buildings across the cease-fire lines. Their effect on Israel's security was troublesome but marginal. Neither they nor Nasser's threats would induce Israel to relinquish the new conditions of her security except for the greater promise and vision of a genuine peace. The Jordan monarch and the Palestinian Arab leaders showed a greater inclination to explore the conditions of a peace settlement. Despite occasional tensions, normal contact between Jews and Arabs across the whole of western Palestine had become possible since the June war. The ordinary commerce of daily life softened the rancors implanted by years of hostile propaganda. If Arab governments were inhibited from negotiating peace it was not impossible that Israel and the Palestine Arab community would adjust themselves to a workable relationship. But the transcendent problem of relations between the sovereign states of the region would continue to challenge the imagination and statesmanship of Middle Eastern leaders.

Whatever the future held, the events of June 1967 promised Israel a broader range of hope than had seemed possible before. If she could not yet attain peace she could at least bear its absence and await its coming in greater security.

There was something casual in the immediate circumstances which led to the Six Day War. Some historians will adduce the blockade of the Straits of Tiran as its central "cause." Others will stress the decision of the Syrian government to activize the relatively passive conflict by terrorist infiltration. All will assign a large role to the action of the Soviet Union in inciting Egypt to mobilize her forces and apply pressure to Israel in the south. The truth is that these were merely the incendiary sparks. Historic events have a broader framework than the immediate one out of which they seem to erupt. The context of the 1967 war, as of its two predecessors, must be sought in the total hostility and negation which marked the Arab policy toward Israel. So long as this accumulated hostility prevailed, like a bonfire soaked in gasoline, the specific motive of conflagration was a matter of chance and time. The world wars were not "caused" by Sarajevo and Danzig, but by the international alignments and emotions from which they evolved. Similarly, an Arab-Israel war was bound, sooner or later, to arise from a situation of belligerency, hostility, and nonrecognition. These considerations inspired Israel's resolve to settle for nothing short of peace. The inflammatory structure would have to be systematically dismantled.

Israel in the World Community

At the outset of her third decade, Israel had struck deep roots in the community of nations. In the early years her international position was narrow and fragile. The United Nations had given sanction to her birth. It had then recoiled from any effort to keep her alive. For many months only a handful of governments maintained relations with her. In May 1949 her admission to the United Nations set the seal on her juridical personality and opened the doors of other international agencies to her membership. In the legal sense this was a more decisive act than the unheeded recommendation of 1947. But until 1960 only one Prime Minister (U Nu of Burma) had risked Arab disapproval by paying an official visit to Israel. There were no peoples, and few governments, whose spontaneous attitude to Israel would not be trustful and benevolent, were it not for the competitive bombardment of an Arab rancor which established hostility to Israel as the price of Arab friendship. No government of conscience could fully pay that price. But the very disposition to strike a bargain in such an invidious market corrupted the true relations of Israel with the world.

Israel's first friends included the strongest nations. The United States showed a general constancy of support, interrupted drastically only by the conflict of 1956. No other relationship brought Israel such enrichment and security over two decades. Memories of immigration and pioneering, of democratic origins and spiritual affinity lent a chivalrous background to this relationship. It was to show its most significant strength in the aftermath to the Six Day War. If Israel had been defeated, the American commitment would have lost its credibility everywhere and a sharp moral crisis would have convulsed American life. After the war the United States strove hard to help Israel build a future more stable than its past. The American attitude was less fluctuating and less dependent on domestic pressures than the Arabs were ready to believe.

The Soviet Union, after three or four years of fidelity, passed, in the early fifties, to an uncritical support of the Arab cause. This, more than anything else, impeded the possibilities of Arab-Israel reconciliation. The motives of the U.S.S.R. derived from its calculations in the Cold War. The Arab states were likelier candidates for an anti-Western posture than was democratic Israel. In the middle sixties Israel made efforts to consolidate her links with Eastern Europe. When these were bearing some fruit, especially in Rumania, the Six Day War brought about a rupture with all Communist capitals except Bucharest and Havana. But Moscow's anti-Israel policy caused deep searchings of heart and much dissent in the Communist world, especially in Czechoslovakia. It was not inconceivable that the U.S.S.R. under pressure of this opinion would find its way back to a more realistic relationship with a state which was manifestly a permanent part of the Middle Eastern reality. But two strong factors were at work against this prospect. Soviet policy had been guided by quantitative concepts. Fourteen Arab states are a more tempting arena in Great Power competition than a solitary Israel. And the Soviet vision of Israel has never ceased to be distorted by a prejudiced view of Jewish qualities and values.

In its relations with Israel Britain passed with typical pragmatism from initial hostility to a friendship which had many historic and sentimental roots. In commercial links and political and social affinities, Britain and Israel were tightly entangled despite occasional estrangements. Israel's parliamentary and juridical institutions reflected the image of a British tradition and experience absorbed during the Mandatory years. As Britain retreated from its positions in the Arab world there was a tendency to judge the Israeli relationship on its own merits and not as a function or consequence of British policy toward Arab states.

France was Israel's mainstay for a full decade and more. The France-Israel relationship evoked a strong public mystique in both countries. The preponderance of French equipment in Israel's armed forces had a powerful emotional effect on the country's youth. Charles de Gaulle's robust view of specific national individuality seemed to make him a natural supporter of Israel's cause. The national rhetoric in both countries took the constancy of this friendship as an unquestioned premise. There was therefore a poignant note in the sudden collapse of support which marked the French attitude to Israel's predicament in the Six Day War. The asperities of President De Gaulle's remarks in his November 1967 press conference sharpened the wound. But there was enough tenacity and faith on both sides to keep better memories alive, and public sympathy for Israel in France never waned.

Israel's effort to consolidate her position in Europe brought her face to face with the agonizing need to adjust her relations with the Federal Republic of Germany. The first turning point came in September 1952 with the signature by Chancellor Konrad Adenauer and Foreign Minister Moshe Sharett of a Compensation Agreement under which Israel's economy was to be enriched by 850 million dollars within the next fifteen years. Over $1000 million was paid by the Federal Republic as personal restitution to victims of Nazi persecution, many of them in Israel. Behind these actions lay a moral idea. What the Jewish people had lost and suffered was beyond remedy or consolation. But Jewish survival could still triumph in the measure that Israel's strength was reinforced. The gravity and precision with which West Germany fulfilled these contracts made a strong impression on Jewish and world opinion. In 1965, when Chancellor Erhard established diplomatic relations with Israel, the movement toward normality was intensified. The Israel governments under Ben Gurion, Sharett, and Eshkol which authorized these measures showed political courage in the face of sharp dissent. By the end of 1968 it was accepted in the Jewish world that the relations between Bonn and Jerusalem had developed an inherent dignity as well as a deeply constructive content. On this foundation Israel advanced toward closer links with the European community.

The most spectacular development in Israel's foreign relations lay in the developing countries. By the end of 1968 Israel had established thirty diplomatic representations in Africa and had signed twenty cooperation agreements. Israeli experts were also at work in Latin America where a warm political friendship had burgeoned in the early years of Israel's struggle and solitude. The "Israeli presence" was a respected element in the development of states in Southeast Asia, the Caribbean area, and the Mediterranean basin. No other country of Israel's size had taken so substantial a part in the effort to close the gap between the advanced and developing nations. In addition to its human qualities this enterprise had a deep political implication. The picture of Israel as an artificial "colonial" intruder had been quietly but sternly rejected by the anti-colonial world. Arab hostility was becoming isolated in the continents where Arab nationalism expected the greatest response to its pressure and influence. For Israel there was a special exaltation in the opportunity to take part in a human and social enterprise outside its borders. A sense of international vocation worked against provincialism and self-centeredness.

Thus the effort to banish Israel from the international community had failed no less decisively than the attempt to destroy her by war. With its flag flying over embassies and consulates in a hundred countries, with contractual agreements linking her to regional organizations in Europe, America, and Asia; with active membership and participation in the multilateral international agencies, and a resounding voice in the United Nations discussions, Israel was a solid political reality. Indeed, among United Nations members more than thirty were smaller than Israel in population, over fifty younger in sovereignty, and more than eighty endowed with a smaller average per capita income. All these advances were won against persistent and vociferous challenge. The paradoxical results of Arab hostility came to vivid expression in Israel's diplomatic consolidation. If Israel had not been harried and assaulted it is doubtful if she would have felt bound to develop such a far-flung network of international relations. In more ways than one, her adversaries were the architects of her strength. The Arab states could not rely on the world community in their effort to bring about Israel's destruction. If they sought this aim they would have to do it themselves, within the severe limits of their own power and efficiency.

Israel's intense international activity was always hedged in by one crucial reservation. Partly because of her own independent spirit and largely through the caution of other states, Israel had no binding security alliances. The physical protection of the state belonged to the autonomous realm of national responsibility. Israel set high store on international sympathies. But advice tendered to her from safe distances on how to be secure without resisting Arab assaults was received with robust scepticism. Popularity was important; but it was more important to be alive than to be popular. A weakened, vulnerable Israel attracted more affection than a strong and resistant Israel. The predicament of Israel's diplomacy lay in the tension between solitary quest for security and a constant ambition for international support. In the direct and concrete dialogue with peoples and governments, Israel prospered more than

David Ben Gurion, Israel's first Prime Minister and one of the founding fathers of Zionism. "His genius lay . . . in the capacity to animate the national will and to create solid and entrenched Israeli facts. . . ."

in the litigation with Arab states on frontier clashes. Beyond the immediate regional environment she could count on a worldwide international interest.

The sources of this fascination were complex and sometimes contradictory. In most affluent countries there was no mystique of struggle. There was a weary feeling that all was accomplished and that there was no further great business to transact. Life had no rhapsodical sense. Israel's atmosphere of perpetual movement reminded the old societies of their younger days. On the other hand, the developing countries drew vicarious consolation from Israel's rapid growth and her challenge to the scientific monopoly of great powers. Thus some admired Israel for what she had already accomplished; others for what she still had to do. Israel was unusual not only in the violence of the hostility which surrounded her, but also in the depth and range of the affections which she evoked.

Leadership and Institutions: The new generation

In her twenty-first year Israel was leaving the pioneering era behind. The torch was being handed on. Before long the majority of the population would consist of those who had no memory of the early years when everything was plunged in doubt and travail. The leading figures of the War of Independence were now receding into the twilight.

The transition was marked in 1963 by the sudden retirement of the first Prime Minister, David Ben Gurion. Like Herzl and Weizmann in the preceding Zionist epochs, he had dominated and overshadowed his political contemporaries. But while Herzl had dealt with a visionary idea and Weizmann with a complex prestate organism groping toward maturity, Ben Gurion brought his powerful historic imagination to bear upon the pragmatic issues of statebuilding. As the Second World War came to an end he perceived and dramatized the prospect of a new dispensation. He had been an ardent partitionist since the days of the Peel Report. He believed that statehood could now be snatched from a variety of sudden circumstances. These included the crushing moral force of Jewish agony, the decline of British power, the rise of American predominance, and the autonomous quality of Palestine Jewry's life. This was not a particularly solitary or original view. A Jewish State in a part of Palestine represented the Zionist consensus. It had respectable support in the political world, not least in Britain itself. But to carry it through against Arab opposition and international inertia demanded that it be articulated, represented and organized with convincing pugnacity. Ben Gurion's natural bent did not lie in international statesmanship, where his strident and abrasive approach was more calculated to disconcert than to impress. His genius lay rather in the capacity to animate the national will and to create solid and entrenched Israeli facts which, in their turn, would pull a decisive weight on the international scales. He was an immensely galvanizing force, sending out sparks of vitality in all directions.

Ben Gurion's greatest work was to improvise and equip a defense force—one which later flowered into the victorious Israel army. Thereafter he exercised his Premiership in a distinctly charismatic vein, laying down the law on everything from defense policy to matters such as science, education, Hebrew syntax, and Biblical history in which his passionate zeal seemed to compensate for deficiencies in specialized talent. He occupied a larger area of the national consciousness than his office strictly demanded; and his short, squat, robust, and explosive presence seemed to symbolize the new Israeli qualities in an era when there was no time for equivocation and the race belonged to the swift. He enjoyed the general confidence, especially among the nation's youth; and yet the electorate, with all its veneration, cautiously abstained from giving a full majority to any party which he led. There was a feeling that he would make the very most of whatever authority he was given, and need therefore not be given too much. In his guidance of Israel's international policies his conduct was fascinatingly complex. He had time only for effort which promised real and swift results. He solved the recalcitrant Arab problem by ignoring it and concentrated all his attention on those forces in the world which were, at least theoretically, available for Israel's reinforcement.

Behind a prickly demeanor and a defiant rhetoric he nourished an essentially moderate and realistic appraisal of Israel's potentialities. In 1949 he drew back from northern Sinai rather than incur British armed resistance and American disfavor. He entered the 1956 Sinai campaign after a period of skeptical caution, and only when he felt assured of support against air attack on Israel's cities. Two days after announcing that Israel would never abandon the occupied territory or allow foreign troops to enter it, he proclaimed Israel's evacuation in favor of United Nations troops. The United States and the Soviet Union had demanded this, and he saw no course but to comply. He somehow contrived to give this prudent retreat the impression of an audacious advance. His people forgave him such vagaries, for they understood the inevitabilities of international life. His immense domestic authority enabled him to advance or retreat within a broad field of discretion. After the spectacular events of 1956 there could obviously be no similar pyrotechnics for some time to come. In the absence of great enterprises to stimulate his interest his sense of priorities became frustrated and diminished. He tended to sharpen personal and party animosities within the nation beyond their real measure of acuteness. He appeared willing to envisage peaceful solutions of domestic and personal problems only if no other solutions were available. As years went on and Israeli society passed from patriotic innocence to greater sophistication there was a growing desire to escape from paternalistic control. People were grateful for Ben Gurion's heroic leadership; but they also wanted to try the novel experience of breathing for themselves. In 1962 he surprisingly defined Israel's moral future as dependent on whether a security blunder in 1954 should be investigated by a judicial committee appointed by the Cabinet, or by a Cabinet committee with legal advice. There was much to be said on both sides of the question, and most of it was said at inordinate length many times over. What the majority could not accept or entirely forgive was the degree of priority and preoccupation which their leader gave to a matter of secondary relevance on which judicial opinion was sharply divided.

Below this subsidiary affair lay deeper causes. Ben Gurion was in a state of alienation from his contemporaries in the Labor party leadership. He had become impatient of Parliament to the extent of virtually boycotting its procedures; and he seemed to find little in Cabinet routine which engaged his deep concern. He turned back to the past. He wrote large chapters of modern Israeli history in a nostalgic spirit with himself firmly in the center. There was now a valedictory tone. In April 1963, when Egypt, Syria, and Iraq announced one of their periodic paper "federations," Ben Gurion reacted, in letters to a hundred governments, with an apocalyptic alarm which contrasted sharply with his traditional confidence. He now openly doubted whether the state would exist after him. Who else could carry it forward? One morning in June 1963, he abruptly resigned. As his successor he recommended his Finance Minister, Levi Eshkol, whom he thereafter began to abuse with an implacable and excessively reiterated violence. Eshkol avoided his predecessor's charismatic mannerisms, but proved able to harmonize conflicts within the Labor movement which he helped to unite, and in the Cabinet, which he managed to enlarge. He also developed a strong and creative control over the security establishment which he tended and prepared for the forthcoming ordeals. He was later to lead a great and well-timed military resistance and a tenacious effort to translate victory into a new security and peace. His humanism came from the tradition of Russian Zionism and Israeli pioneering.

Ben Gurion had been hesitant about entry into the Six Day War which he did not believe could be won by a government in which he had no faith. After the war he showed his old realism by proclaiming more clearly than most that a genuine peace was more important than indefinite territorial gains. An ardent spirit of contention sometimes blurred his vision of men and events at home; but he always looked out on the world with a lucid and a balanced gaze.

Many human tragedies are self-inflicted. This was particularly true of the manner of Ben Gurion's departure from Israel's helm. But his vivid leadership for most of Israel's first fifteen years would live in the nation's memory and gratitude long after the quarrelsome days were lost from mind. Nobody doubted that he was a figure cast in a large and heroic mold.

Sharp internal controversy agitated Israel from 1963 onward. The Six Day War was one of Israel's finest hours; but the days which preceded them were politically among the least noble. There were some disquietingly resolute attempts in May 1967 to make Eshkol and his associates rather than Nasser the main target of Israeli fury and distrust. After some maneuvering of dubious taste and integrity, a broad coalition was established bringing all the Zionist parties into the government and leaving the opposition denuded. The result was far better than the process which led to it. Israel would face its great decisions from the shelter of an overwhelming national unity.

A New Spirit   The conflicts which raged around the problem of leadership were the symptoms of a more general cause of discontinuity in the national growth. The old values were no longer unchallenged. The simple nobility of the *kibbutz* was becoming overshadowed by the hedonistic compromises of urbanism. Egalitarianism was corroded by a widening gap in living standards. The sensual pursuit of individual satisfactions was no longer rejected. Even in *kibbutz* and *moshav* the luxuries of yesterday became the commonplace necessities of today. Social orthodoxy was challenged. Zionist solidarities were impatiently shrugged off. Young Israelis questioned their identity as Jews and their particular links with the Diaspora. Since Zionism, socialism, peace, egalitarianism, altruism, and a measure of pioneering asceticism had been the typical Israeli qualities, their partial or total eclipse would leave a spiritual vacuum behind. There was now a tendency to react with embarrassment to the utopian idea of Israel as a "special" people charged with a somber and elevated destiny. Many young writers and thinkers opted instead for a relaxed normality. The aim was to be like other nations, free from the particular grace and burden of divine election. In political struggle the human frailties were as largely evident as elsewhere, and strident chauvinistic and mass-circulation newspapers reflected the nation's image in its least prepossessing countenance. Educators and social analysts differed about the degree to which the discontinuity had gone. Were these permanent trends or superficial reactions to siege and peril? Was Israel ceasing to be a Jewish nation and a Zionist state?

Across these anxious debates the Six Day War swept like a sudden and revealing wind. In the hour of danger there was a swift return to the old unifying visions. A potent and fierce solidarity gripped the Jewish world. Israelis and Diaspora Jews found themselves and each other anew, and rejoiced in the mutual discovery. The crisis of values was evidently less sharp and drastic than it had seemed in the earlier days. It became evident that modern Israel still looked back to its founding fathers for the ideals which it cherished and the dreams which it carried closest to its heart. Israel would ostensibly be a land like other lands—of cities, automobiles, large hotels, computers, television, violent electioneering, and technocratic realism. Israeli thinking in some quarters seemed at times to have a preponderantly military emphasis and to spurn the old pursuit of intellectualism and spirituality. There even erupted a school of thought which held the very ideal of peace and regional harmony in open contempt. But these very dangers were redeemed by the creative disquiet which they evoked in Israel itself. There was still a brave hope that this people, once freed from fear for its survival, would insist on being expressed, represented, and led in terms of the humane values which had inspired its birth. For while external problems and dilemmas crowded in upon it, the central question about the State of Israel concerned its inner quality. The answer would depend on whether Israel's future could come to terms with its past. It is, after all, no simple thing to be the heir of the Jewish legacy and not to be true to its deeper visions. The gravest of all dangers would be for Israel to live within its narrow geographical limits rather than in the vaster dimensions of its history and culture. Between the two poles of Jewish universalism and national particularism Israel sought a point of balance and reconciliation.

At the end of 1968 the Israel government was firmly entrenched both in its resolve to maintain the cease-fire situation until peace was achieved, and in its refusal to frustrate peace by unilateral and irrevocable commitments to Spartan conceptions and indiscriminate annexations. Beyond the secular aspects of this dialogue lay overriding moral issues. The question was whether or not a Jewish solution would be sought; that is to say, a solution in which respect for principles and an instinct for efficacy could be brought together in a coherent union. If balanced decisions could be taken and patiently maintained, Israel could look forward to a future longer than its past, inspired by a new and spacious vision —a continuing hope fed by continuing achievement.

"For this commandment which I command thee this day, it is not too hard for thee, neither is it far off. . . . But the word is very nigh unto thee, in thy mouth, and in thy heart, that thou mayest do it."

Reflections on the Jewish Destiny

In the larger context of its peoplehood, twentieth-century Jewry faces the same dilemma as in its early dawn. The tension is between the universal and the particular, between matter and spirit, between quantity and quality. The influence of Judaism on the life and thought of mankind bears no relation to the number of its adherents or to their achievements in any domain of temporal power. Its vocation has rather been to preserve and develop an intense vitality of spirit. Religion, philosophy, literature, science, political systems, and moral ideas have all been profoundly agitated by the currents of the Jewish mind. The universal scope of this influence is the more remarkable when we reflect how little was ever done to force it upon other peoples. Judaism has never been carried across oceans and continents by conquering potentates bent on converting the "infidel" to its exclusive concept of truth. It has been the faith of a small close-knit people, which has been content to diffuse its values by example, not by active proselytism. Jewish ideas were first to be vindicated and expressed in the life of the nation which gave them birth. Thereafter, they were offered to humanity, not imposed upon it. The transmission of the Hebrew legacy works not through abstract disputation, but through the illustrative effects of a national history. There is also a Hebraic frame of mind. It is, of course, easier to place Isaiah, Maimonides, Yehudah Ha-Levi, Saadiah Gaon, and Bialik within a Jewish frame than it is to attribute Spinoza, Freud, Marx, and Einstein to a Jewish context. Yet there is something Hebraic in the concentration of Jewish minds in every age on the fundamental questions of purpose and order in the pattern of nature and the life of man. The preponderance of Jews in movements of political liberalism and scientific research has something to do with the Jewish quest for individual self-expression and for some unifying explanation of the natural and human order.

Some writers have professed to see a contradiction between the particularist and the universal element in Judaism. Arnold Toynbee dogmatically declares that Judaism cannot discharge its destiny of becoming a universal religion unless and until the Jews renounce the national form of their distinctive communal identity for the sake of fulfilling their "universal mission." Now this "impossibility" is exactly what the Jewish people has achieved. It is indeed the central thread in the whole tapestry of its existence. A historic situation can be unique without being unnatural. A vigorous sense of identity has not prevented this people from sending the repercussions of its influence far and wide into the oceans of universal history. It is when historic Israel is most persistently distinctive that its universal vocation is enlarged. The lesson of history is plain. There is no salvation or significance for the Jew except when he aims high and stands straight within his own authentic frame of values. The essence of his peoplehood is well summed up in Ernest Renan's definition of nationality:

> A nation is a soul, a spiritual principle. To have a common glory in the past, a common will in the present. To have done great things together, to want to do them again—these are the conditions for the existence of a nation.

p. 3, Editions Arthaud, Paris; *p 6,* Frank Hurley/Rapho Guillumette Pictures, N.Y.C.; *p. 11,* Hassia, Paris; *p. 12,* courtesy of American Heritage Pub. Co. Inc., N.Y.C.; *p. 18,* Peter Merom, Israel; *p. 22,* Dept. of Antiquities, Ministry of Education & Culture, Jerusalem; *p. 28,* S. Shapira, Israel; *p. 31,* Editions Arthaud, Paris; *p. 32,* Israel Information Services, N.Y.C.; *p. 40,* Photographie Giraudon, Paris; *p. 43,* British Museum, London; *p. 44,* Community Service, Paris; *p. 52,* Dept. of Antiquities, Ministry of Education & Culture, Jerusalem; *p. 56,* Editions Arthaud, Paris; *p. 62,* Photographie Giraudon, Paris; *p. 67,* Editions Arthaud, Paris; *p. 73,* P. Gross, Israel; *p. 77,* Refot/Rapho Guillumette Pictures, N.Y.C.; *p. 81,* Dept. of Archaeology, Hebrew University, Jerusalem; *p. 82,* Ephraim Talmi, Israel; *p. 88,* Louis Goldman/Rapho Guillumette Pictures, N.Y.C.; *p. 93,* Israel/Govt. Press Office, Jerusalem; *p. 94,* Professor Y. Yadin, Israel; *p. 98,* Biblioteque Nationale, Paris; *p. 102,* Peter Merom, Israel; *p. 115,* Dept. of Antiquities, Ministry of Education & Culture, Jerusalem; *p. 119,* Israel Information Services, N.Y.C.; *p. 126,* Photographie Giraudon, Paris; *p. 133,* Bettmann Archive, Inc., N.Y.C.; *p. 136,* Inge Morath, Magnum Photos, N.Y.C.; *p. 141,* Editions Arthaud, Paris; *p. 146,* Victor Laredo, N.Y.C.; *p. 154,* Victor Laredo, N.Y.C.; *p. 156,* from a private collection, N.Y.C., Frank Darmstaedter, photographer; *p. 158,* Victor Laredo, N.Y.C.; *p. 167,* Harry Dash, Israel; *p. 168,* Rheinisches Bildarchiv, Kölnisches Stadtmuseum, W. Germany; *p. 172,* Hassia, Paris; *p. 175,* Biblioteque Nationale, Paris; *p. 178,* Louis Goldman/Rapho Guillumette Pictures, N.Y.C.; *p. 185,* Library, Jewish Theological Seminary of America, N.Y.C.; *p. 188,* Biblioteque Nationale, Paris; *p. 194,* Victor Laredo, N.Y.C.; *p. 200,* Louis Goldman/Rapho Guillumette Pictures, N.Y.C.; *p. 206,* Library, Jewish Theological Seminary of America, N.Y.C., Frank Darmstaedter, photographer;

Bohemia, 213, 216, 220, 235
Bolshevik Revolution, 290, 342, 481
Brazil: Marranos settlers, 196; 17th-century Jewish refugees from, 299; present-day Jewry, 488
Britain (and British): early policies toward Jewish resettlement, 312, 322–323, 337, 354; Jewish delegates from, 346–347; and Zionists, 355–357; Palestine Mandate, 359–360, 367, 373, 440, 441, 442; and Arabs, 379–389 *passim*; in W.W. II, 417, 419–426 *passim*; and founding of modern Israel, 429, 431–453 *passim*, 482; and War of Liberation, 462; present-day Jewry, 486, 488; in Sinai campaign, 501, 502; recent attitudes toward Israel, 511
Bulgaria, 315, 349, 489
Bund, 396
Byzantine Empire, 120, 128, 130, 134, 164

Caesarea, 89, 90, 91, 97, 179
Cairo, 163, 236, 374, 407, 500, 501, 503
Canaan and Canaanites, 1, 2, 5, 6, 9, 11–21 *passim*, 27
Canada, 357, 476, 487, 488
Catholic Church and Catholicism, 124, 125, 127, 170–196 *passim*, 208, 223, 226–230, 233–235 *passim*, 285, 407, 480; *see also* Christians *and* Christianity
Central America, present-day Jewry in, 488
charters, 166, 171, 186, 207–208, 335
Christianity: rise of, 83, 84, 87, 105, 107; East-West schism, 87, 174; as state religion, 116–117; and rise of Papacy, 120; in Middle Ages, 121, 123, 124, 125–127, 138, 144, 162–165 *passim*; and Khazars, 149; domination of, 160; during Renaissance and Reformation, 224–230; and Counter-Reformation, 235; and Pan-Germanism, 263; *see also* Catholic Church *and* Christians
Christians: and Moslems, 130, 131, 136; in Palestine, 132; and Khazars, 149; eastern, 132; in Middle Ages, 124–127, 138, 171–196 *passim*, 207, 208, 209; at time of Nazis, 407, in U.S., 480; *see also* Christianity *and* Catholic Church
Churchill White Paper (June, 1922), 379
Committee of Jewish Delegations, 346–349

Constantinople, 120, 176, 199, 203, 236, 237, 324
Cordoba, 131, 144, 145–146, 147, 151, 157
Cossacks, 212, 235, 312, 342
Council of the Four Lands (*Vaad Arba Aratzot*), 211, 241
Cracow, 207, 210, 413
Crusades and Crusaders, 134, 174–179, 354, 375
Cuba, flight of Jews to, 409, 422
Cyprus, 66, 96, 201, 437, 488
Czechoslovakia (and Czechs), 310, 344, 349, 350, 428, 441, 448, 489

Dachau, 415
Damascus, 38, 41, 130, 201, 322, 374, 376, 474, 503
Damascus Affair, 322
Dead Sea Scrolls, 83
Denmark, 341, 397, 400
Dominicans, 229, 230

East India companies, 195, 221, 223, 299–301
Ecuador, 422
Egypt (and Egyptians): ancient kingdom, 1–10, 14–17 *passim*, 21, 29, 30–31, 35, 41, 42, 45–47, 55, 57, 59, 64, 65, 95; Hellenistic, 71–75; Graeco-Roman, 104; Arab caliphates, 128, 134, 176; under Mamelukes, 195; and Palestine question, 354, 355, 375, 380, 445; in W.W. II, 420; in Israel War of Liberation, 458–466 *passim*; armistice, 500; Sinai campaign, 500–502; in Six Day War, 502–505; aftermath, 505–509
Eilat, 495
El Arish plan, 337, 465
England: expulsion from, 170; anti-Semitism in, 177, 289; Marranos in, 193, 195–196, 298; readmission, 223–224; Hebrew study, 228; Jewish Conservatives in, 267; early Palestine policy, 322, 323, 334; Zionist delegates from, 332; in World War II, 420; *see also* Britain
Esdraelon (Jezreel), valley of, 17, 20
Etzion, 447, 448, 449
Exilarchs, 116, 128, 132, 140
Exodus, 10, 13, 14–16
"Exodus, 1947," 441

demonstrations, 423, 437, 444; capital of modern Israel, 453, 459, 460, 462, 463, 487, 497, 499, 501, 505

Jewish Agency, 373, 378, 381, 384, 406–407, 419, 434, 437, 438, 440, 441

Jewish Agency for Palestine, 419, 420, 438, 439, 440

Jewish Brigade Group, 420–421

Jewish Legion, 357

Jewish National Fund, 336

Joint Distribution Committee, 405–406, 408–409, 476

Judah, 5, 25, 27, 36–41 *passim*, 45–47, 48, 64, 66, 72, 100, 101, 342

Judea, 76, 95, 96, 357, 369

Kabbalah, 225, 229, 232, 233, 236, 237, 238, 262

Karaism and Karaites, 142–143, 150, 205

Keren Ha-Yesod, 373

Keren Kayemet, 372

Khazars, Kingdom of the, 145, 148–150, 204–205

Kiev, 205, 268, 403

Kishinev, 337, 473, 474

Kuzari, 149, 153

Lateran Councils, 171–172, 179–180, 208

Latrun, 435, 460

Latvia, 309, 344, 349, 350, 394, 413

League of Nations, 344, 345, 346, 347, 349, 350, 352, 353, 359, 379, 384, 438

Lebanon, 422, 445, 449, 460, 465, 500, 503

Lithuania: medieval, 204, 207, 208, 210; 17th-century, 237; 18th-century, 241, 255; 19th-century, 268, 270, 309; in W.W. I, 342, 344; and Paris Peace Conference, 349, 350, and Nazism, 394

London, 197, 220, 223, 228, 315, 425, 501

Lower East Side, 304, 307, 470, 476

Lublin, 211, 415

Maidanek, 404

Mainz (Mayence), 161–162, 165, 169, 176

Marranos, 189–197 *passim*, 199, 221, 223, 233, 235, 258, 299, 302, 327

Marseilles, 163, 409

Masada, 92, 95, 99, 497

Masorah, 143

Mauritius, island of, 421, 422

Mecca, 128, 129, 374

Medina, 128, 129, 374

Megiddo, 33

Messianism, 97, 104–107 *passim*, 154, 235, 237–238, 243, 245

Metz, 166, 176, 256, 258

Mexico, present-day Jewry in, 488

Mikveh Israel, 324, 335

Mishnah, 114, 117, 118

Mishneh Torah, 159

Mizrachi movement, 388

monotheism, 7, 13, 14, 63–64, 72, 84, 106

Morocco, 135, 474, 486, 488, 489, 504

Morrison Plan, 433

Mortara case, 281, 474

Mosaic code, 27, 46, 84

Moscow, 503, 511

Mount Scopus, 369, 370, 459

Nabateans, 100

Nazis and Nazism, 181, 216, 261, 378, 391, 393, 397, 429, 479, 480, 481, 482, 489, 500

Negev: in ancient times, 33, 65, 497; in modern times, 442, 443, 448, 460–462, 465, 494, 497

Netherlands, 399, 400, 407

New Amsterdam, 299

New World, 298, 299, 471, 476, 480

New York City, 301, 302, 304, 307, 451, 458, 467, 470, 474, 475, 476, 480

New Zealand, present-day Jewry in, 488

Nineveh, 45, 46

North Africa, 130, 144, 148, 159–160, 199, 420

Nuremberg Laws, 399

Norway, 397, 441

Odessa, 315, 316

Ottoman Empire, 187, 193, 199–203, 237, 321, 323, 352–353, 359, 373–374, 423, 444, 477

Pale of Settlement, 267–268, 270, 275–276, 289, 304, 313–316 *passim,* 361, 471

Palestine: early Hebrew settlements, 5, 9–23; Hebrew kingdoms, 23–47; under Roman conquerors, 100, 108–115; under Christians, 115, 116–117, 121–123; under early Moslems, 132–134, 150,

Stern group, 445
Suez Canal, 354, 445, 463, 501, 502–505
Swedes, 212, 236
Switzerland, 341, 400, 409, 474
Syria: ancient, 1, 19, 41, 45, 66, 91, 116; medieval, 134, 161; and Palestine question, 338, 354, 359, 375, 444–445; Arab revolts, 380; and immigration, 422; in Israel War of Liberation, 449, 460, 462; armistice, 500; Egyptian alliance, 501; in Six Day War, 502–505; postwar, 505, 509

Talmud and Talmudism, 118, 119, 121, 141, 147, 151, 159, 173–174, 187, 213, 215, 227–232 *passim,* 235, 236, 237, 241, 253, 254, 270
Tel Aviv, 370, 423, 444, 453, 458, 460–461
Temple, Second, 66, 68, 76, 78, 109, 111, 112, 113, 121, 123, 134
Temple, Solomon's, 30, 33–34, 36, 37, 46, 47, 48, 61, 65, 66–67, 95
Tiberias, 109, 116, 118, 134, 201, 203, 323, 448
Tisha b'Av, 92, 99, 113, 121, 153
Toledo, 147, 186, 187, 190, 199
Transjordan: ancient, 16, 17, 29, 78, 99, 100; modern (Hashemite) kingdom, 375, 379, 445, 448, 449, 463, 501, 504, 505, 509
Treblinka, 404, 410
Turkey: under Ottomans, 161, 199–200, 202–203, 212, 237, 315, 322, 323, 329, 333, 335; in Crusades, 174; in W.W. I, 353, 477; in W.W. II, 423; present-day Jewry, 488; Jewish emigration from, 489
Turks: Fatimids, 137, 138, 176, 198; Seljuks, 174, 176, 177; Ottomans, 199–203, 321, 323, 333–334, 359, 373–374, 423, 477; 16th-century Jewry, 202–203; *see also* Turkey

U.A.R., 509
Uganda, proposed Jewish settlement in, 312, 337, 354, 355
Ukraine, 204, 236, 342, 345, 410
Union of South Africa, 488
United Jewish Appeal, 491

United Nations, 438, 439, 441, 442, 443, 444, 448, 451, 462, 465, 489, 502–510 *passim,* 513, 516
United States: anti-Semitism, 289–290; immigration to, 302; at Paris Peace Conference, 344, 345; and Palestine question, 357, 443, 448, 452; in W.W. II, 407, 409, 424; 20th-century Jewry, 467–485, 486, 488, 489; and Sinai campaign, 502, 516; and Six Day War, 504, 505; aftermath of war, 510–511

Vaad Leumi (National Council), 369, 453
Venice, 171, 176, 193, 195, 201, 204, 212, 213, 225, 228
Vichy (Occupied) France, 399, 409
Vienna, 183, 220, 262, 315, 323, 326, 327, 332, 399, 409, 476
Vilna, 241, 274; ghetto, 413
Visigoths, 121, 125, 144, 162
Volhynia, 211, 236, 238, 241, 268

War of Liberation, 458–466, 515
Warsaw, 210, 399, 402–403, 410–413
White Paper of May 1939, 373, 384, 421–422, 423, 424, 430, 433, 435
White Russia (Byelorussia), 204, 268, 413
World Jewish Congress, 342
World War I, 341–343, 344, 349, 353, 357, 359, 374, 477, 480; *see also* Paris Peace Conference
World War II, 281, 378, 382, 384, 394, 397–429, 430–431, 434, 438, 482, 515
World Zionist Organization, 332, 346, 376, 379

Yavneh, 96, 111, 112
Yemen, 128, 131, 589
Yiddish, 215, 350, 468, 470
York, 179
Yugoslavia, 344, 489

Zaddikim, 238–239, 241
Zealots, 83, 91, 92, 96
Zionism and Zionists, 204, 310, 312, 329–340, 354–361, 370, 376, 377, 378, 379, 388, 427, 432, 475–476, 486, 493, 515, 518, 519; *see also* Palestine
Zippori, 109, 112, 114
Zohar (Book of Splendor), 201, 232, 238